Delhi

A thousand years of building

Humayun's Tomb, Ch. 10

Delhi

A thousand years of building

Lucy Peck

LOTUS COLLECTION
ROLI BOOKS

Photos
Lucy Peck

Roli Collection, 1, 4, 7, 15, 16, 17 (lower right), 36, 39 (top), 42 (bottom), 60, 83 (top), 135, 140, 163 (top), 164, 165 (bottom), 177, 186 (right top and bottom), 188 (top and middle), 189, 204 (right), 206 & 207 (all top), 244, 255, 257 (middle and bottom), 258 (top), 263 (top), 265, 266 & 267, 268, 271, 274, 275, 276 (bottom), 279 (bottom), 280, 281

Tony Paille, p. 288 (top)

By permission of The British Library, map p. 195 from 'A Native Map of Shahjahanabad' (X/1659)

Illustrations
Lucy Peck

Design
Manav Agarwal

Lotus Collection

First edition published in 2005
Third impression 2006
The Lotus Collection
An imprint of
Roli Books Pvt. Ltd.
M-75, G.K. II Market
New Delhi 110 048
Phones: ++91 (011) 2921 2271, 2921 2782, 2921 0886
Fax: ++91 (011) 2921 7185
E-mail: roli@vsnl.com; Website: rolibooks.com
Also at
Varanasi, Bangalore, Jaipur and the Netherlands

ISBN: 81-7436-354-8
Rs 500/-

Typeset in Garamond by Roli Books Pvt. Ltd. and printed at Rakmo Press Pvt. Ltd., Okhla, New Delhi.

Contents

How to use this book VI

Acknowledgements VII

Map listing & Key VIII

Chronology IX

1 Introduction 1

2 Delhi Architecture 7

3 Rajput Delhi 25

4 Early Sultanate Delhi – The Qutb Minar 33

5 Tughlakabad 47

6 Jahanpanah 55

7 Firozabad and Hauz Khas - Firoz Shah's Delhi 79

8 Lodi Mosques and Tombs - Sayyid and Lodi Delhi 99

9 Purana Qila 133

10 Humayun's Tomb and Nizamuddin 145

11 Shahjahanabad 177

12 Mehrauli 217

13 North Delhi – The Civil Lines 239

14 New Delhi – Lutyens's Delhi 255

15 Modern Delhi 283

Bibliography 295

Index & Glossary 298

How to use this book

Delhi can be divided very easily into discrete geographical areas that each relate to a different period of history. Each chapter, therefore, relates to one of these areas and begins with a brief history and a short introduction to the area as a whole and its historical context. This is followed by maps, descriptions of walks (where practical), and short explanations of important buildings in each area. Buildings are also mentioned within descriptions of walks. Wherever a building is described it is in **bold**. The maps have keys, which are referenced with page numbers, where necessary, for each building; if a building is not mentioned in the text it might have a short explanation in the key. The maps should be considered as adjuncts to the excellent Eicher *City Map* of Delhi. Where buildings are accurately marked on that map I have felt it unnecessary to produce another map here, but there are many areas where the Eicher map is not sufficiently accurate. I hope that my maps will fill these gaps.

In exploring Delhi I have been dependent on the valuable INTACH listing, *Delhi, the Built Heritage*, which covers some buildings that are omitted from this book. I have concentrated instead on the buildings specific to each area, seeking to explain the growth of Delhi as well as its architecture.

✦ The INTACH symbol is used to identify those buildings that are classified as Grade A in their listing. These are mostly used in the maps, but appear in the text where necessary.

As well as photographs and drawings many of the buildings are illustrated with Elevations and, sometimes, Sections. These are all at the same scale (approx 1:630) in order to enable comparisons to be made between them. The sample buildings here have the dimensions shown under the drawing.

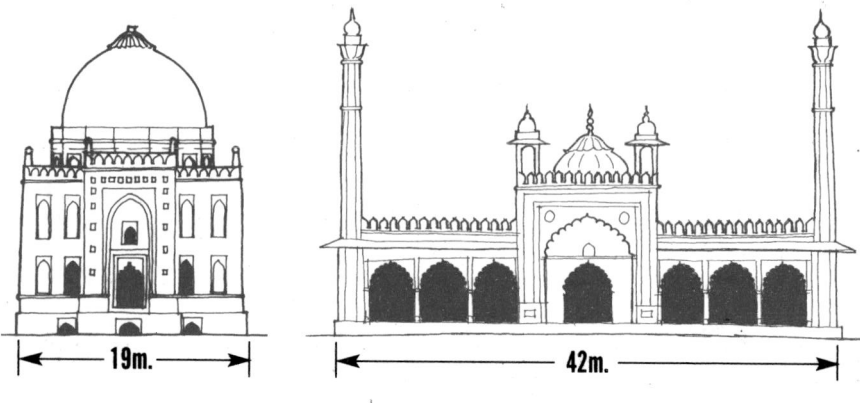

Acknowledgments

First, I would like to thank the Seven Cities of Delhi Group and the friends I made through them. It was working with the group that first showed me what was missing from among the numerous books on Delhi. I would particularly like to thank various friends who visited various parts of Delhi with me and in particular Jane Jones, who joined me over several years in an indefatigable exploration of virtually every alleyway in Shahjahanabad. We were very grateful to the many inhabitants of Shahjahanabad who invited us into their homes.

I would like to thank various people for help and encouragement with this book: Caroline Davidson of the Caroline Davidson Literary Agency, who gave me invaluable help at the beginning of the project; ?atish Nanda and O. P. Jain, Delhi Chapter of INTACH, who produced the INTACH listing, the key to Delhi's buildings; Jeremy Currie, who made for me an excellent translation of the 1840s map; William Dalrymple for information on the early colonial period; Naryani Gupta for some very helpful discussions; Philippa Vaughan for help with the Mughal period; Romila Thapar for invaluable comments on some early chapters. I would also like to thank many friends who have expressed interest in my work and I hope the finished product is as useful to them as intended. I would especially like to thank Shobita Punja of INTACH, who made the publication possible.

Special thanks go to **Reliance Infocomm** for their generous financial support for this project. It is our good fortune that their interest in protecting the heritage and historical character of cities such as Delhi, which are the pride of India, have led them to collaborate with INTACH on this project.

I would like to thank the Staff of the British Library and the ASI Archives at Safdarjang's Tomb; Vincent Rajendran, who drove me, unflappably, into the obscurest parts of Delhi. Many thanks to Priya Kapoor and Renuka Chatterjee of Roli, Rita Vohra for diligent proofreading, and, especially, Manav Agarwal, who designed the book and managed, in such a coherent way, to fit in so much. The inaccuracies and inconsistencies which, no doubt, will still emerge are entirely my fault.

Finally I would like to thank my husband Donald, who was endlessly encouraging, read various versions of the text and vastly improved the style.

Maps

The first map in each chapter shows the development of the city against a simple topographical map. * denotes a walk.

3.2	Lal Kot	30
4.2	Qutb Minar Complex	36
4.3	Siri Fort	44
4.4	Shahpur Jat	44
5.2	Tughlakabad	*50
6.2	Jahanpanah	58
6.3	Jahanpanah Walk	*60
6.4	Chiragh Delhi	*72
6.5	Chiragh Delhi Dargah	76
7.2	Hauz Khas area	*86
7.3	Hauz Khas monuments (plan)	*88
7.4	Qadam Sharif & Ram Nagar	92
7.5	Qadam Sharif village	92
7.6	Qadam Sharif (plan)	95
7.7	Chausath Khamba (plan)	98
8.2	Lodi tombs – the main groups	106
8.3	Western group of Lodi tombs	*108
8.4	Hauz Khas	108
8.5	Northern group of Lodi tombs	114
8.6	Zamrudpur	114
8.7	South Extension	*118
8.8	Kotla Mubarakpur	*118
8.9	Lodi Gardens	*122
8.10	Aliganj	128

10.2	Humayun's Tomb – surroundings and walk	*150
10.3	Humayun's Tomb	*152
10.4	Nizamuddin village	*168
10.5	Nizamuddin Dargah	168
11.2	Shahjahanabad, showing the areas cleared by the British	184
11.3	Shahjahanabad – key map	185
11.4	Red Fort	190
11.5	North of Railway Line	*192
11.6	Lahori Gate, Katra Nil	*194
11.7	Begum Samru's house	*196
11.8	Chandni Chowk	198
11.9	Fatehpur mosque	*200
11.10	Ballimaran	*202
11.11	Dharampura	*204
11.12	Ajmeri Gate	*208
11.13	Turkman Gate	*210
11.14	Delhi Gate	*212
11.15	Daryaganj	*214
12.2	Mehrauli	219
12.3	Mehrauli village	*220
12.4	Qutb Sahib Dargah	224
12.5	Archaeological Park	*228
12.6	Lado Serai	238
13.2	North Delhi Civil Lines area	*248
14.2	New Delhi	*262
15.2	Typical housing layouts (Rabindra Nagar and Nizamuddin East)	292

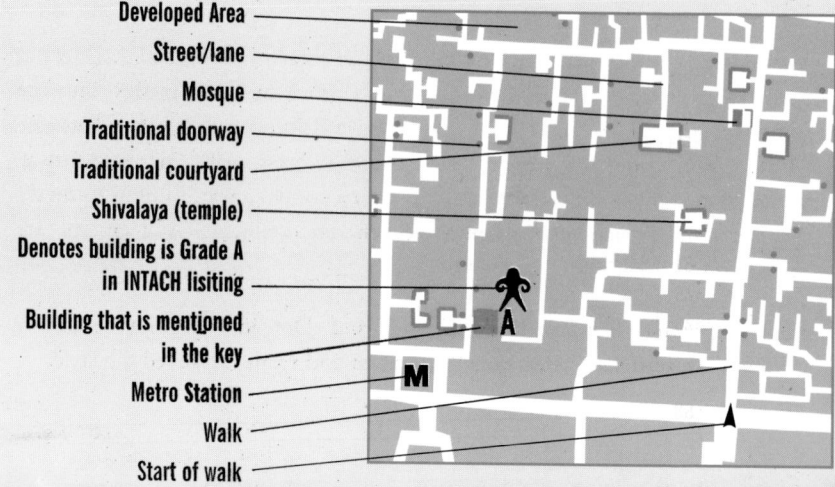

- Developed Area
- Street/lane
- Mosque
- Traditional doorway
- Traditional courtyard
- Shivalaya (temple)
- Denotes building is Grade A in INTACH lisiting
- Building that is mentioned in the key
- Metro Station
- Walk
- Start of walk

Chronology

RAJPUT

1000 BC	Evidence of villages from late-Harappan culture in Delhi area
300-200 BC	Evidence of the first village habitation at the Purana Qila
Mid 3rd c BC	Kalkaji Ashokan Edict carved
700AD – 1160	**Tomar** rule in Delhi area
800s	Suraj Kund dam and tank built
1000s	Lal Kot built
1160 – 92	**Chauhan** rule from capital Ajmer.
	Lal Kot extended to create Qila Rai Pithora

'SLAVE DYNASTY'

1192	Invasion by Muhammad of Ghor. **Qutbuddin Aibak** becomes Sultan of Delhi
	Building of Qutb Minar and mosque
1206	Muhammad of Ghor dies. Qutbuddin Aibak establishes independent state.
1211	**Iltutmish** becomes Sultan. Qutbuddin Bakhtiyar Kaki (Qutb Sahib) arrives in India as disciple of Muinuddin Chisti of Ajmer.
1235	Qutb Sahib dies
	Extension to Qutb Minar and Mosque
	Hauz Shamsi, Mehrauli
	Sultan Ghari's Tomb
	Iltutmish's Tomb
1236 – 45	Several short disputed reigns including the only female Sultan, **Raziya**.
	Shah Turkman and Raziya both buried north of city
1261	Nizamuddin Aulia arrives in Delhi during reign of **Mahmud Shah**.
1266 – 87	**Balban** Sultan of Delhi
	Balban's tomb
1287	**Kaykubad** inherits from Balban
	Builds palace at Kilokri

KHALJI DYNASTY

1290 – 96	**Jalalaldin** seizes power
1296 – 1316	**Alauddin Khalji** assassinates uncle and becomes Sultan.
	Mosque extension, minar stump and *madrasa* at Qutb Minar
	Siri Fort
	Hauz Khas
	Jamaat Khana Mosque at Nizamuddin (?)

TUGHLAK DYNASTY

1320 – 1324	**Ghiyasuddin Tughlak** seizes power
	Tughlakabad and Ghiyasuddin's Tomb
	Nizamuddin Aulia builds *baoli* at Nizamuddin
1324 – 51	**Muhammad Shah Tughlak** reigns.
1325	Nizamuddin dies
1326	Forced removal of most of population of Delhi to Daulatabad
	Jahanpanah walls
	Bijay Mandal and probably Begampur mosque
1351 – 88	**Firoz Shah Tughlak**

TUGHLAK DYNASTY cont.

1356 Chiragh Delhi dies
Hauz Khas restored, *madrasa* built
Firoz Shah Kotla
Qadam Sharif
Numerous hunting lodges
Khan Jahan Tilangani's Tomb
Seven Mosques built by Firoz Shah's Prime Minister
1398 Delhi taken by Timur (Tamberlaine)

SAYYID DYNASTY

1414 – 21 Khizr Khan
1421 – 33 Mubarak Shah
1433 – 45 Muhammad Shah
1445 – 51 Alam Shah
Mubarak Shah's Tomb, mosque and enclosure walls
Muhammad Shah's Tomb
Some tombs built in South Delhi e.g. some of the tombs east of Hauz
Khas village

LODI DYNASTY

1451 – 89 Bahlol Lodi
1489 – 1517 Sikander Lodi
1517 – 1526 Ibrahim Lodi
During Sikander Lodi's reign the court is moved to Agra but Delhi remains
important centre and many fine buildings are erected.
Bahlol Lodi's Tomb
Sikander Lodi's Tomb
Numerous tombs & mosques built north, west and south of city
including:-
Sikander Lodi's Tomb, Bara Gumbad and Sheesh Gumbad now in Lodi
Gardens
Zamrudpur tombs
RKPuram tombs
Tin Burj in South Extension
Tin Burj at Muhammadpur
Moth ki Masjid
Jamali Kamali's Tomb and Mosque
Rajon ki Baoli

MUGHAL DYNASTY

1526 Babur invades India and defeats Ibrahim Lodi. Foundation of Mughal
Empire, ruled mainly from Agra or Lahore.
1530 – 40 Humayun
Walls of Dinpanah (Purana Qila) started
Sher Shah Suri seizes power.
Finishes or rebuilds Purana Qila walls
Masjid Qila Kuhna
Sher Mandal (?)

MUGHAL DYNASTY cont.

Lal Darwaza and Khuni Darwaza

1545 – 1555 Salim Shah

Salimgarh

1555 Humayun regains power but does not reign long before dying after a fall.

1556 – 1605 Akbar

Humayun's Tomb

Athpula in Lodi Gardens built by a courtier

Atgah Khan's Tomb

Adham Khan's Tomb

Khan-i-Khanan's Tomb

1605 – 28 Jahangir

Arab Serai Market & Barapula

Chausath Khamba in Nizamuddin

1628 – 58 Shah Jahan

1638 The emperor starts to build Shahjahanabad: Red Fort, Jami Masjid

Fatehpuri Masjid and other mosques built by his wives

Shalimar Bagh, Hastal hunting lodge built outside the city

Many large mansions built by princes and courtiers

1658 – 1707 Aurangzeb kills his brothers and deposes Shah Jahan, who lives another eight years as his son's captive at Agra

Zinat al-Masjid built by Aurangzeb's daughter

Mosque and Madrasa of Ghaziuddin

1681 Aurangzeb goes south to wage war in the Deccan, never to return to the north.

1707 – 19 Aurangzeb's death leads to civil war between his descendants and the gradual diminution over the next few decades of Mughal power. First *firman* (licence to trade) given to the East India Company.

Mughal Royal Family begin to spend time at Mehrauli, building palace complex near Dargah. Members of the family buried there

1719 – 48 Muhammad Shah

Many temples and mosques built in Shahjahanabad

1748 Qudsia Bagh built

1739 Invasion by Nadir Shah of Persia. The second great sacking of the city and the Red Fort.

1748 – 1803 The final decline of the Mughal Empire, beset by Afghan and Maratha armies, leaves **Shah Alam II** blinded and controlled by the Maratha chief Scindia.

1750 Aliganj built

1753 Safdarjang's Tomb

1779 Lal Bangla tombs in Golf course

COLONIAL POWER

1803 General Lake defeats Scindia outside Delhi. British Resident and other officials installed in Delhi.

1823 Begum Samru's House built

1824 Town Duties Committee established

COLONIAL POWER cont.

1828 European troops move to new Cantonment beyond the Ridge

1830s Development of suburbs west of Delhi – Sadar Bazaar, Kishanganj and Deputyganj.

1835 Sir Thomas Metcalfe's House built

1836 St James's Church built

1848 Part of land on east bank of river included in Delhi territory.

1857 Great Uprising in Meerut, Delhi, Awadh and a few other parts of north India.

1858 The British Government takes over administration from the East India Company. **Bahadur Shah** exiled to Rangoon.

1859 Major clearance of buildings between the Fort and the city

1863 Delhi Municipal Committee formed

1864 Town Hall built

1866 Railway comes to Delhi, necessitating a major clearance of buildings

1869 The poet Ghalib dies

1877 Durbar north of Delhi in which Queen Victoria is proclaimed Empress of India

1903 Coronation Durbar

1911 Durbar at which George V announces that Delhi will become the capital of India.

1912 Bomb thrown at Viceroy, Lord Hardinge.
The Raisina site finally selected for new capital.

1916 New Delhi Municipal Committee formed but only active from 1925

1931 Inauguration of New Delhi government buildings

1940s Delhi University moves to present site

INDEPENDENCE

1947 Independence. Partition causes a massive exchange of populations. The population of Delhi nearly doubles between 1941 and 1951.

1955 Delhi Development Authority (DDA) set up

1962 Delhi Master Plan approved by Parliament

1982 Asian Games held in Delhi.

1985 National Capital Territory created.

INTRODUCTION

Delhi! The name sums up the pomp and power of bygone days.

Count Hans von Koenigsmarck,
1910

Introduction

D elhi is an amalgamation of many cities built at different times in its thousand-year history, and it is this history that has been its fascination for its citizens and visitors for centuries. This book is about the growth and development of Delhi. It concentrates on the scattered remains of the earlier cities, both in terms of actual buildings but also in the way each new 'city' has affected later development and, in particular, the current appearance of Delhi. In one sense several different cities exist now: the city of the political elite based around colonial New Delhi; the city of the business elite, centred on South Delhi; the even larger city of the middle class, which has spread right out to the west, south and east, and finally the city that fits into the interstices of the others, one that is almost invisible to the elite but where millions of people live and work in indescribably desperate conditions. These modern manifestations of Delhi are physically very different but they all, to some extent, overlap with the historic cities. By exploring the old sites many aspect of the modern city are revealed.

In the historical context many people are aware that there were 'seven cities of Delhi' but it is, in fact, plausible to talk of any number up to sixteen. This number includes all known separate foundations as well as the two colonial centres, the Civil Lines and New Delhi, to which, by the same rules, must be

Qutb Minar

added Modern Delhi, that is post-Independence Delhi. In fact, I hope to explain that there were certain areas that remained predominantly urban for centuries, while the majority of the places now considered as 'cities' were either suburban developments or simply failures, sometimes leaving no trace. Effectively, the real centre of power shifted twice, from the Mehrauli area to Shahjahanabad and from there to New Delhi. Modern Delhi's commercial and government centres are still based on the Mughal and colonial cities and the urban area has spread out to encompass virtually all the previous 'cities' as well as numerous villages, which still exist among the residential layouts that supplanted their fields. This legacy has certainly shaped the urban fabric, which varies wildly from the astonishing density of the old city and village areas to the ludicrously spread-out New Delhi and Cantonment areas.

Along with this curious land-use pattern we have also been bequeathed fascinating buildings from every century over the last thousand years. Since at least the 11th century Delhi has been an important urban centre, and there is evidence of continuous occupation in the area for at least a thousand years before that. Rather surprisingly, despite the antiquity of India's urban culture, many of modern India's largest cities do not have long histories; of the six biggest cities only Delhi and Hyderabad existed as important urban centres before the arrival of the British, whose principal cities (Calcutta, Bombay and Madras) were all ports. The colonial economy and external trade gave such places an importance that eclipsed inland cities. Bangalore, although politically important, was only a small city before it became a colonial garrison town, and Hyderabad was only founded in1589.

Even in the next rank down it is surprising how few cities are truly ancient. In comparison with Europe or West Asia, there are only a small number of cities in India that

were important for more than a few centuries. Those that were, such as Varanasi, are often significant centres for pilgrimage as well as being centres of specialist production such as textiles. More common have been medium-sized cities, such as Lucknow or Orchha, which were centres of power for only a hundred years or so as local families rose to power and then were superseded. Some cities in this category

Hauz Khas

continued as local market centres, some dwindled to mere villages, and some were abandoned altogether, either for a site nearby or for political reasons. Often their architectural heritage is preserved only *because* the buildings were abandoned and not, as would otherwise have been the case, pulled down to be rebuilt or used as a quarry. The most moving sites to visit are those of which nothing now remains but defensive walls, ruined palaces, temples and mosques, and these places deservedly attract many tourists. By contrast, Delhi's great interest derives from the fact that it has been an important urban centre for so long. It thus contains ancient pilgrimage centres, abandoned cities, a large medieval city, a colonial capital and urban villages, all within a rapidly expanding and changing modern city. I use the term medieval, which is generally associated with pre-modern Europe, because it effectively evokes a walled city with narrow roads and traditional market areas.

Two of India's twenty-six Indian UNESCO World Heritage Sites are in Delhi and there are approximately 1,200 other monuments listed in INTACH's (Indian National Trust for Art and Cultural Heritage) first survey. These buildings are in various states of repair: some are well maintained, others are ruined; some are well loved and occupied, others are totally neglected.

Because the city has shifted from place to place over the centuries it is logical to follow the old-fashioned dynastic periodisation when discussing the architecture. To some extent dynastic changes led to shifts in style and these are outlined in Chapter 2. Although there were settlements in the Delhi region during the first millennium AD there is very little left to visit from this period. The fragments of buildings left from the Rajput era are discussed in Chapter 3. Because there were Muslim rulers in Delhi from 1192 until the British took over in 1803, most of the early architecture is 'Islamic', particularly so for the buildings that survive from the first three hundred years (1200 AD to 1500 AD), which are of military, educational or religious significance. The first Indo-Islamic style, generally called 'Sultanate', developed very quickly after the 12th century invasions, and was quite different from the local indigenous architecture of the time, but also substantially different from what was being built in Central Asia, North Africa and the Muslim heartland. For instance, whereas the architectural decoration of both Hindu temples in India and Islamic buildings in Central Asia tends to negate the structure of the buildings with a profusion of decoration (typically in carved stonework and tile-work respectively), in Indo-Islamic architecture the structure tends to be expressed quite strongly. The surviving buildings, many of them tombs or mosques, are magnificent stone structures, some in highly ornamented masonry, some built of rubble with stucco surface decorations and some from roughly hewn stone, well proportioned but with little surface ornamentation. The few secular buildings that survive, such as palaces or hunting lodges, are mostly in ruins. This Sultanate period is covered in Chapters 4 to 9.

There is a greater range of buildings in Delhi dating from the second half of the millennium, when large parts of India were ruled by the Mughals, and later by the British. From the Mughal period there are, again, numerous mosques and tombs but also more in the way of secular buildings. Although Delhi remained an important city under the early Mughals, its great renaissance came in the 17th century under Shah Jahan, who built the great walled city of Shahjahanabad (see Chapter 11). Sadly no domestic, non-imperial buildings dating from this time have survived into this century. However, to an extent, the cultural life of the court survived for a long time in the city, even during the early years of British rule in the 19th century, and a traditional urban way of life continued. Handsome houses were constructed in the established style right into the 20th century. At first glance, anywhere inside the walled city (Shahjahanabad), it is difficult to envisage the Mughal city at the height of its glittering wealth when such outstanding buildings as the Red Fort and the Jami Masjid were being constructed. It is even less easy to evoke the colourful elegance of the life led by wealthy courtiers and citizens. However, at second glance, behind the dereliction, the signboards and the frightening tangles of electricity cables, it is surprising how often one notices mosques, temples and finely carved gateways to former *havelis*. The early and late Mughal periods are covered in Chapters 10 to 12.

From the British period there is a more eclectic range of buildings, some of which date from early colonial days, although pre-eminent among them must be the stately Government buildings of Lutyens and Baker (built during the 1920s). These often take visitors by surprise; their magnificence far surpasses modern government centres in most other countries. This period is covered in Chapters 13 and 14. Chapter 15 brings us up to date with a look at post-Independence Delhi and its future.

CONSERVATION

The first concerted conservation work in Delhi was undertaken in the 14th century by Sultan Firoz Shah Tughlak. He carried out extensive repairs to many of the buildings in Delhi and seems to have had a real awareness of the historical importance of old buildings and a general curiosity about the past. He was particularly fascinated by the 3rd century BC Ashokan pillars

Safdarjang's Tomb

found to the north of Delhi and had them moved to his palaces in Delhi. Later rulers were not so interested in antiquities, but the desire to honour the burial sites of ancestors or holy men meant that these buildings were kept in good repair, at least for a time.

Early travellers from Europe were entranced by Delhi's image as the 'ancient seat of kings' and an extraordinary number of books, mostly in guidebook form, were written for visitors during the colonial era. It was also during this time that the history and culture of

North Block entrance

India was investigated through archaeology, numismatics and the decipherment of ancient scripts, adding to the broad body of knowledge already available from the extensive written histories in scripts and languages that were understood. Naturally some of this work was focussed on Delhi and its unparalleled collection of buildings, some intact, some in ruins. The scholar who did most early work on the Delhi monuments was Syed Ahmad Khan in the mid-19th century and it is on his work (sadly not translated fully into English from the original Urdu) that most subsequent writing was based. Once the buildings' historical and architectural importance was recognised (rather late in the day for some of them), measures for repair and conservation were undertaken with increasing professionalism by the Archaeological Survey of India (ASI, founded in 1871). The extent to which the recreational value of the sites was emphasised in the early days is, however, striking. The same amount of money was spent every year on the gardens surrounding the sites as on the buildings themselves.

The movement of the capital to Delhi from Calcutta in 1911 spurred on further work in the conservation field, not least in the compilation of a four volume list under the auspices of the ASI (1916 ASI listing). Many buildings were thereby saved and can now be seen, scattered among the extensive suburbs. The buildings protected by the ASI were mainly those that were in public ownership. It was felt that buildings such as functioning mosques were outside their remit and were in any case being cared for. Equally, in those days, it was felt that buildings in private ownership could not be interfered with, which tended to exclude them from being listed, apart from those that featured because they were 'illegally occupied' such as inhabited tombs.

Following Independence the government's priorities were, naturally, focussed elsewhere for a few decades but recently there has been a revival of interest in Delhi's architectural heritage. The more prominent buildings continued to be maintained, even though the gardens have visibly deteriorated since the time of the garden-obsessed British (there has been a recent revival of some gardens). The private sector, through bodies such as INTACH have tried to fill the gaps left by the cash-strapped ASI. There is also increasing awareness of the importance of educating people to improve their environment from the point of view of general amenity as well as appreciating the cultural value of historic buildings. This has led to a growing concern for the rapidly vanishing heritage of secular and residential buildings in Shah Jahan's walled city and the numerous urban villages that have been engulfed by suburban expansion. The first tentative steps are now being taken to protect private buildings of historical or architectural interest in such areas, but because of legislative and financial constraints it is unlikely that such initiatives will be very effective, unless there is a significant change in the general public's attitude to their environment.

Sprawling Delhi, with its ever-increasing millions of inhabitants, is obviously not as appealing to the senses as many other places in India. It cannot, for instance, compete with the romance of the ruined forts of Rajasthan and Central India. However, it is where millions of people live and, while a few care passionately about Delhi and its history, there are many others who can and should be guided into an appreciation of their city. Most of the main sites are pleasantly situated, so far removed from the urban chaos that surrounds them that the visitor gets an agreeable respite. Those who seek out more obscure buildings will also be rewarded. If they are observant, the curious will notice more and more relics from the past. These monuments are often neglected, so visitors will often find themselves alone, apart from local children who might show them a hidden staircase to the roof or rush off to find the *chawkidar* with the keys.

A WORD ABOUT VOCABULARY, SPELLING AND DATES

This book is written for the general reader and is based almost entirely on English language secondary sources. Because I am writing in English I have chosen to refer to buildings by their English name if that seems to be most frequently used in English, thus Red Fort instead of *Lal Qila*. It also seems peculiar to refer to the 'Rashtrapati Bhawan' rather than the 'Viceroy's House' when talking about its construction, even though the former is in common usage for general purposes. The events of 1857 have been described as the First War of Independence, the 1857 Revolt, and the Sepoy Mutiny among other things. The term Great Uprising is untainted by colonial bias and describes the event well so I have decided on that label. I have come across numerous variations for spellings of names and objects, all being transliterations from the original Persian, Urdu, Hindi, etc. This wild variation can, presumably, be ascribed in part to the very great changes in pronunciation of languages over the decades, so transcriptions accurate at one time become comical a hundred years later. I have decided to stick with the versions that occur most frequently in books that are widely read, on the basis that they will therefore be most familiar to the general reader. Some words are in common Hindi usage in which case I have tried to follow the transliterated Hindi spelling. I have also tried to stick to one short name for individuals, having myself struggled with the multiple names of, for instance, Afghan noblemen, who often had long names that could be variously contracted, and the different contractions used indiscriminately.

I have given dates as frequently as possible, mainly based on the INTACH listing; some are my own guesswork, based on stylistic details. Sometimes different sources give different specific dates; I have generally selected one date rather arbitrarily, but a few years either way makes very little difference to the general chronology. Again, because most dates are 'transliterations' from sources that use a different calendar with different year-ends, it means that the transliterations result in a year that might span over parts of two years of the Christian calendar, thus giving a date of, say, 1370-71. I have elected to quote the earlier year.

Finally, because I am writing for the general reader, I have concentrated on those buildings or aspects of buildings that are easily accessible. It is frustrating to read of the marvellous interior of such and such a building and then find, on arrival, that the door is padlocked and access is prohibited. However, it is highly unlikely that all the buildings that are open (or closed) at the time of writing will remain that way, so I apologise if some buildings are now closed or if others are omitted from description but are now accessible.

DELHI ARCHITECTURE

The gaily dressed crowds who will come in increasing numbers to see the new as well as the old Delhi should grasp the meaning to be read in the stone and marble of their capital.

- Herbert Baker, 1930

Delhi Architecture

In order to avoid going into too much repetitive architectural detail elsewhere, this chapter will look at the most common building types to be seen in Delhi, explaining their features and genesis.

For many centuries the principal public buildings of Delhi were built by Turkish, Afghan and Mughal rulers and their courtiers, often for religious purposes, and it is these that have survived. It is to be expected that important buildings such as those built for court and religious purposes would survive longer than domestic buildings; the building materials and techniques would naturally have been superior and more durable. Religious buildings had an even greater chance of survival, often being endowed for their future maintenance. For this reason we get only a partial view of ancient architecture, the more ephemeral buildings having been replaced many times over. The majority of the population would have built for themselves in a traditional style, one that we know from archaeological excavations did not change much over the centuries. Thus the village courtyard house, still ubiquitous in rural India (and still found in village areas in the city), can be taken as a model of what much of the old cities would have consisted of. Significantly, these builders would also have made up much of the construction workforce and it is not surprising, therefore, that Islamic buildings here contain 'Indian' features. This was done at first because indigenous building techniques were employed to create foreign building types (mosques and tombs) but later because patrons and architects had absorbed into their repertoire of Islamic styles features that they admired on local buildings,

Trabeate lintel

Baoli

Indigenous elements used on an Islamic buliding

Dalan in haveli courtyard

such as highly decorated brackets (corbels) supporting beams. Initially the two traditions were easily distinguishable from each other but they soon adapted to form a marvellous synthesis, commonly known as Indo-Islamic architecture.

Surviving ancient indigenous building forms are those that were built to last and were cherished, such as forts, temples (Hindu, Buddhist or Jain) and structures connected with water collection and supply such as *bunds* (dams), tanks (reservoirs) and *baolis* (stepwells), the conservation of water being as great an issue in the past as it is in modern India. For various reasons few temples survived in Delhi from early times. Obviously a lack of patronage must have affected some, but also, although most Muslim rulers were tolerant of other faiths, temples were sometimes destroyed, either as a political statement of power or by the more fanatical of the Islamic sultans. Recent scholarship has established, however, that this latter phenomenon was much less common than is generally believed while in the former case such destructive statements could as easily be made by rival Hindu powers. Many temples have also been repeatedly rebuilt, adding to the impression that there are few ancient temples. In fact there are several sites where temples have existed for many centuries though little of historical or architectural interest remains. Although residential and community buildings have not survived in great numbers, many of the existing urban villages are ancient settlements where the street pattern and, until recently, traditional building designs and methods prevailed. A very common feature of buildings in hot climates is the open-sided room, called a *dalan*, which can be found free-standing, as part of a courtyard complex or, in effect, as the prayer hall of a typical mosque, the prototype of which was a desert house.

Tank - Gaushala, Mehrauli

Typical village

Traditional village lane

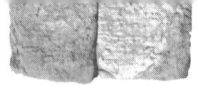

The Rajput and Sultanate Periods

CONSTRUCTION

Apart from three ancient pillars imported from elsewhere (p.32, 85), the earliest structures still visible in Delhi date from the final centuries of Rajput rule, before 1192. At **Suraj Kund** (probably 8th century) there are two relics of an early settlement: a circular tank constructed from massive quartzite (the local stone) blocks and an impressive dam, also built from quartzite blocks. The

Lal Kot walls

settlement at Suraj Kund was replaced by another city nearby, now known as **Lal Kot** (mid-11th century), where the walls are faced with roughly surfaced blocks over a rubble interior. The stone was cut so accurately that it allowed precise alignment in a system that did not use mortar, although the surface of the blocks was not made smooth. At both places there would have been temples; Muhammad of Ghor, who invaded in 1192, claimed to have demolished twenty-seven at Lal Kot (almost certainly an exaggeration but perhaps small shrines were included in this number). The basic construction technique in pre-Islamic times was trabeate or 'post and beam': walls were built in solid masonry but interior spaces and openings were framed by posts (often gloriously carved columns) and beams, the length of the beams dictating the spacing of the columns and the size of the openings in the walls. At the late 12th century **Qutb Minar Mosque** numerous exquisitely carved temple columns were reused, and we can see that they were as fine as any in India.

The earliest buildings after the Turkish invasion are the **Qutb Minar** itself and those grouped around it. Luckily most of the features typical of **early Sultanate** architecture are well represented among the buildings in the Qutb Minar complex, where we can trace its evolution

The earliest part of the **Qutb Minar Mosque** (1192 onwards) is a very good example of an Islamic building constructed with entirely indigenous building techniques (see p.40). The great screen wall of the mosque at first looks entirely Islamic with its huge pointed arches. However, you will see that the construction of the arches is unusual: trabeate, in which flat stones are built one above the other, the inner end of each one projecting further than the one below, as a cantilever, with their non-projecting ends held down by the weight of the masonry above. The shallow domes inside the entrances to the mosque are also interesting because they are the type of domes found in Hindu and Jain temples throughout India, constructed in the same way as the mosque arches, with overlapping rings of cantilevered stones. The internal profile of the dome is therefore governed by the strength

Temple columns - Qutb Minar Mosque

of the stone slabs. This, in turn, is dictated by the slabs' depth and, of course, the depth of the carvings made on their lower surface. Elsewhere, the square spaces between the columns are roofed in a slightly simpler trabeate style, in which slabs are laid across corners, successively reducing the roof opening.

The problem with trabeate construction is that the structural integrity is based on the strength of stone in tension. For instance, the weight bearing down on the centre of a beam will try to make it bend in the middle; the bottom of the beam will therefore be stretched (in tension). The same applies to a cantilevered stone except that it will be in tension on the top surface. Stone is not an inherently strong material in tension. In modern times this problem has been solved using steel, which is strong in tension, either as steel beams or as reinforcement in concrete. Timber is a low-technology alternative but depends on cutting down big trees to make big beams. Although stone is not strong in tension it is very strong in compression, which is the way it is normally used, in solid walls. Arcuate construction was the invention of the Romans and its structural superiority derives from the fact that the arch is made up of blocks of stone that are all in compression. The weight from the wall above bears down on the whole arch, compressing each element in it.

A further benefit of the true arch is that it can be constructed from many small, light blocks, which are much easier to handle than the massive beams and slabs necessary in trabeate construction. From the Romans the technique spread throughout the Mediterranean world and, of course, into the Middle East and then Central Asia, from where India's Turkish invaders came. In India, however, it took several decades for local building techniques to catch up with the architectural style brought with the invasion. You will see good examples of arcuate or 'true' arches in the **Madrasa of Alauddin** (1317 - see p.42), near the Qutb Minar and you can see how the weight is transferred through the stones of the arch. It is clearly important that the joints between the blocks that make up the arch are not vertical or parallel, otherwise the blocks could slide past each other.

Domes in temples were clearly important features, but often expressed differently internally from externally. The interior shallow dome often transmogrified into a different architectural form, typically pyramidal, on the outside, which was the dominant feature. In other words the internal dome was a structurally limited but convenient and decorative way of covering the important central space. Likewise, the Islamic dome was clearly an extremely important architectural element. It is possible that the form of an Islamic dome was seen as a substitute for the sky; this certainly seems to have been the case in the context of tombs, which according to Koranic injunction, were

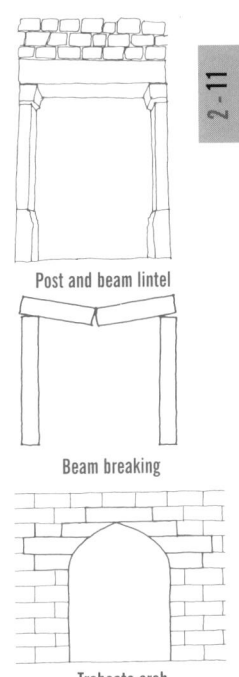

Post and beam lintel

Beam breaking

Trabeate arch

Arcuate arch

Alauddin's Madrasa arches

Qulb Minar detail

supposed to be open to the sky, and dome ceilings often featured star-like decorations on the inner surface.

The principle of the arch can of course be used in exactly the same way for spanning a large space in all directions, creating a full dome. The immediate question arises as to how to put a circular dome over a square building. In simple trabeate construction the corners are bridged with beams and the cantilevered dome built over them. This also occurs in the case of a very common tomb form, twelve-pillared pavilions. In arcuate construction it is easier to construct bigger domes, but this makes bridging the corner even more critical, and impossible with a single, simply supported beam. This is achieved instead in two ways, one based on the arch, the other on the beam and corbel or bracket (the trabeate system). The structure spanning the corner is known as a squinch. Thus, when an arch is used, it is known as a squinch arch and usually contains a half-dome, smoothing out the transition from right angle to arch. Above the squinch arches there is generally an octagonal or sixteen-sided drum with arched niches on each face. Above this there are generally several bands consisting of stone slabs acting as partial beams, transforming the octagon into a circle. The first circle has sixteen slabs, the second thirty-two and there is sometimes a third with sixty-four, which is close to a circle, the base of the dome.

As we have seen, the construction methods of the early Islamic period used both indigenous and imported techniques. The same applied to the decoration. In view of the very high quality of the indigenous temple carvings it is not surprising to find some of the finest carving in Delhi on the two earliest Islamic buildings, the **Qutb Minar** itself and the screen wall of Qutbuddin Aibak's Mosque (the earliest part of the **Qutb Minar Mosque**). It is obvious therefore that highly skilled sculptors and stone masons still abounded in Delhi at that time. The use of sandstone allowed even finer and more intricate carving than on the temple columns. The decoration on both buildings also features the Islamic *nashki* script. The calligraphy is intertwined with arabesque decoration: lovely sinuous foliage that is both traditionally Islamic but also entirely in the Hindu tradition. On the Qutb Minar stunningly intricate sculpture hangs beneath the projecting galleries. This kind of carving can, of course, be seen on the underside of temple domes and, indeed, is visible inside the mosque entrance dome. However, it is also very similar in style to the fabulous *muqarnas* that were a common feature in Islamic architecture from the 12th century.

By the time Iltutmish was ruling (1210-35) sculpture had become rather less exuberant, presumably because sculptors had been imported and the local masons were also learning Islamic restraint. An important decorative feature, the lotus bud and lotus flower motifs, became gradually more prominent and we see them on the more austere later buildings, often the only non-architectural decorative feature, along with the widely used double triangle star, a symbol of great antiquity that has meant different things in different societies.

Iltutmish's Mosque exten detail

The arrival of the **Tughlaks** (14th c.) created quite a sharp break in architectural style. In Delhi there are numerous examples of buildings from the times of the Tughlak sultans. Fortifications were massive: heavily battered (i.e., sloping) walls with roughly cut facing stones like at Lal Kot. In most respects the new forts were similar in design to indigenous ones, although they appear more impressive militarily and were designed, like Islamic forts in other countries, so that the citadel could face attack from the townspeople as well as the surrounding countryside. The walls of most non-military buildings were built using local rock, often uncut but selected to provide a

Ghiyasuddin Tughlak's Tomb

flat surface for the façade, with a rubble infill. The wall was then plastered wherever a more refined appearance was required. Because there is little evidence of what the final plastered buildings were like, we are inclined to think that the Tughlaks were demonstrating their might rather than their sophistication, but contemporary descriptions of the courts rather contradict this. It is likely that we are misled by the non-durable nature of exterior plasterwork; the few Tughlak buildings that are constructed from ashlar (square, close cut) masonry, for instance in **Ghiyasuddin Tughlak's Tomb** at Tughlakabad (1320-24), are in a new, austere style with heavily battered walls and minimal decoration, but indisputably 'refined' (see p.53). These buildings were the precursors of the archetypical style now thought of as Indo-Islamic, which features, among other things, a combination of arches and square frames around distinctively 'Indian' doorways that have heavily ornamented corbels supporting a deep beam.

The style of portal just described is generally found in a bay projecting up and out from the main façade that is sometimes referred to as a *pishtaq*. It is a form found throughout the Islamic world and in the Central Asian context would normally frame an *iwan*, a shallow vaulted hall facing an open courtyard. This was an early architectural feature in Islamic architecture. The *iwan* could be closed at the back or form the portal for an entrance, but in sultanate architecture the *iwan* is normally so shallow that it would be misleading to refer to it as such, although it does occur in a few early buildings.

By the time of the **Tughlaks** much of the carved masonry decoration (calligraphy, lotus buds, etc.) had disappeared (although we cannot tell to what extent the buildings were originally covered with decorated plasterwork) but white marble was sometimes used to outline particular features such as doors, arches and the rectilinear frames that became such an important feature on Indo-Islamic façades. This emphasis on highlighting architectural features is in interesting contrast to the prevailing decorative system elsewhere in the Islamic world where decoration (for instance ceramic tiles) tended to smother all constructional features.

After the turmoil of the end of the Tughlak dynasty and Timur's invasion in 1398 the architecture appears to have become much less forbidding. The Indo-Islamic style reached its climax during the **Lodi period** (1451-1526) and the early

Typical chatri

Mughal interregnum of Sher Shah Suri (1540-55). The basic construction techniques remained the same: the true arch and dome alongside decorated post and beam doorways. The *iwan* disappeared completely, leaving a shallow arch (or several recessed arches) around each entrance. The *pishtaq* remained, but other parts of the façade became more dominant, especially in mosques. Externally the *chatri* as an ornamental feature on buildings also became common. It started to appear in places that once would have had a simple dome but now the dome was lifted onto columns. The architectural concept of a square, open (or screened), domed pavilion had been in existence for some time and had been much used for tombs. It was now used as well to adorn roofs. *Chatri* means parasol or umbrella and the word has been borrowed to describe a small domed pavilion supported on four, six or eight pillars. On roofs they served the practical function of providing shade, where whatever breeze was available could be enjoyed during the endless hot weather.

Internally a charming trabeate variant of the squinch was often used. The corner is bridged with a beam and, below it, small cantilever beams project from the wall to make a flat plane up to the beam. The gaps between the projecting beams were usually highly decorated with carved plasterwork or stucco, a good example being in the **Bara Gumbad Mosque** (1494) in the Lodi Gardens (see p.124). This type of decoration is similar to the glorious *muqarnas* that were in widespread use in Islamic architecture although, in keeping with the more structurally expressive nature of Indo-Islamic architecture, they can be read as coherent elements, unlike the honeycomb-like accretions in Spanish or Persian buildings.

Trabeate squinch muqarna

Stucco in Bara Gumbad

Another manifestation of the flowering of the Indo-Islamic style in the **Lodi period**, was the reappearance of geometric and 'arabesque' designs. The marvellous combination of arches and frames was beautified with a great variety of different coloured stone and decorative features which included coloured tile work and very fine incised stucco that would have been painted in glorious colours. Examples of this can still be seen, the best being in the tomb of **Jamali Kamali** (1528) at Mehrauli (see p.237). The ancient skills of the Indian stonemasons in laying stone without the use of mortar still existed; even the inlaid stone patterns could be made without the use of mortar, a feat that astonished Babur, the founder of the Mughal dynasty.

Tomb façade - Bara Gumbad

The Mughal Period (1526 – 1803)

The Mughals followed in the well-worn path of horse traders and Turkish mercenaries as well as Babur's great predecessor Timur. Nonetheless they brought with them from Central Asia and Kabul new ideas of architecture and decoration, especially after Humayun, the second emperor, had spent some years as an adult refugee in the Persian court. It would be wrong though to claim that a complete stylistic break occurred. Moreover the end result, even for those buildings that were commissioned by the royal court, had as little to do with the architecture of the Mughals' original homeland or Persia as had Sultanate architecture with the architecture of Afghanistan or Turkey. The early Mughal emperors were impressed by some of the buildings they found in India, such as Gwalior Fort, the buildings at Mandu and Sheikh Ahmad Khattu's Tomb at Sarkhej near Ahmedabad. As under the Sultanate, the influential buildings were not necessarily even Islamic; the influence of Rajput and other indigenous styles cannot be underestimated; the influence in both directions was, inevitably, strong.

Hoshang Shah's Tomb, Mandu

Sheikh Ahmed Khattu's Tomb, Sarkhej

Nonetheless, we can still identify a new style that, it is safe to say, is lighter and more delicate than the old. The peak of Mughal architecture was reached under Shah Jahan (reigned 1628-58) with the Taj Mahal and his exquisite pavilions inside the three Red Forts (Delhi, Agra and Lahore) where the extensive use of white marble is probably the most conspicuous element. However, there are other characteristics that distinguish Mughal architecture from previous styles. For instance, the way in which surface decoration was used was different: one sees in Mughal buildings, even as early as the mid-16th century, a greater emphasis on decorating flat surfaces with relief carving, inlaid stonework or tile-work. There was an increasing emphasis on applied decoration rather than the decorative use of architectural features. In other words,

Shah Burj, Red Fort

Applied decoration in Khass Mahal, Red Fort

later Mughal architecture became more Persian. For instance, to consider the treatment of the transition between an octagonal dome drum and the dome itself, in sultanate architecture this was done simply, as described above, with bands of stone slabs that became increasingly circular. While this was a structural solution, the Mughal technique only appears to be structural: 'ribs', that frame each arch, are extended upwards to meet the framing of other arches, forming a net pattern known as 'arch netting'. These ribs might appear to be structural but are purely decorative. This is well illustrated in **Humayun's Tomb** (1563-71) (see p.161-5).

Arch netting was gradually transformed into more exotic net-vaulting,

Arch netting is visible above the upper openings which are, in effect, small i within the main iwan, Humayun's Tomb

which could cover an entire ceiling. This is also an un-spiky version of *muqarnas,* the fabulous ceiling decorations found in other parts of the Islamic world. Of course, when the double dome was introduced early on in the Mughal period, the inner dome, which was generally shallower, was inherently non-structural so this sort of treatment is logically justified.

Double dome

The *iwan* made its reappearance in Mughal architecture, after the long dominance of the shallow arch. The use of an *iwan* created much stronger relief in the façade and, because its ceiling tended to be in the form of a half-dome, a feature that was now dominant in Islamic architecture elsewhere, notably in Persia, it also introduced additional scope for complex decoration, in the form of arch-netting or net-vaulting.

Net vaulting

Muqarnas

Another obvious development was the treatment of the dome, previously either hemispherical or a flattened hemisphere. The dome of Humayun's Tomb is an early, perfect, example of an onion dome. This form became increasingly mannered as time went on, becoming more bulbous and sometimes acquiring ornate decorations. The emphasis on the dome as an external feature led to the dome being elevated high above the main roof. This meant creating a potentially very tall, narrow space below the dome. The inner (double) dome was introduced in order to achieve as pleasing a set of proportions inside the building as outside.

Onion domes

There were other elements that became more mannered as the Mughal style developed. For instance, columns became bulbous and were often fluted. This was possibly under the influence of European pictures of kings and religious scenes set beside fluted columns. The early Mughal reigns saw the first extensive visits by Europeans, eager to trade with the Empire, and one of the gifts they brought were pictures. Cusped arches, which had often featured in early sultanate buildings, made a reappearance, often built in trabeate style with panels carved in the shape of a cusped arch projecting beneath a simple post and beam construction. From

Cusped arches

elsewhere in India came other elements that were incorporated into Mughal architecture. Specifically from Bengal came the curious curved roof (*bangla*), not seen before on north Indian buildings but increasingly common, particularly on domestic buildings such as the later buildings in the Red Fort.

Some of the features mentioned above, such as the bulbous columns and *bangla* roof profile also featured prominently in domestic and secular buildings. However, it is impossible to identify other major changes in domestic architecture because so few pre-Mughal secular buildings survive.

Domestic courtyard

'Bangla' roof with bulbous columns - Jharokha, Red Fort

The Colonial and Post-Independence Periods (1803 onwards)

Like the first Turks and Afghans six hundred years earlier, the British brought with them completely new building forms such as 'bungalows', churches and railway stations. Churches already existed in India but mainly around the coast where European traders had settled (during Akbar's reign Portuguese Jesuits had built a chapel at Fatepur Sikri but it was soon adapted to commercial purposes). Likewise, whereas schools were not a new concept, the new methods of organising education were and required different building types. At first the Europeans in India adapted

St. James's Church

An early bungalow in Bengal

themselves to Indian ways of life in their marriage, dress and living arrangements. However, the increasing number of British people who came, with less adaptable habits (especially among the women), eventually led to a sharp divergence in lifestyles, thereby producing new domestic and commercial building types, something that had not been so much the case after previous 'invasions'. On the whole, therefore, the two kinds of architecture are easily distinguished, both by their built form and their decoration, although European features such as pilasters and classical window surrounds can be found on indigenous buildings such as *havelis*, and typical Indian architectural features were sometimes used on European buildings. Adorning a roof with pretty *chatris* became a popular way of 'Indianising' an otherwise alien building such as a sports stadium.

Alongside the new institutional buildings came the bungalow, so very different from the indigenous Indian house, which tends to present a blank face to the outside world, its rooms facing internal courtyards. The British bungalow evolved in Bengal (hence its name) where the earliest houses were adapted from the local vernacular rural house type. The standard form, which arrived in Delhi in the 19th century, was distinctly un-urban: a sprawling, white-painted, single-storey house with wide verandas that protected the interior from the sun and provided comfortable exterior living space. This was very similar to the *dalan* of Indian houses, palaces and mosques but, instead of facing into a courtyard, the veranda faced out onto a large garden compound, rather in the manner of a Mughal garden pavilion. The obsession for the British was 'good air' and a house in the middle of a large green garden in the extensive cantonment or Civil Lines was supposed to insulate the delicate foreigner from the dangers emanating from the 'native town'.

At first, for institutional buildings, as with domestic customs, the British adapted to the existing administrative buildings in the same way as they adapted to the existing administrative system. However, new methods of government soon emerged, along with their associated buildings. By the time the planning of New Delhi (started in 1912 but built mostly in the 1920s and 30s) was

Bungalow

commenced a huge government system existed and a new building type had been created to house it, exemplified by the old Writer's Building in Calcutta. The New Delhi Secretariat buildings, which replaced the Calcutta buildings, must be some of the finest government buildings in the world (now known prosaically as North and South Blocks).

While a distinction remained in the 19th century between colonial buildings (located mainly to the north of Old Delhi) and indigenous buildings, this difference began to disappear, especially after the building of New Delhi. Although in and around the walled city traditional *havelis* were still built, by the time the capital was transferred there were a considerable number of Indians whose housing was indistinguishable from that built for Europeans, in style though sometimes not in amenity. This was sometimes by choice but often because that was all that was on offer. The trend towards building in a Western style has been inexorable ever since, with numerous estates of public sector housing laid out in 'garden city' style, perhaps architecturally more like a north European than English model. Private housing, by contrast, is laid out in 'colonies' which are constrained by market forces – thus the very affluent have reasonable sized plots in exclusive areas while most of private sector Delhi is highly congested.

Compared with public sector housing styles, the buildings in colonies such as Greater Kailash–II, Vasant Vihar and New Friends Colony, are wonderfully eclectic but are derived more from a wide range of European styles than from any indigenous ones.

Haveli courtyard

PWD housing

The Main Building Types

This short section is an introduction to the types of
buildings you might see. It will not take you long to
'get your eye in' and to be able to identify the most
obvious buildings.

RELIGIOUS BUILDINGS

THE FOUR PRINCIPAL INDIGENOUS RELIGIONS

Hindu temple

By far the most conspicuous buildings in many Indian cities and villages are the
temples. The Hindu, Jain, Buddhist and Sikh religions were all founded in India and
have a common 'ancestry'. Members of all these faiths have built numerous temples
and there are examples of all of them in Delhi. A very simple guide to recognising
the main forms is given below but bear in mind that there are plenty of exceptions
to these general 'rules'.

Hinduism can hardly be described as a religion, being more a vast collection
of highly disparate practices with very ancient origins. The other three religions
arose in opposition to Vedic Brahmanism. While Jain temples are similar in many
ways to Hindu ones, the Buddhist and Sikh religions developed very different built
forms for religious buildings.

Despite the heterogeneity of Hinduism most temples have certain features in
common: the central shrine (*garbha-griha*), to house the deity with space for the
devotee, and a pavilion (*mandapa*) in front of the shrine for gatherings to hear
readings of texts, religious music and dancing. Sometimes, especially in the South,
temples were inside a walled enclosure
with tall and elaborate entrance gateways
(*gopura*). In North India it is the elaborate
roof over the *garbha-griha* that stands out.
This is the *shikhara* and is a representation
of Mount Kailasa (or Meru). It is easily
distinguishable from other temple forms
in being roughly pyramidal in shape
although it will, to some extent, be
elaborately moulded and decorated. In
Delhi this description fits best the many
20th century shrines that are found in
residential neighbourhoods. In Old Delhi

Modern temple

(Shahjahanabad) there are many small shrines, typically roofed with a bulbous dome,
often in the centre of a small courtyard.

The **Jain** religion is among the earliest of those that differentiated themselves
from Vedic Brahmanism, although there were similarities with later forms of Hindu
religion. It dates from the 6th century BC. Hindu and Jain temples are not easy to
distinguish from the exterior, having the same *shikhara* form over the shrine. The
emphasis on white marble in Jain temples helps to distinguish them from more
colourful Hindu buildings. A typical interior has a white marble domed *mandapa* and
the walls are adorned with shining-eyed Buddha-like Tirthankaras, the mainly

mythological 'saints', the last of whom was the most significant teacher of the religion. The extremely wealthy Jain community in Shahjahanabad built a number of temples in which the white marble exteriors and the Tirthankara statues are prominent. The interior walls and ceilings are often decorated with fabulously colourful paintings.

Jain temple, Shahjahanabad

Buddhism (almost contemporary with Jainism in its origin) had more or less died out in peninsular India by the 11ᵗʰ century although it survived in Eastern India until the 14ᵗʰ century. It now survives in the furthest reaches of the Himalayan states. The architecture of the temples in these remote areas derives from local styles. There are a few Buddhist temples in Delhi of which the most noticeable examples are those built recently by the Tibetan community. They generally followed the architectural style of their homeland and the buildings are thus typical of the high Himalayan valleys and conspicuous for their brightly coloured painted decorations. Despite the early demise of Buddhism in Central India its architectural legacy was influential in centuries to come. The *stupa*, unique to Buddhism, was an often huge, generally semi-circular mound built over a relic. The *vihara*, or monastery, also featured in Jainism, and the *chaitya*, the vaulted temple hall, may have inspired similar early forms in Hindu temples.

Guru Nanak founded the **Sikh** religion in 1469. Sikhs believe in one God and are notably egalitarian, both in class and gender terms. Large numbers of Sikh refugees came to Delhi after Partition and their temples (*gurudwaras*), of which there are many examples in Delhi, are easily recognised by their shiny white onion domes springing from square towers that are pierced by arched openings. Many of the largest *gurudwaras* commemorate the sites of specific events in Sikh history.

Unlike Muslims and Christians, Hindus do not bury their dead. Instead the bodies are burned on the banks of rivers. Memorials (often *chatris*) were sometimes erected over the cremation site of important people. In the case of Delhi, because the rulers were Muslim, there are few such examples until modern times.

Gurudwara

Buddhist temple

Gandhi Sthal - where Gandhi was cremated

ISLAMIC BUILDINGS

In Delhi the ancient buildings are almost exclusively Islamic. Although there are a few exceptions, they are mainly religious and are quite easily recognised.

A **mosque** (*masjid*) can be of many sizes and shapes but will always have three characteristic elements: a wall that faces west towards Mecca, so that everyone faces in the right direction when praying, a *mihrab* (prayer niche) in the centre of this wall, and symmetry about one axis which passes through the centre of the *mihrab*. The smallest mosques are for private prayer, typically consisting of a small hall with three arched openings on its east wall. There are subsidiary *mihrabs* on either side of the central *mihrab* and sometimes three domes on the roof. Mosques were often built at first floor level, especially in the late-Mughal period. This would enable the ground floor rooms to be rented out as shop units, thus producing an income for the mosque's upkeep.

Mihrab niche

On Fridays Muslims are expected to gather for their congregational worship. The Jami Masjid (Friday Mosque) will be big, with an enclosed courtyard, generally open to the sky, in front of the prayer hall. This differs only in size and number of bays from the smaller mosques, except that it has a *minbar* (pulpit) to the right of the central *mihrab*. The roof of the prayer hall may also have one or more domes; in addition, in Mughal mosques, there are often slender towers, or minarets, attached to the façade and sometimes to the enclosure walls. In the past the largest of these would have been used by the *muezzin* to call the faithful to prayer; now they are more likely to have loudspeakers attached for the same purpose. Minarets

Mosque

Octagonal tomb

are conspicuously absent from Sultanate mosques but access to the roof presumably allowed the *muezzin* to call from there. For the main feasts (Id al-Fitr and Id al-Adha) the congregation gets even bigger and they will worship at an *idgah*, generally a huge open space outside the city that consists of nothing but a west wall with *mihrab* and *minbar*. The most conspicuous indication of an *idgah* might be the columns at either end of the prayer wall. Smaller **wall mosques** are often attached to burial sites.

There are numerous **tombs** scattered throughout South Delhi. Strictly speaking they should be described as mausoleums, since the bodies are interred in a separate chamber below them. They are distinguished from mosques in being more or less symmetrical about two axes, in other words they are generally square, sometimes octagonal. Two very general types can be identified - first the domed pavilion, generally square with twelve pillars, which were sometimes enclosed with *jalis*. The tombs of saints seem very often to have been of this type. The second kind is a chamber enclosed by solid walls. The main entrance will always be on the south side. In older tombs the west wall is generally closed, with a *mihrab* on the inside. In all other respects each side will be the same and there is almost always a dome over the central chamber. Needless to say tombs vary in size, from a simple, small square chamber with one opening on each face and a plain dome above, to the many-chambered and elaborately-roofed Humayun's Tomb. There are generally one or more cenotaphs inside, indicating the position of the bodies lying in a vault below, the belief being that there has to be enough headroom for the deceased to sit up and reply to the Angels of the Grave who visit on the day after burial. The body is laid to align north-south so that it would face Mecca if turned on its side.

Not everyone was buried below an actual building. The alternative was burial in the open (more correct according to Koranic interpretation), sometimes in a walled compound with a prayer wall on the west side. There was a preference for burial near a holy man or saint; there are several holy sites in Delhi and they attracted burials in proportion to the holiness of the saint, the best-known examples being that of Qutb Sahib at Mehrauli and Nizamuddin Aulia at Nizamuddin. Ibn Battuta, a Moroccan traveller of the 14th century, in Delhi during the reign of Muhammad Tughlak, describes burial customs as he saw them: 'they build domed pavilions in [the cemetery] and every grave must have a *mihrab* beside it, even if there is no dome over it. They plant in it flowering trees' (from *The Travels of Ibn Battuta* – p.59).

Madrasas were religious colleges, but only in the same sense that medieval European universities were religious foundations. They would have taught a wide variety of subjects as well as the Koran. There are not many examples in Delhi but it is safe to say that the pattern of the buildings is broadly collegiate with numerous rooms giving onto common spaces.

CHRISTIAN BUILDINGS

The most obvious example is the church, generally arranged so that the congregation faces east, as in Europe. In the case of Delhi they were, of course, built by the British and look extremely European, with a dome, tower or spire over the 'crossing'. Like in Islam, congregational worship is an important part of the faith and the layout of churches results from their use. They are generally cruciform, with the altar, where the priest officiates, in the shorter,

Church interior - St Stephen's

eastern arm. The congregation sits in the nave, the longer arm, and the side arms are often devoted to small chapels used for private worship. They are commonly surrounded by a churchyard in which there are burials. The constricted sites around churches meant that separate ground was consecrated for further burials; there are several cemeteries in Delhi. Many of the largest schools and colleges were Christian foundations but their buildings were largely secular in use.

SECULAR BUILDINGS

As mentioned before, there are very few extant secular buildings from before the Mughal era. One exception is the *baoli* or step well of which there are several fine examples in Delhi (e.g., in the Purana Qila). There are records of many more that survived long into the 20th century but were, sadly, filled in. The building of *baolis* was a popular form of philanthropy, sometimes mentioned in ancient inscriptions as long ago as the 11th century. *Baolis* were an important feature of northwest India, where there is very little running water and searingly hot summers. Attached to the usual circular well for drawing water, a *baoli* has steps for people to get down to the water level. Apart from the convenience of not having to haul the water to the surface, the daytime temperature in the depths of the *baoli* would have been well below the

Haveli doorway

surface temperature. Further west, especially in Gujarat, there are some astonishingly ornate examples, indicating that much time was spent in them. Most Delhi *baolis* are of a fairly simple design – one long flight of stairs down to the water. Because of the falling water table some are now completely dry.

The other main secular building form, even though most examples in Delhi do not pre-date the 19th century, is the private house, of which the largest type is known as a *haveli*. These are basically mansions, found both in cities and villages and traditionally inhabited by a prosperous, large, 'joint' family, in which all the sons and their families lived with the parents and numerous servants. The largest had

Baoli, Mehrauli

several courtyards with a *zenana* wing at the back for the ladies of the family. *Havelis* are usually identified by a decorative entrance within a high wall, which may have ornate windows and balconies overlooking the street. Inside, most rooms would face onto and be accessible from one or more courtyards. It is now extremely rare to find a well-preserved *haveli* in Delhi, but some fine doorways still exist.

The 19th and 20th centuries saw the introduction of numerous building forms, such as railway stations, office blocks and apartment buildings, that are so universal that they do not need explanation.

RAJPUT DELHI

This is a splendid work, and even in its decay, it retains much of its past grandeur. That a work of such importance was constructed in the desert, where it now stands, is perfectly incredible, and the ruins which still surround it attest a once populous locality.

Suraj Kund,
described by Carr Stephen, 1876

Pre-Islamic

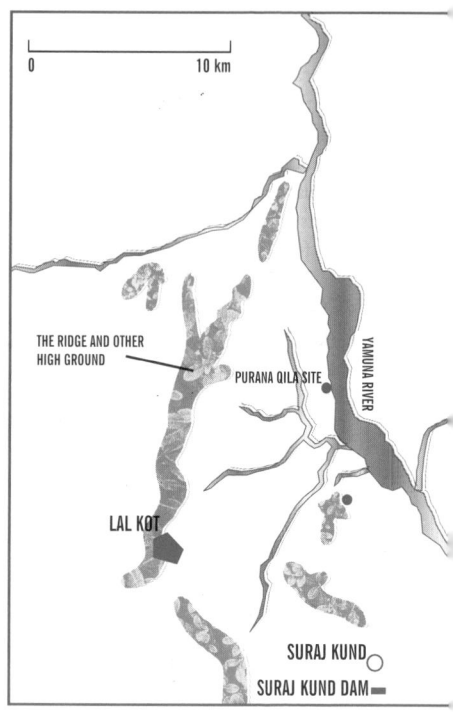

elhi is strategically located on the Yamuna River, in the wide corridor between the mountains and the desert, through which traffic passed between Central Asia and peninsula India. The city is situated where a spur of the Aravalli Hills meets the Yamuna River, and these rocky outcrops were the sites of some early settlements. Archaeological evidence shows that the Delhi area has been inhabited from very early times; stone-age tools, for instance, have been found at several sites. There is also evidence in the area of Late Harappan (Indus civilisation) settlements, by which time the culture, previously urban, had become village based (this Late Harappan phase is dated from the mid-second millennium BC).

For two thousand years after the decline of the Indus civilisation some north Indian history can be gleaned from written sources, but it is from archaeology that historians gain most data and one of the archaeologists' best clues is pottery. Throughout a large area of North India there have been archaeological finds of Painted Grey Ware, the type of pottery most closely linked to the speakers of the Indo-Aryan languages of the first millennium BC, probably a mixture of pastoral incomers drifting down from the northwest and agriculturalists already settled here. Part of what we know about these people comes (via much later transcription) from the legacy of numerous hymns and religious texts as well as the epics, the *Mahabharata* and the *Ramayana*. It is commonly thought that the old village called Indrapat inside the Purana Qila, was the very site of Indraprastha, one of the cities of the Mahabharata legend. However, the crucial archaeological evidence of a Painted Grey Ware 'layer' (indicating an actual settlement) is missing, meaning that it is unlikely that the Purana Qila site has anything to do with Indraprastha of the epic legend.

Before the 3rd century BC India was controlled by numerous competing chiefs and kings, and during this time urban centres of some size developed. One of these became the base of the powerful Mauryan Empire, created by Chandragupta Maurya and consolidated by his grandson Ashoka (reigned 272-232 BC). Ashoka ruled from Pataliputra, modern Patna, but held sway over most of the Indian sub-continent. He aimed at government in a very real sense, controlling affairs, or at least exhorting a certain way of life, through his famous edicts. Again, there is no evidence of a large urban centre at Delhi, but the presence of Northern Black Polished Ware at some sites in the area, including the Purana Qila, make Mauryan-era settlements likely, although the pottery cannot be linked specifically to this narrow time frame. However, the most exciting Mauryan discovery, made in 1966, was of an Ashokan Rock Edict found at Kalkaji (East of Kailash), in South Delhi, indicating that there must have been a reasonably important settlement nearby.

After the decline of the Mauryas, India was again fragmented into a series of variously powerful local states. The excavations at the Purana Qila show continuous occupation throughout this period. From AD 320-540 the Guptas, based in the Ganga Valley, influenced all of India north of the Narmada through a grouping of tribute-paying states. The sophistication of their court can be judged from the literature of the period, which ranged from the plays of Kalidasa to complicated mathematical treatise, while their technical achievements can be judged from the iron pillar, now in the Qutb Minar complex, which is an astonishing feat of both metallurgy and casting.

After the decline of the Guptas the country again disintegrated into warring states. From AD 606 - 647 the powerful king Harsha created a smaller Gupta-type empire, based in Kanauj, about 80 km up the Ganga from Kanpur. For a time he was able to consolidate power and keep at bay the incursions from Huns and Arabs into the northwest. These attacks were mainly after booty and were not much different from fighting between neighbouring Rajput states that were equally predatory. For the next three hundred years Kanauj became the focus of endless fighting between three central ruling families (Pratiharas, Rashtrakutas and the Palas). The Pratiharas controlled a large area that included Delhi. The Tomars ruled under them here, probably based in the Suraj Kund area. It is thought that Anangpur, a village near Suraj Kund, gets its name from Anang Pal Tomar, probably the same Anang Pal who lived around the 8th century.

By the 11th century, the Tomars had achieved independence from a higher authority. They had also moved their capital from Suraj Kund to a new citadel at Lal Kot (where the Qutb Minar was later built), where the extant remains show that there were a number of fine temples and a large tank within the walls. It is calculated that the population of the city amounted to five to six thousand people, growing subsequently when the fortifications were later extended to the east. In 1160 the Tomars came under the sway of their neighbours from Ajmer, the Chauhans. Under the Chauhans the walls of the Tomar city were extended considerably by the construction of the somewhat lower walls that we know as the Qila Rai Pithora, giving a total circumference for the city of about 8 km. (For convenience I will continue to refer to the original Tomar city as Lal Kot even though it had been so much expanded by the Qila Rai Pithora walls.)

Lal Kot walls

Rajput Delhi

Although Delhi as a city is not particularly ancient, there have been settlements in the area for many millennia. The two most significant early archaeological sites in central Delhi are the Purana Qila and the Ashokan rock edict near Kalkaji (there are many other archaeological sites on both sides of the river). Later, towards the end of the first millennium AD, Rajput rulers constructed two urban centres that were clearly of regional importance and contained buildings of considerable sophistication. The first site is at Suraj Kund, the second at Mehrauli.

Purana Qila excavations

PURANA QILA
The later buildings on this site are discussed in Chapter 9

This site was the location of a village called Indrapat, for which reason it is associated with Indraprastha of the *Mahabharata*. However, although excavations have revealed buildings from the early historical period (about the 3rd century BC onwards), so far nothing has been found to link the site with the Epic period. Archaeology has shown that people lived in mud-brick as well as fired brick structures and had moderately sophisticated drainage, with terracotta ring wells that may have functioned as soak-pits. There are many layers of habitation, the houses generally built in a similar style and bricks often reused. The site continued in occupation, probably until it was selected as Humayun's Dinpanah (see Chapter 9).

ASHOKAN EDICT
Correctly marked on Eicher map

The remains of the inscription, on a smooth rock face projecting from the top of a rocky hillock, can be seen under an ugly concrete shelter in a small neighbourhood park in East of Kailash, not far from the ISKCON temple on Raja Dhirsan Marg. It was discovered in 1966 and is an important part of Delhi's history and heritage, because it implies that somewhere nearby was a settlement important enough in the 3rd century BC for an edict to have been carved. Among the cluster of religious institutions on the nearby hilltops, the Kalkaji Temple is said to be of great antiquity, and might have had a settlement around it.

The edict itself does little more than emphasise the importance of a Buddhist way of life:

Ashoka says: It is two-and-a-half years since I became a Buddhist layman. At first no great exertion was made by me but in the last year I have drawn closer to the Buddhist order and exerted myself zealously and drawn in others to mingle with the gods. This goal is not one restricted only to the great but even a humble man who exerts himself can reach heaven. This proclamation is made for the following purpose: to encourage the humble and the great to exert themselves and to let the people who live beyond the borders of the kingdom know about it. Exertion in the cause must endure forever and it will spread further among the people so that it increases one-and-a-half fold.

SURAJ KUND

There is considerable evidence of early settlement, including fortifications, in the area to the south of Suraj Kund. The name of the village, Anangpur, which lies in the midst of these remains, gives a reasonable basis for assuming that the village (or a nearby hill fort) was founded by the Rajput Tomar king Anang Pal, who lived around the 8th century.

Suraj Kund Dam (perhaps 8th century)

One of two significant structures in the area, the dam lies about a kilometre to the north of Anangpur village. A path from the main village street will lead you into flat pastureland. Head for the small rocky hill ahead of you and climb over it. On the other side is another flat area, rather thickly covered in thorn trees. It is worth finding a way through them to the dam that straddles the gap between the two nearby hills.

The dam is an impressive edifice, 50 m wide and 7 m high, built from accurately hewn quartzite blocks. On the inside the dam forms steps that curve round at each end. On the far side the dam drops away steeply, each layer of stones projecting a few inches beyond the layer above. There is a passage for the egress of water at the level of the ground on the dammed side. The flat land across which you have walked is clearly caused by centuries of silt deposits in the lake that once existed behind this dam. The land around has been very heavily quarried recently, so further archaeological finds are unlikely.

Suraj Kund Dam

Suraj Kund Tank (possibly mid-11th century but perhaps earlier)

The stream that runs through the dam feeds the lake at Suraj Kund. Nearby is a circular tank, supposedly built by another Tomar king, Suraj Pal. It is difficult to say how much of the tank is original because it was repaired by Firoz Shah Tughlak in the fourteenth century. We can guess that Firoz Shah would not have shown such interest unless significant remains existed. The platform on the east side may have been the base of a

Suraj Kund Tank

temple as carved temple fragments have been found nearby. Indeed the name of the tank may derive from a Sun Temple connection (Suraj = sun) rather than from Suraj Pal.

LAL KOT (1060)

For some reason, presumably because he needed greater security, Anang Pal II built the strongly fortified town of Lal Kot some ten kilometres away from Suraj Kund, on a more prominent and easily defended outcrop of rock. The foundation of the city is thought to be mid-11th century and at some point the walls were extended on the west side (the part that is best preserved). The Tomars were brought under the sway of the Chauhan clan of Ajmer about a century later and the old town was considerably increased in size, now becoming known as Qila Rai Pithora. The original walls were 3.6 km in circumference with a population, it is speculated, of 5-6,000. The city as extended under the Chauhans was over four times the size, its walls being 8 km round. It is clear from the quality of the carvings on the surviving temple columns that Rajput Delhi was a place of some substance, even though it was not the pre-eminent city in the region.

Lal Kot walls

There is more surviving of Lal Kot than immediately meets the eye. The best place to start an exploration is in the village of Mehrauli, just beyond Adham Khan's Tomb, where it is easy to walk up onto the **Lal Kot wall** (unfortunately via a rubbish dump). This is the later extension wall and, presumably, built stronger and higher than the original west wall, of which nothing but a rise in the ground can be seen. The walls are constructed from random rubble internally but with a facing of quartzite blocks. There are rounded bastions at regular intervals and a few remains of a brick superstructure, which was either built contemporaneously or as a Sultanate addition. From the top of the wall it is possible to follow by sight the line of the wall right round to near the Qutb Minar complex. Following a path leftwards along the top of the wall you will find gateways and, in places, double walls. A path leads down to a tranquil little clearing containing the grave of **Baba Haji Rozbih**. This Muslim saint, who came to Delhi during the reign of Prithviraj Chauhan, converted many Hindus including, tradition has it, one of the king's daughters, reputedly buried nearby. The spot is not very far from the *Idgah* (p.229, 235) and numerous other Islamic burial sites.

Keep following the path until you reach the junction with the older west wall. Follow this to reach, on the left, the excavated site of the **Anang Tal**. This is a deep tank, thought to have been built at the founding of the city and certainly still in use when the city was taken by the Turks. Parts of the tank wall have been excavated and are still visible. The most

3.2 Lal Kot and Qila Rai Pithora

A. Later west wall, late 11ᵗʰ or early 12ᵗʰ c.
B. Grave of Baba Haji Rozbih
C. First walled area, 11ᵗʰ c.
D. Anang Tal, 11ᵗʰ c.

E. Adham Khan's Tomb, 16ᵗʰ c.
F. Qutb Mosque and Iron Pillar.
G. Qila Rai Pithora, 12ᵗʰ c. A section of which can be seen on the south side of Press Enclave Road.

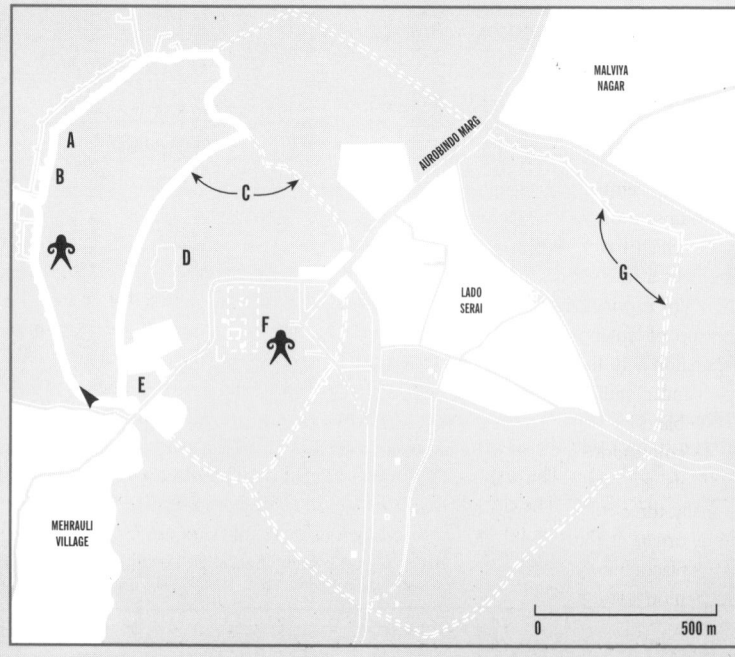

impressive stonework is found at the bottom of the excavation where there are some huge blocks of stone that fit together with perfect precision, the type of work that can be seen in numerous early sites throughout India. It is quite likely that temples were associated with the tank, but no remains have been found. Nearby there is the excavated ground floor of a large masonry building. A few fragments of incised plasterwork show that it was of some importance, and also that it was probably built during the early Sultanate period, and is not therefore a relic from the Rajput town. To leave the area, it is easiest to return to Adham Khan's Tomb.

Anang Tal masonry

QUTB MOSQUE – TEMPLE RELICS (1060 to late 12th century)

The final and most impressive relics from Rajput times are the temple remains built into the mosque in the Qutb complex, mainly consisting of exquisitely carved columns but also including the famous iron pillar (see over). The inscription over the East Gate to the mosque tells of the demolition of 27 Hindu and Jain temples from which this mosque was constructed. This was no communal event; the demolition of temples probably had a greater political purpose than a religious one. It is a historical fact that Hindu conquerors were given to destroying their enemies' sacred places and seizing their principal idols; their loss was seen as a major weakening of the power of the defeated ruler. Among the demolished temples there were clearly a number that were finely carved.

The sculpted columns that support the roof of the prayer hall and colonnades are the most obvious relics. The roof itself is Rajput in style, particularly the domes over the entrance bays, which may originally have come from temple *mandapas*. The lack of mortar in indigenous building techniques must have made such re-use of materials easy. The other pre-Islamic elements are the famous iron pillar and, perhaps, part of the platform on which the mosque was built.

Kirti Mukha

The **columns in the prayer hall** form the most organised array. The matching, central, block of columns are all full height and support temple beams, some of which are still adorned with tiny figures but others of which have been disfigured. The columns themselves feature hanging bells at the top and a highly ornamented section in the middle with bands of carvings, including the popular vase motif. There is another large group of columns of great elegance and restraint that feature a central section with hanging bells over an octagonal shaft. Others nearby are very similar, with one or two bands of hanging bells intersected by a projecting band.

The **colonnades** on the other three sides of the courtyard have higher roofs and are supported on columns made up from two or, occasionally, three columns piled on top of each other. Many of these are at least as ornate as the larger columns in the prayer hall, if not more so. In several places human figures are visible and a stylised face (*kirti mukha*) can be seen on some columns.

Temple column group

IRON PILLAR (4ᵗʰ century)

The pillar is over 7m high with a diameter of 40 cm at the base, 30 at the top. At the top of the column is an inverted lotus capital, which was probably once crowned by a Vaishnavite emblem such as a *garuda*, Vishnu's vehicle.

Inscription

The known history of this pillar comes from its inscriptions. From the longest inscription (a translation of which is on the wall in the northern colonnade) we know the pillar was not made under the auspices of the Delhi Tomars because it was shifted here from its original site, having originally been erected by a king named Chandra on 'the Vishnupada Hill'. A plausible theory is that the king was the Gupta emperor, Chandragupta II (reigned from AD 375 to 415). However, the name of the place is a mystery. While the difficulties involved in moving such an object imply that Vishnupada was nearby, we would expect an artefact of such quality to have been produced at an important centre of power and there was none nearby that we know of. It seems likely, therefore, that the pillar was moved some distance. It might have been a symbol of a former ruler's dominion, important for its political, aesthetic or religious significance and captured by a Tomar to enhance his own legitimacy. The Tomars clearly regarded it as an artefact of importance, as did the Turks, who positioned it in the centre of their mosque courtyard, either moving it here or leaving it in place.

We are in a position to be even more impressed by the pillar than were the Tomars or Turks, knowing now that the workmanship involved in purifying the iron and casting it could not have been achieved in the west until the 19ᵗʰ century at the very earliest. The pillar has been shown to be of exceptionally pure wrought iron. The fact that it has shown so little signs of rusting has been explained recently by the discovery that the early iron-making process produced a high phosphorus content that allowed the iron to react with oxygen and hydrogen to produce a protective film of misawite that has been slowly growing ever since its manufacture.

A legend tells of an early Tomar king pulling the pillar out of the ground in order to check on the accuracy of a tale that claimed that the pillar rested on the head of Vasuki, the king of serpents, and that provided it stayed that way the Tomar dominion would last. When it was drawn up covered in blood the tale was frighteningly authenticated. The king tried to re-fix the pillar but it never held firm and eventually his dynasty fell.

Another, seemingly more plausible myth, was told to Alexander Cunningham, the indefatigable 19ᵗʰ century amateur archaeologist and first head of what is now the Archaeological Survey of India (ASI). He was assured that the depth of the pillar had been investigated and had been found still to be continuous at 35 ft. He ordered this to be checked and discovered the base to be bulbous, extending a mere 20 inches below the surface.

EARLY SULTANATE DELHI

THE QUTB MINAR

'I do not think I have yet seen anything so beautiful – the beauty, though of extreme desolation.'

Fanny Eden, 1838

The Early Delhi Sultanate (1192 - 1320)

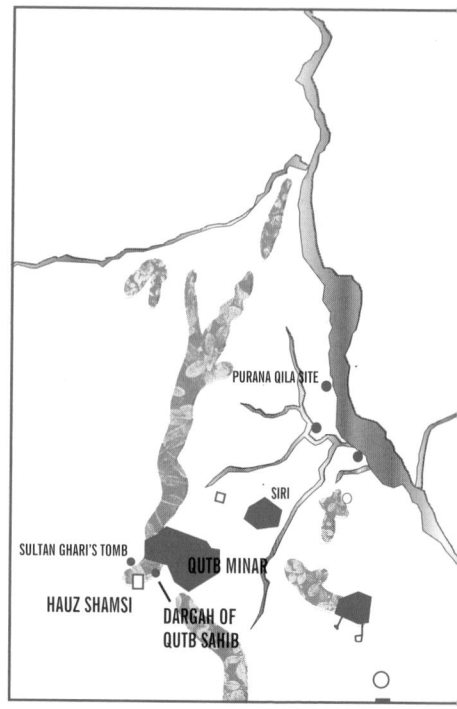

By the end of the 12th century the two most powerful rulers in northwest India were Muhammad of Ghor (Ghor is in present day Afghanistan), by now the conqueror of the Punjab, and Prithviraj Chauhan, leader of a group of north Indian states. Having taken Lahore, Muhammad advanced on Delhi. Prithviraj and his allies managed to fend him off in 1191 but the following year Muhammad returned, met Prithviraj near Panipat, defeated him and went on to capture Delhi and Ajmer. Muhammad returned home, leaving his general, Qutbuddin Aibak, as his deputy in Delhi. Qutbuddin was a highly successful governor and, when Muhammad was assassinated in 1206, he took the opportunity to establish what was an independent state, even though he still struck coins in the name of Muhammad's son.

Qutbuddin was the first of the Slave dynasty, so called because he and his successor had been slaves. Even Muhammad of Ghor's father had been a slave. Slaves in Central Asia could become the most highly trusted and privileged courtiers, well-placed to take over from their masters in one of the turbulent twists of Central Asian history – a bit like a KGB leader becoming head of a former Soviet state. Many of them were Turkish (people from the Turkic-speaking tribes who were found throughout Central Asia), were highly valued, and trained to a high degree. They were usually rewarded with their freedom following good service. Turkish families settled extensively in Afghanistan and most of the landowning and ruling classes there had Turkish origins.

Qutbuddin Aibak cleared the area of remaining Chauhan power and established himself in India, with Delhi as his capital. He built the base of the Qutb Minar and the great mosque beside it, inside the walls of the Tomar city. On his death in 1210 the Afghan nobles in Delhi selected his son-in-law, Iltutmish, as Sultan. Iltutmish continued the building work commenced by Qutbuddin, enlarging Qutbuddin's Mosque and completing the Minar. He also constructed the large Shamsi tank some distance from the city walls.

After Iltutmish's death in 1235, there was a great deal of intrigue and squabbling among weak rulers. Iltutmish's eldest son, to his father's grief, had died in Bengal in 1229. After a bloody succession of other sons and one daughter, Raziya (the only female ruler of Delhi), the court nobles invited Iltutmish's youngest son, Mahmud Shah, to take the throne. He ruled from 1245 till 1265 and was described by contemporaries as possessing 'qualities of saints and characteristics of prophets', perhaps the reason why he was dominated by his father-in-law, Balban, another ex-slave. During this period the original city at Lal Kot continued to act as the centre of power. Archaeological evidence does not give us much information about the interior of the city but outside it we know that there were several important shrines, including the burial place of Qutb Sahib, spiritual descendant of Muinuddin Chishti of Ajmer. The burial places of two of Iltutmish's children are further away from the city.

Balban eventually became Sultan himself and ruled until 1287. It is not clear how this transition came about. We do not know whether Mahmud Shah was murdered or what became of his descendants, especially Balban's grandson, the son of Mahmud

Alauddin's Madrasa

4 - 35

Shah. After Balban's death his grandson, Kayqubad, became Sultan. For the first time the court was moved away from the old city (Lal Kot) and Kayqubad built himself a palace at Kilokhri near the Yamuna. Sufficient people moved with him for it to have been called the 'new town' although nothing of it now remains, unless the Lal Mahal in Nizamuddin was connected with it. There were many rival nobles in his court and when Kayqubad became ill he was deposed and his infant son was placed on the throne by Jalalaldin Khalji, an Afghan nobleman. In 1290 Jalalaldin set the child aside and became Sultan himself.

Despite having been a successful general, as a ruler Jalalaldin turned out to be ineffectual, being pious and merciful, especially to his nephew, Alauddin, who repaid his benevolence by assassinating him in 1296 and soon seized power. The Khalji take-over was not popular with the citizens, who had become accustomed to playing a role in the confirmation of new rulers. A revolt in 1301 caused Alauddin to carry out an extensive purge of the old aristocracy and to move from the old city to the suburbs, to the site of the army camping ground, Siri, where he constructed another citadel. His palace was built outside the walls of Siri and was referred to as the Hazar Sutun ('thousand pillared hall'), a common name for palaces. Outside the walls of the city he also built a new tank to supply water to the city, now known as Hauz Khas. In the old city he commenced two grandiose building projects: a vast extension to the Qutb Minar Mosque and a new *minar* to dwarf the existing one. Clearly this old city continued to be seen as the main religious centre.

Alauddin had a reputation for unusually cruelty, commonly crushing his enemies under the feet of elephants and building towers from the heads of the vanquished. He was also a grandiose builder and contemporary reports speak of 70,000 construction workers in the Sultan's service; judging by the scale of his projects this is not difficult to believe. His military ideas were no less enterprising. He began to establish a real Indian empire, even making several successful sorties into the south, but rebellion nearer home eventually destroyed his ambitions. His military expansionism cost money and he made some radical fiscal reforms, increasing taxation but imposing strict price controls on essential commodities, allowing him to maintain a large army, but also discriminating against the mainly Hindu rural aristocracy in favour of the mainly Muslim urban population. It also encouraged the money economy and craft production, presumably leading to the considerable growth of Delhi.

Alauddin died in 1316. Again, the void created by the death of a powerful Sultan led to a series of bloody episodes in which most of Alauddin's descendants met their ends. One of his sons, Qutbaldin Mubarak Shah, ruled for four years until 1320, before being murdered by his 'favourite', Khusrau Shah. Initially this takeover appears to have been popular among the population, but Khusrau Shah soon got a reputation for being anti-Islamic, although it is likely that he went no further than banning cow slaughter. Probably wilder stories, such as that he used the Koran as a seat, were simply an excuse for intervention by one of Alauddin's former lieutenants, Ghiyasuddin Tughlak.

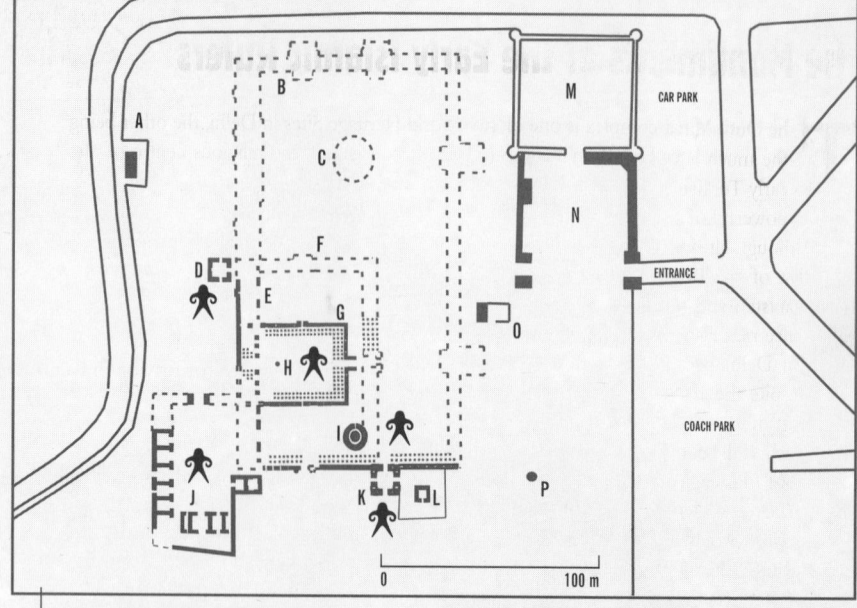

Map 4.2 Qutb Minar Complex

A. Mosque of Wafati Shah, late 18th or early 19th c.
B. Foundations of Alauddin's Mosque, 1311
C. Alauddin's Minar, 1311 (p.41)
D. Iltutmish's Tomb, died 1235 (p.39)
E. Screen wall of Iltutmish's Mosque, early 13th c.
F. Line of enclosure of Iltutmish's Mosque extension
G. Original Mosque, started 1192 (p.40)
H. Iron Pillar, 4th c. (p.32)
I. Qutb Minar, 1202 (p.38)
J. Alauddin's Madrasa, 1310 (p.42)
K. Alai Darwaza, 1310 (p.42)
L. Tomb of Imam Zamin, 1539 (p.43)
M. Late Mughal garden (p.43)
N. Serai, 18th c. (p.43)
O. Late Mughal mosque
P. Cupola from misconceived restoration of Qutb Minar, 1828

The Monuments of the Early Islamic Rulers

The Qutb Minar complex is one of two World Heritage Sites in Delhi, the other being the much later Humayun's Tomb (p.162). It consists of the religious centre of the early Turkish / Afghan city and contains buildings constructed by three of the most powerful of the early Sultans.

Although already a regionally important urban centre, Delhi only became a capital with the arrival of the Turkic Afghan, Muhammad of Ghor in 1192. Because his power base was in Afghanistan and the Punjab, Delhi was of great strategic importance to him. The city's importance may also have been enhanced because Qutbuddin Aibak, the commander left in charge of Delhi, became the most powerful of Muhammad of Ghor's sultans.

Despite the arrival of a seemingly alien political and religious culture, for the ordinary inhabitant of the city the changes may not have been as traumatic as we might think. Many things such as the currency remained the same, and they would already have been familiar with the culture and religion of traders from Central Asia. The local people would have witnessed the destruction of temples and the erection of some astonishing new buildings in their place. Local masons would have been involved in the construction and, while the new work would have surprised them, the political symbolism of the new buildings effacing the old would not. Moreover, despite the newness of the building forms, there was much architectural continuity, because of the adaptation of indigenous materials and construction techniques to these new Islamic buildings.

In the present setting of the Qutb Minar it is difficult to keep in mind that these monumental buildings were originally in the heart of a city, presumably a relatively open space hedged in by other structures of which some, such as the Sultans' palaces, must have been a considerable size. There would also have been ordinary houses, markets and all the other necessities of urban life. Not far from the religious centre we know that there was a large tank, Anang Tal (p.30), which would have been another refreshingly open spot among the city buildings. The immediate surroundings, being the oldest part of the Rajput city, were probably the most densely built up part of the fort, although there is insufficient archaeological evidence to be sure. The area to the east of the religious centre, then only recently enclosed by the Qila Rai Pithora walls, was probably not so urbanised; the fact that there are some later Sultanate tombs and graves in that area may mean that it was never densely inhabited.

These buildings continued to be an important part of Sultanate Delhi for several centuries, even though grandiose building projects were undertaken at various times elsewhere in the Delhi area. This continuing significance is evident from the number of important shrines, mosques and tombs that were built outside the city walls during the Sultanate and Mughal periods. One of the earliest, and the magnet for much of the rest, was the shrine or *dargah* of the *sufi* saint Qutb Sahib (these buildings are discussed in Chapter 12). During later Mughal times, when the residential area had shifted southwards to the area around the *Dargah* (Mehrauli village), the old city had become ruined and was used as a site for burials and the construction of gardens, one of which is inside the present enclosure.

The buildings in this area are used to illustrate the evolution of early Indo-Islamic architecture, described in Chapter 2.

Alauddin's Madrasa

Qutb Minar (Construction started 1202)

The name appears to come from 'Qutb Sahib ki Lath', in honour of the local saint Bakhtiyar Kaki, whose popular name is Qutb Sahib. The tower was thought of as his staff (lath), which connected earth with heaven.

This astonishing building stands 72.5 metres high with a diameter at the base of 14 metres while at the top it is only 3 metres, a difference that, together with the 4 projecting circular balconies, gives the tower its superbly distinctive profile. The tower bears a striking resemblance to victory towers in Afghanistan and it seems certain that this was partly why it was built. It was probably also a functional part of the mosque complex. By this time a minaret had become a standard fixture for mosques throughout the Islamic world, signalling their presence from afar.

It is thought that the first level, 29 metres high, was built by Aibak (ruled 1192-1210) while his successor, Iltutmish (ruled 1210-35), built three

Qutb Minar detail

more, altered by subsequent damage and repair. During Firoz Shah's reign the tower was damaged by lightning. He seems to have partially demolished the top layer and added two in its place, mainly in white marble. The next major repair work was carried out by the British in 1828 following earthquake damage. The entrance was extensively repaired and the inscriptions incorrectly repositioned. The clumsy parapets were also added to the balconies along with a cupola on the top. Doubts about the authenticity of the cupola led to its removal twenty years later and it ended up at the edge of the garden.

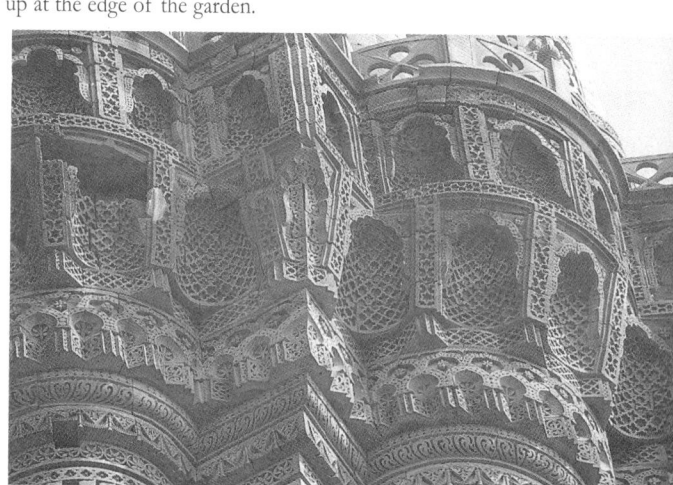

Qutb Minar

Qutb Minar detail

There was considerable scholarly debate in the 19th century about the origins of the Qutb Minar – some people maintained that it was a Rajput building, citing Devanagiri script found on the inside and its non-minaret like appearance, but this view has long since been rejected. A more current issue is stylistic: whether this is an Islamic building with indigenous decorations or whether all the inspiration came from the west with the invaders. The hanging

Qutb Minar and Alai Darwaza

decorations under the balconies do at first glance bear a striking resemblance to the *muqarnas* of Islamic buildings elsewhere, but their inspiration could equally (and more plausibly at this early date) come from the local masons' skills in carving highly intricate decorations under the domes of temples. It has been argued convincingly that the Qutb Minar is a good example of the synthesis that occurred in the early days of the invasion between an alien architectural style and local craftsmen who continued to employ traditional skills and techniques.

Iltutmish's Tomb (1235)

Behind the Qutb Minar Mosque is a building believed to be his own tomb. This, incidentally, is one of the few tombs where one can clearly see that the burial chamber is separate from the upper chamber containing the cenotaph; on the north side steps lead down to a chamber beneath the tomb. The exterior of the tomb is quite austere, only the double-arched entrances being ornamented. Inside, the walls are lavishly decorated, on the west wall with three highly decorated *mihrabs* and on the other three sides from the midpoint upwards. We see here many of the features that recur on later sultanate buildings: the *pishtaq* (entrance bay) with framed arches within it, the engaged columns on external corners, and cusped arches.

The square is transformed into an octagon with uniform trabeate ogee squinch arches. There is no dome and it is not known whether one ever existed. Compared with later tombs the walls are relatively thin, perhaps incapable of counteracting the outward thrust of a dome. A dome might have collapsed or the cenotaph might have been left deliberately open to the sky, in accordance with a generally ignored belief that a grave has to be exposed to rain and dew to be blessed.

Iltutmish's Tomb interior

Qutb Minar Mosque
(started 1192)

Popularly known as the Quwwat-al-
Islam (Might of Islam) Mosque, the
mosque actually acquired the name
relatively recently, having been
corrupted or misread from Qubbat al-
Islam, meaning 'Sanctuary of Islam', a
term that we know was used historically
to describe the environs of Qutb
Sahib's shrine. Early records produce
no mention of the triumphalist epithet.

Qutb Minar Mosque prayer hall

The Turko-Rajput synthesis noticed on the Qutb Minar is seen again in the oldest and
best-preserved part of mosque, the central courtyard built under Aibak. The mosque follows
the original Arabian pattern of a hypostyle prayer hall, a courtyard and surrounding
colonnades. The actual details however are unusual because, in common with other very early
Indian mosques, temple columns and other elements were reused in its building. The reused
columns of the prayer hall were carefully selected to match in groups. On the right side of
the prayer hall there is a very ruined collection of smaller columns supporting a raised
chamber, probably the private prayer hall for the Sultan and his family. Curiously, this roof
aligns neither with the roofs of the prayer hall or the adjacent colonnade.

The prayer wall itself must have been built new but unfortunately it is mostly ruined.
One remaining projection on the rear of the wall indicates the presence of a *mihrab* in this
off-centre position, which in turn indicates two or three *mihrabs* either side of the main central
one. Multiple *mihrabs* are a uniquely Indian feature, so it is interesting to see it in such an early
building. It is thought to derive from temple design, where the worshipper expected to
encounter an object of veneration through every opening.

The great arched screen was erected in 1199, after the building of the prayer hall. The
openings do not align with the layout of the hall. It is a lovely piece of work, combining the
robust wide arches of Islamic architecture with delicate local sculptural traditions. The
structural features of these arches are discussed in Chapter 2 but, in brief, the system of
arcuate construction, invented by the Romans and used in West Asian buildings, was yet to
arrive in India. Nonetheless, the local craftsmen used their superb masonry skills to achieve
the desired shape. The
wall was then carved, by craftsmen
who were clearly at the peak
of their profession, with
glorious bands of the lovely
nashki script threaded through
with creepers (a common
Islamic calligraphic device
known as arabesques) as well
as other panels adorned with
purely decorative sculpture
that would look totally at
home on a Hindu temple.

Qutb Minar Mosque courtyard

The north and east colonnades are well preserved; the southern one is only partly complete and seems to have been built using much plainer or even newly carved columns. At the rear of the courtyard the colonnade is four bays deep with two-storey pavilions in the corners. Traditionally the colonnades were used as temporary shelter for travellers; one can assume that the upper rooms were rather exclusive accommodation, containing as they do some of the best sculptured columns, just visible from the lower steps.

There is a widely accepted theory that the builders of the mosque would have plastered over all the columns, beams and anywhere else that showed carvings of animate life, such things being idolatrous, especially in mosques. However, this theory is contradicted by the 14th century description of Ibn Battuta who said it was built of white stone and converted from an 'idol temple', implying that he saw it in the same state as we do.

The original courtyard appears large enough to have held a good-sized congregation. Nevertheless Aibak's successor,

East arcade of the mosque

Iltutmish, proceeded to enlarge the mosque with a surrounding colonnade and an extension to the screen wall on either side. Part of the original enclosing wall survives on the south side. The screen wall contrasts dramatically with Aibak's. The flowing *nashki* is sometimes replaced by a strange knotted square *kufic* script. Gone are the sinuous intertwined plants; instead the decoration is geometric and formal, the high relief contrasting with the low relief of the carving on the earlier screen. It is impossible to know whether this part of the mosque was completed and, if so, why the original exterior wall of the first mosque was left, blocking the view of worshippers in Iltutmish's extension.

Iltutmish's mosque extension may indeed never have been finished, but Alauddin got even less far with his grandiose enlargement of the mosque at the beginning of the 14th century. This was to have been a vast enclosure with four entrances. It would also have contained a massive *minar* designed to overshadow the Qutb Minar completely. Its rubble base still stands and shows that it would have been at least twice its height. The base of the

projected enclosure wall is exposed, as are the bases, an extension of Alauddin's screen arches. The only finished building is the southern gateway known as the Alai Darwaza (see over).

The mosque was in use when Ibn Battuta wrote about it and it may have remained in use until Shahjahanabad was built in the 17th century, when there was a major population shift northwards. This area became the location for gardens and burials during the later Mughal period.

South Gate of Iltutmish's mosque extension

Alai Darwaza (1310)

The third Sultan to contribute to the complex was the self-aggrandising Alauddin Khalji. As already mentioned, his plans were stupendous but the only buildings that materialised were one superb gate to the vast mosque extension, and an austere *madrasa* behind the mosque.

The completed gateway is known as the Alai Darwaza and is attached, albeit clumsily, to a section of the pre-existing wall on either side; judging by the inept conjunction of wall and gateway it is unlikely that this wall was part of Alauddin's final conception. Apart from the Qutb Minar itself, the Alai Darwaza is in many respects the most architecturally satisfying building in the complex. By the early 14th century Islamic architecture and decoration had been fully assimilated and a unique Indo-Islamic style had evolved. The arches are true and the decorations combine indigenous Indian and Islamic motifs.

Alai Darwaza (below) and detail (abo

It is likely that the exterior wall once projected above its present height, forming a significant parapet around the dome. If so, the already fine proportions would have been considerably enhanced. The alternating use of white marble and red sandstone is very effective, particularly where the two are reversed as in the three exterior façades where red predominates over the bottom half and white above. The recessed arches of the three exterior openings are particularly charming, with red columns supporting a white arch, followed by white columns and a red arch. On the underside of the red arch, white marble lotus buds (or spearheads) create a sort of cusped arch design that frames the opening. On the north side the exterior is plain red sandstone. The doorway is not as lofty as on the other sides and the shape of the arch is very unusual: entirely of marble, it is made up of three shallow arcs connected to form a slightly cloverleaf shape, elaborately decorated with circular beading.

Inside, the very slightly horseshoe-shaped arches are repeated as recessed squinch arches framing a tiny domed squinch. The centre of the dome ceiling is open and capped by a small white marble dome, a feature not seen again in Delhi.

Alai Darwaza - elevation and section

ALAUDDIN'S MADRASA (1317)

Unlike the Alai Darwaza, Alauddin's *Madrasa* is hardly ornamented at all. The original design seems to have consisted of a courtyard with, on the north side, the remains of a large gateway and, on the south, three separate chambers. The central chamber, it is thought, was Alauddin's tomb. These chambers were enclosed at the back by a wedge-shaped room with unusually wide stairs built into the end wall. Unfortunately, the facing stone has been comprehensively removed from all these walls, presumably for reuse, so it is impossible to guess at its original decoration.

On the other two sides were wings containing rows of separate chambers, generally exaggeratedly vaulted, although the central ones on each side are domed. The transition from square to octagon is made, in this case, in the simplest and plainest way, with square projecting

Alauddin's Madrasa

corbels. The eastern wing seems always to have ended at the central domed chamber, above the 'moat' around the mosque platform, a window on this north side showing that this was built as an external wall. On the west side some of the chambers have haphazard openings at the rear. Behind these, incidentally, is an unfrequented bit of ground that contains some attractive trees that are native to the Delhi region, such as the gnarled *piloo* (Salvadora oleoides) – a less common sight than would be expected.

TOMB OF IMAM ZAMIN (1539)
This tomb was built on a platform beside the Alai Darwaza. Nothing is known of the Imam but it is supposed that he was connected with the Qutb Minar Mosque. The tomb has a typical design with twelve pillars forming a square. *Jali* screens enclose the chamber, apart from the solid *mihrab* screen on the west and the entrance on the south.

LATE MUGHAL GARDEN (18th century)
This is one of the many gardens and tombs built during late-Mughal times, when Mehrauli was the royal family's only other dwelling other than the Red Fort. *Chatris* stand on three of its four corners. Gardens were an extremely important part of Mughal life, many hours and indeed days being spent camping in the comparative comfort created by plenty of shade and water. They were often unattached to particular houses or palaces but were positioned in suitable resting places for travel. This garden probably had a simple layout of four garden plots bisected by paths and a pond or perhaps running water at the centre. Although no gardens have survived intact from Mughal times, the garden around Humayun's Tomb (p.165) gives some idea of what they might have looked like.

SERAI (18th century)
In front of the garden enclosure are the remains of a *serai* from roughly the same time. The two gateways remain, one of them now acting as the entrance to the complex. Part of the enclosure walls and rooms survive, as well as a small mosque, typical of late Mughal architecture. *Serais* were built to help long distance travellers. There was provision for secure storage, the stabling and feeding of animals, and facilities such as water and food for the traveller and his servants.

Serai

OTHER BUILDINGS
Scattered across part of the site are numerous graves, including a few inside the Qutb Minar Mosque courtyard. These are mostly from the late Mughal period.

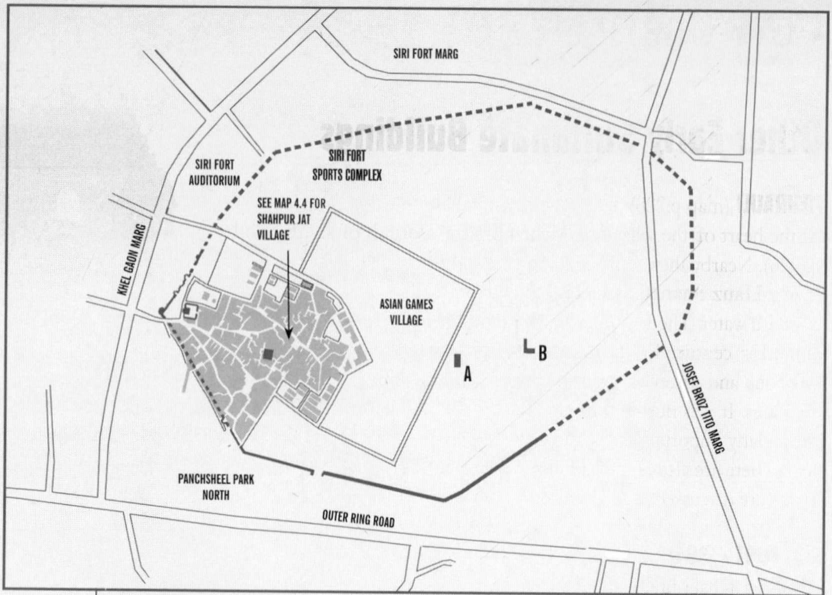

4.3 Siri Fort

A Ruin in nursery area at back of Asian Games village
B Ruin in Siri Fort Park

4.4 Shahpur Jat

A City walls
B Tohfe Wala Gumbad
C Baradari

Other Early Sultanate Buildings

MEHRAULI (map p.228)

At the heart of the village of Mehrauli is the **Dargah of Qutb Sahib** (p.226). Nearby there is a *baoli* and further south there are the remains of the **Hauz Shamsi**, both said to be built by Iltutmish to supply the city with water. The **Idgah** to the west of the village was probably built in the 13th century. From later centuries there are numerous tombs and mosques and an even greater number of late Mughal and colonial buildings. It was during the late Mughal period that Mehrauli became particularly important, which is why it is relegated to Chapter 12.

There are also some Khalji-era buildings in **Nizamuddin** village. These are discussed in Chapter 10.

Ruin in Siri Fort Park

SIRI FORT (1304)

Alauddin Khalji built Siri Fort on the site of the military camp northeast of the city. The construction follows a common pattern, with slightly battered walls (i.e., with a wider base on the outside) and a protected passage within the width of the walls. A few ancient buildings of some size can be found within the walls, but they are all probably from a slightly later date.

Alauddin Khalji also constructed a great tank to supply the new city with water: this was later restored by Firoz Shah and is known as **Hauz Khas** (p.87).

Tohfe Wala Gumbad (early 14th century)

Visible from outside the walls in front of Shahpur Jat, this mosque has to be approached through the village from the east. It seems to have been an early prototype for the Begampur Mosque, built by the Tughlaks. The central prayer hall is well preserved, with a huge arch (*iwan*) on the east side containing three equal arched entrances (although this might be inaccurate restoration – the 1916 ASI listing (p.5) describes a single door supported by modern pillars because of its dilapidated state). On the north and south sides similar openings once led through to double-aisled pillared chambers on each side, only the foundations of which remain. These halls seem to have turned at least part of the way along the sides of a central courtyard. The whole building is constructed from rubble masonry with a rendered surface inside and out, minimally decorated. If it was built by Alauddin it is a far cry from the delicacy of the Alai Darwaza or even the slightly plainer Jamaat Khana Mosque in Nizamuddin (p.174). The rubble masonry construction also distinguishes it from Alauddin's *Madrasa* at the Qutb.

Tohfe Wala Gumbad

Baradari (early 14th century)

In the centre of the village, only visible in a few places (see map) is a large structure, known as the *baradari*. It is described in the 1916 ASI listing as a rectangular building with a nine-bayed central hall, and side chambers to the north and south. Arched openings are visible on the east and west sides and on the north side several vaulted bays are visible, the remains of Tughlak plasterwork still attached in places. The ground level has now risen to just below the column capstones; it is easy to see that this was once a large and impressive building.

Baradari

SULTAN GHARI'S TOMB (1231)

Near Vasant Kunj, this is shown on the Eicher map

The inscription informs us that this tomb was built for Nasiruddin Mahmud, Iltutmish's eldest son, who died before his father. It is thought that the tomb, which stands some distance from the city, was built by Iltutmish in 1231 and is therefore reckoned to be the first Islamic mausoleum in India. The name probably derives from the cave-like burial chamber (*ghar*) and it is not known who else was buried here.

Sultan Ghari courtyard interior

The materials used are very similar to the contemporary Qutb Minar buildings, even including some reused temple pieces that probably came from a nearby demolished or ruined temple. The design is quite unlike any other tomb that was to be built in the next few centuries, the main difference being the enclosure itself, built rather like a small courtyard mosque, and the ambiguous design of the octagonal burial chamber, which projects up into the courtyard. It therefore combines the function of an underground crypt, existing under all tombs, and the standard domed tomb that is now ubiquitous in the Delhi landscape. The tomb chamber is reached down steep steps and consists of a smoke-blackened room with four columns supporting beams projecting from the walls. The graves inside are considered to be highly sacred and are visited by local villagers *en masse* every Thursday.

The entire tomb chamber construction is based on the indigenous trabeate method. Upstairs the design is more Turkish / Afghan, with a tiny white marble prayer hall in the middle of the west wall and white marble at the entrance and around the tomb itself. The fact that Firoz Shah claimed to have extensively repaired the building, as it had 'fallen into such ruin that the sepulchres were undistinguishable', makes it difficult to assess how much is original. For example, on one side of the tomb chamber's roof a red sandstone decorated cornice has been exposed, which might have been original, while the more visible white marble could have been added by Firoz Shah.

Beside the main building is an octagonal *chatri*. This is one of two that formerly stood here and were said to be the tombs of two more of Iltutmish's sons, the ones that ruled either

Sultan Ghari's Tomb entrance

side of their more talented sister Raziya. Both men were deposed, one dying soon afterwards, the other being killed. The chatri was restored by Firoz Shah.

Surrounding these tombs are the ruined remains of a village which appears to have contained some quite fine buildings that are said to be mainly Mughal, apart from a Tughlak mosque some distance away, opposite the entrance to Sultan Ghari's Tomb. Ruins of a Jami Masjid and a *khanqah* have been found to the south of the tomb.

5

TUGHLAKABAD

The relics of palaces, baths, &c., many of which are still sufficiently entire to excite our wonder, induce us involuntarily to put the question; 'Were there giants in those days?'

Thomas Bacon, 1837

Ghiyasuddin Tughlak

Three strong Tughlak Sultans followed the Khaljis. The first, Ghiyasuddin Tughlak, overthrew Khusrau Shah in 1320 and took the throne himself, supposedly because all members of the Khalji family had died or been killed. Ghiyasuddin is described as being a just and competent ruler, as successful as Alauddin but without resorting so much to bloodshed. During his short reign Ghiyasuddin completed the construction of the massive fortified city, Tughlakabad, beside which he or his son built an exceptionally handsome tomb. He was Sultan for only four years.

In 1324 Ghiyasuddin died in famous and mysterious circumstances (see next page).

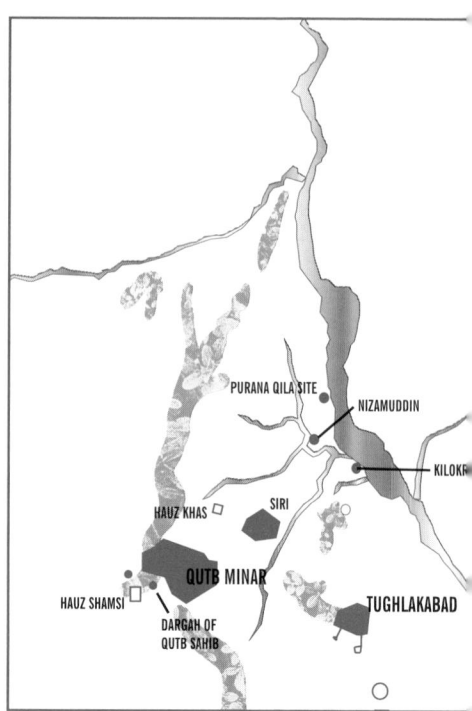

Tughlakabad

Tughlakabad is generally considered to be the third city of Delhi, after Lal Kot and Siri, although another less durable city had already been constructed beside the river at Kilokri, a pattern of building that has to be considered as aggrandisement by a new ruler. The history of Tughlakabad is difficult to believe. However, it is a fact that much of the city was built over a period of only two years during Ghiyasuddin Tughlak's short reign (1320-24), and yet its outer walls are 6.5 km in length, inside which are a further two walled areas. The outer one appears to have contained the palace, while the innermost one was the citadel. The large outer area contained the ordinary residential and commercial neighbourhoods, which even spilled out into an extensive suburb to the east. An aerial photograph taken in the 1940s shows the layout of the city, especially the main residential area. Here there was a straightforward grid pattern, apart from where it was interrupted by a road leading directly from the central gate on the east side of the city to the main gate

Tughlakabad walls

into the palace area. Halfway along this road on the south was the Jami Masjid, still a large clear space in the photograph but now built over. Uncontrolled development (and, in some places, the prevention of grazing that kept down the undergrowth) has meant that virtually all the remaining ruins have now been built over or buried under vegetation.

The secret of the incredibly fast construction (not unusual in medieval India) is thought to be that each army commander was assigned a length of wall between the points at which the gates were to be located. The gates, built from a different stone, were constructed afterwards, ironing out the non-alignment of different sections. The street layout of the city was also established by the positions of the gates; thus a great deal of construction could take place simultaneously.

Joined to the city by a causeway is Ghiyasuddin's mausoleum, built in 1325 inside a miniature fort. Further east are the remains of a dam that once created a huge lake in the middle of which stood the tomb. On the far side of the dam is a substantial fortified area, Adilabad, which is supposed to have been built by Muhammad Tughlak, Ghiyasuddin's son.

Some well-known stories are attached to the building of Tughlakabad. It is said that Ghiyasuddin proposed to his then master, Mubarak Shah Khalji, that he should build a fort on this easily defended outcrop. Mubarak Shah laughed and told him to build it himself when he became Sultan, not realising that his words were prophetic. Another story relates to Ghiyasuddin's bad relationship with the *sufi* saint Nizamuddin Aulia. While Tughlakabad was being built Nizamuddin was engaged in constructing his *baoli* (step-well) and was depleting the labour force at Tughlakabad. Ghiyasuddin forbade the labourers to work for Nizamuddin but after working at Tughlakabad by day they went and worked at the *baoli* at night. Enraged, Ghiyasuddin prevented the sale of oil to Nizamuddin but the saint was undeterred; the water from his *baoli* miraculously gave off sufficient light. Nizamuddin put his famous curse on Tughlakabad 'Either it will be inhabited by Gujjars or it will remain barren' (actually both these things happened; not so long ago barren Tughlakabad was used only by Gujjars - traditionally nomadic cattle herders). Another legend has it that when Ghiyasuddin was returning to Delhi from a campaign his son, Muhammad, went out of the city to meet him and erected a temporary pavilion. While Ghiyasuddin was inside the pavilion it collapsed, killing the Sultan and another of his sons. Muhammad was absent and was saved. Because Nizamuddin had seemed to predict Ghiyasuddin's death when he said, on Ghiyasuddin approach, 'Delhi is yet far off', Muhammad and Nizamuddin were suspected by some of plotting his death.

Tughlakabad citadel walls

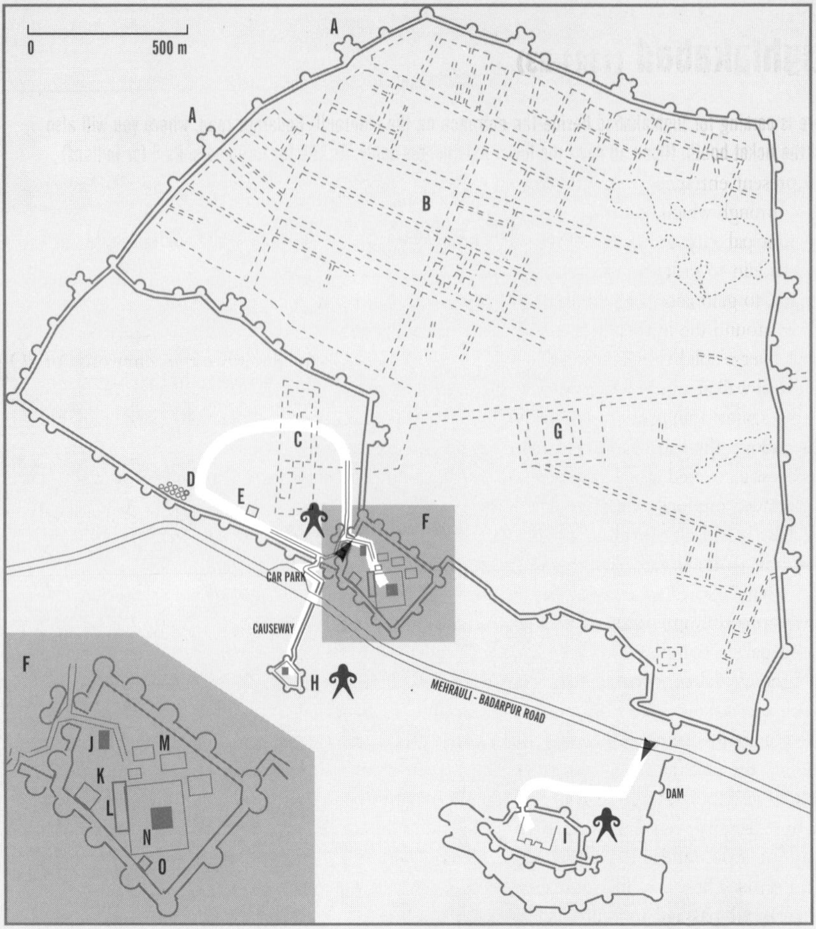

Map 5.2 Tughlakabad

A. Gates
B. Layout of city streets as revealed by excavation
C. Palace
D. Underground pits
E. Tank
F. Citadel
G. Jami Masjid (position of)
H. Ghiyasuddin's Tomb
I. Adilabad

Inset map of citadel

J. Mosque
K. Tank
L. Storerooms
M. Village houses (Mughal)
N. Burj Mandal
O. Secret passage

Storerooms

Tughlakabad (1321-23)

There is parking for Tughlakabad beside the entrance on the Mehrauli- Badarpur road, where you will also find the ticket booth. (Open all day - the lower ASI charges apply: Rs 100 for foreigners; Rs 5 for Indians)

The present entrance to the Tughlakabad Fort is from the causeway linking the city to the tomb, through which the road slices. This gate does not have the great fortifications found on the principal city gates because it was only a subsidiary and private entrance, used by Ghiyasuddin to visit the site of his tomb (these were often built in advance of death) and, possibly, to gain access to the lake. The walls are particularly impressive at this point, being highest around the inner city and citadel. They are distinctively battered, with a facing of cut stones over a solid rubble core. The base of the walls was further reinforced by a glacis, an additional wall at an even greater slope that served to buttress the higher walls, to increase the security against mining and make it more difficult for attackers to lay their ladders against the walls. Above, the fortifications are similar to those at Siri (p.44).

There was a covered walkway with arrow slots at regular intervals and rounded merlons along the skyline.

The gate brings you to a point below the **citadel walls**. Follow the path ahead, beside the wall, to the citadel gate. On the left is a large excavated area that supplied stone for construction and was probably intended to be a lake. Beyond it are the ruins of a large palace complex, probably Ghiyasuddin's public palace, while the citadel contained his private rooms. Go right into the citadel and follow a path towards a prominent mound. The citadel contains some interesting buildings, but confusion is added by the fact that there was a late Mughal settlement inside the walls and most of the standing walls are from that date. The principal Tughlak buildings are the **Burj Mandal**, the mound ahead of you, and the platform below it with basement **storerooms**. These can be explored on the right of the path. The

Tank in palace area

underground passage is quite well preserved with chambers either side. These are often described either as dungeons or as a market. It is difficult to reconcile the idea of a market in such a narrow, dark passage and local guides delight in turning any dark hole into a prison. Storerooms seem a likelier possibility. Interestingly, it appears that the dividing walls between rooms were added later, the original plan being long galleries either side of the corridor.

Above the storerooms is a large open area (partly built upon in late-Mughal times), which might have formed a courtyard in a building that also included the nearby Burj Mandal. It is possible that there are further storerooms between the known ones and the Burj Mandal, an arrangement seen at the similar Bijay Mandal in Jahanpanah (p.64). Just beyond the storerooms is a **tank**, which lies right up against the outer wall. Fine stonework survives on that outer side while the other three sides are disintegrating quite fast.

The **Burj Mandal** seems to have been a solid structure that may have once served as the base for a permanent superstructure, the foundations of which are just discernible. This superstructure might have been a single room with openings on each side. A similar arrangement can be seen at the Bijay Mandal in Jahanpanah. Near the Burj Mandal, built within the outer wall, is a **secret passage**, only visible now as steps leading down into the ground. Despite what is commonly believed by local guides here and at other ruined medieval cities (who will tell you fantastic stories about secret passages going miles to the nearby

Palace remains

city/fort/palace), this is the only proven incidence of a secret passage of this nature throughout India, Iran or Central Asia. Excavations carried out in the 1990s revealed an elaborate passageway with storage chambers and a disguised entrance and exit, the latter being a small opening emerging from the outer face of the wall that looks much like an innocent drain.

Leaving the citadel it is possible to explore parts of the **Palace enclosure** by turning right and following a path through thorn trees. The most impressive buildings in Tughlakabad were probably not those inside the citadel but those that are now nothing more than mounds of overgrown masonry. It is difficult to get close to many of them because of thorn bushes, but previous excavation has revealed a series of large courtyards on a north-south orientation. In one place, inside the gateway that connected two of the courtyards, some fine incised plasterwork was found, indicating that the palace buildings, at least, were far from austere. The most prominent remains now are two sides of what appears to have been an open courtyard looking onto the 'lake'. These are not very Tughlak in appearance and there is clear evidence of alterations to the original fabric, indicating a longer occupation of the site than tradition allows. Current excavations in front of this building are revealing more buildings and courtyards to the south of the main mound.

It is difficult to reconcile the austere remains visible today with Ibn Battuta's description of the palace at Tughlakabad:

In [Tughlakabad] was the great palace whose tiles he had gilded, so that when the sun rose they shone with brilliant light and a blinding glow. He deposited in this town vast stores of wealth and it is told that he constructed a tank and poured into it molten gold so that it became a single block.

This was written after his visit in the 1330s, after the city had been abandoned as the main seat of the Sultan, although its strong defences meant that it remained in use for storage. Perhaps the 'tank' is the one beside the palace, probably as dry then as it is now. It is possible local people were just as ready with tall stories about molten gold as they are now about secret passages.

Beyond the palace, near the outer wall, are the remains of **underground pits,** located beside one of the original entrances to the city. Similar pits have been found beside other city gates. Each one has a round access hole in the roof, leading into a large beehive shaped chamber. These chambers were once unconnected but the walls have been broken between most of them, presumably by people in search of treasure. The vast size of these pits makes it unlikely that they were built to contain treasure, even the 'vast stores' spoken of by Ibn Battuta. Although their use as dungeons is of course a popular idea, grain seems a more likely commodity to have been stored here. Returning to the entrance gate you will pass another deep **tank**, overgrown and crumbling away on most sides.

Underground pits

Ghiyasuddin's Tomb (1320-24)

From the car park it is necessary to brave the increasingly heavy traffic to rejoin the causeway to the Tomb. The strongly defended entrance takes the visitor left, up steps into the small enclosure. The tomb itself stands in remarkable contrast to the rest of the buildings of Tughlakabad. It is not known whether the tomb was in fact built before Ghiyasuddin's death; it might have been built, or finished, by his son, Muhammad. Instead of the dressed quartzite and rubble masonry of the outer walls and the city, the tomb is built from finely cut red sandstone and white marble. The one feature that it shares with the fortification walls is their pronounced batter. The architectural interest of the building is considerable, for here we are seeing an early version of the Indo-Islamic style that would become ubiquitous in sultanate tombs in the next century. Typical are the diminishing framed arches within the *pishtaq* (central bay). The small niches either side of the *pishtaq* develop in later buildings, increasing in number and size.

Ghiyasuddin's Tomb

Ghiyasuddin's Tomb - elevation and section

The unusual enclosure is roughly triangular. The narrowest point is towards the east, where the large round bastion is left open to the sky. Below the main level is a large storage pit similar to the ones inside the city. At the other angles the bastions are smaller and roofed, containing subsidiary unknown graves. The northern chamber is surmounted by a small white marble dome, the stonework elaborately inscribed in places. One of the inscriptions states that this is the tomb of Zafar Khan and goes on to say that, as a mere child, he 'seized the country as far as the boundary of Lakhnauti [northern Bengal] in a short time, and was subduing another kingdom when suddenly by the decree of God he received a wound from the evil eye of that age and repaired from this transitory world to eternity.' Nothing further is known of this hero.

View of Tomb and city walls. Since this photo was taken the area in front of the tomb has become a container storage site.

ADILABAD, probably built early in Muhammad Tughlak's reign (1324-51)

Access to Adilabad is easiest from the car park of the small recreation area below it. Walk down the steps from this area onto the open area that is used for informal games of cricket and follow the fence until you get to an opening from which an old road goes up through the northwest gate.

East of the causeway linking the city to the tomb are the remains of the dam that once created the lake surrounding the tomb. The remains of the sluice can be seen at the Tughlakabad end. At the other end the dam was connected to a rocky hillock on which is situated Adilabad, thought to have been built by Muhammad Tughlak. In most respects, such as the exterior walls, Adilabad is identical to Tughlakabad, except that it is unclear how it was used. Like Tughlakabad it contains an outer and

Adilabad walls

inner enclosure. There are no visible signs of buildings inside the former; presumably it was never developed or construction was non-permanent (i.e., mud-brick, timber and thatch). The inner enclosure contains one large building, presumed to be the palace but, as an 1946 archaeologist's report says 'as a palace, the plan leaves much to be desired', having only two rooms and a large courtyard. A mystery is the northwest gate, which can only have been accessible by crossing the lake created by the dam. Moreover the ramp leading from the outer to the inner gate stops awkwardly a good four feet below the doorsill.

Beyond Adilabad there is yet another small fort, known as the **Nai ka Kot**, very unlikely to have had anything to do with a barber (nai). It is thought that perhaps it was built by Muhammad as his residence while he was building Adilabad.

Adilabad Main Gate

JAHANPANAH

From the fort of Siri to that of Old Delhi, which is a considerable distance, there runs a strong wall, built of stone and cement. The part called Jahanpanah is situated in the midst of the inhabited city.

Timur's description,
as translated by Henry Miers Elliot

Muhammad Tughlak's reign

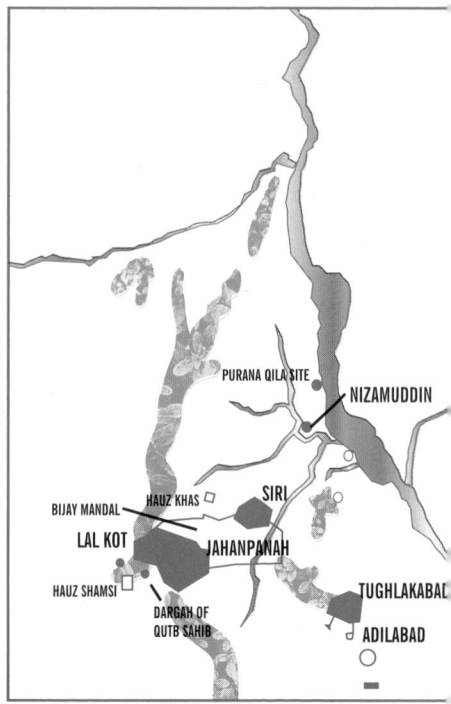

Muhammad Tughlak, Ghiyasuddin's son, has an extraordinary reputation for megalomania. Since the contemporary histories were written either by those working in his court who had reason to praise him, or by those who were writing later with reason to discredit him, it is difficult to decide where the truth lies. He seems to have been clever and interested in philosophy. He was inspired by a Syrian scholar to reinvigorate Islam by a fresh interpretation combined with holy war against infidels. He invited, and attracted, scholars and soldiers from all over the Islamic world to his court, among whom was the Moroccan traveller Ibn Battuta, who has left a particularly vivid description of Muhammad's reign. Ibn Battuta covered pages in descriptions of Muhammad's generosity (often to strangers whom he preferred over his own subjects), his humility and his sense of equity. For instance, Ibn Battuta was very impressed because the Sultan accepted a court judgment and paid compensation for wrongfully killing a Hindu chief's brother. However, this same killing indicates the darker side to his character of which there are an equal number of examples under the heading 'this Sultan's murders and reprehensible actions'. As Ibn Battuta himself says, Muhammad was 'far too free in shedding blood'.

Muhammad conceived of some extraordinary and unpopular schemes, all more or less failures, and ended with a much smaller empire than he had started with. The mistake for which he is best known is the removal in 1326 of the population of Delhi to Daulatabad in the Deccan, well over a thousand kilometres south of Delhi, near Aurangabad in Maharashtra. It is unclear how sweeping a clearance of the population this was and it was probably mainly the Muslim population that was involved. From other sources we know that, despite the clearance of so many families from Delhi, there were still many Hindu families living in and around the city after the exodus. It is certain, though, that the families of Muhammad's principal courtiers were moved and they had a tough time, with many deaths as a result, although it seems that they were well compensated in financial terms. The move had happened by the time Ibn Battuta arrived in 1333. According to him the entire population had left, some of them only after an example had been made of a reluctant old man, who was dragged on the forty day's journey and 'fell apart' on the way, only his leg arriving. Muhammad summoned people from other parts of his provinces, but the new population was nowhere near sufficient to restore the city.

The whole enterprise is shrouded in mystery but the reasons for the move were probably twofold: firstly in order to establish a solidly Muslim power base in the Deccan, secondly to allow the buildup of a large force in Delhi for a campaign in Khurasan (part of modern Afghanistan) that eventually proved a catastrophe. To add to the riddle of the population movement we also know that Muhammad built extensively in the Delhi area, most notably the walls linking Old Delhi with Siri, creating the 'city' known as Jahanpanah. When Ibn Battuta arrived in Delhi in 1333, two years before the exiled citizens were recalled, Muhammad was living in Jahanpanah. It seems, therefore, that Delhi remained the main city of Muhammad's empire.

During the 1330s, in order to finance his large army, Muhammad introduced a token currency because of the chronic shortage of silver. The currency was easily forged in the countryside and the forgeries used to pay the land tax. Eventually the currency had to be recalled and gold and silver given in exchange. By this time inflation had set in, making the burden of supporting an army even more difficult for Muhammad. To make matters worse, there was a seven-year drought during the 1330s and there was severe famine in Delhi. At the end of the period Muhammad had to allow migration to Awadh until the drought was over. Adding to his problems there had been epidemics in his army and widespread revolts.

After a decade or so of rule it is not surprising that, following such a series of tribulations not all of his own making, Muhammad was in considerable difficulties. To compound them, he had also run up against the problems of maintaining a large empire: the expenses were greater and the revenue less than when outlying areas were simply used as foci for raiding parties. The officers that were left in the provinces to collect revenue found that they could not raise the amounts they had promised. They were forced into rebellion in order, quite literally, to save their skins (one of their number had been flayed alive for failing in his revenue collection). It must have been a difficult time for courtiers. According to Ibn Battuta, Muhammad was unpredictable in the extreme and while he could be lavishly generous to some, he could be exceptionally cruel to others. It was as a result of exceptional oppression that many of his provincial governors revolted and broke away from central control. In 1347, for instance, Hasan Bahman rebelled at Daulatabad, soon shifting his capital to Gulbarga to found the Bahmani Sultanate, a province that would never again be held by a Delhi Sultan. It must have been with some relief among the noblemen, therefore, that Firoz Shah, Muhammad's cousin, accepted the throne when Muhammad died while campaigning in Gujarat in 1351.

Bijay Mandal

Jahanpanah

Jahanpanah is considered to be the fourth city of Delhi, founded by Ghiyasuddin's son, Muhammad Tughlak, in 1326-27, and created by linking Lal Kot and Siri by two walls, thus enclosing a large area between them. It is, in a way, the most mysterious and haunting of the cities of Delhi in that there is very little left, even of walls or gateways, to give one any idea of what it must have been like when first built. Yet there are extensive remains from later centuries, scattered among the villages and colonies of South Delhi. To come across these buildings, either accidentally or after a search, gives one a sense of discovery that is lacking in other, better-known places.

There are numerous mysteries surrounding the character and activities of Muhammad Tughlak and these have been outlined in the history section. Here it is only necessary to say that Delhi seems to have remained Muhammad's centre of power for most of his reign. The physical appearance of his city is uncertain. Ibn Battuta, who lived in Delhi from 1333 to 1341, gives us a description of the city, although in nothing like the detail that he provides for the pomp and ceremony of court life (see box). He is very clear about the demarcation of

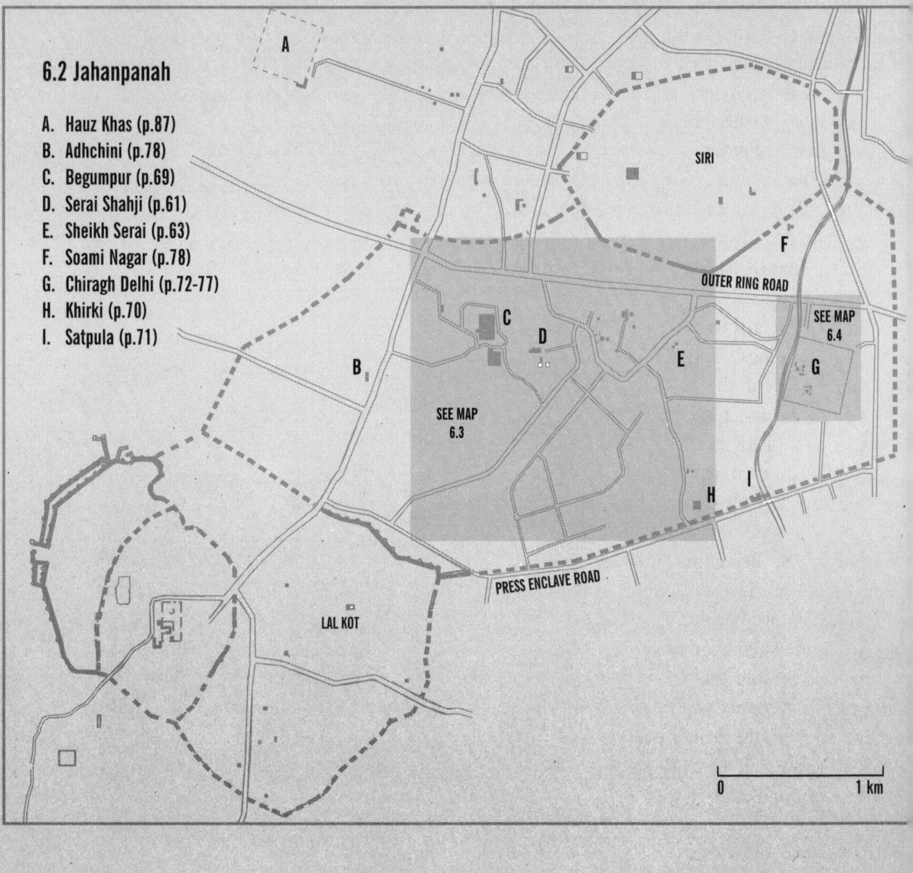

6.2 Jahanpanah

A. Hauz Khas (p.87)
B. Adhchini (p.78)
C. Begumpur (p.69)
D. Serai Shahji (p.61)
E. Sheikh Serai (p.63)
F. Soami Nagar (p.78)
G. Chiragh Delhi (p.72-77)
H. Khirki (p.70)
I. Satpula (p.71)

SIRI

OUTER RING ROAD

SEE MAP 6.4

SEE MAP 6.3

PRESS ENCLAVE ROAD

LAL KOT

0   1 km

Jahanpanah, Siri and Lal Kot (which he refers to, significantly, as Delhi ('Dihli')). He also mentions Tughlakabad (see Chapter 5). Ibn Battuta has most to say about Lal Kot, remarking on its exceptionally wide city walls, the 'lofty' walls of the houses and the beauty of the mosque. About Jahanpanah, the area enclosed within the new walls, he tells us that it was 'set apart for the residence of the Sultan', and says that Muhammad had also intended to incorporate Tughlakabad but the expense was too great. Our best guess, therefore, is that the old city of Lal Kot was still the main urban area, Siri was the military zone, and the remaining area was reserved for the royal palace, of which we assume the Bijay Mandal to be a part. It was out of Lal Kot, in 1326, that the Muslim population was expelled to Daulatabad for reasons that are far from clear. Despite the absence of the families of Muhammad's senior courtiers, it appears that Delhi remained the centre of Muhammad's empire.

Jahanpanah may originally have been reserved for the Sultan's palace, but it is clear that this situation did not prevail for long. The palace was soon joined by several tombs, mainly of saints or holy men. We know, from casual observation and documentary sources, that tombs were generally built outside city walls. For instance, Ibn Battuta describes the cemetery outside one of the gates of Delhi. It appears, however, that extremely exalted individuals, such as Sultans and saints, could be buried inside the walls, which then attracted satellite burials. It could be that the preponderance of saints' tombs within Jahanpanah follows the same pattern. Alternatively, perhaps, the area was seen as rural and therefore was used for burials. There are certainly plenty of examples throughout India (e.g., Mandu in Madhya Pradesh) of fortified walls so extensive that they enclosed large areas of farmland as well as the urban centre. Tombs are found inside such walls. The existence of several extremely large mosques in Jahanpanah, built not very long after the walls, suggests a rapid increase of population, but it is reasonable to suppose that there continued to be a large area of cultivated land or jungle inside the walls.

Whatever the size of the urban population during Tughlak and later Sultanate times, it was much reduced when the population shifted to Shahjahanabad, built in the 17th century. By the 19th century contemporary maps show us that this area had become a scatter of villages based in or around older buildings. This situation prevailed into the second half of the 20th century, but since then the area has been engulfed by modern colonies such as Panchsheel Park and Malviya Nagar.

What then remains of the city from Muhammad's time? Very little actually. The buildings that do are the Bijay Mandal, perhaps the Begumpur Mosque, and part of the city wall. The wall can be seen at various points along Press Enclave Road. At the westernmost end, on the southern side of the road, is the old wall of Qila Rai Pithora to which it is connected. The road cuts through the start of the Jahanpanah wall near Hauz Rani and it can again be seen at the Satpula (just east of Khirki, p.70).

IBN BATTUTA'S TRAVELS

It has to be pointed out that Ibn Battuta's travels were dictated by him to a secretary of the Sultan of Fez, many years after the events. Their absolute veracity cannot, therefore, be assured, and it is certainly true that some of the journeys do not make sense geographically. On the other hand, it has been found that the details of people and places are well corroborated by other contemporary sources so that, as far as our purposes are concerned, they make an invaluable contribution.

Begumpur Mosque

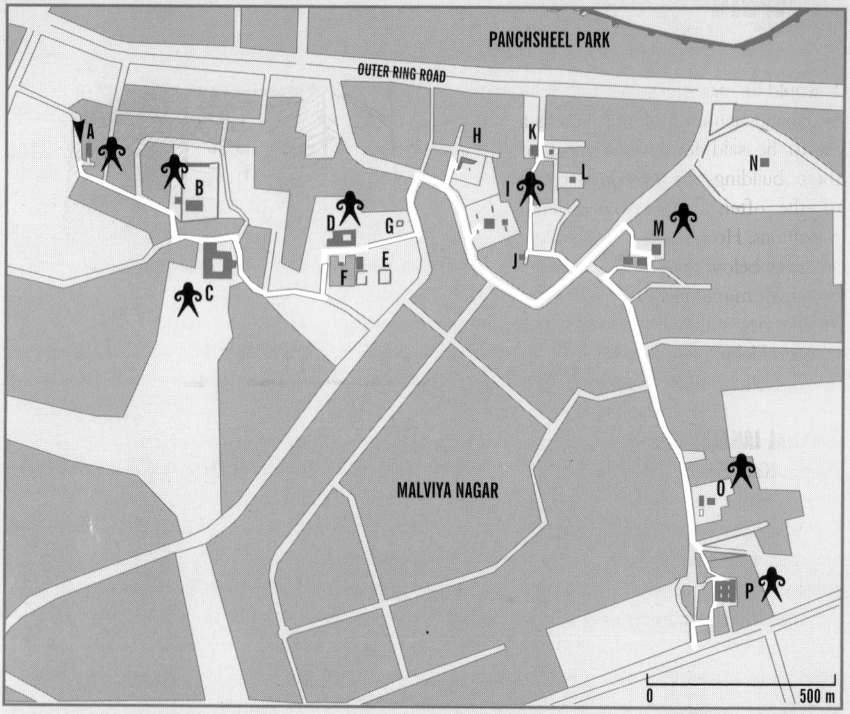

PANCHSHEEL PARK

OUTER RING ROAD

A

B

C

H

K

I

L

N

D

G

F

E

J

M

MALVIYA NAGAR

O

P

0   500 m

6.3 Central Jahanpanah Walk

A. Kalu Serai Mosque, late 14th c. (p.61)
B. Bijay Mandal, early 14th c. (p.64-68)
C. Begumpur Mosque, mid 14th c. (p.69)
D. Serai Shahi Mahal, ? early 16th c. (p.61-62)
E. Mosque and burial grounds, mainly 17th c. (p.62)
F. Ruined gateway, 15th c. (p.62)
G. Ruined grave platform
H. Kharbuze ka Gumbad, before 1397 (p.62)
I. Lal Gumbad 1397 (p.63)
J. Gateway once leading into enclosure 14th c.
K. Baradari and tomb, early 15th c. (p.63)
L. Gurudwara (ex-tomb)
M. Sheikh Serai tombs, early 16th c. (p.63)
N. Tomb of Sheikh Salahuddin Darwesh, early 14th c.
O. Tomb and mosque of Yussuf Qattal, 1520s (p.63)
P. Khirki Mosque, late 14th c. (p.70)

Bijay Mandal

It would be masochistic to explore all of Jahanpanah on foot and there is a lot to be said for visiting most of these buildings by car on account of the often disagreeable walking conditions. However, two suggestions are given below, the first taking in the principal monuments in the heart of the city and the second around Chiragh Delhi, one of the least spoilt of the Delhi's urban villages.

Serai Shahi Mahal

CENTRAL JAHANPANAH

Start at **Kalu Serai**, which is reachable by car. From Aurobindo Marg turn left immediately after passing Essex Farms at the IIT crossing. The road turns to the right at the village. A little before the road turns left leave the car and walk into the lane beside Thapar Arcade.

Walk up this lane a short distance and then go up a steep path to your left, turn right and follow the path to a derelict and inhabited **mosque**. It is believed that this is one of the seven mosques built by Khan Jahan Junan Shah during Firoz Shah's reign. The building is inhabited by several families and is in a very poor state of repair, approximately half the mosque having fallen; the 2003 monsoon rains brought down another couple of bays. It was originally three bays deep and seven wide. The ground level has risen over time, concealing the column bases. The architecture is undoubtedly similar in style to that of other mosques built by Khan Jahan Junan Shah, although the *mihrab* decorations are more elaborate.

Kalu Serai Mosque

Return to the road, which continues left round a corner and then straight to the **Bijay Mandal** (p.64-68). Picturesque but not beautiful, this is one of the most intriguing buildings in Delhi. Continue on the same road, and turn left through the village, passing the great walls of the **Begumpur Mosque** on your right until you reach the entrance (p.69). Having visited the mosque, follow the road out of the village into a wasteland of nasty concrete walls and rubbish-strewn open spaces. Beyond these can be seen the **Serai Shahji mahal** and the various buildings surrounding it that once formed part of **Serai Shahji** village (this is probably the filthiest part of the walk). Most of the buildings here seem to date from the Mughal period. Approach the rear of the *mahal* and, by crossing a huge rubbish heap, you can enter another building, attached, but not connected internally. There are several bays and it is just about possible to make out that the ceilings were once ornately decorated.

Serai Shahji Mahal archway

Take the lane to the right of the **Serai Shahji mahal,** passing on the right the very dilapidated remains of a **gateway** into a walled enclosure now housing a slum. It has a row of recessed arches over the opening and fragments of green and blue tilework in the alcoves. The lane brings you to another open space with several ruined mosques and graveyards. On the right is a **late Mughal mosque** with curved bengali-style (*bangla*) roofs over each bay. Behind it a well preserved arched gateway leads into the enclosure and grave of **Sheikh Farid Murtaza Khan,** a prodigious builder who lived during Akbar's reign, among whose projects was a *serai* and mosque on the road to Agra, the probable origin of Faridabad. His grave is the one with a railing, with an elegantly carved white marble headstone. Behind it is a prayer wall forming the western boundary of the enclosure. There are many other graves inside the burial ground. Opposite is another burial ground with a **wall mosque,** in an even worse state of repair.

Serai Shahji Mahal interio

Here you can find the entrance to the *Mahal,* which has a large courtyard with arched openings to rooms on all sides. On the west side the three central bays have been used as a mosque and there are remains of graves in and around the walled enclosure in the centre of the courtyard. Steps near the entrance lead up to the roof, from where you can enter the tower. This contains a central square room with an ornate incised plaster ceiling decoration, and two smaller lobbies. From the entrance lobby gently winding steps follow the curve of the inner wall up to the roof, where remains of red sandstone brackets once supported balconies at the present roof level. The date of this building is unknown and its features could come from a variety of periods. This should not surprise us; secular buildings go through many transformations, whereas mosques and tombs are likely to go on serving their original purpose, so little alteration is called for. This *mahal's* original use may have been as a *khanqah* although it clearly became a graveyard at some moderately distant time. An interesting feature on the outside of the *mahal* is that, on the corner to the left of the entrance, the stonework has been cut away in order to round off the corner. This feature is common in the narrow lanes of the Walled City (Shahjahanabad), where such chamfering helps people to manoeuvre loads through the city, and implies that this area was once closely built up.

Serai Shahji Mahal corne

From here you can walk out to the main road where you should turn left and then right along another busy road. Make a short detour along the second road to the left to see the tiny **Kharbuze ka Gumbad** in the garden behind the Panchshila Public School. This is a bizarre little structure, named so because of its resemblance to a melon (kharbuza). A small platform supports four quartzite pillars and on top of these is a ramshackle pile of stones carrying a tiny, solid, stone dome. Tradition has it that Sheikh Kabiruddin Auliya (buried in 1397 in the Lal Gumbad) would spend his days under the dome and

Kharbuze ka Gumbad

his nights in a cave below the platform. Although this little edifice has the appearance of having been created from scraps yesterday, it has actually been standing for quite some time, being mentioned in ASI reports from the 19th century.

Lal Gumbad

Visible from the Panchshila Public School is the open space that contains a group of buildings surrounding the Lal Gumbad, reachable further along the main road. The **Lal Gumbad** itself is very similar to the tomb of Ghiyasuddin Tughlak (died 1324) (p.53), although it was built much later in that century for Sheikh Kabiruddin Auliya, a disciple of Chiragh Delhi. Nearby is a rubble-built **gateway**, which might have been an entrance to the tomb enclosure. In the same compound are no less than four **wall mosques** and various grave platforms in various states of decay. They are from approximately the same period (Lodi) and were probably built as private burial grounds.

Lal Gumbad

Further round on the main road you come to the entrance to **Sadhana Enclave**, which contains several ancient buildings. These are marked on the map. The two most interesting are found by following the main road past the central garden. On the left is the **Baradari**, probably from the late 14th or early 15th century. The building seems to have survived intact and could have been a mosque, although little remains on the west wall to confirm this apart from niches that could have contained *mihrabs*. Opposite is a **tomb**, believed to be of the Lodi period, a simple square building that once stood inside a small walled enclosure.

Tomb Sardana Enclave

On the other side of the main road from Sadhana Enclave is Sheikh Serai. Take a lane that leads directly into the village, opposite the Madrasa Talimul-Quran. The three tombs around which the village grew are soon visible in a small open space. The best preserved is that of **Sheikh Alauddin**. He was a descendant of Baba Sheikh Fariduddin Shakarganj of Pakpatan, Nizamuddin's *pir*. Sheikh Alauddin built this

Bardari Sardana Enclave

tomb during his lifetime and was buried here in 1541. The square tomb originally had three openings on each side, with *jali* screens between the columns; these are now filled with rubble masonry. The **adjacent tomb** is in a worse state. The design was very similar in many respects to Yussuf Qattal's tomb near Khirki, built at about the same time. A third tomb is inhabited.

A wide road opposite Sadhana Enclave eventually passes the **Tomb of Yussuf Qattal**: a tomb, its attached mosque, and a much more ruined mosque beside it. Shaikh Yussuf Qattal was a popular saint during Ibrahim Lodi's reign (1517-26). The **tomb** is a very ornate twelve-pillared pavilion built from red sandstone with a plastered drum and dome, and geometrical *jali* work in contrasting designs between the columns. The **mosque** is small but elaborately decorated, the interior being ornamented throughout with fine plasterwork. The mosque is very different from the tomb, although its appearance would have been a little more similar when fully plastered. Even so it would be difficult to leap to the conclusion that the two buildings were built as a single whole. That is not unusual; there are other examples where clusters of seemingly related buildings are stylistically very different and probably not built together, for example the Bara Gumbad complex in the Lodi Gardens (p.124).

The road continues and skirts **Khirki** village before joining Press Enclave Road. The spectacular **Khirki mosque** is in the centre of the village (p.70).

Bijay Mandal (First half of 14th century)

(Map p.60)

The Bijay Mandal is perhaps the most puzzling building in Delhi, mainly because we know relatively little about ancient secular buildings, but also because it clearly went through numerous transformations over time. There are several reasons for supposing this to have been part of Muhammad Tughlak's palace, but without an extensive archaeological investigation we can only speculate as to how it functioned as a building. Ibn Battuta's description of Muhammad's palace gives us no clues as to what it was like, except that visitors had to pass through three gates to 'a vast hall called *hazar sutun*, which means "thousand pillars". The pillars are of painted wood and support a wooden roof, most exquisitely carved'.

It is very difficult to envisage how this hall would have looked, as we know little of domestic buildings at this time. It sounds like a hypostyle hall, with many rows of columns (but not as many as a thousand (*hazar*), which would have been a figure of speech and was anyway a common name for palaces) and a flat roof. One question is how a flat roof that was supported on a timber frame, which was constantly moving due to changes in heat and moisture content, could have remained water-proof? As far as the interior is concerned we know little more: we are only told that the pillars and roof were highly ornamented. It is possible that the walls were decorated with paintings, as there are references to paintings being removed from palaces (which might have included this one) during Firoz Shah's anti-idolatry campaigns a few decades later.

To draw any conclusions from the buildings as described in the following pages is difficult. However, insofar as we can comprehend them, it is clear that they were used over a considerable period, judging by the archaeological finds as well as signs of many alterations. This has a bearing on our comprehension of the development of the city. For instance, it is mentioned that Alauddin Khalji had a *hazar-sutun* as well as Muhammad Tughlak. It seems probable that they were one and the same (although Ibn Battuta mentions, perhaps erroneously, that Alauddin's palace was in Siri). We can therefore speculate that the stone hall dates from Alauddin's time whereas the tower beside it was almost certainly built by Muhammad Tughlak. Archaeological finds that seemed to be the remains of 'treasure' show that the buildings were still in use after Firoz Shah's reign, and its occupation by Sheikh Hasan Tahir in the early 16th century brings the story of the buildings' use right up to the time of the Lodi Sultans.

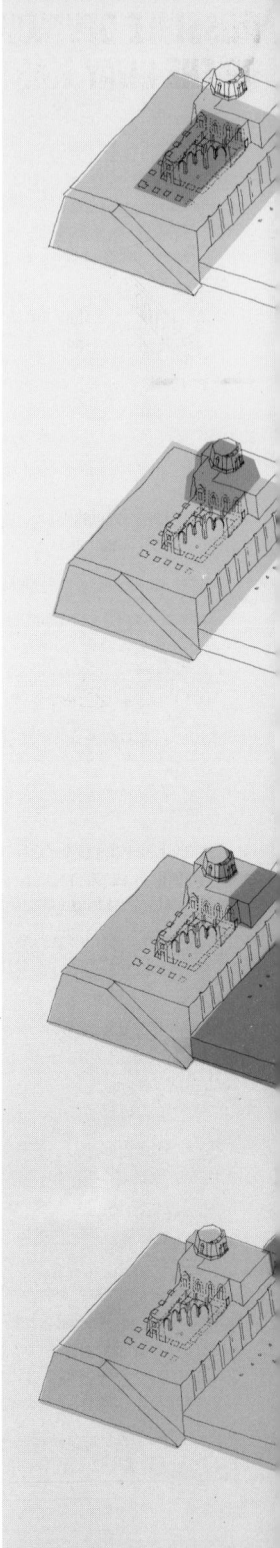

POSSIBLE DEVELOPMENT OF THE BIJAY MANDAL SITE

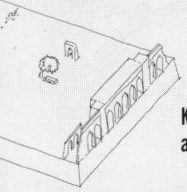

Khalji Period: Main platform and hypostyle hall.

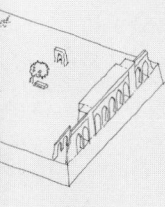

Early Tughlak: Additional platform built beside hall and octagonal pavilion built.

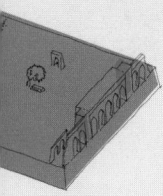

Later Tughlak: Extension to upper platform and enlargement of octagonal pavilion. Large low platform built, perhaps for timber columned hypostyle hall (as described by Ibn Battuta). Twin towers built at east end of low platform.

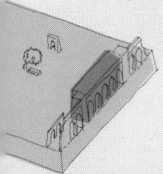

Lodi: Domed building and pavilion at east end of low platform.

DOMED BUILDING (15th century)

This building, right beside the Bijay Mandal, is thought to be of a later date than the adjacent palace. Its purpose is unknown and its architecture is unusual, with two openings on each of three sides while the east side is solid. It appears that this building once adjoined another building on its west side, where there is evidence of extensive basement passageways.

Domed building

BIJAY MANDAL

The earliest part of this complicated building is probably the **upper platform**, which is raised considerably above its surroundings; the battered (sloping) retaining walls can be seen on the west, south and east sides. Under the flat surface at

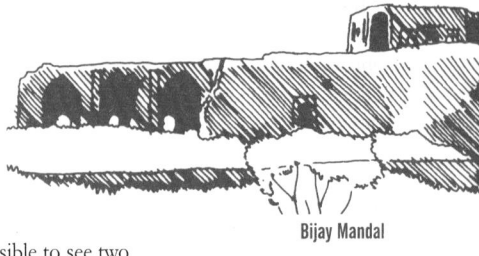

Bijay Mandal

the eastern end of the platform it is possible to see two levels of barrel vaulted basement rooms by scrambling a little way down the southern slope. At the other end of the platform it appears that there were similar barrel vaulted chambers. Between these slightly raised areas there must have been a forecourt to the main building.

From the platform you can see the façade of a single-storey **hall**, with an octagonal tower on the massive masonry base on its left. In front of the hall are the remains of a veranda, which appears to have wrapped around the east end of the building as well; the large square bases of the arcade columns are visible, with a few steps between each of them. Doorways led from this arcade into the main apartment, three bays wide and five bays long. The roof is supported by stone columns, single apart from those in the second north-south row, which are, inexplicably, double. Behind the first row the floor level drops about half a metre, with two large circular pits. When the area was excavated during the first part of the 20th century numerous precious objects were found in these pits: fragments of ivory, porcelain, glass beads, pearls, red coral, gold, rubies and coins from the reigns of various Sultans from 1296 up to about 1390. It is reasonable to suppose, therefore, that these were treasure stores, with a storage capacity that would again confirm the identification with Muhammad's palace. It is also likely that they were concealed under a false floor, compatible with the main floor and door levels.

Verandah bases

The hall seems once to have had arched openings on all sides. When the massive platform supporting the octagonal tower was built against the hall these end doorways were

Pavilion from roof

blocked up. The first doorway on the north wall, beside the platform, also seems to have been altered, perhaps to adapt to a new room layout on the north side of the hall, now only indicated by different levels and foundations, showing that there were once buildings along the edge of the platform.

A ramp and then unusually wide and shallow steps lead up to the base of the **octagonal pavilion**. There is plenty of evidence that the original octagon was extended on the north side and that the triple doorway (framed in quartzite) and the narrow stairs to the roof are later additions. Inside is a symmetrical, vaulted, cruciform room with identical openings on each side. At the height of summer the interior is considerably cooler than outside and catches every breeze. Upstairs, on the roof, there are two well-preserved sockets, one of which still has a recess round the rim, indicating that it would have been fitted with a cover. Close inspection reveals that there were once similar sockets beside the top of each staircase. The depth of these sockets implies that they would have been used to hold posts of considerable weight and height, perhaps the frame for a temporary *baradari* (pillared pavilion), thought to have crowned the tower. At regular intervals along the very edge of the roof are smaller sockets that may well have held smaller posts. We can easily suppose that this tower was used by Muhammad Tughlak as a private retreat or to watch happenings below, but many questions remain, not least whether the Sultan would have come up the same way as us, squeezing, in his finery, through the narrow gap between the steps and the tower. It seems likely that there was another way up which led more directly to the entrance of the tower, although Indian palaces in general are not noted for fine staircases; they are commonly tucked into the solid masonry of structural walls.

Altered doorway

From the upper platform it is possible to climb down to the larger lower one. On the east and west sides of the **lower platform** the retaining walls are visible. Interestingly, there are signs that there have been two stages of construction here: the base of the walls are battered and built from large quartzite boulders with well cut flat surfaces on the outside. Above this level is a vertical wall built in the kind of masonry construction typical of Tughlak buildings.

Treasure pit

Pavilion door

Pavilion and hall

Excavations in the 1920s uncovered what appeared to be stone column bases at regular intervals, a few of which can be seen in the southwest corner of the platform. At the other side of the platform, near the crumbling east retaining wall, there are the remains of an area of polished plaster flooring. Both these facts are some sort of confirmation that this could have been the site of the *hazar sutun* as described by Ibn Battuta.

Pavilion on lower platform

Between the two platforms there is a retaining wall of considerable height, with vertical slots at regular intervals, perhaps slots for timber posts or part of a decorative scheme. The immediate question is whether the two platforms were linked in any way, there being no trace of a connection now, apart from a ramp on the east side of the upper platform. It is very difficult to work out in what way the two levels could have fitted together, given the great difference in their floor heights. It is possible that timber columns at the lower level supported a floor at the higher level that, together with the stone hall at the southern end, formed the *hazar sutun*. Alternatively, the lower level might have been where the *hazar sutun* stood, the upper level being the Sultan's private quarters, physically separate from the hall below.

Roughly halfway along the platform there is a considerable rise in the level of the ground, which might indicate the extent of the 'hall' at this level. At the far end there is a small burial ground where are interred Sheikh Hasan Tahir and his descendants. The Sheikh lived at the time of the Lodis and died in 1503, having settled in Delhi, it is said in the Bijay Mandal.

Beyond the graves is another puzzle: an arcaded building, collapsing off the edge of the platform. On the north side are the remains of a long arcaded wall, broken in two places by solid towers. This arcade seems to have formed the northern edge of the lower platform. The finely dressed battered columns and arches have a Lodi appearance, although the solid towers with their blackened plaster coating appear distinctly Tughlak, with their very low entrances and tiny windows at first floor level. Between the towers a vaulted hall appears to have been built at a later date, probably replacing an earlier structure. The new arches and vaults were clearly not bonded well with the original arcade, which is pulling away and is in danger of collapsing, while two of the vaults have recently begun to collapse. The three central bays of the hall are at a lower level. There are no signs of steps either up from the outside or within the hall itself, but every other feature gives it the appearance of a gateway. Alternatively, it is plausibly suggested, this was a *khanqah* (a residential religious centre), built while Sheikh Hasan Tahir lived here. Beyond the towers, on either side, are the remains of yet another stage of building, rows of joined or single rooms with access on the south. Two arches remain of this south wall and its alignment bears no relationship to that of the hall or the towers.

Grave of Sheikh Hasan Tahir

Begumpur Masjid (mid-14ᵗʰ century)
(Map p.60)

The mosque is a magnificent piece of architecture. The arcaded courtyard is vast, with square domed chambers at the centre of each side, three of these being gateways, although that on the north is closed. On the west side is the prayer hall, consisting of a central square chamber, larger than the gateways, with a three-by-eight-bay hall on each side. It has a tall *pishtaq* flanked by attached minarets, inside which there is a large arch or *iwan* containing three doorways. Originally there were arched openings in the outside walls on all three sides except the prayer wall, although there were fewer openings on the north side,

Begumpur Masjid roof -Bijay Mandal beyond

opposite the palace. The masonry columns and arches are plain, the only concession to decoration being the modest carving on the capitals in the prayer halls. The remaining stonework and the many domes were once covered with gleaming white *chuna* plasterwork now deteriorated into black roughness.

From a very low doorway in the northern arcade, it is possible to get into a nine-bay prayer hall, thought to have been the *zenana* prayer room. It has a view down into the main mosque and is in the same position relative to the prayer wall as private prayer rooms in many other mosques. It can be assumed that the Sultan's household had an alternative entrance, perhaps the blocked door that can be seen at road level.

There has been considerable discussion on the date of construction. There are two schools of thought: many scholars believe that it was built by Muhammad Tughlak, which would make it part of the original Jahanpanah, while others believe that it was one of the seven mosques built later by Khan Jahan Junan Shah, Firoz Shah's prime minister. On the side of the first opinion is the mosque's proximity to the supposed palace, Bijay Mandal, and, to some extent, its style, which sets it apart from those mosques that are definitely considered to be Khan Jahan Junan Shah's (and two of which are close to Begumpur). Supporting the second position is the fact that it is clear that the mosque had not been built by the time of Ibn Battuta's visit, although he left in 1341, time for the mosque to have been built by 1351, the year of Muhammad's death.

The mosque probably remained in use while Jahanpanah was occupied (until the 17ᵗʰ century). In the 1920s the ASI cleared the courtyard of a village that probably established itself here during the anarchic 18ᵗʰ century, when vulnerable communities moved into any available walled site.

Begumpur Masjid

Khirki Mosque inside

Khirki Mosque

Khirki Mosque (Map p.60)
(late 14th century)

Khirki, along with Begumpur, is the most striking of the Tughlak mosques. This mosque, unlike Begumpur, was undoubtedly one of the series built by Khan Jahan Sujan Shah in the 1370s. Like Begumpur, the Khirki mosque is raised above the original ground level, now seen at the bottom of the 'moat', excavated out of the layers accumulated over centuries of habitation around the mosque. There are projecting entrances on the north, east and south sides, each framed by narrow minarets. The corners of the mosque are reinforced by large round towers.

Inside, the feature that sets this mosque apart from virtually all other mosques in India is that it is almost completely covered (the only completely covered mosque from the Sultanate period is in Gulbarga, northern Karnataka). The mosque is arranged as a regular grid of 15 bays each way, with the outside and central sets of three bays in each direction roofed. Thus left over

Khirki Mosque interior

Khirki Mosque - elevation above, section below

are four three-bay-square courtyards, letting in all-important light. The bays in front of the prayer wall are the darkest since they receive no light from the grid-patterned windows that pierce the exterior walls on the other three sides, probably giving the mosque its name (Khirki = window). The geometrical patterns created by the combination of single and double columns within a regular grid give rise to fascinating and extremely photogenic views across the interior of the mosque. From the east

Khirki Mosque entrance

gate steps go up to the roof. It is well worth the climb to see the elegant geometry of the clusters of domes at each crossing.

Not far from the village, to the east, is the **Satpula,** part of the original Jahanpanah walls. This is an interesting structure, built to allow a stream to pass underneath the wall but still providing security. The stream has now been diverted and runs slightly further east. There are seven arches (giving the structure its name) flanked by two further sets of arches at slightly higher levels, which each led to a long barrel–vaulted passageway. Those at the higher level appear to have been gates, but the intermediate ones are closed on the outside. Either side of these are fortified bastions containing octagonal rooms with elegant plasterwork decorations. Above the culverts and passageways there were platforms at appropriate levels, with access, via identical narrow stairs, to the latter. At the back of the lowest platform it is possible to make out the way in which the sluice gates were lowered into position, defensively or to act as a dam. It is likely that the wide flat land south of the wall is formed by silt deposited by the dammed stream.

6 - 71

Satpula pavilion

Satpula sluices

Satpula

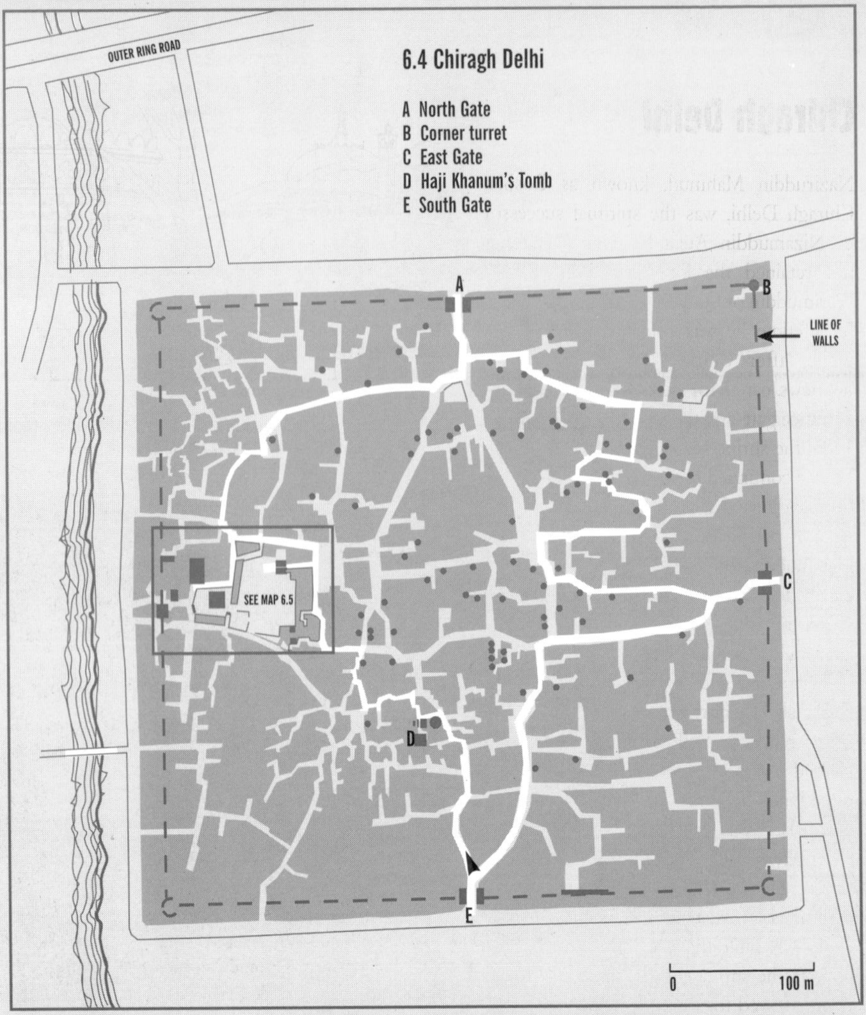

6.4 Chiragh Delhi

A North Gate
B Corner turret
C East Gate
D Haji Khanum's Tomb
E South Gate

OUTER RING ROAD

LINE OF WALLS

SEE MAP 6.5

0   100 m

Chirag Delhi shrine

6 - 72

Chiragh Delhi

Naziruddin Mahmud, known as Roshan Chiragh Delhi, was the spiritual successor to Nizamuddin Aulia. Chiragh Delhi has not retained the long-term following of Nizamuddin or Qutb Sahib, although during his lifetime he was equally famous. For a while, after Chiragh Delhi's death, his

Chirag Delhi's shrine on the left. Most of the other Tombs are unkown

nephews cared for his tomb and it was patronised by Firoz Shah, who built the existing entrance gate and the original tomb over the Saint's grave. However, after Timur's invasion in 1388, the shrine seems to have been abandoned by his descendants, who moved to Gujarat. People continued to be buried within and near the *dargah,* but it is clear, from the simplicity of

the buildings, that it did not benefit from the same level of patronage as the shrines of Qutb Sahib or Nizamuddin. Interestingly, at some point, probably before the end of the 15th century, the orientation of the buildings shifted by almost 20 degrees. The later buildings, including the nearby tomb of Bahlol Lodi, are all aligned more or less east-west although facing slightly northwards (towards Mecca) as with most religious buildings. The earlier ones are aligned so that they face in a rather more northerly direction. The shrine had a revival under the later Mughals. It was visited by large numbers of people, especially for the Urs (death commemoration) and around Diwali. They bathed in a curative tank, now no longer in existence. Muhammad Shah Rangila (1719-48) built the wall and gates around it, to contain the shrine and the camping ground where people stayed for the festivals.

Haveli with traditional doorway

Chiragh Delhi is a delightful place to visit. The shrine, with trees scattered among the white and pale green buildings is in many ways a lot less stressful than Nizamuddin (this is acknowledged in the film *Fire* by Deepa Mehta, in which Chiragh Delhi (the place) stands in for Nizamuddin!). The village itself is far less over-developed than most urban villages and contains a number of open squares, often with attached *chaupals,* and courtyard houses with attractive traditional doorways. So far it has escaped overwhelming commercialisation but how long this situation remains can only be guessed. There is the usual development pressure on the village and the shrine itself is, of course, prone to the kind of doubtful 'improvements' that beset so many functioning places of worship.

Ruined haveli

Village and Dargah

This is described from the South Gate of the village, which can be approached easily from Press Enclave Road, past the College of Vocational Studies. Turn left at the end of the road and the gate can be seen on your right.

A road encircles three sides of the village and from it you can see parts of the **walls and gates**, built mainly in brick but with sandstone ornamentation. The gates are all still standing, in various stages of decay, along with one corner turret on the northeast corner and a few stretches of quite insubstantial wall. The enclosure would have been effective in keeping the occupants secure from common robbers at night, but was clearly not built with any military purpose. From the **South Gate** you

South Gate

should take the road straight ahead and then take the third turning to your left. The lane zigzags slightly but after a short distance you should spot on the left a circular **turret**, with exaggerated fluting on the roof and the remains of vertical triangular mouldings on the walls. This once formed the corner of the 14th century **Haji Khanum's Tomb** enclosure, accessible through the **gate** nearby. Nothing is known about Haji Khanum.

Corner turret

Haji Khanum's enclosure turret

Haji Kahnum's Tomb

Gateway to Chiragh Delhi dargah

Village square

From the tomb walk northwards a short distance and turn left then right down a market lane. Ignore one turning backwards on the left, then go left and immediately right to a large open square (detours to the left will take you to two tombs that lie outside the Chiragh Delhi's dargah). The entrance to the **Dargah,** the **gateway** built by Firoz Shah, is past the modest group of shops selling religious artefacts. Architecturally, the most interesting buildings in the dargah are the **Mahfilkhana (Assembly Hall) and tomb,** probably built in the 14th century and with fewer alterations than other buildings in the enclosure. It is not clear whether this complex was built together or separately. The detailing of the substantial twelve-pillared tomb in front is certainly slightly different, but the parapet and *chajja* are

Wall mosque

Dargah tombs

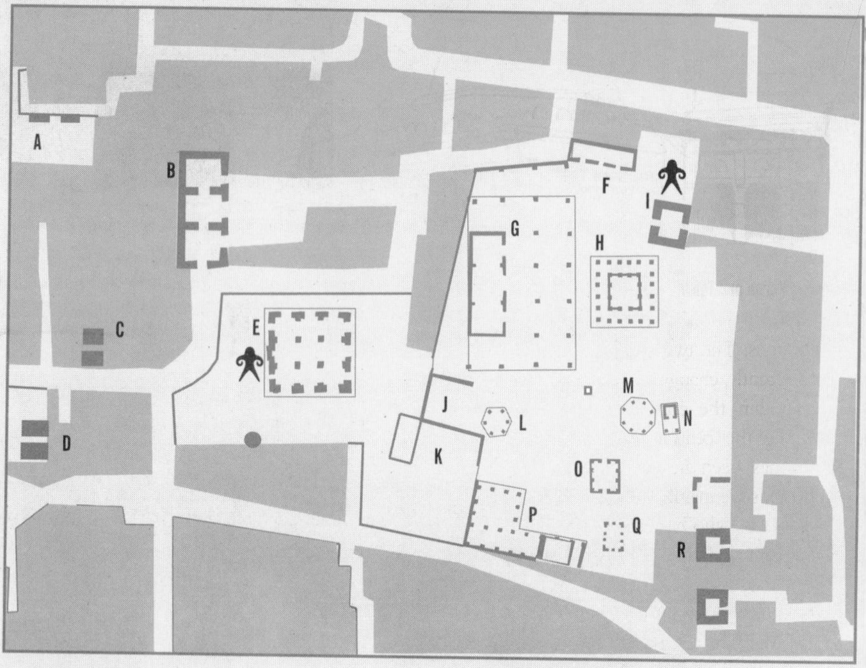

6.5 Dargah of Chiragh Delhi

A. Part of ruined arcaded wall, ?16th c.

B. Pahar, 15th c. In plan rather like the Tin Burj in Muhammadpur (p.111), it is thought to be an unfinished mosque

C. Gateway to Bahlol Lodi's former tomb enclosure, 16th c. This vanished recently

D. West Gate of village, 1729

E. Tomb of Bahlol Lodi, died 1489

F. Majlis Khana, 1720 - meeting room attached to Dargah

G. Mosque (Built by Emperor Faruksiyar, reigned 1713-19)

H. Tomb of Chiragh Delhi (modern - the original tomb was built by Firoz Shah 1351-88)

I. Main Gateway to Dargah (built by Firoz Shah)

J. Wall mosque, ?14th c.

K. Grave enclosure with an elaborate late Mughal grave platform

L. Tomb supposed to be that of the granddaughter of Sheikh Farid al-Din Shankarganj (unlikely since he was born in 1173)

M. 'Tomb of Sheikh Kamluddin' (much altered - now modern in appearance)

N. 'Tomb of Sheikh Zainuddin', ?late 14th c.

O. Tomb, 14th c. - it has been enclosed quite recently

P. Mahfilkhana (Assembly hall) and Tomb, 14th c.

Q. Tomb enclosure (late Mughal probably altered)

R. Two inhabited Lodi tombs, 15th c.

Pahar

Majlis Khana and Tomb

Bahlol Lodi Tomb interior

continuous. The two southern bays have been filled in quite recently, changing the appearance and layout.

Within the compound there are various tombs including the central one of Chiragh Delhi himself, which has been heavily restored. Of the others, the ascriptions are mainly by tradition. The Japanese scholar, Matsuo Ara, who has studied the Sultanate buildings of Delhi, cautiously describes them simply as 'tombs'. On the west side of the compound is a small **wall mosque** that, with the long return wall, encloses a graveyard. This building shares the non-alignment of the Mahfilkhana. It may originally, have been a Tughlak building with later repairs altering the style: the parapet merlons have a Mughal appearance, while the elaborate decoration above the main *mihrab* is seen on earlier buildings such as the tomb of Mubarak Shah (died 1433).

On leaving the *dargah* follow the walls to the left to the very untypical **Bahlol Lodi's Tomb**. With nine equal bays instead of one central or dominant one, it has a central *mihrab* and two small arched openings on the west wall. The three other walls each have three arched openings between substantial columns.

Bahlol Lodi was the highly competent grandson of an Afghan trader. He was orphaned at a young age and brought up by Sultan Shah of Sirhind (west of Chandigarh), later marrying his daughter. He inherited Sirhind in 1431 and took the Delhi throne in 1451. He died in 1489 after considerable territorial gains, the final victory being the annexation of Jaunpur. There is no direct evidence or oral tradition for this being Bahlol Lodi's Tomb. However, history relates that his body was brought to Delhi and buried near the shrine of Chiragh Delhi, the tomb being erected by his son Sikander. Babur, the first Mughal emperor, visited both Bahlol and Sikander's tombs when he first entered Delhi.

Beyond Bahlol Lodi's Tomb you can see several other buildings in various stages of perilous decay. The Lodi gateway shown on the map has recently disappeared. From Bahlol Lodi's Tomb it is possible to make a circuit round the back lanes of the village, with short diversions to inspect the other village gates.

East Gate to village

OTHER AREAS

The two remaining areas in which there are old buildings dating from the period when Jahanpanah was inhabited, are Adhchini and Soami Nagar (see map p.58).

ADHCHINI

This village, beside Aurobindo Marg, contains quite a complex of buildings. In the south is the much-visited shrine that contains the grave of Nizamuddin's mother, Bibi Zulaikha Sahiba, and many relatives and followers. A sign to the Dargah of

Adhchini - Lodi Mosque rear

Bibi Zulaikha Sahiba indicates the passageway to take for the shrine around which the village grew, roughly in the middle of the shops along the west of Aurobindo Marg. One of the entrances to the shrine, a plain pointed-arch gateway, may date from the foundation of the site in 1250. The rest of the buildings have been rebuilt in modern times. Near the shrine to the north is a Lodi-era gateway to a large mosque.

Lodi Mosque (1509-10)

This was originally within the outer enclosure of Bibi Zulaikha's shrine. There is a large modern extension in front of the original prayer hall. The ground level has increased by several feet, as can be seen by the curious proportions of the *mihrab* and the entrance gate outside. At the back it is possible to see the original exterior, with large turrets at each end of the prayer wall. There are various later buildings attached to the mosque.

Adhchini Gateway

SOAMI NAGAR TOMB (15th century)
Accurately marked on Eicher map

Very near the walls of Siri, this is a twelve-pillared tomb with fine red sandstone pillars and inner dome lining, the latter being laid in alternating wide and narrow bands. It was once inside an enclosure, the west wall of which formed a prayer wall. The whole complex now houses a small *madrasa* and the buildings have been considerably altered.

Soami Nagar tomb interior

FIROZABAD AND HAUZ KHAS

FIROZ SHAH'S DELHI

*So many buildings were erected that from the
kasba of Indrapat to the Kushi-i-shikar, five kos
apart, all the land was occupied.*

Shams-i-Siraj Afif, 1388

Firoz Shah

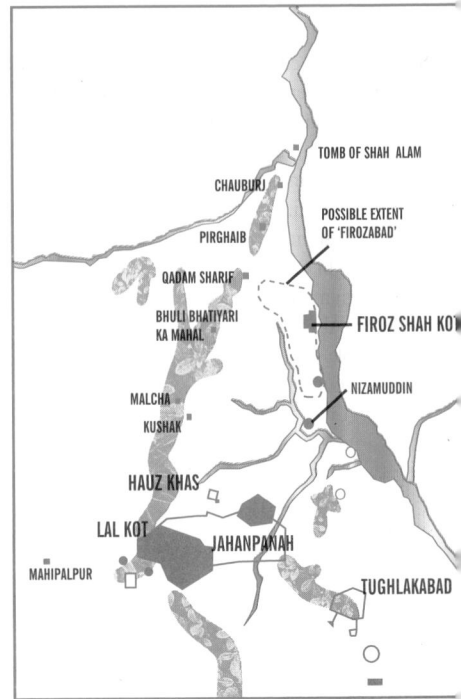

Firoz Shah, who inherited from his cousin Muhammad in 1351, was of a different temperament, reluctant at first even to take the throne. Although Firoz Shah was militarily unsuccessful, his reign was clearly far more peaceful than previous ones. His emphasis seems to have been on improving his existing dominion rather than on reconquering the provinces lost by Muhammad. He even lost some of the remaining provinces such as Bengal. On the whole he was a popular ruler, although his more orthodox Islamic ideas must have made life more difficult for Hindu subjects. It is the first reign in which we know for certain that the poll-tax (*jizya*), as levied on Christians and Jews elsewhere in the Islamic world, was demanded of the Hindus. However, apart from the poll-tax, Firoz Shah lowered taxes considerably, with the land tax falling, perhaps, to as little as 10 per cent. Cultivators also benefited from major irrigation works, enabling them to produce two crops a year. His revenue-raising system was also changed, the officers' posts becoming largely hereditary, for the first time in over a hundred years. This hereditary attachment to land probably helped in the subsequent break up of the sultanate after Firoz Shah's death. The money raised from taxation went towards major irrigation, building and charitable purposes rather than maintaining a huge army.

One of the most appealing things about Firoz Shah was his genuine interest in ancient buildings and history. He transported two Ashokan pillars many miles from the countryside to install them in Delhi, one at his out-of-town palace citadel, now known as the Firoz Shah Kotla, and one at one of his hunting lodges, on the northern Delhi ridge. He also restored the Qutb Minar and the Hauz Khas, where he built a large *madrasa* (religious school). Compared with Muhammad's reign, it is less easy to envisage what the city looked like under Firoz Shah. It seems that the centre of power was still the Jahanpanah complex, but there were also considerable settlements over a wide area around the palace citadel. The size of some of the mosques built during his reign attest to considerable populations within and outside the walled city.

Middle-aged when he came to the throne, Firoz Shah was eighty-one when he died in 1388 after four years of illness. Throughout his reign he had been highly dependent on his two *wazirs*, Khan Jahan Tilangani and his son, Khan Jahan Junan Shah, the later of whom, like Firoz Shah, is supposed to have been an enthusiastic builder, erecting seven large mosques throughout the Delhi area. Just before Firoz Shah's death Junan Shah had tried to turn the Sultan against his son, Muhammad Shah (not to be confused with the the former Sultan, Muhammad). Other courtiers, loyal to Firoz Shah, expelled Junan Shah and Muhammad Shah was made *wazir*, and then later joint Sultan. Later, however, Muhammad

Shah was turned out by the noblemen and went to his mountain power-base at Nagarkot (Kangra Fort). On Firoz Shah's death in 1388 his nominated heir, his great-grandson, Tughlak Shah became Sultan. The following year both Tughlak Shah and his *wazir* were murdered and Abu Bakr, a grandson of Firoz Shah, was put on the throne. At this point Muhammad Shah returned and ordered his allies around Delhi to put to death all Firoz Shah's old slaves, thus enabling him to take control of Delhi and defeat and imprison Abu Bakr. The internal situation then became more stable although the new Sultan was still involved in endless fights with local Hindu chieftains.

In 1394 Muhammad Shah died and the political situation deteriorated again. One son inherited the throne but died soon after. Another son, Mahmud Shah was then enthroned by a powerful nobleman Mallu Khan in Jahanpanah, but a rival group of courtiers put Nusrat Shah onto the throne at Firozabad (Firoz Shah Kotla). Neither of the Sultans, both ruling as puppets from a few miles apart,

Hauz Khas

had much control over the surrounding provinces, which were held by rival noblemen. This was the perfect moment for the most serious Mongol invasion ever in India. Timur the Lame (Tamberlaine) swept into India from Central Asia and arrived outside the walls of Delhi at the end of 1398. From a Turkish tribe, Timur was leading a Mongol army that had converted to Islam. Luckily we have Timur's rather self-satisfied record of his exploits and, from a detailed account, the following bare facts are taken. Despite this being the first time that Timur's men had encountered war elephants, they defeated Mahmud Shah's army and the Sultan fled back to the city, Jahanpanah, while Timur set up camp nearby at Hauz Khas. Overnight the Sultan escaped and Timur soon after had the *khutba* (Friday prayers) read in his name at the main city mosque, thus legitimising his rule in Delhi.

Before entering Delhi, Timur had met the local officials and all the Islamic scholars and clergy. He had agreed with them to spare the population of the city and to let them go about their business. Unfortunately, although the army was based outside the walls, various errands took groups of fierce Turkish soldiers into the city and it was not long before fighting had broken out between the Turks and the Hindu population. Soon the city was aflame and the troops, by now completely out of control, went on a three-day rampage, killing, looting and taking prisoners. In Timur's account there is a tone of mild regret at what had happened but he justified it by saying that 'It was ordained by God, however, that the city should be ruined, and he accordingly inspired the infidel inhabitants with a spirit of resistance, so that they brought on themselves that fate which was inevitable.' Timur then settled down to fifteen days of 'pleasure and enjoyment' before starting back for some more infidel-slaughter on his way back to Samarkand. He took with him great numbers of Indian craftsmen because he wanted to construct a handsome mosque on his return to Samarkand (p.84).

Timur left a more or less deserted city. Many artisans had been forced to leave with him and much of the rest of the surviving population had fled and did not return. For three years there was no Sultan in Delhi, Mahmud Shah having established himself at Kanauj and his rival's champion having fled the scene before Timur's invasion. Mahmud Shah's very powerful minister, Mallu, reigned in Delhi until 1405 when he was defeated and killed by Khizr Khan, an adherent of Timur's. Mahmud Shah then returned to Delhi as Sultan until his death in 1412.

Firozabad and Hauz Khas

Firoz Shah Kotla Mosque

The two main sites of Firoz Shah's Delhi are delightful to visit. There is nothing difficult about finding them and yet they are much less frequented than other large historical sites in Delhi. At both there is a profound sense of tranquillity, almost as if Firoz Shah's scholarly and unaggressive nature has been imbued into his buildings. The only exception to this is the weekly visitation of Firoz Shah Kotla by hundreds if not thousands of people who arrive on Thursday afternoons to pay their respects to or appease the *djinns* said to lurk there. Besides the two main sites there are a number of other very interesting buildings, some of which are far more challenging to visit.

Firoz Shah reigned from 1351 to 1388. It is difficult to imagine a more prodigious builder than his cousin Muhammad but, amazingly, Firoz Shah was just such a man. Not only did he undertake his own projects, which included massive irrigation schemes as well as diverse buildings, but he was also passionately interested in earlier buildings, undertaking extensive repairs to previous Sultans' works (e.g., the Qutb Minar).

To recap: when Firoz Shah came to the throne in 1351 Delhi consisted of three contiguous walled enclosures: Lal Kot, containing the main mosque and other ceremonial buildings, Siri, and the area enclosed by the Jahanpanah walls that contained Muhammad Shah's palace and, probably, the great Begampur Mosque. This very large mosque and the construction of at least two more here during Firoz Shah's reign implies a population within the walls of a considerable size, although the building of numerous tombs not much later suggests that there was also a good deal of open space. Further away was Tughlakabad, to some extent abandoned, at least by the court, and a number of small settlements that existed around religious centres such as the *sufi* shrines in Mehrauli and Nizamuddin.

It seems that none of this satisfied Firoz Shah who, like other rulers before him, needed to have his own new quarters. These were mostly built very early in his reign. Dating from 1354, the Sultan's main building project in Delhi was his fortified palace complex beside the river, now known as Firoz Shah Kotla, while the city he is supposed to have built around it is referred to as Firozabad. He also repaired Alauddin's great tank at Hauz Khas and constructed a grand *madrasa* there that included his own tomb, built in advance of his death. Apart from these two huge projects he built the

Firoz Shah Kotla ruins

Qadam Sharif, a large fortified enclosure and tomb for his eldest son, Fateh Khan, and a number of hunting lodges on the Ridge. His Prime Minister, Khan Jahan Junan Shah, is also thought to have built seven large mosques; it is not entirely clear which buildings these were (see under Chausath Khamba below), but on the basis of educated guesswork most have been identified and their widespread locations are an indication of the extensive nature of the 'city' in Firoz Shah's reign: it encompassed the Kalan Masjid in Old Delhi as well as the Khirki Masjid near Saket. Common sense tells us, however, that the land was not solidly urban over such a huge area. While Khirki was built within the walls of the existing city, obviously to serve a sizeable urban population, it is probable that the Kalan Masjid was built because it was near a holy shrine (Shah Turkman's grave) and the main route to the northwest.

Firoz Shah Kotla Mosque

Hauz Khas Madrasa

It is really very difficult to get any idea of what Firoz Shah's Delhi was like. Apart from the evidence of the mosques, we know that before the building of New Delhi there were extensive remains of ruined buildings around Firoz Shah Kotla that might have been remains of Firozabad, Firoz Shah's new 'city', but this was also the site of an equally nebulous 'city' built by Sher Shah a century and a half later. Another problem with the notion of Firozabad, based around the Kotla, as a huge, brand new, self-sufficient city is that other evidence tends to point to the main city still being Jahanpanah. For instance, Timur, when writing about the city he conquered a mere ten years after Firoz Shah's death, quite clearly described Jahanpanah. It seems most likely that the buildings around Firoz Shah Kotla were suburban estates, perhaps built by noblemen to be near the Sultan's various palaces.

Firoz Shah Kotla

Correctly marked on the Eicher Map.

High walls surround a generally peaceful green area. Much of the area is open, although ruined courtyards can be made out in the southern part, where two blocked gateways can be seen in the outer wall, one of which led into a subsidiary walled enclosure that is now densely populated. Once overlooking the river were the mosque and the Ashokan pillar building, near which was the *baoli*. All these are clearly visible.

Firoz Shah Kotla ruins

This fort seems to have been a walled palace rather than a small city. It is possible that it was never even built for defensive purposes. Despite the high walls there is no evidence of a walkway from which soldiers could have fired from the wall-top and some of the arrow slits look as if they may have been decorative rather than functional. The river frontage would also have been highly vulnerable to attackers. Contemporary descriptions of the Sultan's court mention three separate palaces, in which different administrative activities took place, although it is not clear where these were. An extraordinary building, a large affair with circular bastions surmounted by *chatris*, sketched by the Daniells on their first tour of India (1789-90), was described by them as being Firoz Shah Kotla but it appears, from its surroundings, to have lain outside it. It has now vanished completely, although it may have become the pile of ruins seen near the Kotla at the very beginning of the 20th century. Clearly, the most obvious site for his palace(s) would have been inside the Kotla, but there is not enough left of the various ruins inside to identify them as such.

MOSQUE (1354)

For some reason it is generally believed that the mosque inside the Kotla was the Jami Masjid that Timur so admired in 1398. It is difficult to understand how this misapprehension came about since it is crystal clear from Timur's description that he spent all his time, following his victory, at the main city of Delhi (Jahanpanah, Lal Kot and Siri). In that city there were several mosques that might have impressed him more in size and ornamentation than this one. In fact the Begumpur Mosque closely resembles that of Timur's unfinished Bibi Khanum Mosque in Samarkand. Of course we cannot be sure of the quality of the decoration in this mosque, but it appears, from the rather scant remaining ornamentation, to have been quite an ordinary building, perhaps rather like the Kalan Masjid in Old Delhi. Like other mosques it was raised above ground level and on each side, below, there is a colonnade giving access to vaulted chambers extending some distance under the mosque

Passage under Mosque

Mosque

courtyard. These chambers are among the many places that are visited by people who go to assuage the *djinns;* it is a dramatic sight to see dark figures crouching over a few lit tapers at the far end of these cave-like rooms.

Djinns are the same as genies. The idea derives from pre-Islamic beliefs. They are generally thought of as demons or supernatural beings variously credited with the misfortunes of life. They are represented by the pillars at Mina that are stoned during the Haj. Interestingly the ancient Persians believed in 'kind *djinns*' who relished the odour of food and perfume.

The only entrance to the mosque was on the north side, rather uncomfortably close to the Ashokan pillar building. Although convenience would suggest it, there is no physical evidence of a high level linkage between the two.

e two Delhi pillars were still standing in ir original positions when Firoz Shah st saw them. They were, of course, two of eries of seven stunningly carved and ished monolithic stone pillars erected the third century BC emperor Ashoka to mulgate his newfound Buddhist faith. A lennium and a half later the local ple had come to believe that they were walking sticks of Bhim, one of the dava brothers from the Mahabharata, t as memorials to him when he died. The tan was desperate for a translation of inscription but the Brahmi script had en forgotten. Nonetheless, he ognised them as something special and anged for them to be carefully lowered o a pile of silk cotton and transported a forty-two-wheel carriage to the river k, from where they were moved to a t of several boats and sailed down to hi, along with the original base stones. building on which it stands was cted around the pillar, which was raised he next level as each was completed.

ASHOKAN PILLAR BUILDING (1354)

It appears that this building was constructed purely to support the pillar. At every level there are linked rooms but they are all so small that it seems unlikely that they were ever intended as anything more than part of the Sultan's route to the roof. Unfortunately the building is very ruined now, but it was sketched in 1800 or thereabouts and we can see that on the first and second floors there were small, square, domed rooms attached to the main block at each corner. The rooms on each floor form an arcade around a solid core and some of them are now used for *pujas.*

The pillar itself is about thirteen metres high with over a metre sunk below the platform. When built it would have had a capital, perhaps like the Sarnath lion capital that is now used as the Indian national emblem. This, presumably, had vanished, so Firoz Shah is said to have had the top decorated with friezes in black and white stone, surmounted by a gilded copper cupola. All that is visible now is the astonishingly smooth surface of this huge monolith, with the inscriptions visible as if carved yesterday. There are a few later additions including a charming elephant.

BAOLI (1354)

This would have been arcaded at ground level and the level below, with access underneath this to the water level. As with other *baolis,* the shaded underground colonnades would have been an agreeable place in which to sit out the heat of the day.

While visiting the Kotla it is convenient to look at the **Khuni Darwaza** (mid-16th century – p.144) situated between the carriageways on the main road.

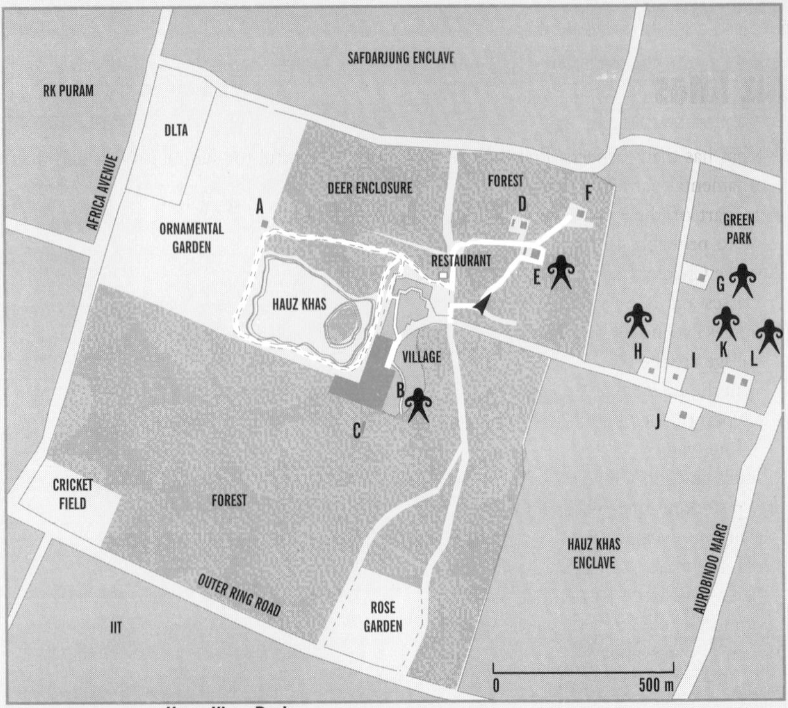

Hauz Khas Park

A Munda Gumbad late 14th c. (p.87)
B Madrasa, tomb etc. mid - late 14th c. (p.88-89)
C Lodi Mosque 15th c. (p.110)
D Kali Gumti 14th c. (p.110)
E Bagh-i-Alam ka Gumbad late 15th – early 16th c. (p.110)
F Tuhfewala Gumbad 14th c. (p.110)

G Biran ka Gumbad late 15th c. (p.109)
H Sakri Gumti late 15th c. (p.109)
I Chhoti Gumti late 15th c. (p.109)
J Barah Khamba 14th c. (p.109)
K Dadi ka Gumbad late 15th c. (p.109)
L Poti ka Gumbad late 14th c. (p.109)

Frioz Shah Tomb with adjoining madrasa

Hauz Khas

Hauz Khas has many aspects: first there is the forest, wonderful for summer walks, and the large ornamental garden that occupies much of the area that was once the tank. In the northern part of the forest and on the entrance road there are some fine tombs, some of which were probably built during or fairly soon after the final extinction of the Tughlak dynasty (see Chapter 8). Second, there is the village, which has been taken over by the Delhi upper classes and is now dominated by expensive fashion and antique shops. A number of poor families live in shacks on the south and west fringes of the village. Finally, on the far side of the village are the remains of Firoz Shah's *madrasa*.

From the *madrasa* buildings it is possible to appreciate the original vast size of the tank. Nearby, a part of the old tank has been re-landscaped, a smaller water body being more viable than the long vanished original one, which would have lapped at the walls of the *madrasa*. A rubble-built pavilion, known as the **Munda Gumbad**, is visible on the far side of the lake. This once stood in the centre of the tank, linked to the southern edge by a causeway. At the far side of the deer enclosure (see map) are ruins that would have stood at the northeast corner of the tank. When Firoz Shah restored Alauddin's abandoned tank he had streams unblocked and constructed stone embankments, thereby returning the tank to use. On the east and south sides he constructed a magnificent array of buildings and placed his own tomb at the corner. A contemporary poet, Mutahhar Kara, describes the *madrasa* in these swooning terms:

> I saw an even space as wide as the plain of the world. The courtyard was soul-animating and its expanse was life-giving. Its dust was musk-scented and its fragrance possessed the odour of amber. There was verdure everywhere and hyacinth, basil, roses and tulips were blossoming and were beautifully arranged so far as the eye could reach… Nightingales, so to say, were singing their melodious songs everywhere. It appeared as if they had guitars in their talons and flutes in their beaks. (Quote from Banerjee – see Bibliography.)

Walk

Cars can be left on the road into the village. Take the path into the deer park area and turn right into the woods on a jogging path, then left for the **three tombs** that stand close together in the forest. The first is one of the finest Lodi tombs in Delhi. Because these are mostly slightly later in date than Hauz Khas, and in historical and stylistic terms relate more closely to the nearby Lodi tombs, they are described in detail in the next chapter (p.110).

Walk back on the main path towards the deer enclosure. Turn left down the park road and then take the path on the right for the Park Baluchi Restaurant. Turn left just before the restaurant; this path takes you through a fence to the Hauz Khas lake and garden. Walk straight ahead so that you walk round the lake counter-clockwise, passing the **Munda Gumbad**, which used to stand in the middle of the original lake, to the *madrasa* on the far side. Here you get a good view of the lovely pavilions that once lined the water's edge, and from here it is possible to climb some unprotected steps to the 'Residential building' (see map over). Alternatively continue on the path until you return to the point at which you entered the lake area. Turn right along a narrow path with railings on your right. This will bring you out into the village not far from the entrance to the monuments, which are to your right.

Hauz Khas monuments (all built in second half of 14th century)

A Residential building
B Remains of residential wing of madrasa
C Triple domed building
D Open pavilions above, residential units below
E Tughlak tombs
F Firoz Shah's tomb
G Open pavilions above and below
H Possible courtyard complex with southern range of buildings missing. Residential units at lower level in northern range.

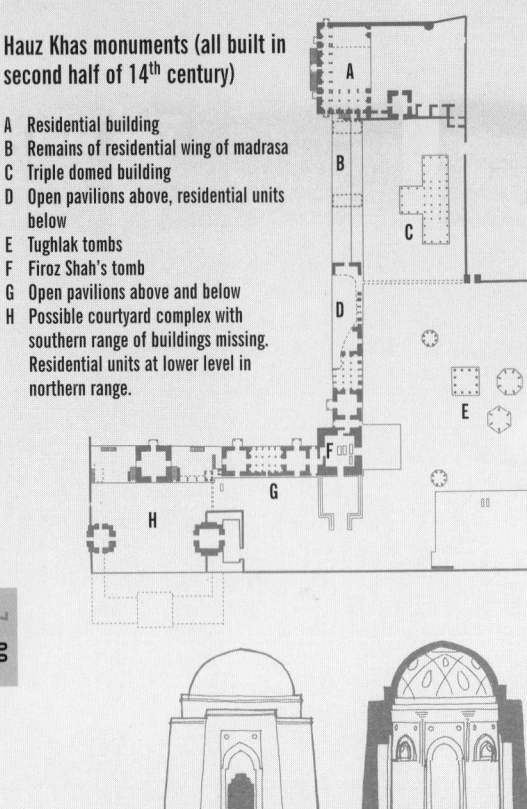

Firoz Shah's Tomb

Firoz Shah's Tomb - elevation and section

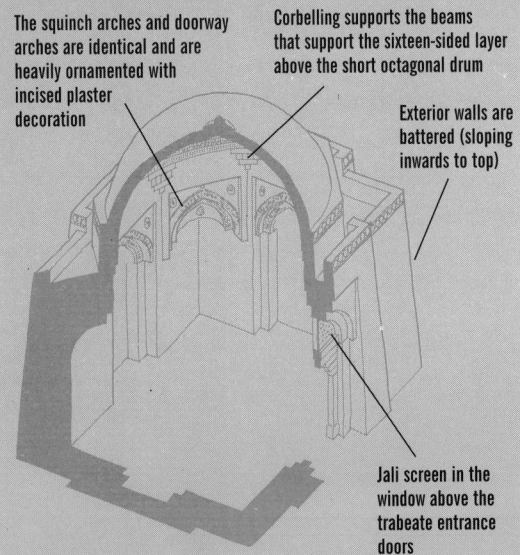

FIROZ SHAH'S TOMB

The shallow drum is octagonal on the outside

The squinch arches and doorway arches are identical and are heavily ornamented with incised plaster decoration

Corbelling supports the beams that support the sixteen-sided layer above the short octagonal drum

Exterior walls are battered (sloping inwards to top)

Jali screen in the window above the trabeate entrance doors

Hauz Khas Monuments 🦑

FIROZ SHAH'S TOMB (1354)

The most ornate building in th complex is Firoz Shah's own tom which connects the two wings of th *madrasa*. The main entrance is on th south, with a small yard in fro enclosed by stone railings, a featu not found anywhere else in Delh The tomb has the same gener proportions as Ghiyasuddin's Tomb Tughlakabad but, instead of re sandstone and marble, it is built fro local quartzite rubble and finishe with a plaster surface that would ha gleamed white when first applie Grey quartzite was used for do pillars and lintels and red sandsto for the more delicately carve elements.

TUGHLAK TOMBS (late 14th century)

This group, opposite the entrar gate, all follow a similar pattern pillared cupolas, but with differe numbers of pillars, sometim single, sometimes double. T **small eight-pillared** chatris ha a curious feature: they have ve heavy cantilevered beams that on supported a flat projection around t tiny dome; could they have been p of a larger building?

View of madrasa looking east

Madrasa cells

MADRASA (1354)

The main buildings flank the tomb on either side. On the west a fairly simple one-storey façade conceals a complex two-storey interior, consisting of open pillared rooms facing the tank and intervening enclosed domed chambers with balconies projecting out over the tank. This wing adjoins a further complex beyond it, probably part of a courtyard that included the two similar tomb-like structures nearby and, perhaps, a matching building on the south side that has now vanished

Tombs in monument enclosure

(see plan). Below this extension can be seen a residential section with narrow cells.

On the north side of Firoz Shah's tomb is another row of interconnected buildings, rather more ruined. This wing terminates in a building projecting further into the tank area. Entered through a plain, square, domed building, on the left is a hypostyle L-shaped hall (once U-shaped). This hall has been described as a mosque but this seems slightly unlikely given the fact that the central bay (always the main *mihrab* niche) opens onto a balcony that originally had steps leading down to the tank. Presumably this could have been a more private part of the *madrasa* buildings.

TRIPLE-DOMED BUILDING (late 14th century)

This complex building is unlike anything else in Delhi. It is widely thought to have been a tomb, but its position, located centrally in part of the *madrasa* complex, might indicate that it was some sort of meeting hall; it stands in what would have been its own enclosure, with a mainly residential part of the *madrasa* to its west.

Small pavilion

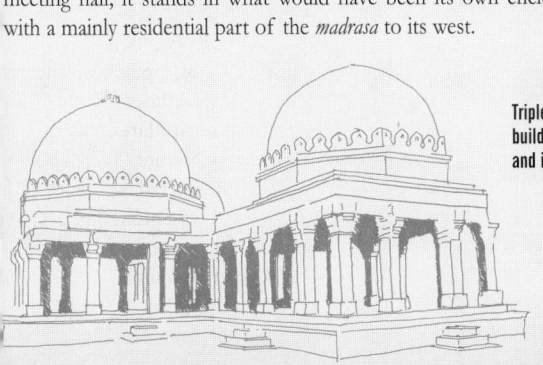

Triple-domed building (left) and interior

Other projects

Elsewhere in Delhi there are a considerable number of buildings that were constructed in Firoz Shah's reign. Most of these are strung out along the Ridge and many were connected with hunting, along with the damming of streams to form water bodies. Starting from the most northerly building, near the river, they will be described below, working southwards (mainly shown on map p.248).

Tomb and mosque of Shah Alam
(late 14th century)
Correctly marked on the later versions of the Eicher map, at Wazirabad, near the river in North Delhi.

Beside a nine-arched contemporaneous bridge is the tomb and attendant mosque of Shah Alam, believed to have been a well-known saint (and not to be confused with the much later Mughal kings). The **bridge** was once a handsome structure, built from rubble masonry with a plaster finish. The bridge abuts the rear corner of the mosque.

The mosque courtyard was entered through a plain square gate and in front of the mosque is the **tomb** itself. This is very similar to many other such tombs, with twelve pillars and a dome. The **mosque** is a charmingly simple building. An

unusual feature for such a small mosque is the private prayer chamber occupying the back right hand bay of the prayer hall.

Chauburji Mosque (1354 or1373)
Nineteenth century restoration has disguised its former appearance but, according to early descriptions, this seems originally to have been a square tomb with four domed chambers on the roof. A multi-chambered tomb is unusual for this date but there are precedents, such as the Barah Khamba in Nizamuddin (p.170). It was subsequently converted to a mosque and has plain late-Mughal decorations.

Shah Alam Mosque interior

Shah Alam Tomb and gate

Chauburji Mosque interior

Pir Ghaib (1354 or 1373)

This is probably the only remains of Firoz Shah's hunting lodge on the Ridge, referred to as Jahan Numa (meaning world-like). It is described both as having been built early in the Sultan's reign, and also as built by the Sultan to assuage his grief after the death of his eldest son, Fateh Khan, in 1373. Perhaps the complex was extended then. This building was probably only a small part of the lodge, which also incorporated the second Ashokan pillar (not on its present site) and presumably the *baoli,* which is not far away.

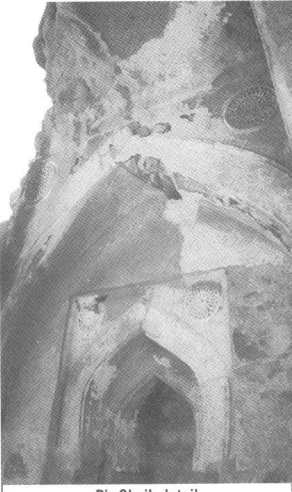

Pir Ghaib detail

What remains of this building is fascinating. A small part of the exterior wall is visible. On the ground floor are several unadorned rooms and passages, the most interesting of which lies in the centre of the building and has a hole in the ceiling that aligns with a hole in the roof above the upper room. On the upper floor there was a wide veranda on the eastern side, with arched openings to small chambers on the west with an opening to the sky (now covered by a small protective 'cap'). On the south, two very steep flights of parallel steps lead up to first floor and roof levels. It is highly likely that this particular building served some sort of astronomical purpose, judging by the strange double steps and the vertical hole passing right through the building.

Baoli (1354)

Like the Pir Ghaib, it is difficult to make out the original form of this *baoli*. Situated just to the north of the main Hindu Rao Hospital buildings, it is worth scrambling down the steps to see the northern wall of the well. At the lowest visible level there are some typical Tughlak double pillars that appear to support the end of vaulted rooms facing east into the well. There are some

Pir Ghaib

mysterious arches and openings above this level. One of these was found to lead to a long tunnel, described in the 1916 ASI survey. It did not appear to lead anywhere and had eight shafts to the surface for light or air: a mystery.

Ashokan Pillar (3rd century BC)

This is the second pillar brought to Delhi by Firoz Shah and was placed in his hunting lodge. Because the pillars were moved early in his reign it seems likely that the lodge was partly built at that date. The pillar was severely damaged in an explosion at the beginning of the 18th century. The five fragments were restored to an upright position in 1866, but without the inscription, which had been sent to the Asiatic Society in Calcutta. In the early 17th century it was described by an English traveller, William Finch, with a 'globe and half moon at top, and divers inscriptions upon it'; clearly a similar adornment to the other pillar in Firoz Shah Kotla (p.85).

Baoli

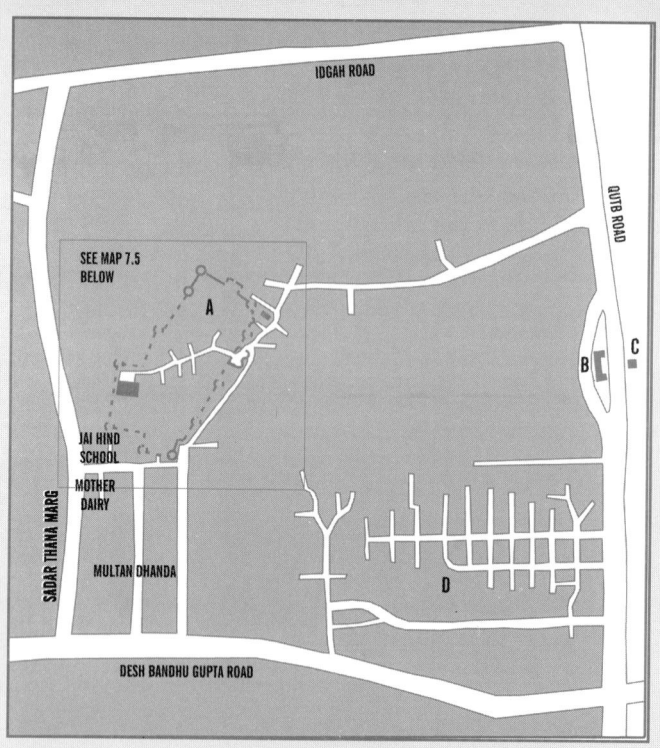

7.4 Qadam Sharif & Ram Nagar

A Qadam Sharif village
B U-shaped building
C Tomb
D Ram Nagar

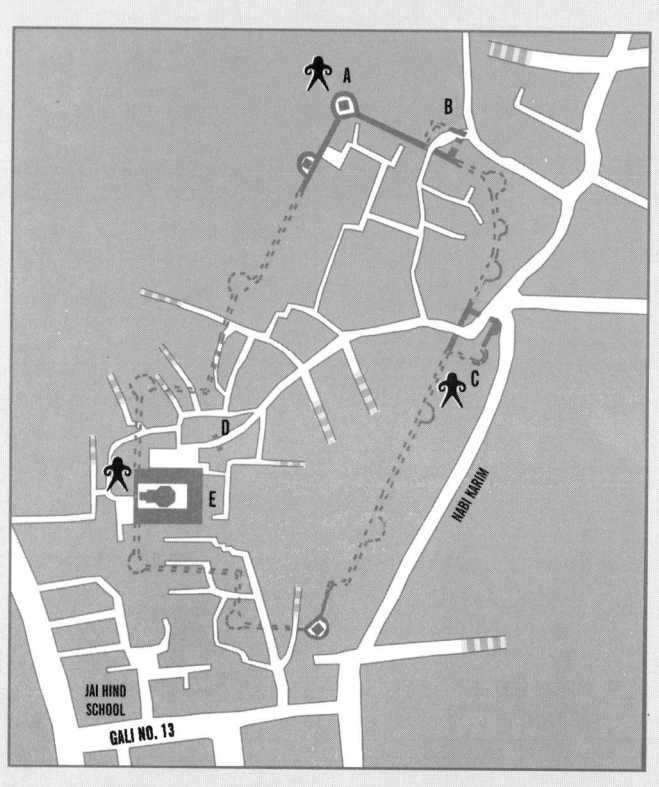

7.5 Qadam Sharif village

A Existing walls and chatris
B North gate
C East gate
D Inner gate
E Qadam Sharif

Qadam Sharif (1376)

This is another private project of Firoz Shah's. It is one of the most challenging historical places to visit in Delhi, being in the heart of one of its poorest and most congested areas, just north of New Delhi railway station. It is the burial place of Firoz Shah's son, Fateh Khan, who died in 1374. The Sultan had him buried here with, above him, a small slab of marble, believed to bear the imprint of the Prophet Muhammad's foot.

Fateh Khan's Tomb

This is said to have been acquired from the Caliph, on Firoz Shah's behalf, in exchange for substantial gifts. It was met, with great pomp and ceremony, by the Sultan and all his nobles 20 miles from Delhi and deposited in the Royal Treasury. Later, when Fateh Khan was offered a choice of what he considered most valuable from the treasury, he selected the footprint. The Sultan said he could not have it, but it would form the burial stone of whichever of them died first. Thus, it was his painful duty to bury his much-loved son beneath it. The stone is now kept separately, in a box.

FINDING IT

At the time of writing, the Eicher map is totally inaccurate for this area.

7 - 93

The easiest way of finding the Qadam Sharif is to drive up Sadar Thana Marg (it becomes Dr Ram Manohar Lohia Marg) and stop where the road bears leftwards. Go down Gali No 13, between Mother Dairy on one side and the Jai Hind School on the other. This road narrows before meeting a busy lane. Turn left here, along a lane called Nabi Karim. On the left the houses are built against the **Tughlak walls**, parts of which still exist but are largely invisible. It was a wide wall with a walkway along the top and large bastions projecting out at intervals. These were ornamented with *chatris*, some of which still exist (one can be glimpsed from this road but the others can only be seen from the roofs of houses near the North Gate). In due course, behind you on the left you will see the main **East Gate**. This gate is an

East outer gate

North external gate

Chatri

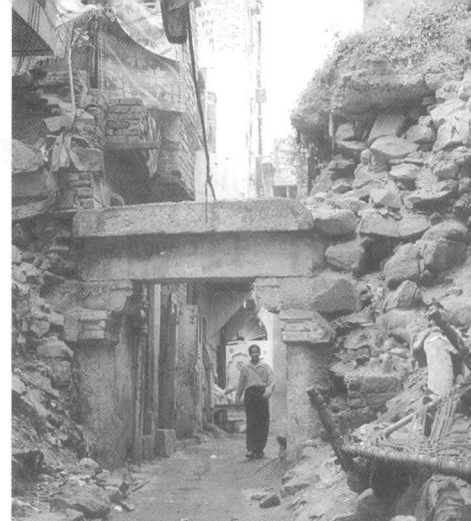

Gate to inner enclosure

important access point to the village. It is double, with the gateways at right angles to each other. Further on, taking one turn to the left, you come to the **North Gate** (see map), which is similar but exists in a different state of preservation. Although it is rather more ruined in general, some of the original features still survive, such as a little plaster decoration, and stone rings and 'saucers' for holding staves, perhaps lanterns, behind the battlement merlons. There is a small tunnel entrance to the right of the outer main gate that is still in use and would have been used when the main gates were closed.

Enter through this gate and follow the lane straight ahead back to the main path from the East Gate, where you should turn right for the tomb. Just before reaching the tomb there is a very **ruined gateway**, marking the location of an inner enclosure. It is clear that the whole walled area was built up for many centuries, because of the considerable rise in ground level, evidence that there has been a long cycle of masonry buildings that have been erected, pulled down and rebuilt. The route to the tomb from the East Gate seems to have remained clear throughout, with paths off it climbing steeply either side.

Lantern holder inside East Gate

FATEH KHAN'S TOMB

The tomb of Fateh Khan is a highly unusual building inside a colonnaded enclosure. The whole building appears to have been constructed on a natural hill, the platform being well above normal ground level (visible from outside on the west). From here we can also see that the solid enclosure walls are not necessarily contemporary, and that the stone columns supporting the corner domes were in-filled at a later date. The platform's original design was an open area with a pillared pavilion at each corner. In the centre was a rectangular chamber covering the grave of Fateh Khan. This was extended on the east, north and south sides with an octagonally shaped projection carrying a *chatri* identical to the ones on the outer fortification walls. On the west side of the tomb there is an attached four-pillared building with a *chatri* above it. It is interesting to note that the pillars of the lower part of this pavilion are carved as if they are simple temple columns.

A significant alteration was probably the building of a roofed colonnade, linking each of the corner pavilions, perhaps to cover further graves. An unusual feature of the more recent columns is that they have pronounced bands encircling them a bit over half way up. At some point before the 19th century the spaces between all the outer

Fateh Khan's Tomb

pillars were filled in, enclosing the tomb. Surrounding the main chamber (but cutting through the pavilion on the west) is a low wall made from sandstone slabs set on end. Although it is shown in 19th century drawings, again it was not necessarily part of the original building. The entrance to the grave chamber was on the east side, where the space between the columns are filled to form a solid porch; early sketches show this covered with painted decoration (perhaps Mughal). A further change was made when a late Mughal Majlis Khana (Assembly hall) was added on the east side. Finally another major alteration, after the 19th century drawings were made, is the square structure in the middle of the roof of the tomb building, completely altering the design, and adding to the claustrophobic feel of the space.

Grave inside tomb

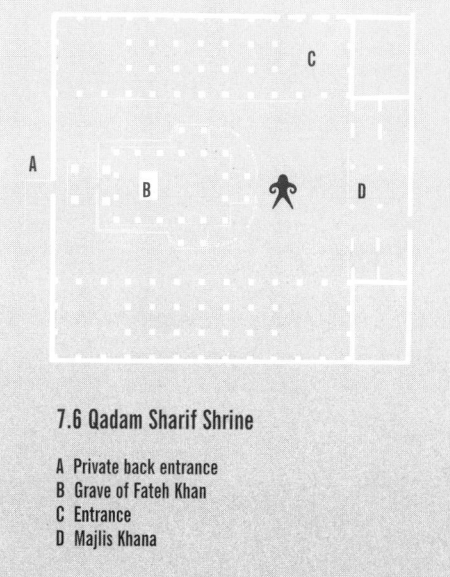

7.6 Qadam Sharif Shrine

A Private back entrance
B Grave of Fateh Khan
C Entrance
D Majlis Khana

NEARBY BUILDINGS

Not far from the Qadam Sharif, but easier to find because it is on the very crowded Qutb Road that runs north from New Delhi railway station, is an interesting **U-shaped building.** It would be tempting to suppose that this was one of the seven mosques built by Firoz Shah's Prime Minister, Khan Jahan, one of which was

U-shaped building

thought by Carr Stephen, the first person to write a visitor's guide to Delhi (1876), to stand near the Qadam Sharif, 'near [the] wall of Shahjahanabad between Lahore and Ajmer gates'. However, there are problems with this idea because the slender columns and the narrower arches indicate that it is probably a bit later, perhaps from the Lodi period. Originally the building had open arcades on all sides but these were filled early in the 20th century to provide more accommodation when the building was used as a Municipal Infectious Hospital. It is now used for storage. Opposite it is another building, thought to have been a **tomb**, originally inside the walled enclosure (now demolished) of the U-shaped building. This second building is in very poor repair, but the features that are visible appear to be Tughlak, for example the slightly battered walls and low dome drum.

North of these buildings is the large cemetery enclosure around the **grave of Khwaja Baqi Billah**, an early Mughal-era saint who was born in Kabul in 1570

Tomb   U-shaped building

and came to India after becoming a disciple of Khwaja Amkanki in Medina. He is believed to have introduced the Naqshbandiya sect (a Sufi reformist movement that originated in Mongol-ruled Central Asia) to India and is said to have had the habit of reciting the whole Koran twice every night.

HUNTING LODGES

Bhuli Bhatiyari ka Mahal (late 14th century)

This is thought to have been one of Firoz Shah's hunting lodges. It is a small, fortified enclosure of which nothing much remains but the outer walls and gates. It was originally built on a *bund*, one of several built by Firoz Shah. As has already been pointed out, the Sultan was a great improver as well as builder and the water supply was fundamental. As well as *bunds* he built canals and, as we have seen, repaired old tanks. Another *bund* that is still visible is the one at Mahipalpur.

Malcha

Another hunting lodge, built on a *bund*, is buried in woodland on the Ridge not far off the road up to the Satellite station. It is ruined and illegally occupied by a paranoid descendant of the Awadh royal family (on a notice: 'Proclamation: Intruders will be gun down' (*sic*)).

Kushak Shikargah (late 14th century)

This hunting lodge, in the grounds of Teen Murti (on the right as you approach the house), is more complete than any other. It stands on a small platform that itself stood on a wide *bund*. A passage, presumably for the dammed stream, passes through the upper platform. The building itself consists of a central hall with verandas either side facing north and south. On the west side, towards what would have been water, there are indications of two flights of steps leading down from each veranda. On the east side arched openings led out onto an open terrace.

Kushak Shikargah

MAHIPALPUR (see Eicher map)

This is a village that seems to have grown up around another of Firoz Shah's hunting lodges, this time to the west of the Ridge. A long wide *bund* was built, mostly north-south but turning east at the south end (where it can be seen on the north side of the Mehrauli – Mahipalpur road). This trapped water on the east side. The hunting lodge must have been built behind the *bund* so that it overlooked the irrigated land behind it. Later, a village seems to have grown up immediately beneath the *bund*; several old rubble-built houses can be found in the area closest to the *bund* so this must be the core of village. It is an interesting village to visit, because there are still a number of traditional houses on quiet clean lanes.

To find the **hunting lodge** (known as the *mahal*) take the road north from the lights on the main road. At a complex junction turn half right, leaving a building with a highly ornamental plastered façade on your left. Follow this lane until you get to the rear of a large white building on your left. The steps up beside it lead to the top of the *bund*. Ignore them and turn right after passing the white building. The *mahal* is through gates on the left. It is

typical of its date, with solid columns supporting the main chamber, a two by three-bay *dalan*, with enclosed rooms on each side. A staircase on the left leads to the roof, the edge of which is protected by a stone railing, similar, but with heavier elements, to the railing in front of Firoz Shah's Tomb at Hauz Khas.

If you take the left turn at the complex junction and keep going you will eventually come to steps up through a narrow passage on the right to the top of the *bund*. Here you can walk along for some distance and go down steps to examine the *bund* from below.

Mahipalpur hunting lodge

CHAUSATH KHAMBA (1370s)
Map p.262

This building is found north of Mirdard Marg, near the southern entrance to the Lok Nayak Hospital. The sign over the gateway is marked Al-Jamiatul-Islamia.

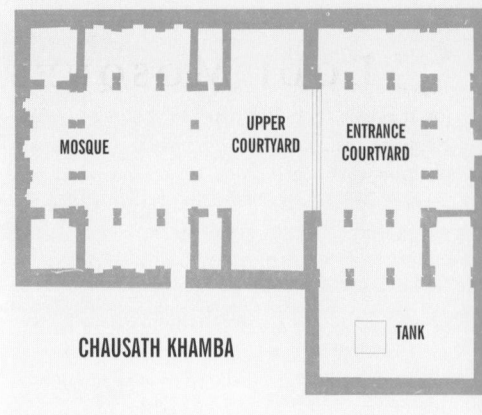

CHAUSATH KHAMBA

As mentioned above, Firoz Shah's second Prime Minister, Khan Jahan Junan Shah, was said to have built seven mosques. These are supposed to be the Kalan Masjid (now inside the walled city of Shahjahanabad – p.209), the Khirki Masjid (p.70), Begumpur Masjid (though this is doubtful for various reasons–p.69), Kalu Sarai Masjid (p.61), the Masjid in Nizamuddin (p.173), a mosque near the wall of Shahjahanabad (p.96) and the Chausath Khamba. Three of these mosques lie within the walls of Jahanpanah. Of these, those at Khirki and Kalo Serai, along with the Nizamuddin mosque and the Kalan Masjid, bear a striking stylistic resemblance, shared to some extent by the Chausath Khamba. This building has a curious layout, and seems to have consisted of a lower level entrance courtyard with access on one side to an ablutions pool, then a step up to an open area, which forms the mosque apron. The mosque itself is exactly the same shape as the lower courtyard except for the addition of niches in the sidewalls. The mosque has been so altered by doubtful improvements that at first the similarities with other Tughlak mosques are not obvious. One clear difference is that there are only three arches in each arcade and these are strikingly uneven, with the central arch much wider than the other two.

Nearby are two late Mughal buildings, one a *dargah* with a bulbous dome and the other a rather pretty but dilapidated enclosure, probably for a grave.

Conservation

Firoz Shah was, in effect, an early conservationist. As well as repairing many tombs belonging to previous dynasties, he also repaired secular structures such as the tanks at Hauz Khas and Suraj Kund. He instinctively knew that the Ashokan pillars were special, even though he did not know why. It seems appropriate, therefore, to mention in this chapter the importance of preserving the heritage that still exists in Delhi (and elsewhere). Some of the structures that date from Firoz Shah's reign are in particularly grave danger. It would be a real loss to future generations if, for instance, they could no longer see such buildings as the Qadam Sharif or the baoli at Hindu Rao hospital, both of which are markedly different from other better known tombs or baolis.

Chausath Khamba

LODI MOSQUES AND TOMBS

SAYYID AND LODI DELHI

Saw no end of other tombs, all more or less close together in a sort of village. Some of these are most exquisite as to architecture, and finished ornament, and some of great interest

Edward Lear, 1874

Sayyid and Lodi Sultanates (1414 - 1526)

In 1414, soon after Mahmud Shah's death, Khizr Khan took over the Delhi throne, establishing the next Sultanate, the Sayyids (so called because the family claimed direct descent from the Prophet). Khizr Khan himself ruled, in name at least, as a tributory of Timur's son, Shah Rukh, who was based at Herat (Afghanistan). The Delhi Sultanate, presumably based at the Jahanpanah / Siri complex, was no longer pre-eminent in north India, and was surrounded by powerful Muslim states such as Jaunpur, Gujarat and Malwa and Hindu states in Mewar, Alwar and the Doab. The other Muslim rulers even had the same standing in the eyes of the Caliph, who previously, in better times, had sent his Diplomas to Delhi alone, this being the ultimate legitimisation for Islamic rulers.

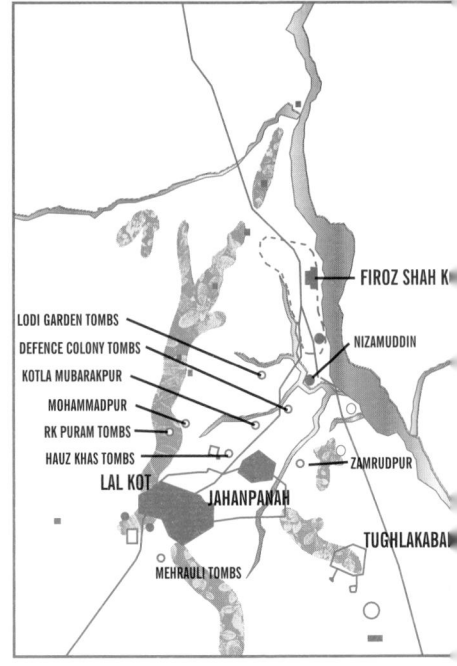

The power of Khizr Khan and his descendants was limited by their dependence on powerful Afghan nobles, and by the fact that their state was so small. Khizr Khan's son Mubarak Shah made the not very bold step of assuming sovereignty over Delhi when he inherited the Sultanate in 1414 - Timur being little threat having died fifteen years earlier. He campaigned endlessly to bring outlying areas into tax-paying submission and was beginning to see results towards the end of his reign. He had started to plan his new city beside the river but was murdered in his new mosque by one of his courtiers, Sarwarul Mulk, disgruntled that his own family was being eclipsed by that of another nobleman's. He put Mubarak's adopted son Muhammad Shah on the throne as a puppet, but found him not as pliant as expected.

In the civil war that followed Muhammad Shah killed Sarwarul Mulk and assumed power. However, his indolent and pleasure loving nature did not suit the nobles that surrounded him and they eventually lost patience and invited Mahmud Khalji of Mandu to take the throne. Muhammad Shah sent for Bahlol Lodi, then ruling Punjab, to help him. Much to Bahlol's displeasure, however, Muhammad Shah then made disadvantageous terms with Mahmud Khalji, at the cost of leaving himself only a tiny kingdom around Delhi. Indeed, a contemporary mockingly described the last Sayyid, Alam Shah, as holding sway from Delhi to Palam. Despite their penurious condition, however, the Sayyids seem to have had the funds to bury themselves in some style: Mubarak Shah (Kotla Mubarakpur) and Muhammad Shah (Lodi Gardens) were buried in handsome octagonal tombs and it is likely that several other tombs in Delhi date from the same period, for example, some at Hauz Khas.

Bahlol Lodi eventually returned to Delhi and seized power in 1451. The Lodi dynasty subsequently regained some of the territory lost under Firoz Shah and the Sayyids. Bahlol Lodi himself annexed Jaunpur, a powerful rival state. His son and successor, Sikander Lodi made further gains and was particularly keen to capture Gwalior. For this reason he made the decision to move his capital closer, down the river to the present site of Agra. Despite this, he himself was buried at Delhi, as was his father (their tombs are in Chiragh Delhi and the Lodi Gardens respectively). Although Bahlol Lodi had ruled as the 'first among equals' like the Sayyids, his son Sikander and grandson Ibrahim were more ambitious, Ibrahim tactlessly so, provoking an invitation, resulting from his overbearing behaviour, to invade India from one of the Afghan nobles to Babur, a descendant of Timur.

Like the Sayyid dynasty, the Lodis did not rule a rich state. Nonetheless the Sultans and their nobles seem to have had the wealth to construct several handsome mosques and numerous tombs in Delhi, evidence of the importance of the city of Delhi even when the court had transferred to Agra.

DELHI DURING THE SULTANATE - A SUMMARY

Throughout the Sultanate period the dominant class was Muslim while the majority of the population were Hindus. The effect this had on relations between the two communities varied but it seems that for most of the time problems were few. From very early days Muslim rulers had adapted to Indian customs. Some Hindus converted to Islam but there were clearly many who did not. Men sometimes converted for political reasons while their families remained Hindu; under Sharia law non-Muslims were allowed to follow their own forms of worship and, although they were not in theory allowed to build new temples, even this restriction seems to have been abandoned quite frequently.

Muhammad Tughlak was interested in Hinduism and went as far as celebrating some of the Hindu festivals such as Holi. It is an indication of his permissiveness that Firoz Shah complained that new temples had been constructed around Delhi before his reign. Firoz Shah was probably the most fanatically Islamic ruler of the Sultanate period and claimed to have demolished new temples, building mosques in their places, although even he left older temples standing. Unfortunately subsequent history makes it impossible to say how many Hindu temples there were in Delhi during the Sultanate period, partly because of later demolitions by Aurangzeb, but also because of a general habit of rebuilding. Several ancient temple sites exist, even if the buildings on them are of no great antiquity (e.g., the Kalkaji Temple and Jogmaya at Mehrauli), so it can be assumed that there was continuity at these sites, in order for tradition to be maintained. The fact that ancient Islamic buildings outnumber Hindu ones distorts our image of Sultanate Delhi, which was probably a much more pluralist place than its physical remains would indicate.

It is sad that there is so little evidence of what Delhi looked like during the Sultanate period. The remains are overwhelmingly of Islamic or military origin and we do not know what surrounded them. We know that early foreign travellers were impressed by the size and opulence of what they saw of urban India and we can tell, just from the distances we have to cover within them, that Indian cities were large, but we do not have much idea of how the population lived: how dense it was, what sort of houses they inhabited and whether there were gardens and orchards within the walls.

Sayyid and Lodi Tombs and Mosques

Muhammad Wali Masjid

Compared with the series of 'cities' founded by the Sultans in Delhi, the Sayyid and Lodi dynasties appear to have left very little behind. In fact, two of the Sayyids did build new capitals but nothing remains of them. Khizr Khan (reigned 1414-21) built a city called Khizrabad beside the Yamuna. It is a possibility that the present village of Khizrabad near New Friends Colony is its descendant. The centre of the village is significantly higher than the surrounding land, indicating occupation over a long period. Nearby are the severely damaged remains of an ancient bridge, which crosses what is now a drain in a slum area. This bridge would have linked Kilokri (Kayqubad's palace) with Khizrabad. Another city, Mubarakabad, is supposed to have been built south of Khizrabad by Mubarak Shah (reigned 1421-33) but absolutely nothing remains of it, not even a name. The remaining Sultans seem to have been content to use the existing urban centre (Jahanpanah, etc.) until Sikander Lodi (reigned 1489-1517) shifted his capital to Agra for strategic reasons, in order to be closer to Gwalior, which he hoped to capture.

Despite the disappearance of their 'cities', the Sayyids, Lodis and their courtiers left us a legacy of truly wonderful buildings, some of the most handsome in Delhi. Because India was now divided into many competing sultanates (and Hindu kingdoms), it did not mean that social or cultural life was less remarkable than what had gone before; indeed, there is abundant evidence that the very opposite was true. Elsewhere in North India there were powerful rulers, with whom the Delhi Sultans were intermittently at war: to the west and south were Mahmud Khalji of Malwa, Ahmed Shah of Gujarat, and Rana Khumbha of Mewar; further to the south was Muhammad Shah Bahmani and, to the east, the Sharqi dynasty.

Sakri Gumti

Each of these rulers left superb architectural legacies in, respectively, Mandu, Ahmedabad, Chittor, Bijapur and Jaunpur, even finer than anything built at the time in Delhi. In the wider cultural sphere as well, there were great achievements, in literature (classical and regional languages), social behaviour, and in socio-religious changes. It was during this period that inspired leaders, such as Kabir, Guru Nanak in the Punjab and Chaitanya in Bengal, began their reformist movements.

Bridge near Khizrabad

In Delhi, what is left from the Lodi period is a large number of tombs, as well as some very fine mosques. The majority of these were built in what we can assume was open ground around the urban areas, although a few of the tombs (and quite a lot of adjacent graves) are found inside Jahanpanah. These intra-mural tombs generally belonged to Muslim saints, as has already been observed in Chapter 7. It seems that most ordinary mortals were buried outside the walls, especially if they wished to erect a large mausoleum, which often happened in advance of their deaths. It should be mentioned that few tombs have inscriptions relating to the occupant. Most ascriptions are by tradition or guesswork.

The main disposition of Lodi tombs seems to have been west from Siri, past Hauz Khas and beyond. Another group extended

Mubarak Shah Tomb

north from Siri, in the area between the old city and Firoz Shah's ill-defined 'city'. A third cluster occurs south of the old city, in the area around Mehrauli. Because this last group falls into the area examined in Chapter 12, these buildings will be discussed there. This chapter deals with the buildings that lie in what is now known as South Delhi.

A fascinating 1849 map of the surroundings of Delhi gives a very good idea of how the landscape looked then: quite empty, with small villages and many ruins. Nearly a hundred years later, in 1931, Robert Byron could still describe the area south of New Delhi (which he was 'reviewing') as 'A flat country – brown, scrubby, and broken… This country has been compared with the Roman Campagna: at every hand tombs and mosques from Mughal times and earlier, weathered to the colour of the earth, bear witness to former empires.' The 1916 ASI listing (Zafar Hasan's 4 volumes), prepared in advance of the development of New Delhi, describes all these South Delhi tombs with reference to each other; at that time they were all visible on the broken plain and this state of affairs prevailed more or less into the 1960s. Since then development has been rapid all over the area and beyond. Now it is rather more difficult to locate the buildings, hidden as most of them are in over-developed urban villages or residential colonies, but many of them are well worth finding. Some are accurately marked (but not often labelled) on the Eicher City Map; where this falls short the maps in this book attempt to fill the gap.

Bara and Chhota Khan ka Gumbad

Bagh-i-Alam ka Gumbad

Typical Features of Lodi Tombs and Mosques

These are described in the following drawings. The major variations are pointed out on individual buildings.

The corner is spanned by a beam and the octagon is transformed to a circle with several rows of masonry layers with ever increasing numbers of sides.

Kangura battlements surro the square base and the octagonal drum supporting the dome.

A chajja protects the interior the tomb from rain and sun.

Twelve pillars support the structure. They sometimes filled with jali screens. and the is sometimes a mihrab on the west side.

The sixteen-sided drum has niches, like in square tombs. Four of these are open for light and are offset, not placed over the doors because here the light would be blocked by the external chatris. Because the openings are not placed above the doors there is a curious asymmetry involved in choosing to open only four niches as windows instead of the possible eight.

Chatris are placed over each entrance. It is interesting that these chatr were always placed above the centre of each wall, despite that fact tha the geometry of a near circle within an octagon allows more space at th corners (where chatris occur on square tombs), and also despite the fac that it results in the curiously offset windows in the drum.

Guldastas emphasise the corners of the parapet walls.

There are heavily battered buttresses at each corner of the veranda.

Mihrab niche.

The columns between the entrance arches are double counteract the sideways pressure of the roof and do

Steps up to the roof from the small lobby formed in the depth of the central chamber wall.

Jalis screen the central chamber from the veranda.

A sixteen-sided drum with blind niches on every face is surmounted by narrow bands that eventually become a circle.

A Lotus finial crowns the dome.

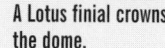

Each façade has a pishtaq (central bay) and the doorway is set back slightly inside a large arch. The pishtaq is higher than the main walls and projects out a small distance.

Squinch arches similar to the arches over the entrances and mihrab niche span the corner to support the dome drum.

The parapets are generally decorated with merlons, as here, or kanguras.

In larger tombs the internal corner niches align with a niche on the façade and are open.

The niches either side of the pishtaq are mostly blind. Some will give light to stairs to the roof or will connect with the interior corner niches.

Mihrab niche.

The doorway generally has a trabeate lintel with a small arched opening above it.

Octagonal tower at rear corners of prayer hall.

External drum may have windows to central chamber.

The treatment of the ceiling of each chamber will depend on whether or not there is a dome above it.

16-sided drum with blind niches.

Squinch arches above main arches, which span full width of wall.

Different treatment of entrance arches.

The mihrab in the central chamber is the most important one, and will have a minbar to its right if the mosque is congregational.

When the main arches are full width and the celing is low, the squinch is often achieved with corbelling between the arches.

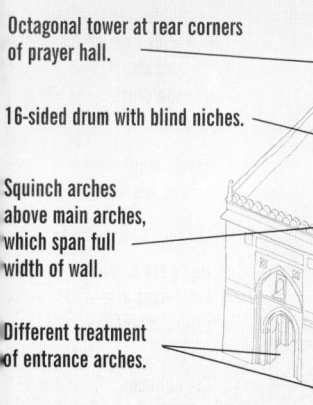

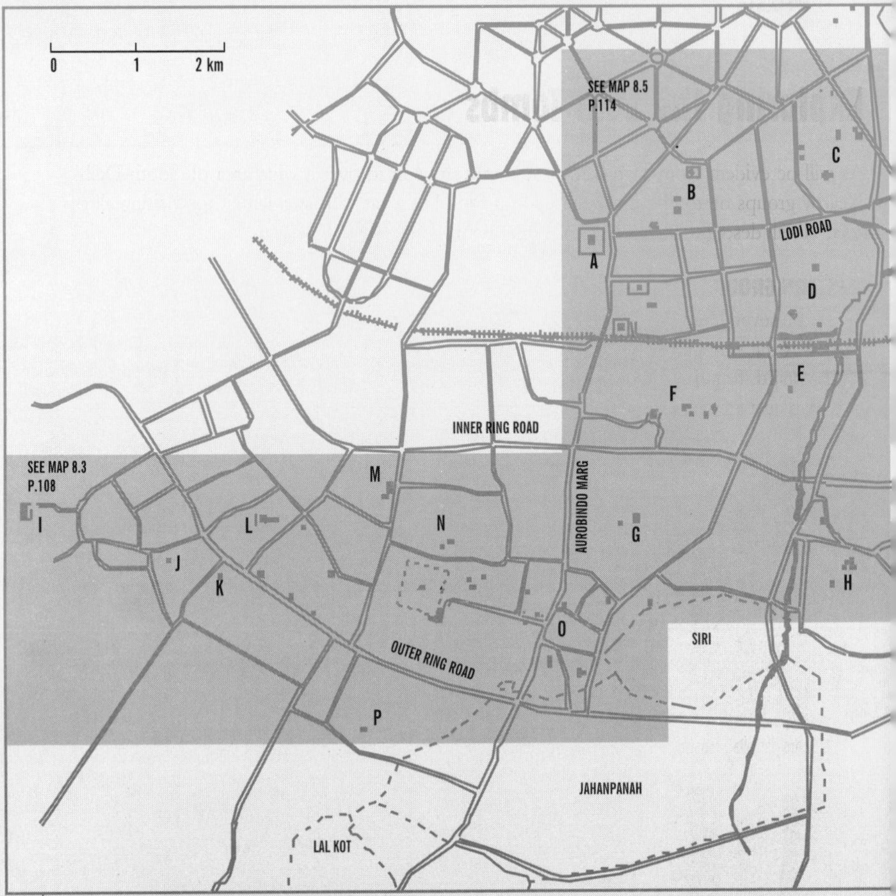

8.2 LOCATIONS OF MAIN GROUPS OF SAYYID AND LODI MOSQUES & TOMBS

A. Aliganj and Safdarjang's Tomb, 18th c. (p.127-130)

B. Lodi Gardens tombs, late 15th & early 16th c. (p.121-126)

C. Golf course tombs, 14th to 18th c. (p.131-132)

D. JN Stadium tombs, 15th – 17th c. (p.121)

E. Defence Colony tombs, early 16th c. (p.120)

F. Mubarakpur tombs, late 15th c. (p.117-120)

G. Moth ki Masjid, early 16th c. (p.116)

H. Zamrudpur tombs, 15th – 16th c. (p.115-116)

I. Muradabad Pahari Fort, 14th & 15th c. (p.113)

J. Vasant Vihar tombs, 14th & 16th c. (p.113)

K. Munirka, 15th c. (p.112-113)

L. RKPuram tombs, 15th c. (p.111-112)

M. Mohammadpur, 15th c. (p.110-111)

N. Humayunpur, 14th & 15th c. (p.110)

O. Hauz Khas tombs, 14th & 15th c. (p.107-110)

P. Katwaria Serai, 15th c. (p.113)

Makhdum Sahib

Exploring the Lodi Tombs

As will be evident from map 8.2, these tombs are spread over a wide area of South Delhi. Nearby groups of tombs can be visited on foot, but a car will be essential for visiting all of them. I will describe itineraries that take in both the main groups of tombs (p.103).

WESTERN GROUP

There are several buildings that were built just outside the walls of Siri. Closest is the very pretty, typical, three-bay Lodi mosque **Muhammad Wali Masjid**, found by taking a litter-strewn path on the outside of the wall (here just an overgrown mound) on the left of the road into the Siri Fort Sports Complex. The gateway to the mosque will soon be visible, leading into a large enclosure once full of graves, now a pleasantly shaded green area. Not far away, over August Kranti Marg, in the Gulmohar District Park, is the late 15th century **Mosque of Darwesh Shah**, a wall mosque and grave enclosure on a high platform. On the other side of the park turn left towards Hauz Khas market and right at the crossing. The **Nili Masjid** (1505-06) is a short distance on your right. Less typically proportioned than some mosques, the central bay is raised quite prominently in front of the single dome and the entrance arches are unusually flat.

Muhammad Wali Masjid

Muhammad Wali Masjid

South of here, in the southern part of Hauz Khas are three interesting buildings. The first, on the circle at the entrance to Q block, is a tower, the **Chor Minar,** believed to have been built in the early 14th century by Alauddin Khalji, who also built Siri Fort. The wall of the circular tower has holes, supposedly for displaying the heads of thieves. Just north of the Chor Minar, in the middle of Padmini Enclave, is an **Idgah** (1404-05) with five niches either side of the central *mihrab* and large round towers at each end. This building can be accurately dated to 1404-05, from an inscription that states that it was built by Mallu Khan, the virtual ruler of Delhi during the final years of the sultanate. The inscription, like most such things, is full of self-congratulation for the builder, who claimed to have been 'able by great efforts and endeavours to restore all the charitable foundations, and repopulate the capital of Delhi and other parts of the country' following the devastation of Timur's invasion.

Nili Masjid

Mosque of Makhdum Sahib

Between these two buildings and Siri there is a small complex of attractive buildings, now surrounded by Mayfair Gardens, called the **Tomb and Mosque of Makhdum Sahib**. Little is known about Makhdum Sahib, who is said to be buried in one of the graves to the north of the tomb. The entrance is through a small domed building, probably, judging by the battered walls and

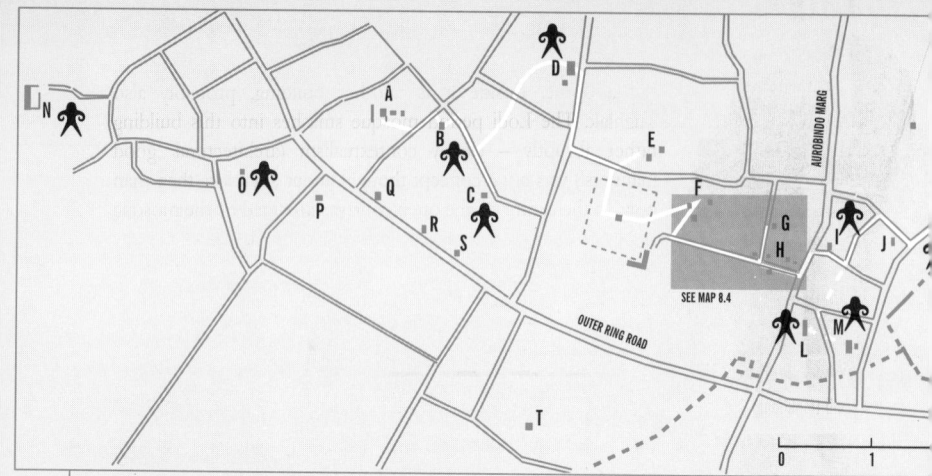

Map 8.3 Walk - Western Group

A. Wazirpur tombs, late15th c. (p.111-112)
B. Munda Gumbad, 15th c. (p.111)
C. Bijri Khan's Tomb, 15th c. (p.111)
D. Mohmmadpur -Tin Burj, late 15th c. (p.110-111)
E. Humayunpur (p.110)
F. Hauz Khas forest tombs, 14th and 15th c. (p.110)
G. Biran ka Gumbad, late 15th c. (p.109)
H. Hauz Khas road tombs, 14th and 15th c. (p.109)
I.   Nili Masjid, (1505-6) (p.107)
J. Mosque of Darwesh Shah, late 15th c. (p.107)
K. Muhammad Wali Masjid, late 15th —early 16th c. (p.107)
L. Chor Minar, early 14th c. & Idgah, (1404-5) (p.107)
M. Tomb and mosque of Makhdum Sahib, mainly 15th c. or early 16th (p.107, 109)
N. Muradabad Pahari Fort, 14th and 15th c. (p.113)
O. Vasant Vihar tombs, 15th c. (p.113)
P. Malik Munirka Mosque, 15th c. (p.113)
Q. Mosque (p.112)
R. Mosque (p.112)
S. Haji Langa Group, 14th c. (p.112)
T. Katwaria Serai Tomb, late 15th c. (p.113)

8.4 Hauz Khas Tombs (p.109-110)

A. Burial ground wall mosque, 15th c.
B. Kali Gumti, 14th c.
C. Bagh-i-Alam ka Gumbad, late 15th – early 16th c.
D. Tuhfewala Gumbad, 14th c.
E. Biran ka Gumbad, late 15th c.
F. Sakri Gumti, late 15th c.
G. Chhoti Gumti, late 15th c.
H. Barah Khamba, 14th c.
I.   Dadi ka Gumbad, late 15th c.
J. Poti ka Gumbad, late 14th c.

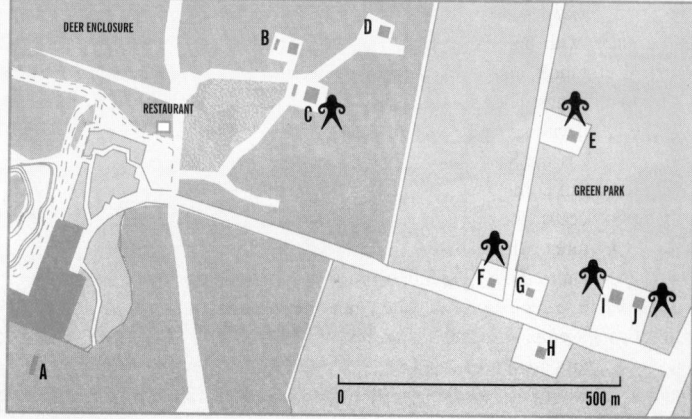

twelve-pillared tomb (Makhdum Sahib)

Dadi ka Gumbad

fluted dome. Beside it is another building, probably also Tughlak. The Lodi period mosque smashes into this building rather abruptly – clearly contextualism (architectural 'good manners') was not a concept thought about any more then than now. In the centre of the open courtyard formed by the mosque is a **twelve-pillared tomb**, its most interesting feature being the remains of extensive painting over the surfaces inside – pretty floral patterns as well as geometric designs.

The next area to explore is the road leading from Aurobindo Marg to Hauz Khas village. Opposite, on Aurobindo Marg, is a high stone wall, which once enclosed a village called **Kharera**. The villagers were bought out and the walls now contain the compound of private corporate offices, as well as an attractive Lodi mosque, unfortunately inaccessible. The tombs that line the road to Hauz Khas are interesting for their heterogeneity, coming in various shapes and sizes. Some of them are thought to be among the oldest of this type in Delhi. First on the right are the two large tombs known as **Poti ka Gumbad** (Granddaughter's Tomb – late 14th century) and **Dadi ka Gumbad** (Grandmother's Tomb – late 15th century). They have been popularly linked because of their proximity, but their fanciful names are shown to have nothing to do with history by the mere fact that the first tomb is clearly of an earlier date, from the late Tughlak or Sayyid periods, indicated by the lack of niches on the façade and the small lantern on top of the dome, a feature that is only seen once elsewhere, on the tomb of the Sayyid Sultan, Mubarak Shah (in Kotla Mubarakpur). Inside, the squinches and drum niches spring rather arbitrarily from the walls, without the fixed relationship with the doorway arches that is more common. Both tombs lack traditional doorways.

On the left you will find the **Barah Khamba** (Twelve pillars), a very unusual, *mihrab*-less, tomb that may well be pre-Lodi. It has openings on all four sides, with one large arch dominating each façade, enclosing three arched entrances and a single window. Almost opposite are two small domed buildings. The first is the **Chhoti Gumti** (Small dome), probably a gateway and without a projecting *pishtaq*. On the other side of the road into Green Park is the **Sakri Gumti** (Narrow dome – perhaps muddled with Chhoti Gumti in the 1916 ASI listing). The exterior of this small tomb is untypical because the *pishtaqs* and dome are unusually dominant because of the low stature of the main walls. A diversion at this point into Green Park will bring you to the **Biran ka Gumbad** (it is not known from where the local name came), another Lodi tomb, but with curiously vertical proportions, emphasised by two arches inside the central bays. Inside, the squinch arches are high above the floor, where two very insignificant little niches crouch in each corner.

Poti ka Gumbad

Dadi ka Gumbad

Chhoti Gumti   Sakri Gumti

Biran ka Gumbad

Bagh-i-Alam ka Gumbad

The next group of tombs are those inside the Deer Park forest. As described in the previous chapter, they can be included in an exploration of Hauz Khas. The first and largest tomb is the **Bagh-i-Alam ka Gumbad**. This is one of the finest Lodi tombs in Delhi. Unusually, the façade is built entirely from dressed local stone with touches of imported red sandstone and blue ceramic tiles. One niche is open to the interior on each side of the doorway. Nearby is its **wall mosque**, typical of the genre. Beyond it to the right is the austere **Tuhfewala Gumbad**, undoubtedly Tughlak, being very plain on both the exterior and interior except for the rather striking cenotaphs inside, made from well-carved quartzite. This is another tomb without a *mihrab*. Near the Bagh-i-Alam ka Gumbad is the **Kali Gumti** (Black dome), probably also 14th century. This has typical proportions, but without the pronounced batter typical of Tughlak buildings. Adjoining it is a small wall mosque.

Another Lodi monument is a ruined 15th century **Wall mosque**, found beyond the slum, behind the *madrasa* monuments. Turn left just before the monuments and then take a brick paved path beside the slum. It appears that the ground level has risen quite considerably from consecutive burials since the mosque was built.

From the Hauz Khas Park it is possible to walk out to Safdarjang Enclave, which envelops another old village, **Humayunpur**. On the edge of the village there is a small domed building, clearly Tughlak, with entrances on all four sides. In the centre of the village there is a well-preserved well, probably dating from Mughal times. Opposite the well there

Bagh-i-Alam exterior

Wall mosque behind madrasa

is a brick platform with steps up to an attractive *dalan* (p.9) that has two rows of Shahjahani-style columns with rooms behind. There are a few other traditional houses and, down a passage beside the *dalan*, a Lodi tomb called **Maluk Chand ka Gumbad**, without a *mihrab* but containing a grave.

From Humayunpur you can walk out through Safdarjang Enclave to Africa Avenue. A little way down on the right the **Mohammadpur Tin Burj** is clearly visible across the road. The rather humdrum façade belies a ruined but ornate interior; this is an exceptionally interesting building. From the Tin Burj it is possible to visit a very derelict and humble **Lodi tomb**, now used for storage, found by taking the road into the village immediately to the left of the Tin Burj. The first significant turning to the left takes you to the north face of the tomb.

Many of the tombs described in this chapter are or were in villages, and constituted the foci around which, presumably, the

Tuhfewala Gumbad   Kali Gumti

Maluk Chand ka   Humayanpur
Gumbad   Tomb

MOHAMMADPUR TIN BURJ (late 15th century)

This is one of the largest and most architecturally sophisticated Lodi buildings in Delhi. It is not entirely clear for what purpose it was originally built. Although full of graves, the building is completely untypical of tombs built at any period. The layout is in a way more like a mosque: it has three bays and originally had three entrances on the east side, although the side entrances have now been partially blocked. Unlike any other mosque, however, is the fact that originally the two end bays had large arched openings on the west side (making it rather like Balban's Tomb at Mehrauli (see Chapter 12), although there the orientation is different). One of these is still visible at the northern end of the building, where the dressed stone plinth disappears into the building, a rubble wall having been built across the opening.

The façade is severe and far less articulated than any other mosque; an ornamented surface would certainly have been planned, if never built. On either side of the main façade the dressed stone plinth of the main building clearly runs round the foundations of what can only have been octagonal minarets. On the northern side there is evidence that the minaret here once reached some height, as stones projecting from the flat surface of the wall must once have tied the minaret into the main building.

villages grew. Beyond Mohammadpur there were a number of tombs that remained forlornly in the countryside until the growth of Delhi swallowed them. In R K Puram there are several. From Mohammadpur it is possible to walk or drive south, beside Sector 1 of R K Puram to Venkateshwara Marg. Here you should turn right for the large 15th century **Bijri Khan's Tomb.** This seriously dilapidated tomb has lost a great deal of original masonry at the base of its walls, probably because it was faced with valuable dressed stone. The base of the wall has recently bean restored. Crouching at the southwest corner of Bijri Khan's Tomb is a small, severely plain **Tughlak Tomb.** Returning back along Venkateshwara Marg, turn left into Sector 4. Near the Kendriya Vidyalaya is the domeless **Munda** (bald) **Gumbad** (15th century). In overall design this is very like Bijri Khan's Tomb except that there are openings in the dome drum above the entrances, unusual for this date.

On the other side of Vivekanand Marg, and visible

Munda Gumbad

Tughlak Tomb

Bijri Khan's Tomb - elevation and section

Wazirpur ka Gumbad

Wazirpur tombs

from it, is an attractive group of five tombs and other buildings. These are known as the **Wazirpur Tombs**. They were built unusually close together, with an associated wall mosque and, nearby, a *baoli* and another small wall mosque. Although the name implies a village, Wazirpur does not seem to have existed at the time of the 1849 map or the 1916 listing (when the tombs were described as being on the land of Munirka village). The buildings are all archetypical for their age and size. The largest tomb, known as **Wazirpur ka Gumbad,** has arched doorways, a variant on the more normal trabeate lintels. Its interior is typical except for one surprising feature: the drum supporting the dome contains a row of thirty-two blind niches instead of the more normal sixteen.

Just southwest of the Wazirpur Tombs, in the centre of the Government Senior Secondary

Wazirpur Baoli

School there is a fine Lodi **Wall mosque** on a raised grave platform. It is quite well preserved internally, although threatened by tree growth. Less well preserved are two nearby **mosques**. The first is near the shopping area in Sector 5, R K Puram. Originally on a high platform with graves in the courtyard, it has been much altered. Back in Sector 4, near the Outer Ring Road opposite the DDA flats is another mosque, only the back of which is visible in its original state.

Eastwards, some distance along the Ring Road is the 14th century **Haji Langa** group of buildings. This is a small complex, now serving as a *madrasa*. The name Haji Langa is associated with it, but nothing is known about this person. The three buildings all appear to be Tughlak. There is a tall gateway with battered walls and a fluted dome. Inside the compound is a stolid unornamented tomb and opposite this a three-domed mosque. Modern additions have somewhat obscured the original façade.

Opposite R K Puram Sector 4 is **Munirka**. This is one of the largest urban

Haji Langa group

Wall mosque in Government Senior Secondary School

Munirka Tank

villages in Delhi. It has been heavily redeveloped and now consists of the usual narrow lanes with four or five storey buildings somehow crammed onto the irregular plots between them. In places, particularly towards the west of the village, traditional houses can still be found, but not, perhaps, for much longer. In the middle of the village there is quite a pronounced rise in ground level. At the top of this hill is an extremely decrepit but ancient mosque known as **Malik Munirka Mosque** (15th century), only the heavy *chajji* brackets indicating its existence. Even in 1916 the side bays were in residential occupation, as they still are, with only the central bay unoccupied. It would appear, from the paltry vestiges of ornamentation, that this was never a very grand building.

On the west side of the village there are the remains of a large **tank**. Although dry now, it must once have been quite deep, with a fine *ghat* on the far side and various remains of platforms around the edges. At the top of the *ghat* is a small *dalan* with rooms either side, of which the right hand one is a temple. Behind this building is the conspicuous Sri Munirka Baba Ganganathji Maharaj Temple.

On the near side of Vasant Vihar is a group of buildings in the District Park opposite the Basant Lok Market. Most obvious is a large Lodi tomb, the **Bara Lao ka Gumbad**. This neglected tomb is inaccessible, inside a walled compound, but can just be seen over the wall. An unusual feature is the intersecting bands on the exterior of the dome that would once have been tiled. These are very similar to the red bands found on the interiors of many tombs. Inside the adjoining walled enclosure a domed *chatri* on a large platform has recently been demolished. Behind these are the ruins of a small three-bay

Bara Lao ka Gumbad

mosque, perhaps Tughlak, judging by its heavy construction, but more likely Lodi. The erstwhile courtyard in front of this mosque once contained a grave and beyond this were the remains of what is thought to be a Tughlak-era garden.

On the other side of Vasant Vihar is the **Muradabad Pahari Fort**, accessible through an ornamental modern gate from the lane opposite the Vasant Vihar Club. Inside is a thriving *madrasa* where 125 boys are taught the Koran for the prescribed period of three years. The main school hall / dormitory is inside a large **Lodi mosque** that is, strangely enough, built right beside an earlier mosque, the **Qasai Wala Gumbad**, with a doorway between them. The older mosque has three entrances leading into three bays, the central one being roofed with a hemispherical dome that springs straight from the surrounding flat roof, an unusual detail. To the north of the mosques there is a conventional twelve-pillared **tomb**; on the south there is a stretch of the old boundary wall which once had arched chambers within it. One of these is currently being used as the *madrasa* kitchen.

Katwaria Serai Tomb

Rather remote from the other areas is the **Katwaria Serai Tomb**. This Lodi tomb faces a large open space on the northwest side of the village and has been much altered, now acting as a gateway to the village and a storehouse.

8.5 Northern Group of Lodi Tombs

A. Safdarjang's Tomb, 1753 (p.130)
B. Lodi Gardens, mainly 15th &
    early 16th c. (p.121-126)
C. Golf Course Tomb, 18th c. (p.132)
D. Mughal Golf Course Tomb, 16th c. (p.131)
E. Barah Khamba, 14th c. (p.131)
F. Lal Bangla, 1779 (p.131)
G. Mir Taqi's Tomb, late 16th (p.132)
H. Aliganj, mainly18[th] c. (p.128-129)
I. Tomb with chatri, 16th c. (p.121)
J. 16-sided tomb, 16th c. (p.121)
K. Tomb, 14th c. (p.121)
L. Tomb of Khwajah Sara Basti Khan,
    early 16th c. (p.120)
M. Gumti of Sheikh Ali, late 15th c. (p.120)
N. South Extension tombs, 15th c. (p.117-120)
O. Moth ki Masjid, early 16th c. (p.116)
P. Tomb, after 1494 (p.115)
Q. Zamrudpur tombs, 14th and 15th c. (p.115-116)

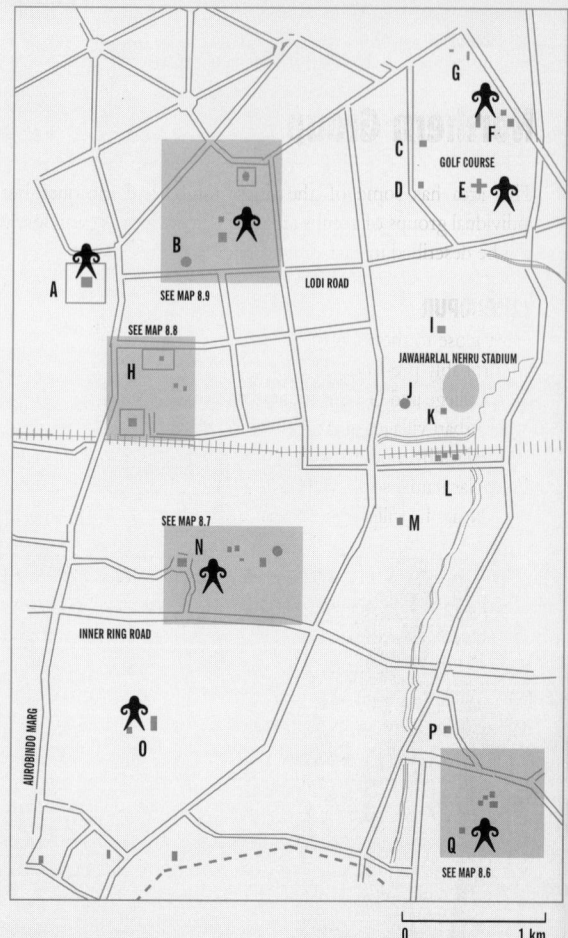

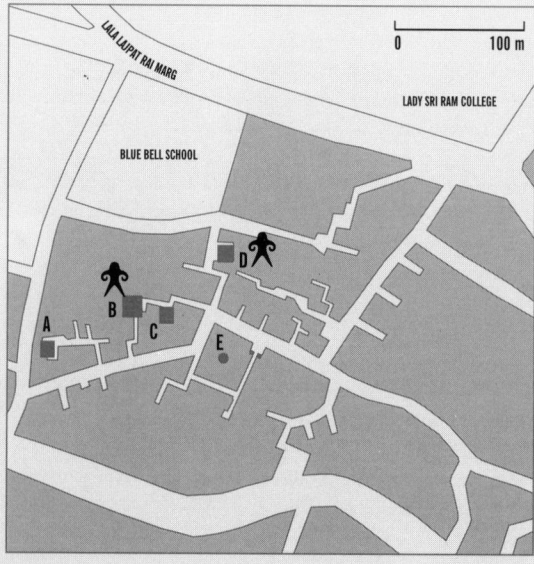

8.6 Zamrudpur Map

A. Tomb, late 15th – early 16th c.
B. Tomb, 15th c.
C. Tomb, late 15th – early 16th c.
D. Tomb, 15th c.
E. Tomb, 15th c.

Northern Group

This area has some of the finest tombs and mosques but the individual groups of tombs are too far apart for easy walking. Walks will be described in each area instead.

Mahavir Library, Central Park GK-1

ZAMRUDPUR

Fairly close to the walls of Siri, this area contains a few tombs that are probably pre-Lodi. The village of Zamrudpur is near Lady Sri Ram College and Greater Kailash - I N Block Market and, like most other urban villages, it is a deeply deprived ghetto being eaten into at its edges by modern commercialisation. None of the tombs has a popular name, so they are labelled in order to locate them on the map.

Near the village, on the most northerly part of Lala Lajpat Rai Marg, is a **Tomb** that seems to have been built inside the tomb enclosure (dated 1494) of Langar Khan, one of Bahlol Lodi's courtiers. The nearby ruined gateway was also part of the enclosure. The twelve-pillared tomb is inhabited by a sadhu so cannot be seen.

Zamrudpur Tomb B

Walk into the village opposite the corner of N Block, along the road behind Blue Bells School. You will soon see **Tomb D** on your right. This is the most typically Lodi of the tombs here but, like the Tomb B, it is hybrid. On three sides (only one is easily visible) there is a wide arch enclosing three doorways, the central one being much larger than the other two. There is no *pishtaq,* but four small niches frame the main arch, two above and two below a stringcourse. Unusually, this tomb is built entirely from dressed stone, rather than rubble.

Walk past this tomb and turn left. This lane will take you into the centre of the village. Take a tiny lane to your right to see **Tomb C**. This was a twelve-pillared tomb but it has been inhabited and the openings have been walled-up, making the interior dark. Just beyond it you can get access to the dark interior of **Tomb B**. Very difficult to see, this is quite a large tomb in a style similar to Tomb D. The interior is used as a cattle shed and there is very little light, so internal features are invisible.

You will need to return to the village centre where, if you turn left on the main road, you will shortly come to an attractive traditional doorway. Go through it and turn right, where you should be able to see the abused remains of **Tomb E**, a six-sided-*chatri* that is inhabited and recently added to with a concrete framed building. Continuing in the same direction and then turn right, back to the village centre, and then turn left. The first tiny lane on the right leads to a better view of Tomb B, but access here is impossible. The next turning takes you to the gem of Zamrudpur: **Tomb A.** This

Zamrudpur Tomb D   Zamrudpur Tomb B

twelve-pillared tomb is unusually ornate, with finely carved pillars and an elaborate *kangura* design around the dome. However, its true glory is inside, above the dung-cake stores: the ceiling is decorated with incised plaster and is exceptionally well preserved. Radial bands converge on the central roundel, with tear-drop roundels supported on elaborate columns in low relief between them. These bands are not seen elsewhere in Delhi but are very similar to those in the Jami Masjid in Champaner (Gujarat). Below the dome there is a narrow drum ornamented with tiny niches.

Central Park Tomb

Just south of the village, in the middle of Central Park, GK-I, is another **Tomb** that is probably Tughlak and very reminiscent of Haji Khanum's Tomb in Chiragh Delhi. The excrescence above the projecting *mihrab* bay was presumably put there when the building was converted into a library – a good use for an old building but one that has apparently failed.

SOUTH EXTENSION PART II

Just to the south of South Extension Part II is the village of Masjid Moth, built in front of the beautiful early 16th century **Moth ki Masjid**. This is undoubtedly one of the loveliest mosques in Delhi. The mosque is entered on the eastern side through a handsome gateway decorated in red sandstone and white marble. Steps lead up into a raised courtyard with *chatris* at each corner. There are two trees and the remains of graves inside the courtyard, as well as another structure that is not aligned with the well-preserved mosque.

This mosque was built by a courtier of Sikander Lodi's called Miyan Bhoiya. One version of the tale that describes the foundation of the mosque goes like this: The Sultan found a grain of *moth* (a pulse) on the floor of the Jami Masjid and gave it to Miyan Bhoiya, who considered that a seed from such illustrious hands (and, perhaps, its sacred place of discovery) merited planting. He put it into his orchard and it did extremely well, producing two hundred grains, which were again sown. Eventually this excellent strain of *moth* made a fortune for Miyan Bhoiya and he built this mosque in gratitude.

Beyond the mosque to the south take the turning on the right and follow it until the road turns quite sharply right. A **Lodi era building** is immediately on your left. This is a tomb or perhaps a gateway (because it had projecting balconies on the east side) that has been almost engulfed by neighbouring buildings.

Moth ki Masjid

Moth ki Masjid

Lodi era tomb

Moth ki Masjid elevation

SOUTH EXTENSION PART I

South Extension was built to the south of an old village called Kotla Mubarakpur, which developed inside the tomb enclosure of the second Sayyid Sultan. Near it are a number of Lodi tombs, now scattered among residential neighbourhoods.

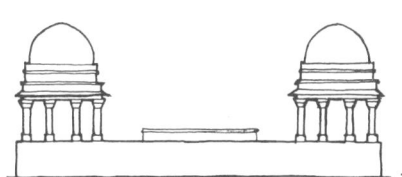

Tomb of Darya Khan Lohani

Kale Khan ka Gumbad

From the northwest corner of the main market walk in one block and turn left on a long through road. Soon on the right you will find **Kale Khan ka Gumbad** (1481). This is an archetypal Lodi

Tomb of Darya Khan Lohani

Tomb. Unusually, it has an inscription, so we know the occupant and date: it was built in 1481 by a courtier of Bahlol Lodi, Mubarak Khan, probably the father of Darya Khan Lohani, buried in a fine tomb not far away. Perhaps its only unusual feature is the very tall cenotaph inside. From here turn right, northwards and then turn left and cross a drain. On the other side of the small market building is the ruined **Tomb of Darya Khan Lohani** (early 16th century). Darya Khan Lohani was chief justice under Bahlol Lodi and vakil under Sikander Lodi. This is an uncommon style of tomb, although it would have had much in common with the Qadam Sharif Tomb (p.94-95) in its original form. The cenotaph was set on a circular platform in the middle of a larger platform that had 12-pillared *chatris* at each corner. This platform was in turn set on another platform, very little of which remains.

Return over the bridge and take the second turn on the left. At the next junction cross almost opposite and you will find two of the Tin Burj (three domed), once prominent features on the open plain (not to be confused with the Tin Burj in Mohammadpur). The nearest is the **Bare Khan ka Gumbad**, with an unusually elaborate façade. Either side of the conventional central bay are

Chhote Khan ka Gumbad

three rows of three niches, the central ones being larger than the other two. Beyond these there are slender octagonal corner turrets, a feature not seen on any other Lodi tomb. Above them there were once *chatris* on each corner of the roof. Beside it is the exquisite **Chhote Khan ka Gumbad.** The classic proportions of this tomb are beautifully enhanced by incised

Bare Khan ka Gumbad

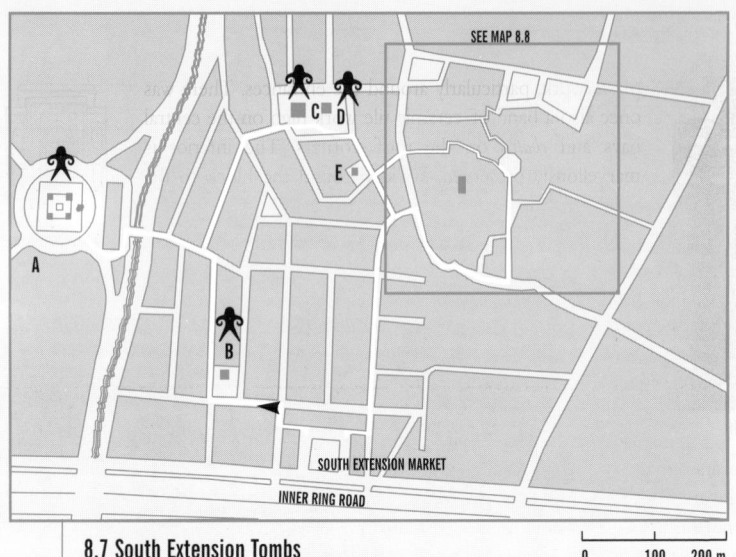

8.7 South Extension Tombs

A. Tomb of Darya Khan Lohani, early 16th c.
B. Kale Khan ka Gumbad, 1481
C. Bare Khan ka Gumbad, late 15th – early 16th c.
D. Chhote Khan ka Gumbad, late 15th – early 16th c.
E. Bhure Khan ka Gumbad, late 15th – early 16th c.

0   100   200 m

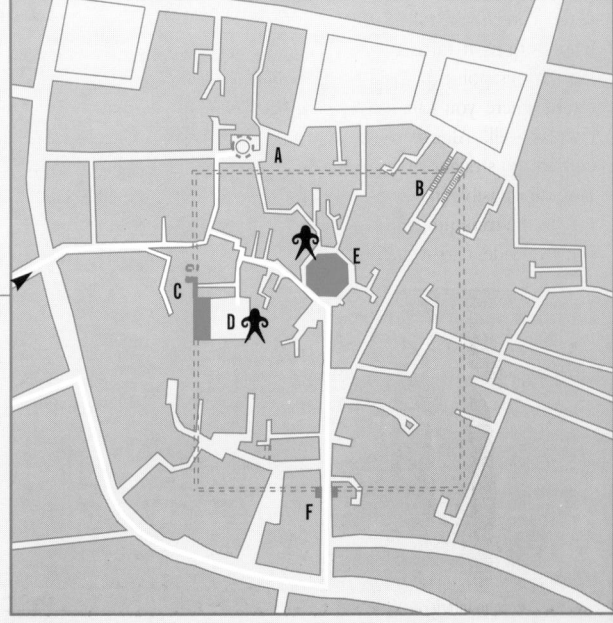

8.8 Kotla Mubarakpur,
   mid 15th c.

A. Baoli
B. Both these lanes have quite
   a number of steps, indicating
   the limit (wall) of the old
   village
C. West Gate
D. Mosque
E. Mubarak Shah's Tomb
F. South Gate

Mubarak Shah's Tomb

Bhure Khan ka Gumbad

plasterwork, particularly around the entrances. There was once also a band of ceramic tile work high on the central bays and *chatris* on the roof corners. The interior is marvellously preserved. Walking round the block to the south will bring you to the third member of the group, the disappointing **Bhure Khan ka Gumbad**. Once part of the Tin Burj group it has been separated from the others by a group of temples.

From here take the road opposite the east side of the tomb. This meets a wider street that you should cross and walk up the lane opposite, leading into the old Kotla Mubarakpur. **Mubarak Shah's tomb** was built inside a walled enclosure that had gates on the south and west sides. Although it is shown on an early map as being octagonal it appears that the layout was rectangular, with the tomb standing towards the north end of the enclosure. Although there is no visible sign of the north wall it is likely to have been near the northern edge of the village, where the ground slopes down quite steeply, indicating the limit of the higher ground resulting from centuries of demolition and rebuilding within the walls. Compared with villages such as Mohammadpur and Munirka there are a good number of traditional houses left (until recently there was even one thatched building left beside the tomb), although this is likely to change soon.

A turning on the right will take you along what would have been the outside of the enclosure wall, where it is just about possible to see the remains of the **West Gate**. Return and follow the main path as it turns to the left. At this point the lane ahead takes you to the remains of a **baoli**, where you can still see the stonework surrounding the circular well. Alternatively turn right and, after a couple of corners, go straight ahead down a narrow, dirty lane. Part of the old wall is visible in one place on the right, before you reach the gate to the **mosque**, which was built as part of the west wall of the enclosure. Two bays deep and five wide, narrow arches span between the moderately slender pillars, while rather clumsy wedges carry the vaulted ceilings of each bay.

Mubarak Shah's Tomb

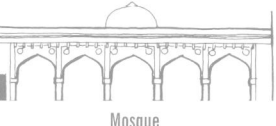

Mosque

Returning to the main lane turn right and this will soon bring you to **Mubarak Shah's Tomb**. This is the oldest and also, historically, the most important of the tombs in this area. Mubarak Shah was the second Sayyid Sultan, the son of Khizr Khan, and he died in 1434. His tomb was only the second octagonal tomb to be built in Delhi, but the older one, that of Firoz Shah's Prime Minister, Khan Jehan Tilangani (d.1368), is barely visible (p.173). Unfortunately the ASI has recently enclosed this **tomb** inside an ugly fence so the façade, although

Mosque interior

not actually obscured, is spoilt. Curiously the exterior columns are made from a solid block, but carved to appear as twin columns. The dome is crowned by a red sandstone lantern instead of the more normal lotus finial.

From the south face of the tomb a wide lane leads down to the **South Gate,** which is just visible, particularly on the right where the thickness of the wall, the pillars, and corbelling can be made out. Shortly after passing the gate you reach a busy road where you should turn right. This will take you back to South Extension, where the first turning on the left will lead back to the main market.

South Gate

DEFENCE COLONY

Tomb of Khwajah Sara Basti Khan (early 16th century)
Accurately marked on the Eicher map between the railway line and Defence Colony

On the northern edge of Defence Colony there is a pleasant, seldom-visited group of buildings that now serve as a *madrasa*. Because of its use, many layers of blinding whitewash have smothered the buildings, but their basic forms can be seen even if architectural details are less clear. Khwajah Sara Basti Khan, a eunuch during Sikander Lodi's reign, built the entire complex,

Khwajah Sara Basti Tomb

consisting of a gateway, a mosque, his tomb and a *baoli*. The west enclosure wall is now used as a prayer wall and there is a simple *minbar* (pulpit) attached. The *baoli* has been long abandoned and is not visible. The **gateway** is the least altered building. Like the Bara Gumbad in the Lodi Gardens (p.124), it is tomb-like in plan, but the niches on the western side are replaced by projecting balconies. The exterior of the **mosque** has been altered by the extensions recently built in front, dividing the three arched openings from the frieze of niches above them, only visible from the tomb platform. The **tomb** itself is the most prominent

Khwajah Sara Basti Khan Tomb   Gateway

building, on a high platform with access through an arched gateway on the east side. There is a central twelve-pillared pavilion and, originally, a square *chatri* on each corner of the platform (similar to the larger tomb of Darya Khan Lohani in Mubarakpur), only one of which now remains.

Gumti of Sheikh Ali (late 15th century)
Correctly marked on Eicher map in the centre of the distinctive circle

This is an unusual tomb. It was originally open, with eight pillars supporting arched openings that have now been filled in to create the office of the local residents' association. The detailing makes it more like a small octagonal tomb than an eight-pillared *chatri*.

Khwajah Sara Basti Gateway

JAWAHARLAL NEHRU STADIUM

The stadium was built in 1982 for the Asian Games. Three nearby tombs were preserved, which are very different from one another. The two southern tombs are not far from Kotla Mubarakpur and are described as being outside it in the 1916 ASI listing. The easiest to find is the **tomb with a chatri** to the north of the stadium. It is early Mughal and has a rectangular chamber with the remains of arch-netting on the vaulted ceiling. A plain and moderately featureless **14ᵗʰ century tomb** can be found between Gates 9 & 10 of the stadium. The most interesting of the three is the **16-sided tomb,** probably 16ᵗʰ century. It is beside the running track, which can be reached off the main approach road to the stadium. This unusual tomb has an arched niche on each of its sixteen sides except on the south where there is a locked entrance to the burial chamber. On the roof is an octagonal platform with three cenotaphs, the central one of which has some calligraphy.

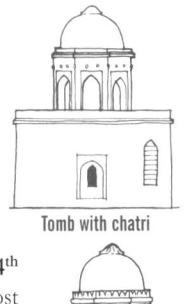

Tomb with chatri

14ᵗʰ c. tomb

16-sided tomb

THE LODI GARDENS

Despite the architectural perfection of the Chhote Khan ka Gumbad near Kotla Mubarakpur (p.117), the climax of the Sayyid and Lodi tombs is clearly to be found in the four tombs in these eponymously named gardens. We do not know why this area was chosen for such a rash of special tombs, although plainly they are part of the scatter extending northwards from Siri. The 1849 map helps us a bit: Mubarak Shah's Tomb was near a road between Nizamuddin and Jahanpanah. Likewise Muhammad Shah's Tomb was near a road from Firozabad to Jahanpanah, and also near a stream. Both the roads are marked on the 1849 map and it seems likely that the roads dated back to the 15ᵗʰ century. The ascription of the two royal tombs happened at some point in the 19ᵗʰ century in the absence of actual documented proof. What records are available do not necessarily confirm the ascriptions. For instance, a contemporary history says that Sikander Lodi was buried 'together with his father, in a garden which [he] had enclosed and prepared for the purpose', while another states that Bahlol Lodi was buried near the shrine of Chiragh Delhi (hence the guess at that tomb).

Following the construction of the four principal tombs there were various additions to the scene during the Mughal period. First, a bridge was built during Akbar's reign, shown on the 1849 map but with no sign of a road for it to carry. Perhaps it was connected in the past with Nizamuddin and Humayun's tomb, both important sites for the Mughals. Later several smaller Mughal buildings such as mosques, garden pavilions and a *baoli* were built. There were also a lot of burials, usually on raised platforms. At some point a village called Khairpur developed around the two central tombs, shown as a tiny place on the 1849 map. In 1936 the area was turned into a park on the edge of New Delhi. The population was moved out of Khairpur, some of them moving to Kotla Mubarakpur, and the park was laid out around the tombs. Photographs from the early years of the park show a preponderance of native trees in a fairly unfussy and natural landscape. The park was re-planned in 1968 with a great deal of new planting and the unfortunate addition of a lake, in truth unsustainable in water-short Delhi and detracting from the landscape when dry.

Garden gateway

8.9 Lodi Gardens

A. Remains of octagonal platform
B. Sikander Lodi's Tomb, early 16th c. (p.126)
C. Athpula Bridge, late 16th c. (p.123)
D. Remains of garden enclosure, 18th c. (p.123)
E. Sheesh Gumbad, late 15th – early 16th c. (p.125)
F. Bara Gumbad, late 15th c. (p.124-125)
G. Round tower, ?14th c. (p.123)
H. Remains of grave platform
I. Late Mughal mosque, 18th c. (p.123)
J. Glasshouse, 1968 (p.123)
K. Muhammad Shah's Tomb, died 1445 (p.124)
L. Remains of grave platform
M. Remains of grave platform

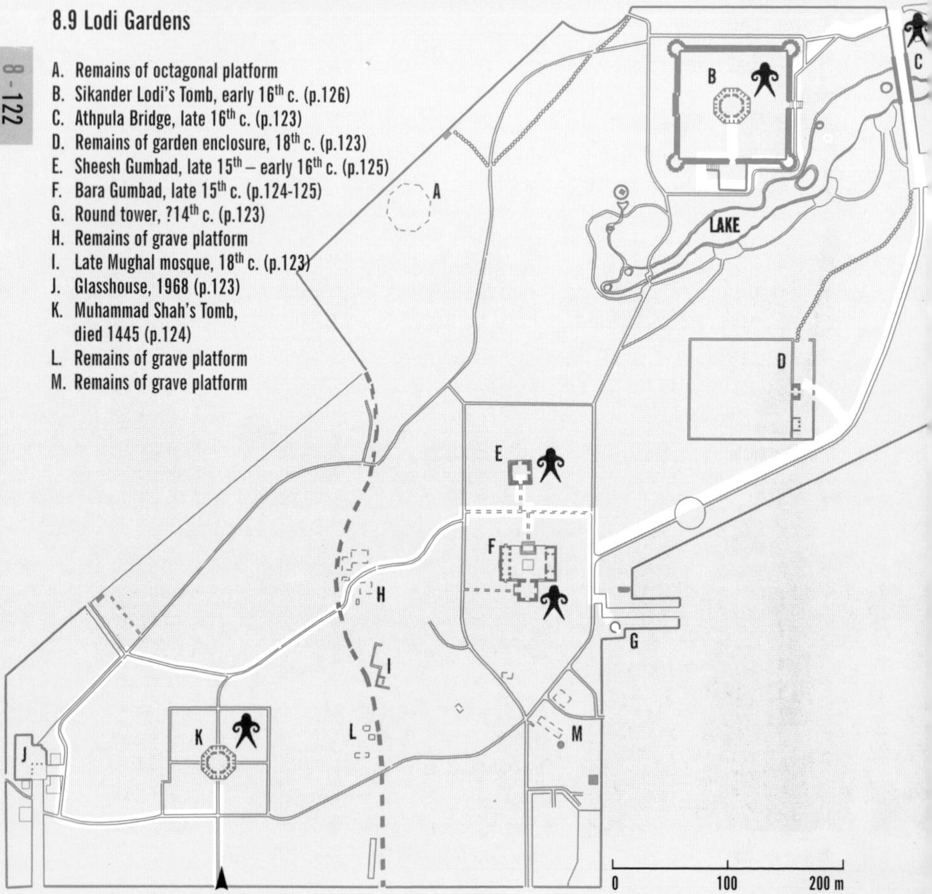

Round Tower

This walk takes in the principal tombs, but it also passes some of the lesser monuments. These will be mentioned in the walk while the main monuments are described below. The walk should start at **Muhammad Shah's Tomb** (over), surrounded by Royal Palms, part of the 1968 garden renewal. From here walk west towards the **Glass House** and its formal entrance path. This was designed in 1968 by Joseph Stein, who built many of the institutional buildings in the area. Turn right here and walk along beside the nursery area until you get to a path leading to another entrance. Turn right and follow a gently curving path through attractive trees, until you cross the cycle path. On the other side, there are a number of very over-grown **grave platforms** and, a little way off to the right, a small **18th century mosque** and burial ground. Continue on the same hard-surface path to join a wide path at a point between the two central monuments, the **Bara Gumbad** on your right and the **Sheesh Gumbad** on your left (see over). After visiting them join the path on the other side. To the right a wide entrance path near the India International Centre (IIC) passes close to a **Round Tower.** This is, perhaps, the oldest building in the gardens. The battered walls, heavy projecting opening and fluted dome suggests Tughlak construction, probably from Firoz Shah's reign. It was probably the corner turret of an enclosure that no longer exists. A path to the north of this exit takes you through a wooded area, passing a group of **Late Mughal buildings** on the left. These were probably part of a walled garden complex, of which only a tiny part of the wall, two buildings, a small mosque and the entrance gate, survive. The uninspired layout of rose beds surround the site of a small brick building that no longer exists, but which might have been a tomb. There appears to have been a forecourt that also contained a *baoli* but it has been filled in.

Garden enclosure mosque

The main path eventually crosses the late 16th century **Athpula** bridge, undoubtedly the most attractive bridge in Delhi, said to have been built during Akbar's reign by a Nawab Bahadur. The *ath* (eight) of the name refers to the number of piers. Walk into the car park and turn left for **Sikander Lodi's Tomb** (p.126). Follow the walls clockwise to the entrance on the south side.

Athpula

MUHAMMAD SHAH'S TOMB (died 1445)

This octagonal tomb is a slightly grander version of the tomb of his uncle, Mubarak Shah, at Kotla Mubarakpur. The small territory that Muhammad Shah inherited was reduced by mismanagement to an even smaller area. Lack of an empire does not seem to have reduced Muhammad Shah's ability to construct a very fine tomb. The only octagonal tomb in Delhi without a walled compound, this perhaps indicating a shortage of funds, but perhaps simply the collapse of a wall that could have surrounded the distinctly raised platform on which it sits.

Muhammad Shah Tomb - elevation and section

In the tomb there is evidence that the *mihrab* was an afterthought; the stonework at the rear is not bonded into the structure. It also appears that *jalis* (now gone) were introduced into the remaining openings (apart from the south entrance) post-construction, since decorative features were chiselled off to accommodate them. The 16-sided drum has particularly intricate niches and four offset openings for light. The opening that most nearly faces west is especially elaborate on the inside, and is at the top of the stairs to the roof.

BARA GUMBAD (late 15th century)

This is a group of three buildings consisting of the large domed Gumbad itself, the most conspicuous building in the gardens, along with a mosque and a residential pavilion. In the raised courtyard between them there is a mound of rubble; in the past there were clear signs that this had been a grave platform. The history of these buildings is, like most others, a mystery. It is dimly illuminated by an inscription inside the mosque that states 'this noble edifice was erected by ...Mughal Abu Amjad... the defunct of happy memory, in the building of the jami masjid... during the reign of the emperor of emperors, the king of the inhabited fourth part of the globe, ... Sikander Shah, son of Bahlol Shah, the emperor... on the first of Rabia 1 of the year 900 [30th November 1494].' The definite date for the mosque does not help us with the other buildings, which are stylistically very different.

An unanswered question is exactly what was the domed building? In many respects it

Bara Gumbad - elevation and section

is similar to the gateways to great mosques, such as the Alai Darwaza at the Qutb Minar or the entrance to Firoz Shah's mosque in Firoz Shah Kotla. Furthermore, no evidence of a burial below the building has been found. Certainly, the lack of a *mihrab* makes it less likely that it was built as a tomb, although there are instances of tombs at this date without them. But, if it was a gateway, what did it lead to? Not, presumably, the diminutive and probably later mosque at its feet.

Bara Gumbad Mosque

The **Bara Gumbad** is built entirely from dressed stone, with no sign of plasterwork. In the façade great use is made of different coloured stone, setting off the delicious creamy grey colour of the local stone. Inside, the design is what would be expected, except that again the interior is finished in dressed stone rather than being plastered. Satisfactorily, four niches are open in the drum and positioned over the four entrances, an uncommon feature at this time. Decorative detail was used as sparingly on the interior of this tomb as on the outside, but one charming and unusual feature is the row of tiny niches at the base of the squinch arches.

...sed plaster decoration in mosque

The connection between the Bara Gumbad and the two adjoining rubble-built buildings is uncertain, especially as the plinths they sit on were not built together. The **mosque** is glorious, almost baroque in its design, in that some of the ordinary conventions have been altered in subtle ways. For instance, the common layout of a five-bay mosque emphasises the middle and end bays, while here the three central bays are dominant. Inside, there is a riot of incised plasterwork where the few plain surfaces only serve to enhance the splendour of the rest. The amount of decoration in the central chamber is possibly too much, with two rows of niches and several calligraphic bands. The rather crude painted decorations on the domed ceiling appear to be a later addition.

Pavilion interior

Opposite, the **pavilion** has slightly more in common with the Gumbad stylistically. It is built from the same dressed stone and the simple proportions of the arches are similar, with red sandstone spandrels on the façade. The façade bears a slight resemblance to the mosque, in that the three middle entrances are wider than the end ones. Inside there are three main chambers linked together by narrow bays between them. Doors at either end of this long space lead into distinctly domestic rooms, with shelving inside the large wall niches. The ceilings are fluted. It is likely that this served as residential accommodation for mosque attendants.

SHEESH GUMBAD (late 15th – early 16th century)

This tomb is noticeably out of alignment with the Bara Gumbad. The name means 'glazed dome', because the dome was once covered in ceramic tiles. There are a few tiles left on the walls, especially above the main entrance arch, where two rows of tiles once framed a series of decorated ones, of which only a few remain. Either side of the *pishtaqs*, it appears that the masonry below the string-course was designed to be seen, while above it the work is inferior and traces of plasterwork show that this part was probably plastered. The exterior of the Sheesh Gumbad is very attractive, a more cheerful version of the Bara Gumbad, but the interior is a sad disappointment because of its poor condition: the walls are so streaked with bird droppings that it is difficult to focus on the architecture.

Sheesh Gumbad

SIKANDER LODI'S TOMB (early 16th century)

It is interesting that Sikander Lodi chose to be buried in Delhi rather than Agra - it shows that Delhi was still regarded as an important place dynastically. Sikander Lodi was a good administrator and delegated power well to his fellow Afghans. He and his nobles built a great many mosques.

The south entrance to Sikander Lodi's tomb is from a platform that appears to have

Wall Mosque

been an earlier construction, perhaps rather like the tomb of Khwajah Sara Basti Khan (Defence Colony). The peaceful garden enclosure includes a wall mosque on the west side. The tomb itself is similar to Muhammad Shah's tomb, the most noticeable difference being the lack of *chatris* on the roof. It is likely that these were planned (or were removed) because the windows in the dome drum are still offset, as if to avoid external *chatris*. Another difference is that there is greater disparity in width between the entrance arches, barely detectable in earlier tombs. The interior, likewise, is similar. *Jalis* appear to have been removed from all the doorways apart from the already open south entrance. Curiously, the underside of the northern entrance arch is particularly ornately decorated, suggesting that this was also

Sikander Lodi's Tomb

an entrance. Stonework now closes the western doorway, implying there was never a *mihrab*; perhaps the view through to the wall mosque was sufficient. The greatest difference in the interior of this tomb is the use of patterned tiles around the doors and niches.

Sikander Lodi is considered an almost ideal monarch: handsome, brave, charitable and just. He administered Delhi when his father Bahlol Lodi went campaigning, and the city remained important to him, even after he had transferred the capital to Agra for strategic reasons. During his 29-year reign he hugely expanded the sultanate and administered his lands in an exemplary fashion. His main defect was considered to be bigotry, unusual repression of Hindus and incitement to conversions, even though he himself indulged in drink and enjoyed music. However, it seems that much of the repression was politically rather than religiously motivated and was only remarked upon because of the extreme liberalism prevailing at that time. What was not so much remarked upon was his ruthlessness in military campaigns, a more or less constant feature of his life. In 1499, in fact, in a campaign in Baghelkhand (northeast MP) he so devastated the land that he 'blotted out all traces of cultivation' and had to withdraw because of lack of provisions. He faced a similar problem in his unsuccessful sieges of Gwalior.

Sikander Lodi's Tomb

Later Tombs and Mosques

After the great spate of building in the 15th and 16th centuries in the South Delhi area the pace of construction of tombs diminished somewhat during the early Mughal era, although we know of many tombs and grave enclosures that were constructed near the tombs of Nizamuddin and Qutb Sahib. There was a revival of building during the reigns of the later Mughals and there are many buildings in South Delhi from this period, some well known, others not. The fashion for tomb building seems to have abated somewhat, with important people often choosing to be buried under the sky, in accordance with Koranic instruction.

The landscape of South Delhi during the 18th century can be supposed to have been dotted with tombs, mosques and villages, many of the latter inside walls, newly built or inside pre-existing tomb enclosures. Many other walled enclosures contained *serais* and gardens.

ALIGANJ (mainly 18th century)

This neglected area was once part of the estate of the Awadh Nawabs (Safdarjang's family) who were Shias. It contains a number of buildings based around the Dargah of Shahi Mardan, that contains a relic of Ali, the Prophet's son-in-law. This is a very important place for the Shia community; the Muharram Tazia processions (commemorating the death of the Prophet's grandsons at Karbala) end here at the **Karbala**, a large walled enclosure built at the end of the 18th century. The west end of the Karbala is now used as a plant nursery (immediately to the south of Jor Bagh). In the centre of the wild area there is an older tomb, built in 1726-27 for one **Mah Khanam**, whose epitaph reads: 'the sun of the zodiac of chastity, by heaven's decree hid her face under the cloud of compassion, and turned her heart towards God'. There is a rectangular entrance pavilion that gives access to steps down to the burial chamber, underneath the platform behind it. This is an unusual arrangement. Outside the Karbala, on the east side, is a **wall mosque**.

South of this there appears to have been a late Mughal royal garden, traces of which are described in the 1916 ASI listing. The only remaining building now is in an open space on the left of the access road to the Dargah, where there is a half buried **brickwork pavilion**, which appears to have been quite an ornate open-sided building.

At the end of the access road is the **Dargah of Shahi Mardan**, which houses a 'footprint' of Ali. An inscription over the north entrance says that the complex was built by Qudsia Begum (who was a Shia and widow of Muhammad Shah) and Nawab Jawid Khan in 1750-51. All the buildings have been altered quite radically so the place is of more historic than architectural interest. The Dargah was once surrounded by massive enclosure walls but these have now vanished and the area has been considerably encroached upon. The north gate to the *dargah* is known as the **Naqqar Khana**. Outside, on its left there are the remains of a late Mughal building, probably another gateway, inside which visitors to the *dargah* were accommodated. Beyond the Naqqar Khana turn right for the **Qadam Sharif** itself (not to be confused with the Qadam Sharif built by Firoz Shah – see Chapter 7), which

Qadam Sharif and Bibi ka Rauza

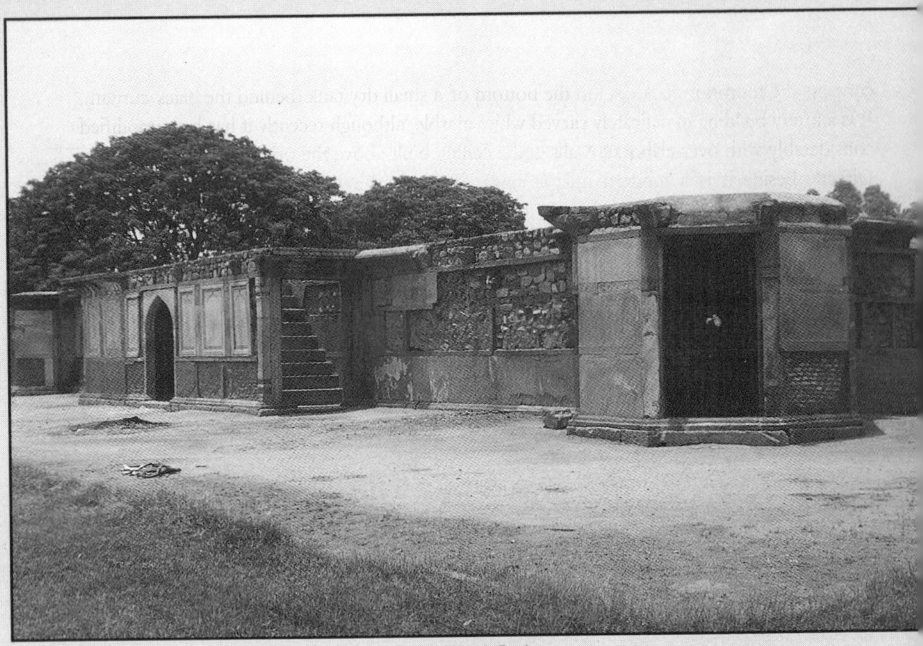

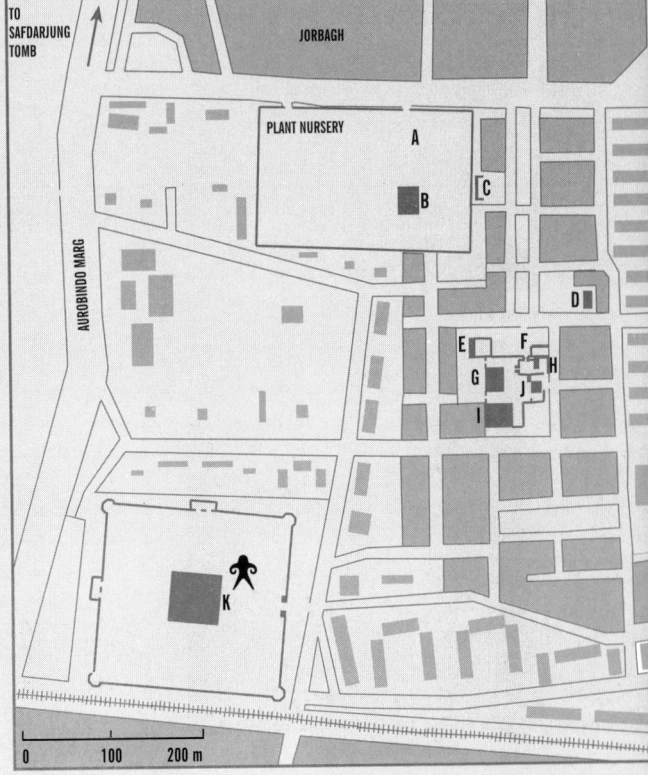

Najaf Khan's Tomb

8.10 Aliganj, mainly 18th c.

A. Karbala
B. Mah Khanam's Tomb
C. Wall mosque
D. Brickwork pavilion
E. Mosque
F. Naqqar Khana
G. Qadam Sharif & Bibi ka Rauza
H. Lal Masjid
I. Imambara
J. Tomb of Arif Ali Shah
K. Najaf Khan's Tomb

TO SAFDARJUNG TOMB
JORBAGH
PLANT NURSERY
A
B
C
D
E
F
G
H
I
J
K
AUROBINDO MARG
0
100
200 m

contains the footprint of Ali, set in the bottom of a small dry tank (behind the black curtain). It is a pretty building in delicately carved white marble, although recently it has been modified considerably with over-elaborate walls and a ceiling built above the original screen enclosure. Directly beside it is a modern mirror image building, the **Bibi ka Rauza,** an honorary mausoleum for Fatima, the wife of Ali (and the Prophet's daughter). Instead of the footprint there is a grindstone. No men are allowed inside out of respect for the laws of *purdah*. Beyond the Bibi ka Rauza is a **small mosque**, typical of its late-Mughal foundation. Just south of the Qadam Sharif is the **Imambara**, a fairly large hall with double Shahjahani columns supporting the roof. It was built in 1808-09 but has been extensively restored. Conspicuous from the Imambara is the **Tomb of Arif Ali Shah,** a child saint who died when he was only twelve. The tomb has been covered all over, inside and out, with bathroom tiles. A **small mosque** is in the corner of the compound but is no longer used. North of this compound is the **Lal Masjid**, another small late Mughal mosque.

Najaf Khan's Tomb

From the south side of the Aliganj Dargah walk west, out of the densely built up area around it into an area more typical of this neighbourhood, with individual blocks of flats and older, low-density government housing. Turn left on a wide street, which will bring you to the gate of **Najaf Khan's tomb** (1782). He was a powerful minister during the decline of the Mughal empire and controlled large parts of North India. He built a mansion and township at Najafgarh. The tomb is in a big garden and is a large building, consisting of nothing but a square tomb platform with octagonal projections at the corners. There is a low platform on the roof that has two cenotaphs, one each above the two chambers below, which are lit through openings in the side of the platform. It is possible that a tomb like Safdarjang's was planned but it would have been incompatible with the shape of this upper platform. The burial chambers contain several finely carved marble gravestones.

Safdarjang's Tomb

Safdarjang's Tomb garden

The tomb enclosure backs onto Aurobindo Marg. On the other side of this arterial road, some distance to the north, is **Safdarjang's Tomb** (1753). This enormous and magnificent tomb, inside an equally vast garden, has been considered inferior to Humayun's Tomb: for the purist European architectural historians of the early 20th century it was considered a debased and mannered affair, although early travellers admired it greatly, probably painting it more frequently than Humayun's Tomb (though this may have been more because it was conveniently situated on the well-worn tourist road from the Civil Lines to the Qutb).

The entrance is through a double storey pavilion with an arcaded veranda above it. Its façade is quite lavishly decorated, the best-preserved part being the painted net-vaulting under the main entrance arch. To the right of the entrance is a handsome mosque, unfortunately inaccessible to visitors.

The tomb is constructed from red sandstone and white marble, some of which is supposed to have been taken from Khan-i-Khanan's Tomb, near Nizamuddin. The building is similar in layout to Humayun's Tomb, with a central tomb chamber surrounded by two storeys of subsidiary rooms. The façade is different, as the subsidiary rooms dominate the elevation, each one looking out through ornate windows onto the garden. Finely detailed circular columns frame each façade, with elegant *chatris* at roof level. The central bay has a parapet screen very like those at the Red Fort and the Jami Masjid. The interior of the tomb is more engaging than Humayun's because of the well preserved and exuberant plaster decoration that covers every surface.

Safdarjang's Tomb - corner turret

Safdarjang was the nephew of Sa'adat Khan, Nawab of Awadh. He inherited the title in 1739 but continued to live partly in Delhi, where he became prime minister to Ahmad Shah and lived in half of the vast mansion of Shah Jahan's eldest son (see Chapter 11). He served under Muhammad Shah, deserting his military command just before the battle with Ahmad Shah Abdali in 1753. He died the following year and his body was brought to Delhi to be interred.

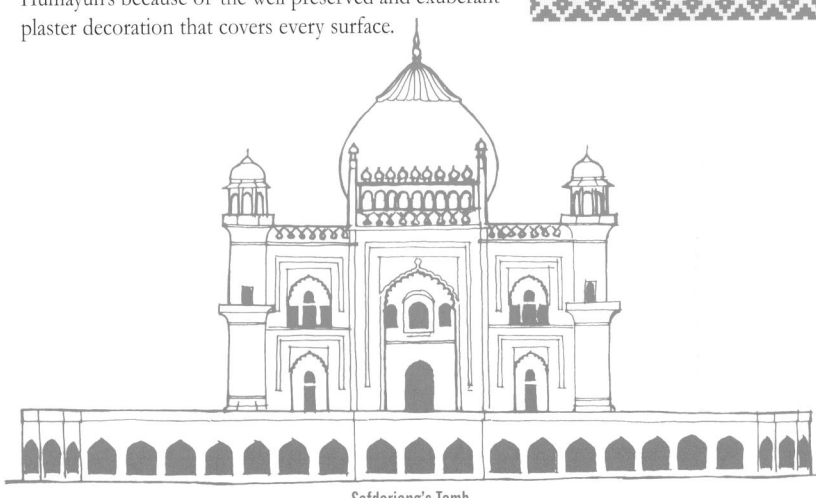

Safdarjang's Tomb

GOLF CLUB TOMBS
Non-members wll need permission to visit the tombs.

The finest of these can be glimpsed from the roads
outside the club walls and are Mughal, although there is
one older one. Visible from the Clubhouse is the **Tomb of
Sayyid Abid** (1626). Sayyid Abid was a companion of one
of Jahangir's courtiers.

Sayyid Abid Tomb

Lal Bangla Tomb

Just beyond the Clubhouse is a fine late Mughal
gateway, which partly encloses the swimming pool.
It was originally the entrance to a large enclosure
containing three tombs that was known collectively as
Lal Bangla (1779). The **gateway façade** is quite well
preserved, with a central entrance pavilion surmounted

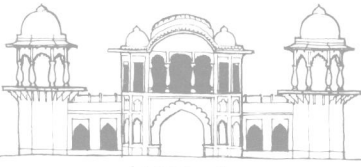

Lal Bangla gateway

by a *bangla* roof. Either side of this the corners of the enclosure are
emphasised with substantial octagonal pavilions with domed *chatris*. One
of the tombs, a small octagonal affair that might actually be a little earlier
in date than the bigger tombs, is inside the pool enclosure and the other
two tombs stand right beside the entrance to the club and can be seen
quite well from the flyover. These are
attractive buildings. In layout they
follow the pattern of larger tombs,
with rooms around a central chamber. The domes appear
relatively small as a result, especially as they are not
surrounded by anything else such as *chatris*. Tradition has it
that one of those buried here was Lal Kunwar, the dazzling
concubine, later Empress, of Jahandar Shah.

Barah Khamba

Centrally placed in the south of the course is the
Barah Khamba. This tomb dates from the Tughlak
period. The cruciform plan is most unusual. It has a central
bay with four vaulted bays attached on each side (the
eastern one has fallen and the others are in a precarious
condition), supported on solid monolithic columns.

Up the western edge of the course are the two finest
tombs, first the serene **Mughal Tomb** visible from

Tomb interior

Barah Khamba

Lal Bangla gateway

18th c. Mughal tomb

Mir Taqi's tomb

Archbishop Makarios Marg. It is a tomb with a highly satisfying Baghdad octagon plan and an equally charming interior. North of this is a deliciously baroque **18th century Tomb.** Here the corners are emphasised by square 'towers' with rather chunky little *chatris* above them. The faces of the towers are ornamented with zig-zag patterns in plaster and the underside of the arches over the doors are decorated with net-vaulting, picked out in red and cream paint. This is repeated on the interior dome, while below it the arches, and particularly the arched pediments over the doors, are decorated with lush foliation. In the northern part of the course are a **Late Mughal mosque,** not dissimilar to the one in the Lodi Gardens, and **Mir Taqi's tomb,** a small Baghdad Octagon tomb. It is not known who Mir Taqi was.

18th c. tomb interior

ELSEWHERE
Also in South Delhi are two sites of some interest.

Lalit Kala Academy Studios (18th century)
This is a little known ruined garden at Garhi (East of Kailash), marked as Artists Studio on the Eicher map.

These studios, the first purpose-built ones in Delhi, were built by the DDA in 1976 inside the walls of a ruined Mughal garden, a rare example of a thoughtful reuse of an old building. Artists' studios were built along the wall either side of the gate and perhaps the main point of a visit is to see these and the newer residential rooms in a pleasant curving block on the right. Of the original garden the gateway survives, along with part of the central garden pavilion (not, unfortunately, conserved).

Lalit Kala gateway

Kalkaji (1764)
This is a very ancient site but the temple is supposed to have been entirely rebuilt in 1764 and renovated and altered much since then. Amidst the revolting squalor of the temple's surroundings there are some late Mughal buildings, built at various times to serve the priests and visitors to the temple.

The mythology attached to the site is that Kali Devi was born from the eyebrows of the Goddess Parvati's daughter, Kushki Devi, who was created to fight thousand of giants. Kali Devi drank the blood that poured from their wounds and between them the goddesses achieved victory. About 5,000 years ago Kali Devi is supposed to have settled here.

Kalkaji Temple

PURANA QILA

*A grey curtain of stone, immensely thick, with a
cavernous old hall, a yawning gateway, lead into
the long deserted market place and to a network
of small dim rooms beneath the inner walls*

Norah Rowan Hamilton, 1915

Early Mughals and Sher Shah

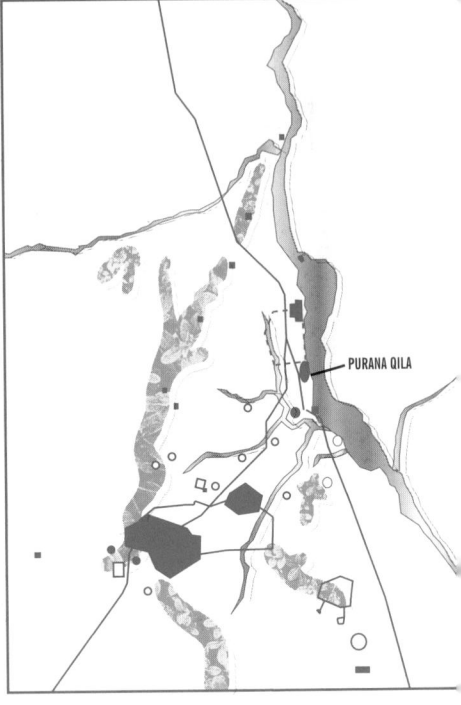

PURANA QILA

As we have seen, by the beginning of the 16th century India was fragmented into several independent states or sultanates. The Delhi Sultanate had regained some power but Sultan Ibrahim Lodi's autocratic behaviour had resulted in the invitation from one of his noblemen to the Kabul-based Babur to invade.

Babur's is an amazing story, which he told himself in Turkic and which illustrates well the extraordinary fluidity with which kingdoms came and went in Central Asia. Babur was descended from both Genghis Khan (died 1227) and Timur (Tamburlaine). It is difficult to be clear about the remoter origins of the Central Asian clans to which Babur's family belonged but, to be brief, Genghis Khan was the globally successful Mongol warrior whose origins were in present day Mongolia. By the time of his death Genghis Khan controlled a vast empire extending from China into northeast Persia. His descendants built on his successes: famously, the Mongol hordes caused great alarm when they reached eastern Europe in the mid-13th century. Timur was the successful Turko-Mongol leader who took Delhi in 1398.

Babur was well aware of his ancestry and had ambitions beyond the small princedom of Ferghana (now at the eastern end of Uzbekistan) which he inherited from his father in 1484 when only eleven years old. He failed to win Timur's old capital Samarkand but captured and held Kabul. After his third expulsion from Samarkand Babur turned his eyes in the other direction, to India. He felt he had a claim to the country because of Timur's success in India, even though Timur himself had spent so little time there. The nominally tributary state had soon become independent of Timurid authority, but nonetheless Babur claimed that he was entitled to his ancestor's conquered lands. His first move was to send the Delhi Sultan, Ibrahim Lodi, a goshawk and ask for 'the country which from old had depended on the Turks'. Not surprisingly, he was rebuffed. He then set about acquiring guns and artillerymen, still a novelty in those days as far as north India was concerned. This was the one crucial advantage that he would have over the Sultan's forces because, although guns were known along the west coast of India, they had not penetrated into the north. He finally marched into India at the end of 1525.

After defeating Ibrahim Lodi at Panipat Babur advanced on Delhi and had the Friday Prayers read in his own name, as Timur had done. During the necessary consolidation of his empire Babur took the forts at Chanderi and Gwalior and was struck by the architecture at both places. Because it had recently been the Lodi capital Babur stayed in Agra rather than Delhi. However, Babur and his men, who originally came from Kabul and similar places,

Purana Qila and boating lake, created from the former moat

found the summer climate in North India disagreeable and amenities like gardens sadly lacking. Babur died in 1530 and the throne was inherited by his son, Humayun, who lost it after a ten year reign to a powerful Afghan nobleman, Sher Shah Suri.

After his victory over Humayun (p.146) Sher Shah settled down to create a new order and he should have become the first of a glittering new dynasty that might have achieved all that the Mughals did. He was certainly talented, leaving, for instance, an administrative system by which every subsequent government organisation seems to have been foreshadowed. During a short reign, he managed to achieve an astonishing amount in the way of administrative reform as well as building numerous roads (including extensive repairs and improvements to the Grand Trunk Road from Dhaka to Lahore), well-appointed *serais* and several forts, mosques and tombs. He established a highly effective police system, enabling travellers, according to the historian Abbas, to sleep anywhere with 'minds at ease and free from care, as if in their own house'. Not surprisingly there were also building projects: he planned more than he actually achieved during his short reign, but what he did complete is impressive. His most magnificent building is in Bihar, from where he came: his own vast tomb in a huge tank at Sasaram. In Delhi it appears that he either completed or rebuilt the walls of Humayun's new city Dinpanah, renaming the citadel Shergarh and, inside it, built the wonderful Qila-i-Kohna Masjid. Sher Shah Suri died after a reign of only five years and was succeeded by his son Salim Shah, builder of the Salimgarh Fort.

Purana Qila ☆

Considering that Sher Shah Suri was in power for a mere five years (1540-45), before passing on the throne to his less effectual son, the legacy left by him is astonishing, both administrative and physical. In Delhi his biggest project was the fort or citadel, now known as the Purana Qila, which was built beside his new city. This has been known as Delhi Sher Shahi, but of it there remain only two gates, one outside the Purana Qila and the other in the centre of Bahadur Shah Zafar Marg, opposite Firoz Shah Kotla. However, while these gates are identified with his reign, it is not entirely clear how much of the Purana Qila, was built by Sher Shah and how much had already been constructed by Humayun (1530-40),

North Gate of Purana Qila

who had started to build his Dinpanah (asylum of faith) on the same riverside site. It is thought, however, that the Qila-i-Kohna Masjid was definitely built by Sher Shah.

The site was the location of a village called Indrapat, for which reason it is associated with Indraprastha of the *Mahabarata* (p.28). However, the concrete evidence tells us that, apart from a village or two, Humayun would

Qila-i-Kohna Masjid

have considered that he was developing a virgin site. Work started in 1533 after the necessary astronomical calculations and, according to Khond Amir, Humayun's historian, it was far advanced after only ten months, with walls, bastions, ramparts and gates nearly finished. We have no further information about Dinpanah and do not know whether Sher Shah's citadel was one and the same thing or whether it was newly built. The historian who chronicled the life of Sher Shah's son, Salim Shah Suri, maintains that Salim ordered walls to be built around 'the fort of Humayun' after completion of Salimgarh (further up river, opposite the Red Fort). On the other hand Sher Shah's own

South Gate from the zoo

historian seems to imply that he (Sher Shah) ordered the building of the Governor's fort (Purana Qila) and the wall around the whole city, which was not finished at the time of his death. Perhaps Salim's project was only to complete the city walls, his father having augmented (or finished) Humayun's citadel walls. Having said that, it has to be pointed out that there is absolutely no evidence of any city walls apart from two gateways (p. 142,144).

Although we cannot be sure of the builder, we know that the walls were built in the mid-16th century. In many ways the ruins of the Purana Qila are the most impressive in Delhi, combining as they do considerable height, some superb architecture (the three gates) and a pleasant setting. There are a few places where the wall is complete enough for us to see how it once looked: not dissimilar to the walls of Siri, although higher and without the pronounced batter. The construction was in rubble masonry with two rows of arrow / gun slits and two stringcourses at the top of the wall. Above them are rubble masonry battlements. The effect, on the whole, must have been forbidding, although evidence in one or two places of a projecting balcony supported by heavily ornamented corbels, as well as the three magnificent gateways, hint at a less military ambience.

Inside the fort there is an eclectic mixture of buildings: a *baoli*, the mosque, the Sher Mandal, and a Mughal-era bathhouse. At the beginning of the 20th century 1,900 people lived inside the fort, mainly in village houses at the south end, but also in the rooms built into the walls. They were moved out in 1913 (with compensation) and the fort was turned into the archaeological site we see today, although it briefly served as a sanctuary for refugees during the turmoil of Partition.

The **Northern Gate** of the Purana Qila can be seen from the outside by walking around the boating lake. It is a handsome structure, massively tall, with the main decorative architectural features happening at and above the first floor level, where there is a higher opening that gives every appearance of being an actual gateway. While the ground level entrance is through a humble quartzite arch, this one is framed in red sandstone; stone hinge brackets indicate that doors once closed this opening. A clutch of three *chatris* adorn the roof.

Purana Qila walls

This is the most complete gateway and its interior can be seen (with difficulty) from inside the fort. There is access to one of the rooms inside the bastion, while the first floor ceilings can be seen from a distance. The impression that the main entrance was at first floor level is reinforced here, where the floor aligns with the ground level inside the fort and the ceilings are decorated with incised plaster and inlaid roundels. Inside the lower gateway the ceilings were decorated in a very different style from the floor above, with simple arch netting as found in buildings from Akbar's reign. The two gateways, one above the other, are baffling, especially as the upper one is so very far above the level of the ground outside. Yet it is impossible not to entertain the notion that they were both designed as entrance gates and that there must have been a bridge to the higher gate that crossed the moat, while perhaps the lower gate gave access to the water.

North Gate interior

9 - 137

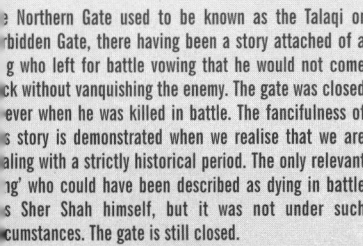

e Northern Gate used to be known as the Talaqi or rbidden Gate, there having been a story attached of a g who left for battle vowing that he would not come ck without vanquishing the enemy. The gate was closed ever when he was killed in battle. The fancifulness of s story is demonstrated when we realise that we are aling with a strictly historical period. The only relevant ng' who could have been described as dying in battle s Sher Shah himself, but it was not under such cumstances. The gate is still closed.

North Gate

South Gate

South Gate interior

To see the exterior of the **Southern Gate** it is necessary to go into the **Delhi Zoo** (inside which there is also the well-preserved Jahangiri Kos Minar, a badly-preserved Tughlak twelve-pillared pavilion and a ruined Mughal tomb built mainly in brick). It is quite like the Northern Gate and exactly the same puzzle attaches to this gate, as there are entrances at two levels. It has two *chatris* on the roof. The interior of the gateway is too ruined for us to be able to compare it with the others. The **Western Gate** gives access to the fort but it is the least impressive of the three. There is the same general arrangement, with projecting balconies but, instead of marble panels above the main arch, there are three windows to light a vaulted room behind it, the remains of which can be seen from the back.

The interior of the fort is mostly open, with lawns and trees. There are some ASI offices in the northern part of the fort but most of the monuments are in the south. The most prominent building is the **Qila-i-Kohna Masjid**, directly ahead as you enter. For many people this ranks as the finest mosque in Delhi and is the largest and most elaborate of the Lodi-style five-bay mosques. These have many common features and the Qila-i-Kohna Masjid exemplifies most of them (p.140-141).

Before you reach the mosque you will pass the *Baoli*. It is deep, with recessed arches built into the walls on the way down. At the back is a vertical well for drawing water, now used for watering the lawns. Beyond the mosque to the north it is possible to explore the curious remains of **underground chambers** that partly form the foundations of the mosque and its courtyard. There are a series of

South Gate

Qila-i-Kohna Masjid

Rooms under wall

Underground chamber

chambers, probably once linked to the double arcade provided within the walls themselves, all of which were once plastered, making it likely that they served as residential accommodation of some sort. From here you can walk up to see the interior of the Northern Gate.

South of the Qila-i-Kohna Masjid is the **Sher Mandal**. This building has very little, stylistically, to do with the very late flowering of Sultanate architecture as exemplified by the mosque but, instead, seems very Mughal in its close resemblance to Persian pleasure pavilions. The building is clearly domestic, or at least not religious or military, making it one of the earliest such structures in Delhi. Despite its Mughal appearance it is thought that it was originally built by Sher Shah as part of his palace, and renovated by Humayun to house his library and make a good astronomical observatory.

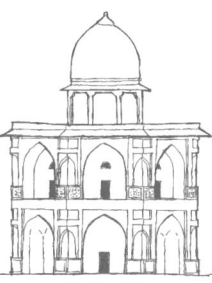

Sher Mandal

Sher Mandal from Hammam

The Sher Mandal is an octagonal building, with two layers of deeply recessed arches on each face and an octagonal *chatri* on the roof. The Mughal appearance comes from the lightness of the detailing: compare, for instance, the simple arches with the much heavier double arches of the mosque. The simplicity results from the reversion to a more Persian style, effectively using small *iwans*. The decorative detail, although in places similar to that of the mosque, is also very discreet. An unusual feature is the way that the arched niches and panels between the *iwans* turn the corners, giving a continuity at each corner that would be difficult to achieve in any other way, with so little space between each *iwan*.

Beyond the Sher Mandal the ground drops quite steeply and, depending on the covering of vegetation, it is possible to see the remains of the **archaeological excavations** that took place from 1954: the ancient brickwork from modest houses is exposed (p.28). In front is a low brick building, a bathhouse or **Hammam**,

It is thought that it was in Sher Shah Mandal that Humayun met with his fatal accident, when he answered the call to prayer too hastily, and fell headlong down the awkward stairs. The generally graceless quality of most Indian staircases has been a matter for comment; Ebba Koch (the Mughal art history pundit of our era) observes that they were seen by Mughal architects merely as a necessary evil. Perhaps in this case they can be praised for having brought to an end the obscurantist reign of Humayun, and ushering in the enlightenment of Akbar.

Qila-i-Kohna Masjid

The central bay is domed. The build-up to the dome is an elaborate version of the typical squinch arched progression. The sixteen-sided drum niches are decorated with ceramic tiles and the dome itself still shows signs of intricate painting on the stonework itself.

The delicate carvings in the interior are all in stone, a feature that sets this mosque apart from others, where most of the fine detail is in incised plaster.

Looking at the entire façade it can be seen that the entrance arches increase in size towards the centre, but so subtly that it is barely noticeable.

The façade is a scintillating combination of all the styles we are already acquainted with but with far more elaborate surface decoration than seen elsewhere up to this date. A new architectural development, however, are the deeply recessed doorways inside the three central arches. In a sense this a reversion to the iwan, seen in earlier buildings such as the Begumpur mosque, except that the walls and ceiling between the two planes are articulated differently: this could not quite be read as a vaulted but shallow open hall.

Mosque central entrance

Main Mihrab

Mosque detail

The intermediate bays are slightly smaller in plan than the central one; they have very shallow domed ceilings under a flat roof supported by an exceptionally fine set of trabeate squinches, with the top row of niches continuing round to form a sixteen-sided drum.

The elaborate stepping back and forward of the façade, and the spacing of the doorways gives rise to differently shaped chambers inside and, therefore different ceiling treatments. The end bays are rectangular, so half domes and shallow arches support the small dome over the centre of the space.

The rear facade features engaged columns either side of the central projecting bay, a small balcony, an elaborate string course, and open corner turrets.

A doorway on both sides of the prayer hall is surmounted by a projecting balcony.

Mosque interior

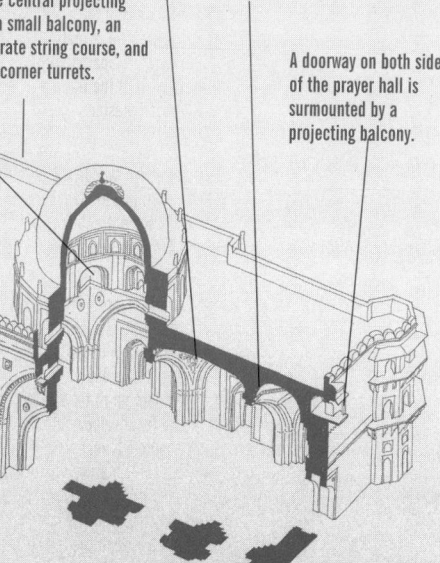

Mosque from side

which probably dates from the late 16th century. Steps lead down to a plastered room with ornamental wall niches and a steep cascade down where water would have trickled. The ridges in the face to give it the appearance of a mountain stream are still visible in places. On the roof it is possible to speculate (but difficult to guess with any confidence) about the way the water system worked. From the South Gate there is a good view towards Humayun's Tomb.

On leaving the fort it is well worth visiting the buildings opposite it, on the other side of the Mathura Road. There is a Mughal-era mosque as well as a gateway that marked the southern entrance to the city known as Delhi Sher Shahi. The northern gateway is near Firoz Shah Kotla and is known as the **Khuni Darwaza** (bloody gate, so called because it was here that Lieutenant Hodson shot the Mughal princes while taking them back to Shahjahanabad in 1857 (p.144). Rather like

Lal Darwaza

Firozabad, Delhi Sher Shahi is a much less defined place than earlier or later cities. Some early descriptions suggest that it extended from Firozabad (presumably the Kotla) to Kilokri, but this latter boundary is contradicted by the position of what appears to be the southern gate, the magnificent gateway opposite the Purana Qila, known as the Lal Darwaza.

The **Lal Darwaza** is approached along a wide street with rows of ruined shops on either side of the road. The outer face is a pretty combination of dressed quartzite and red sandstone, with highlights of white marble. Most of the details are conventional, but there is one exceptional piece of decoration: either side of the relieving arch there are three red sandstone sculpted panels, framed by quartzite borders. Above them yellow sandstone arches intersect, with the spaces between them filled with ceramic tile patterns. Above these were projecting balconies, which have collapsed. The interior face of the gate is now totally ruined but luckily there is a superb 19th century watercolour that reveals its original appearance. If anything, the interior seems to have been even finer than the exterior, with first floor arcaded rooms on each side of the gate looking down onto what would have been the city.

Lal Darwaza

One question that immediately presents itself is: what was the relationship between this gate and the Purana Qila? It would appear that any wall that extended from the eastern bastion might have linked up with the northern end of the fort, but it could equally have missed it altogether and would, anyway, have had to span the moat. This, and the fact that there is not much evidence for supposing that these city gates were connected to a wall, means that we need not expect an actual physical connection between the two buildings; they obviously served very different purposes. Cunningham, an enthusiastic 19th century amateur archaeologist and first head of the ASI, speculated that the real city walls ran around a much larger area than is implied by these two gates, the total length of the walls adding up to nine miles. However, there was little enough archaeological

Ruins behind Lal Darwaza

evidence to help him then; there is even less to go on now. Two twelve-pillared tombs inside the National Stadium enclosure, that would have stood just to the south of the city, indicate, perhaps, that this was not a heavily inhabited area, especially if they were built, as claimed, contemporarily.

Given the highly decorative and non-defensive nature of this gateway, it does not preclude the city from having extended southwards, perhaps as an uncongested suburb. Evidence of a quite heavily built-up urban area inside the gate lies just behind it: the remains of several **ruined houses**, two of which are sufficiently complete to enable us to see their layout (we have to make an assumption that these buildings date from this period, but it seems likely). They seem to have backed onto each other, each containing a central courtyard surrounded by rooms of various sizes. In some of these rooms the walls were lined with three rows of deep niches. There is a basement beneath each building. In places, it is easy to see where the good facing stone has been ripped away from the rubble interior, presumably for building purposes elsewhere, most likely in Shahjahanabad.

Khairul Manazil Gate

It is this quarrying of old houses that probably accounts for the lack of remains of domestic buildings in any of the ancient cities.

Finally, it is worth walking into the adjacent ruin to see the **Khairul Manazil** (1561). This mosque, whose name means 'the most auspicious of houses', lies just in front of the Lal Darwaza and was constructed only a few years later, with an attached *madrasa* built around a courtyard. The complex was built in 1561-62 by Maham Angah, Akbar's famous wet nurse,

Khairul Manazil courtyard

mother of Adham Khan; these two together played a powerful political role during the early years of Akbar's reign (p.175, 223). The entrance gateway, facing the Purana Qila, is a handsome, typically Mughal building. The façade is mainly in red sandstone and features an entrance doorway that is set right back within a deeply recessed main arch. The

Khairul Manazil elevation

half dome that roofs the niche is supported by corbelled beams that flank a small window above the entrance gate. This type of *iwan* has of course already been noticed at the Sher Mandal and, as we have seen, it is entirely untypical of Sultanate architecture. The mosque itself, however, follows a Sultanate pattern.

The courtyard contains a large central pool and is surrounded on three sides by the *madrasa* buildings, uncharacteristically built on two levels. There were small rooms on the first floor, with access from a narrow open passage, and slightly larger rooms below them.

Khairul Manazil interior

Khairul Manazil Mosque

KHUNI DARWAZA (mid-16th century) 🏃

This is much further away and not worth visiting except at the same time at the Firoz Shah Kotla. The building is plain on the interior, south-facing side, with undecorated rubble masonry walls. The northern face is finer, in dressed quartzite and red sandstone. This is finely carved in places, for example the colonnettes attached to the entrance arch. Like at the Lal Darwaza, there is no evidence of a curtain wall having been attached to this gate; it was probably used to control traffic on the road into the city rather than defensively.

Khuni Darwaza

HUMAYUN'S TOMB
AND NIZAMUDDIN

With the dust of the road still clinging to me I paid a visit to the blessed tomb of his Majesty Jannat-Ashyani [Humayun] and asked for his spiritual help. I gave money with my own hands to the poor and needy.

Emperor Jahangir, 1607

Humayun

I n 1525 the seventeen-year-old Humayun accompanied his father, Babur, when he invaded India, and fought in the decisive battle of Panipat. In 1527 Humayun left Babur's court to go and govern the remote province of Badakhshan, beyond the Hindu Kush. He was not happy to go but the appointment was routine; powerful Mongol and Turkish rulers generally appointed their sons as Governors, the oldest often being sent furthest. While away, Humayun wrote complaining of his lot to his father, who replied sternly, reminding his son of his duty as a king and also criticising his flowery letter-writing style. Humayun provoked his father's wrath again when he returned prematurely, having heard that Babur was ill, but the son's charm

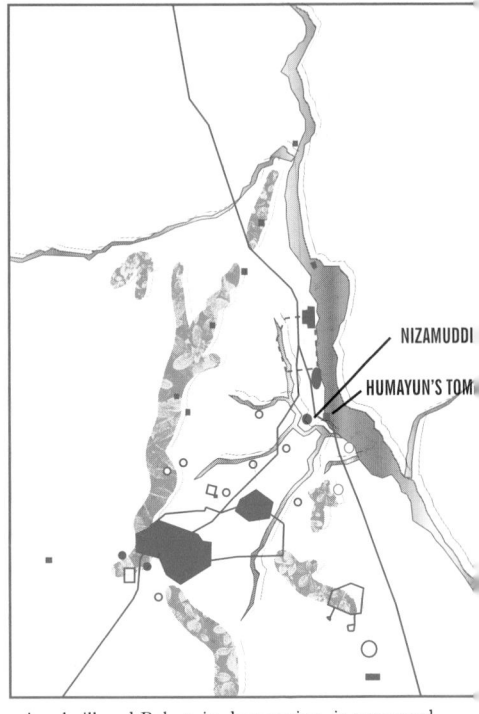

NIZAMUDDI

HUMAYUN'S TOM

won Babur over. Soon Humayun became seriously ill and Babur, in desperation, is supposed to have offered his own life in place of his son's. Humayun recovered and Babur did indeed fall mortally ill, but only after an interval of several months.

Despite some shortcomings Humayun became Emperor in 1530. Unlike Babur, he was hopelessly superstitious, taking astrology very seriously, but he was also charming and had inherited his father's unbloodthirsty nature; Babur had implored him to be affectionate to his three brothers and he was so, possibly to excess when he had tearful reconciliations with them after their numerous acts of treachery. Another defect was love of leisure, which probably helped him lose his Empire when he retreated all too often into luxurious indolence, indulging in wine, opium and poetry instead of pursuing his military campaigns.

Humayun was highly religious and in 1533 he started to build a new city at Delhi, Dinpanah ('Asylum of Faith'–now the Purana Qila), to be a home to all Islamic faiths. However, he was not left in peace to complete the project, being troubled on two fronts, by Sultan Bahadur in Gujarat and from the east by Sher Khan Suri. Over the next few years Humayun struggled to control his two neighbours. Eventually Humayun found himself stuck behind enemy lines in Bengal, after too long an interval of rest and recuperation. Two of his brothers were plotting against him in Agra while Sher Khan stood between him and his capital, calling himself Sher Shah and claiming the Empire. Humayun's army was defeated on the banks of the Ganges and the Emperor barely escaped with his life. Sher Shah followed slowly on Humayun's heels and defeated him finally in 1540. Humayun, with his family and treasure, retreated to Lahore and thence into a fifteen-year exile, at first on the borders of the empire, later in Persia. During the tedious early years of exile the most significant event was his marriage to Hamida who subsequently gave birth to Humayun's first surviving son, Akbar.

In 1544 the exiled Humayun began to prosper after he was welcomed to Persia by the Shah. Among other places, Humayun visited the great Islamic city, Herat, and thoroughly absorbed the culture of the Persian court. When he eventually returned to Hindustan he took two famous painters with him, thus introducing to India the techniques that developed into the exquisite Mughal miniature style. With assistance from the Shah, Humayun began to make inroads into Sher Shah's Empire and his prospects improved further when Salim Shah (Sher Shah's son) died, leaving three rival claimants to the throne in India. The discord created a good opportunity for Humayun to march back under the generalship of Bairam Khan (whose son's huge tomb is on the modern Mathura Road, not far away from Humayun's). Humayun eventually remounted the Delhi throne in 1555.

Barber's Tomb

From then on Humayun's life was easier. He returned to Dinpanah and installed there, along with his painters, the precious library that had accompanied him on his arduous journeys. He also resolved to build upon Sher Shah's excellent administrative system. Unfortunately his life was to be cruelly terminated by a curious accident. According to one account, while on the roof of the Sher Mandal, observing the movement of Venus (his superstitious nature had not left him), he heard the call to prayers. In his haste to observe his religious obligations, he tripped on his robe and fell down the steep steps from the roof and died three days later. Because of his long exile and premature death, Humayun had not embarked on a tomb for himself and it was several years after his death that construction began.

Akbar succeeded to the throne at the age of thirteen and reigned long and successfully, expanding his Empire through conquest, treaty or marriage alliances, one of which was with the daughter of the Hindu Raja of Amber, the wife who gave birth to Jahangir, Akbar's eldest surviving son. Because he preferred Agra

Atgah Khan's Tomb

and his new capital Fatepur Sikri, his reign impinged little on Delhi, although there are some splendid tombs, besides Humayun's, that were built during his reign.

Akbar was brave, intelligent, and intellectually curious, although he could not read. His interest in other religions was a torment to his Muslim clergy and also to those of other faiths who thought, wrongly, that they had him on the path to conversion. Trouble came to Akbar towards the end of his reign when his two younger sons both died from drink, leaving only Jahangir, who rebelled in 1600, setting up his own power base in Allahabad. The ladies of the court brought father and son together again in a reconciliation and, on his deathbed in 1605, Akbar was obliged to acknowledge Jahangir as his successor.

Akbar's distrust of Jahangir was not in the end justified. Although Jahangir led a more dissolute life than Akbar would have approved, he was, like Akbar, exceptionally interested in intellectual and artistic pursuits. His favourite place was Kashmir where he adored the natural beauty. He seldom visited Delhi and then only to hunt and visit the tomb of Humayun and the nearby shrine of Nizamuddin.

Perhaps the most powerful person in Jahangir's court was his wife Nur Jahan. Her father was Jahangir's Chief Minister, Itimad-ud-daula, and her niece was Mumtaz Mahal, the wife of Jahangir's third son, Khurram (Shah Jahan), who became Jahangir's heir. Khurram was Akbar's favourite grandson, liked and trusted by Jahangir, who felt that his birth at the start of the new millennium (by the Islamic calendar) was remarkably auspicious.

Humayun's Tomb and Nizamuddin

There are probably more graves in the area around the urban village of Nizamuddin than in any other part of Delhi. The reason for this is the presence of Sheikh Nizamuddin Aulia's shrine in the heart of the urban village that bears his name. It was desirable for Muslims to be buried near the graves of holy men (and women) and thus we find tombs and graves spread around Nizamuddin's shrine up to about a kilometre in distance. These range in size and importance from Humayun's Tomb to nameless mounds scattered around the surviving open ground.

Sheikh Nizamuddin Aulia was born in 1236 and came to Delhi at the age of twenty-five. He became a disciple of the branch of Sufism introduced by Muinuddin Chishti of Ajmer and was fourth in the line of spiritual descent from Muinuddin.

Nizammudin's shrine

When Nizamuddin first came to Delhi the Sultan's court was at Lal Kot. We know that Balban had a palace in this area, possibly the Lal Mahal (p.169). Balban's successors and the early Khalji rulers based themselves nearby, at Kilokri, of which nothing historic now remains. At times, therefore, Nizamuddin lived close to the court; it is known that he attended prayers at the Jami Masjid in Khilokri. Among numerous other saints and holy men, Nizamuddin has always been particularly venerated, making his shrine a popular centre of pilgrimage.

Sufism is a mystical form of Islam, which emphasises an inner spiritual connection between man and God rather than the proscriptive relationship expounded by the *ulama* (Islamic jurists). The *sufis* rely on *pirs* for advice and, to some extent, intercession with God. Some of these *pirs* have gained great spiritual status and their burial places are venerated, in a way that has been highly criticised by some Orthodox Muslims. These aspects of Sufism make the faith more accessible to non-Muslims and *pirs* often have followers from other faiths.

The Chishtis, the most widespread *Sufi* order in India, accept music and dance as a means of becoming closer to God. They follow down-to-earth, empiricist methods, common throughout Islam, in which observations of natural phenomena are used to enhance knowledge, and the telling of parables play a major role in religious education. The Chishtis are against involvement in state affairs, but nonetheless they have sometimes been seen as a serious threat to state power because of their popularity.

Islamic burial sites were selected because of their beauty (ie. potential approximation to paradise, enhanced by garden enclosures) and their sanctity (proximity to a holy shrine). Judging by the number of Sultanate tombs that are spread out all over South Delhi, beauty was more important during the Sultanate era. By contrast, there is a significantly greater concentration of tombs from the Mughal era around the shrines of Nizamuddin and Qutb Sahib at Mehrauli. Near Nizamuddin's shrine, the availability of land must have influenced the design of tombs: some people chose to be buried within small compounds close to the saint while others preferred a large garden further away.

Humayun's Tomb

The Mughal Tomb

There are a number of tombs near Humayun's Tomb that demonstrate the new Timurid style brought by the early Mughals and their courtiers from Central Asia. As in Chapter 8, a generic description is given here and variations pointed out below.

SQUARE TOMB

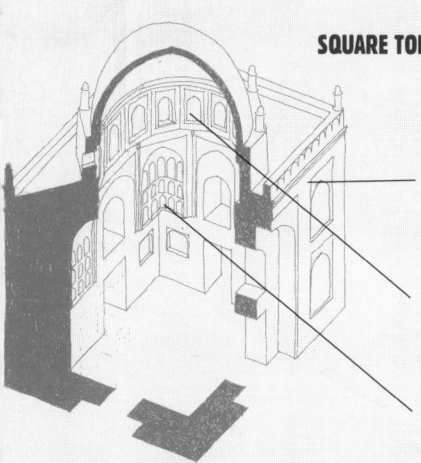

There is often no pishtaq so the parapet is continuous.

There is often no sixteen-sided internal drum. When there is one there are generally windows, sometimes as many as eight. This, and the general absence of mihrabs and screens gives the tomb interiors better light.

The squinch arches are often divided internally with niches that sometimes reflect the architectural pattern of the rest of the tomb, for instance with mini-arch netting in the half dome.

...GHDAD OCTAGON TOMB

...ere will often be a double dome (shown dotted) so that the ...erior is perceived more easily as a single space, unlike in ...tanate tombs, where there is a sharp distinction between the ...n chamber and the volume enclosed by the dome.

... use of an inner dome, thereby ...arating the external dimensions from ...se of the interior, made it possible to ...ld much taller dome drums, raising the ...me itself elegantly above the main ...mb chamber.

... internal plan is effectively ...ure octagon inside the ...ghdad Octagon exterior. ...wever the corner arches are ...ectively squinches, springing ...m the floor. Thus the internal ...n has square corners.

...aghdad Octagon is a square with ... corners chopped off, thus making ...unevenly sided octagon. The long ...e often projects forward slightly as ...hey were a pishtaq.

Arch netting forms the transitional zone between the dome drum and the inner dome.

The entrance is inside an iwan, a deep arched open 'hall' that features in many early Islamic buildings in Central and Western Asia.

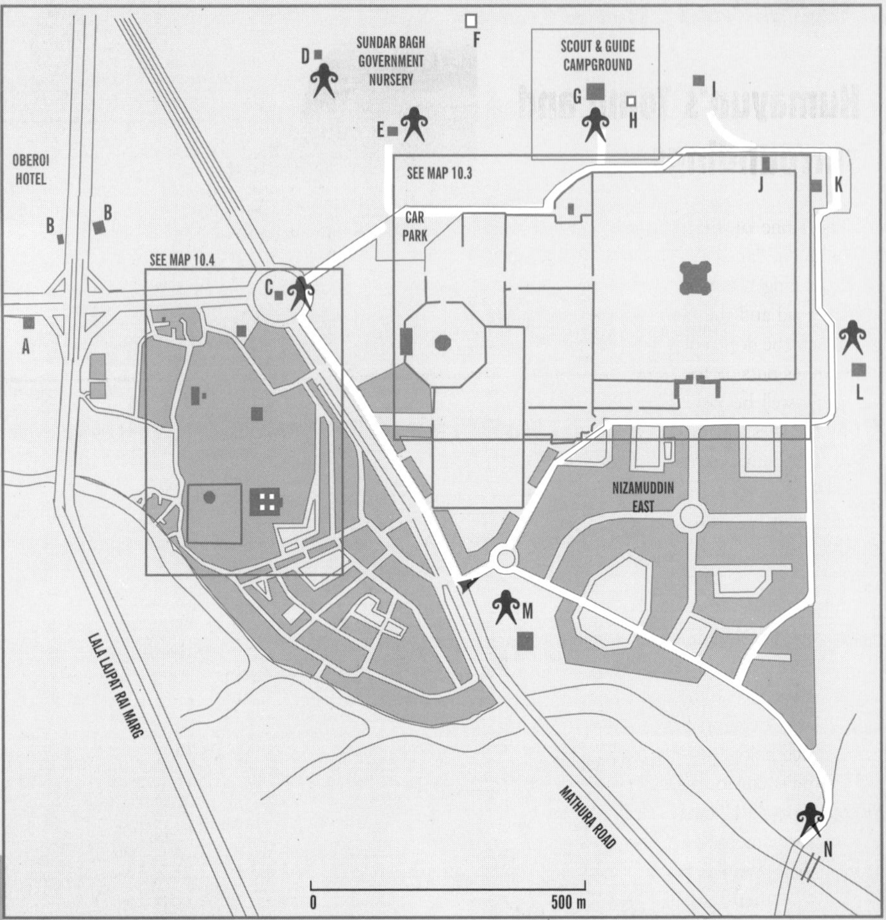

Map of Humayun's Tomb and Nizamuddin area with labeled locations including OBEROI HOTEL, SUNDAR BAGH GOVERNMENT NURSERY, SCOUT & GUIDE CAMPGROUND, CAR PARK, NIZAMUDDIN EAST, SEE MAP 10.3, SEE MAP 10.4, LALA LAJPAT RAI MARG, MATHURA ROAD. Scale bar: 0 to 500 m.

Labeled points: A, B, B, C, D, E, F, G, H, I, J, K, L, M, N.

Map 10.2 Humayun's Tomb and Nizamuddin

A. Gol Gumbad ?14th c. (p.176)

B. Gateway and Tomb 15th c. (p.176)

C. Sabz Burj, late 16th c. (p.159)

D. Tomb in corner of nursery 17th c. (p.159)

E. Sundarwala Burj 17th c. (p.159)

F. Sundarwala Mahal 17th c. (p.159)
   Beyond this tomb there is a late Mughal pavilion or tomb in the forest.

G. Bara Batashewala 1603 (p.158)

H. Chota Batashewala (p.158)

I. Tomb in 'DDA Green Area', late 16th – early 17th c. (p.157)

J. Chilla Nizamuddin 14th c. (p.157)

K. Gurudwara, modern (p.157)

L. Nila Gumbad, circa 1625 (p.156)

M. Khan-i-Khanan's Tomb, late 16th c. (p.166)

N. Barahpula 1611 (p. 156)

Bu Halima's Garden Gateway

Humayun's Tomb and surroundings

This is one of the most pleasant places in Delhi, and marvellously tranquil considering it is situated between a very busy road and the main railway line. The walk can be done entirely on foot, but the buildings outside the tomb enclosure can equally well be visited by car. A tour on foot involves leaving the tomb compound via Mihr Banu's gate and turning right for Khan-i-Khanan's Tomb, something that the security guard sometimes takes exception to. The route will therefore be described as if a car is used outside. It is necessary to start the tour by buying a ticket and walking around Humayun's Tomb and the other buildings in its enclosure.

Isa Khan's Tomb and Mosque

Start with the Sultanate-style **Isa Khan's Tomb** through a gate on the right. This important building, set in a large octagonal enclosure surrounded by trees, is described below (p.160). Further along on the left is **Bu Halima's Tomb and Garden** (late 16th c.). Nothing is known of Bu Halima, said to be buried here. The tomb is of the same pattern as two other tombs nearby (see Bara Batashewala, p.158). At the north end of the enclosure there are highly decorated square *chatris* at each corner, perhaps pre-dating the Mughal tomb. The layout of this area is curious because Isa Khan's compound wall seems to project into Bu Halima's rectangular garden at the south end. It could be that the garden pre-dates the Isa Khan compound, even if the tomb was built later. The puzzle continues when one considers the **gateway**, the east entrance to Bu Halima's garden. Although not aligned centrally in the garden enclosure it aligns perfectly with the western, subsidiary gateway of Humayun's Tomb, indicating that it was built

Isa Khan's Tomb

Bu Halima's Garden Chatri

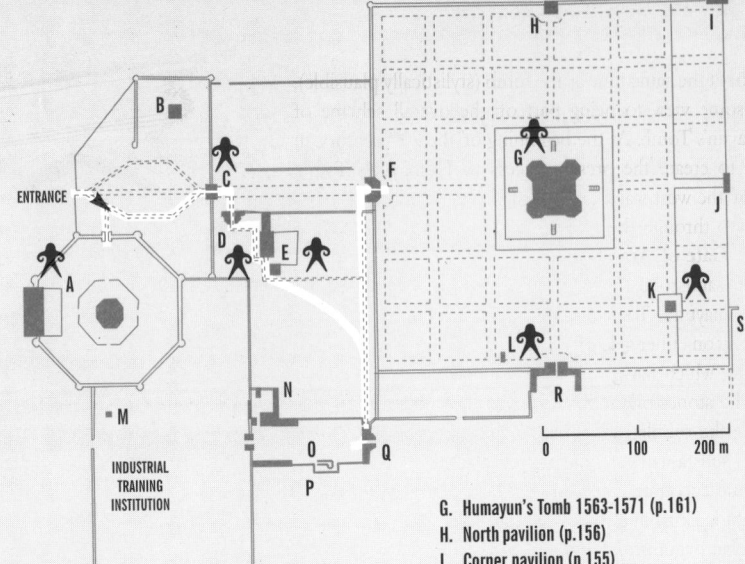

Map 10.3 Humayun's Tomb enclosure

A. Isa Khan's Tomb and Mosque 1547 (p.160)
B. Bu Halima's Garden, late 16th c. (p.151)
C. Bu Halima's Gate, late 16th c. (p.151)
D. North Gate of Arab Serai 1560s (p.153)
E. Afsarwala Tomb and Mosque, before 1566 (p.153)
F. West Gate of Humayun's Tomb 1560s (p.154)

G. Humayun's Tomb 1563-1571 (p.161)
H. North pavilion (p.156)
I. Corner pavilion (p.155)
J. East pavilion (p.155)
K. Barber's Tomb 1590 (p.155)
L. Mosque 18th c. (p.155)
M. Twelve-pillared tomb (p.154)
N. Enclosure
O. Mihr Banu's market 1612 (p.154)
P. Baoli (p.154)
Q. Mihr Banu's gate 1612 (p.154)
R. South Gate of Humayun's Tomb 1560s (p.155).
S. Prayer wall of Nila Gumbad (p.156)

Humayun's Tomb

after or at the same time as the tomb (stylistically plausible), with some view to being part of the overall scheme of Humayun's Tomb. At the beginning of the 20th century, in order to create the present access to Humayun's Tomb, part of the west wall of the garden was demolished.

Go through the gateway and turn right through the **North Gate of Arab Serai** (1560s). Built in pale quartzite and red sandstone, the style of the gateway is similar to that of Humayun's Tomb except for the small projecting *jharokhas* on either side of the door and the heavy sill to the window, which hark back to a more Afghan style. At the rear, the stonework has been stripped or crumbled away, leaving the rubble-built skeleton of what must have been quite a substantial gatehouse. The eponymous Arabs were, by some accounts, three hundred reciters of the Koran brought back from her pilgrimage to Mecca by Humayun's wife, Haji Begum, who was appointed administrator of the tomb complex.

It is not entirely clear which of the existing compounds was actually the Arab Serai because there have

Arab Serai Gate

been alterations to the compound walls. This gate probably led into an irregularly shaped compound that was later incorporated into the Mihr Banu complex (see over), while the **Afsarwala Tomb and Mosque** inside were probably built within a separate compound with their own entrance (shown on a Daniells painting of 1789). Because one of the cenotaphs mentions the date 1566 we can be confident that the Afsarwala buildings were constructed before that time, but nothing more is known about them. For what it is worth, *afsar* means officer so it is assumed that the tomb was that of an army commander, but that would apply to most tombs in an age when many courtiers were also soldiers. Steps to the roof allow you to view the upper surface of the inner dome. The interior of the mosque is airy and spacious and has a *minbar,* indicating that it was once used as a congregational mosque. On the other side of the mosque there is a low, vaulted chamber with doorways on each side, thought to have been a *hammam.*

Afsarwala Tomb and Mosque

Afsarwala Mosque interior

In the far corner of this large green compound there is an entrance to **Mihr Banu's gate and market** (1612). It appears that the whole complex, comprising a gateway, the market and the walled enclosure at the far end was an addition to the enclosure entered by the Arab Serai gateway. They were built by one Mihr Banu, so far unidentified. There are remains of market buildings along both sides of the first enclosure, and at the far end there is a very ruined gateway that once led into a large compound that now houses an Industrial Training Institute. The Institute was founded soon after Independence. Initially Japanese technicians trained young refugees in twelve different crafts to replace Muslim craftsmen who had left for Pakistan.

The interior of the main gateway is decorated with quite elaborate net vaulting, badly damaged but, in places, still sufficiently intact to give a good idea of the richness of such decoration during Jahangir's reign. It is worth stepping through the small wicket gate to see the exterior, decorated in white polished stucco and coloured tiles.

The other buildings of note in the market area is an L-shaped *baoli* on the left hand side, probably built at an earlier date since the exterior wall of the market was realigned to contain it, and an **enclosure** on the far right hand side which appears to have contained a number of rooms around a small courtyard, with a small wall mosque in the southwest corner. Inside the Industrial Training Institute there is one **twelve-pillared tomb** but no other buildings survived.

Walk back along the main path towards the **West Gate of Humayun's Tomb** (1560s). Before

Baoli

Twelve-pillared tomb in Industrial Training Institute

West Gate upper floor

leaving the Afsarwala Tomb and Mosque, it is worth glancing up at the half-courtyard that formed part of the accommodation above the West Gate. Here we see a style of architecture that is surprisingly different from either façade of the gateway, much more like Lodi architecture (or indeed Akbar's buildings at Agra or Fatepur Sikri).

Go through the gate for the breathtaking view of Humayun's Tomb (p.161) in the middle of its serene garden. Having explored the tomb walk down to see the **South Gate of Humayun's Tomb** (1560s). This was designed as the principal entrance to the tomb. Later it was used as a rest house, then by the police, but it is now being restored as part of the tomb complex. It is a well-proportioned building in pale quartzite and red sandstone, with the same delicate white marble inlay in the spandrels as has been seen on other buildings. Near it is a small 18th century **Mosque**. Its interest lies in the deep blue quartzite stone with which it is built, obtained locally but not used exclusively in any other historical buildings.

Walking on round the garden you first see the **Barber's Tomb** (1590). Tradition has it that this was the tomb of Akbar's barber, necessarily the most trusted of all imperial servants. It has some unusual features, particularly inside. Like Humayun's Tomb it has a double dome, but here the lower 'dome' does not have anything to do with the shape of the outer dome.

Beyond this is the **East garden pavilion** (late 16th – 17th c.), which would originally have overlooked the river, viewed from a cusped-arch arcade in front of a shallow veranda. The pavilion consists, in addition, of one room, ornamented with deep alcoves, and two arched entrance bays. At the corner is a dilapidated late 16th century **garden pavilion** with an arcade on the

West gate of garden (pre-restoration)

South Gate

Section

Elevation

Barbers Tomb

10 - 155

east side, overlooking the modern Gurudwara Damdama Sahib. On the north wall is the **North garden pavilion** (1560s). Just outside the wall is a well, one of the principal sources of water for the garden. The interior has one large room, in the centre of which is a deep pool, once perhaps fed by a fountain, from where the water cascaded into the garden channels below.

North pavil from side (pre-restoration)

Now return to the entrance and drive, turning left into Mathura Road and then left towards Nizamuddin Station. Opposite the entrance to the quiet neighbourhood of Nizamuddin East is **Khan-i-Khanan's Tomb** (p.166). Beyond it, on the busy main road past the station is the **Barapula** (1611). This old bridge once carried the main road to Agra. According to an inscription that is now lost it appears to have been built by Mihr Banu, who also built the Arab Serai market and east gateway (nearby, p.154). The bridge spans a tributary of the Yamuna, now nothing more than a vast open sewer. A modern bridge has recently been erected right up against it and the old bridge is used as a market place. It was generally reckoned to be the handsomest bridge in Delhi but, needless to say, it has now lost its looks.

Barapula

Drive through Nizamuddin East Colony to the wall of Humayun's Tomb. At the right hand corner a narrow lane passes round the back of the tomb. On the right is the **Nila Gumbad** (circa 1625). It is said that this tomb was built by Abdur Rahim (Khan-i-Khanan) for Fahim Khan, a loyal attendant. It once stood in a walled enclosure and part of the long prayer wall on the west remains, forming part of Humayun's Tomb enclosure. The tomb is decorated on the north side with geometric patterned tilework, highly unusual in this area. The nearest similar example can be seen at the Chini ka Rauza in Agra.

Nila Gumbad

Nila Gumbad detail

Beyond this you get a good view of Humayn's Tomb east pavilion before passing the modern **Gurudwara Damdama Sahib**. This Sikh temple commemorates the meeting of the last Sikh Guru, Gobind Singh, and Aurangzeb's son, Bahadur Shah. Guru Gobind Singh agreed to support Bahadur Shah in his fight for succession against his

Chilla Nizamuddin

brother. Turn left here. Soon on the left is the **Chilla Nizamuddin** (14th c.). The name means Nizamuddin's meditation place. Legend has it that Nizamuddin himself performed devotions here so, judging by this tradition as well as its style, the building must be from the early Tughlak era or before. Its importance is indicated by an entrance directly into Humayn's Tomb enclosure, through a ruined but once substantial gateway complex. The shrine is still in use and is remarkably atmospheric.

Opposite is a **DDA Green Area**. Go in and follow the path that veers to the left up a slight rise, to a rather charming **Tomb** (late 16th – early 17th c.) on a very ruined platform. Upon retracing your steps you will notice that there is a heavily worn path going on into the trees. This takes you to a surprisingly bucolic burial ground containing the well-tended tomb of a *pir*, a Muslim saint or holy man, likely to have been attached to Nizamuddin's shrine.

Further along the road on the right is the **Bharat Scout and Guide Compound**. In this enclosure there are remains of two tombs.

Tomb in Green Area interior

Also of interest are the modern buildings, a series of simple huts with naturally ventilated brick walls and bengali-style roofs. Called **Bharatiyam Gram**, they were built in 1989 by Laul and Associates as a demonstration of low cost construction using

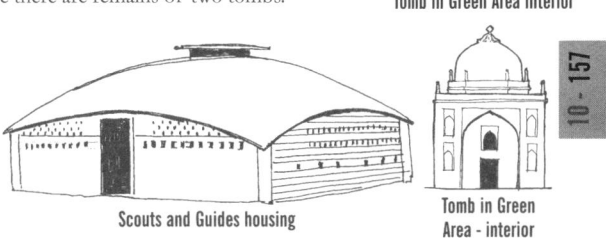
Scouts and Guides housing

Tomb in Green Area - interior

10 - 157

Old photo of Bara Batashewala

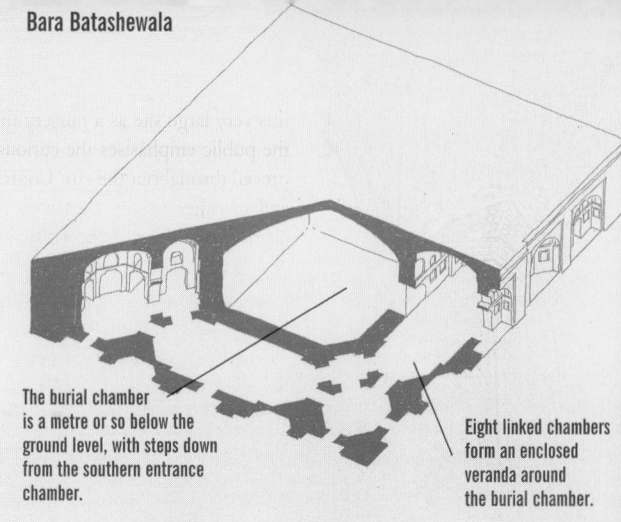

Bara Batashewala

The burial chamber is a metre or so below the ground level, with steps down from the southern entrance chamber.

Eight linked chambers form an enclosed veranda around the burial chamber.

Bara Batashewala interior

Bara Batashewala

Tomb in Sundar Bagh Nursery

Nursery tomb interior

locally available materials. The main tomb is the **Bara Batashewala** (1603). Eight linked chambers surround a sunken burial chamber beneath a flat roof. It is a plan form derived from Persian prototypes and exists elsewhere in contemporary tombs and garden pavilions (Itimad ud-Daula's marvellous tomb at Agra is a good example). The chambers were once elaborately decorated with incised and painted plaster; enough remains for us to get a good idea of how it once looked. The cenotaph may have been on the roof, open to the sky with a stone screen surround. This was common at the time. Alternatively, following Persian tradition, there would have been a textile canopy over the flat roof. The ASI guidebook of 1964 (Sharma) claims that this platform supported a domed tomb, whereas the 1916 ASI survey does not. Both sources, however, concur in saying that this was the tomb of Mirza Muzaffar, great-nephew of Humayun, who was married to Akbar's eldest daughter and buried here in 1603. Nearby is the **Chota Batashewala**. This is now in ruins but both sources mentioned above concur in stating that there was a conventional domed tomb with fine incised plasterwork decorations inside. Much damage was clearly done quite recently.

The road ends at the car park for Humayn's Tomb. On the right is the entrance to the **Sundar Bagh Government Nursery**. This is closed on Sundays and other holidays, which means that access to the exceptionally ornate 17th century tombs inside is sometimes impossible. The use of

Nursery tomb - squinch

Sundarwala Burj detail

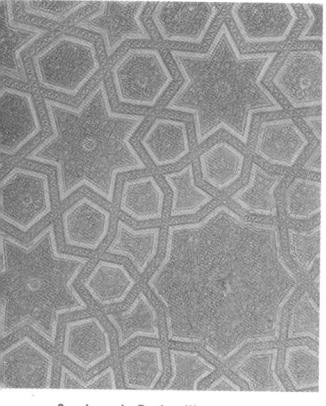
Sundarwala Burj ceiling

this very large site as a nursery that is only semi-open to the public emphasises the curious land-use patterns that prevail throughout the city. Contrasting the land use here and in other nearby sites with poorer neighbourhoods nearby should make the citizens of Delhi question the wisdom of current city 'planning' that tolerates such pointless inequity. The first tomb is the **Sundarwala Burj**, with very fine plasterwork decorations inside, which are well preserved where they are out of reach. To the right is the **Sundarwala Mahal**. This is similar in layout to the Bara Batashewala but more damaged. The burial chamber is closed. In the far left hand corner and seen, tantalisingly, from Sundar Nagar, is another **Tomb.** This combines many of the features of the Sundarwala Burj and the tomb inside the DDA Green Area, in this case even more elaborate and extremely pretty. On the west side there is a later addition: a small chamber that appears to have looked out onto the enclosure wall, which seems to have been built as a wall mosque, with a *mihrab* niche visible opposite the chamber.

On the roundabout at the entrance is the **Sabz Burj** (late 16th c.). This is a Mughal-era tomb but its occupant is unknown. The ceramic tile-work on the drum is original, as is the remains of painted decoration that can be seen inside the arched recesses. It is thought that it dates from early Mughal times because of its style.

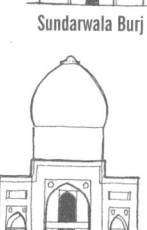
Sundarwala Burj

The name means 'green covered' - the ASI renewed the roof with blue tiles in the mid-1980s. This seems to have been controversial at the time: there is a pointed reference in the ASI report to the tiles being of the 'original colour and texture'.

Sabz Burj

Sundarwala Burj interior detail

Isa Khan's Tomb and Mosque (1547)

Map 10.3 (p.152)

Isa Khan's Tomb

Clearly, the site was chosen for its relative proximity to Nizamuddin's shrine, but without having to sacrifice space to achieve glorious paradise-like surroundings. Isa Khan was a grandee of Sher Shah's time, so he was among the last nobles to be buried beneath an Afghan-style tomb, like Sher Shah himself. It is not surprising, therefore, to see some advanced stylistic features, such as the large *chatris* that replace the two subsidiary domes on the mosque, which in other respects matches the tomb.

Isa Khan's Tomb is a particularly fine example of an octagonal tomb (other examples are discussed in Chapter 8), and follows the typical pattern of octagonal tombs in Delhi. The exterior still has the remains of incised stucco and glazed tile-work around the arches, the finest example being on the south side, over the entrance; there are good examples on the mosque. The *jali*-work screens of the inner doors are attractive, but

Isa Khan's Mosque

have the defect of reducing the light inside the chamber, making it hard to see the particularly fine and well preserved carved and painted stucco ceiling. The stairs are normally open to the roof, from which there is a view of the dome of Humayun's Tomb.

The **mosque** is a fine building with quite well preserved tile-work on the exterior, giving a good idea of the building's original appearance. The red sandstone *mihrabs* are in place in each bay. There is access to the roof, up steps visible on the front façade or up a staircase at the right hand end of the prayer hall.

Isa Khan's Mosque (left), Tomb (below left) and Mosque interior (below)

Humayun's Tomb

The central chamber has three well-proportioned storeys of arched openings, with adequate daylight filtering through jalis in the top layer. The clarity of the interior chamber's design is enhanced by the lack of a mihrab, but here, unlike in most other Mughal tombs, a notional mihrab is indicated on each of the west-facing jalis. As we have seen, the other jalis do not appear to have been contemporary but it could be that these mihrab ones were.

The dome's very slightly bulbous profile has a Persian appearance as well as being reminiscent of other domes in Delhi and elsewhere (e.g. Ghiyasuddin's Tomb at Tughlukabad or Hoshang Shah's tomb at Mandu, Madhya Pradesh). However, while the Mandu dome, like many other contemporary domes in Delhi, departs from a perfect hemisphere in that it looks as if the finial has pushed the centre of the dome downwards, in the case of Humayun's Tomb the finial appears to draw the dome upwards.

From a distance the dome drum is just visible either side of the tall central bay.

The walls that surround the arches are harmoniously decorated with yellow sandstone spandrels and white marble, which is used variously: as narrow bands to frame each arch, as quoins, and to provide surface decoration.

Roof pavilions, chatris and guldastas surround the dome.

Most of the ground floor openings are closed with rather chunky jali screens. It is possible that, when originally built, the tomb could have been processed around, using the passageways that divide the octagons. If so, it would mean that the screens that now close these passages were not built then. Evidence of door hinges across the north, east and west doors to the main chamber suggests that there were once no jalis here either: it could be that the ground floor jalis were later additions.

On three sides the tall central bay is set back and contains one large iwan with a two-storey arrangement of smaller iwan-style arches within it.

On the south side a doorway within a shallow arched recess leads into the lobby. This has a shallow domed ceiling adorned in a style seen again at the 18th century Safdarjang's Tomb.

The plan of the tomb itself consists of five linked Baghdad octagons, the central one being taller, domed, and containing the main tomb chamber. This is the first example in India of a multi-chambered tomb where the linked chambers are so visually independent of each other.

Mihrab in jali

Humayun's Tomb - southeast corner

Humayun's Tomb (1563-1571)
Map 10.3 (p.152)

The history of Humayun is given in greater detail in the history section of this chapter. Here, it is enough to say that he is probably the least known of the early Mughals, which is hardly surprising: he was emperor for only ten years before being ignominiously ousted by the Afghan Sher Shah and again for a mere six months from mid-1555, after his recapture of the Empire. He is also unfortunate in coming between the two most illustrious Mughal emperors, his father Babur who founded the dynasty and his son, Akbar. The site of the tomb was no doubt chosen carefully. Close to Nizamuddin's shrine, it was even closer to the river, which ran beside the east wall at that time. The river's proximity was important for access and helped moderate the climate locally.

Steps up to tomb platform

THE TOMB

There are very few architectural experiences that can rival one's first awe-inspiring sight of Humayun's Tomb. Built sixty years before the even more astonishing Taj Mahal, it was highly innovative. To appreciate its novelty one only has to compare it with Isa Khan's Tomb next door, built only a few years earlier. It was

Muqarnas in tomb lobby

constructed on the instructions of Akbar, Humayun's son and heir, long after his death and was finished in 1571 after about eight years' work. The architect was probably Mirak Mirza Ghiyas who had worked in Bukhara (in present-day Uzbekistan) and came to Delhi in 1562.

The building stands on a high platform that contains seventeen arched openings on each side, giving access to small burial chambers. The corners of the platform are cut at an angle to match the corners of the tomb above, while a central archway gives access via steep steps to the tomb platform.

Close external inspection of the tomb does not add anything to its architectural merits; these all reside in the superb external proportions and unfussy ornamentation. Interestingly, as in earlier Islamic buildings in India, the decoration emphasises the tomb's structural form (eg., arches and beams) instead of negating it. Most of the major buildings that Humayun would have seen and admired in Persia and Afghanistan were covered in elaborate tilework, the decorative patterns not necessarily having much to do with the construction underneath.

Having climbed the steep steps to the platform, turn to your right for the entrance to the tomb. This

Humayun's Tomb - jali with mihrab

Humayun's Tomb main chamber

leads into a lobby whose ceiling is ornamented at the edges by the sort of *muqarnas* decoration that is seldom found in India. Unfortunately the main chamber cannot fail to disappoint, despite its exceptionally fine proportions, because it is sorely in need of cleaning and maintenance. The very poor state of the walls, scarred, and seriously water-stained in one place, distracts from the architectural form. It is unclear whether the interior was always as austere as this; it certainly seems unlikely that Humayun's family would have been happy with the tomb's present appearance. A description by Nicolao Manucci, a Venetian who lived in Delhi during Shah Jahan's reign, tells us that there were 'many paintings and stones of various kinds, and the roof of the dome is gilded'. There is also a reference to some remains of decoration in the 1916 ASI survey. However, as against these accounts, there are no references in 19th century travellers' descriptions to decorations other than the formal adjuncts (cloth covering, etc.) to the cenotaph.

Humayun's cenotaph is a plain marble block in the middle of the main chamber. Most of the cenotaphs are unidentified but a few are known or are inscribed. In the northeast corner chamber are the cenotaphs of Humayun's wives, Hamida Begum (Akbar's mother) and Biga Begum. The southeast chamber has three cenotaphs, supposed to be those of Humayun's daughters, and the southwest chamber has the cenotaph of the seventh Mughal emperor, Bahadur Shah (reigned 1707-12), and his wife. Numerous members of the Mughal dynasty were buried here and some of their cenotaphs are found on the tomb platform. Dara Shikoh, Shah Jahan's eldest son who was murdered by Aurangzeb, was one of them; most of the others were members of the Imperial family after its glory had been eclipsed in the 18th and 19th centuries.

HUMAYUN'S TOMB GARDEN

Gardens were the places of relaxation and were therefore the natural setting for tombs, the permanent resting place of the dead and, indeed, the Islamic conception of heaven or paradise (the Persian word *paradise* actually means 'walled garden'). The tomb set within a garden was clearly not an innovation in India. In his memoirs Babur mentions visiting the tombs and gardens of both Bahlol and Sikander Lodi. Even earlier tombs have enclosures that might have contained gardens (Khan Jahan Tilangani's in Nizamuddin and Mubarak Shah's in Mubarakpur Kotla). We have no idea what these gardens looked like but we do know that they did not measure up to Babur's standards; he lamented particularly the lack of running water in India. Soon after

Garden detail – before restoration

his conquest of Hindustan Babur had built gardens with running water at Agra, Dholpur and Sikri (to become Fatepur Sikri in Akbar's reign). Babur, describing the building of his first garden near Agra, mentions the formal layout and the water bodies and summarises: 'Thus, in unpleasant and inharmonious India, marvellously regular and geometric gardens were introduced'!

Humayun's Tomb is located in the centre of a huge garden, occupying the central four squares in a grid of thirty-six (six by six), the divisions being marked by raised walkways, each of which has narrow water channels leading to pools at most of the intersections. On the east side of the tomb, towards the river, the ground drops away, the change of level incorporated into the grid pattern. Extensive work has recently been undertaken jointly by the ASI and the Aga Khan Foundation to restore the garden. This has included lowering the levels of the lawns, the planting of fruit trees and shrubs and the investigation of the original hydraulics. Although the recent work has gone some way to improving the garden's authenticity, the overall design (the pathways and sandstone channels) was created at the beginning of the 20th century, based probably on not very much evidence. However, the way the tomb fits into the geometry of the six-by-six squares is persuasive.

Khan-i-Khanan's Tomb
(late 16th century)
Map 10.2 (p.150)

Abdur Rahim, Khan-i-Khanan (Akbar's prime minister, died 1626), held the same position as his father Bairam Khan, who was Humayun's General when he marched back into India after his fifteen years' exile, and was subsequently the young Akbar's guardian and prime minister. Bairam Khan fell foul of rivals at court, in particular Akbar's powerful ex-wet nurse, Maham Angah, when Akbar was still in his teens and was exiled and murdered, leaving Abdur Rahim an orphan of four. The boy was brought up in Akbar's harem and was well educated. As a result Abdur Rahim was a highly cultured man who wrote poetry and spoke several languages. Like his father he was in charge of a future Emperor's education, being tutor to Jahangir.

In style the tomb would be rather old-fashioned if it had been built at the time of Abdur Rahim's death; it is therefore likely that it was

Detail of interior plasterwork

originally the tomb of his wife, who died in 1598, though of course it might even have been built before her death. It is a handsome building but, sadly, most of its exterior stonework was stripped off and taken away for the construction, it is said, of Safdarjang's Tomb. It is difficult to tell whether the tomb was ever surrounded by a walled garden. A possibly inaccurate 1849 map shows a confusing number of walled enclosures in the area but none appear to be the square enclosure we would expect: they are probably unrelated to the tomb.

Khan-i-Khanan's Tomb - elevation and section

Nizamuddin

In many a story told to children, the adventurer has passed through a mysterious doorway in a wall and has found himself in an unfamiliar land; and here, it would seem, is a realisation of the tale...

The shrine is the tomb of Nizam-ud-din....
Frederick Treves, 1904

Out of the 22 saints of Delhi, Nizamuddin is one of the most revered and his shrine is always full of visitors. During Ramadan there is a daily Iftar 'breakfast' when hundreds of people visit for free food, eaten the moment the bell sounds for the setting of the sun and the end of that day's fast (tourists and other visitors are very welcome). At other times of the year Thursday is the day that *fatiha* (prayers for the saint) is offered by devotees at all shrines; Nizamuddin's shrine is particularly busy, especially for the evening prayers, after which *qawwalis* sing to an informal gathering. This is a nice time to visit and a good way of hearing traditional music. On these evenings and to a lesser extent on others, the enclosure is full of people, quietly sitting under the shrine's veranda or out in the open around the *qawwals*, who address their songs to the shrine. Every now and then a member of the audience will be moved to donate some money and then slip back into the crowd.

Among the many 'urban villages' of Delhi Nizamuddin is one of the most interesting, partly because of the number of historic buildings but also because of the numerous visitors. Although the majority are Muslim, there are many Indians of other faiths who come as tourists or pilgrims, *sufism* traditionally having had very wide appeal. There are always large number of beggars as well, attracted by the charitable institutions here.

Jamaat Khana mosque and Nizamuddin's shrine

Although there is no compulsory fee at the Dargah, this can be an expensive place to visit because the attendants of the Shrine produce a book with six columns, each representing a separate fund (charity, feeding the poor, school, prayers, etc.) to which you are invited to contribute. You can decide into which funds your money goes. You can also pay for meals for poor people at the Mehboob Restaurants at the main entrance to the Dargah.

If you carry a bag with you for your shoes you can walk through the Dargah, an advantage if you want to visit all the buildings (see over for map). Note that women are not allowed inside Nizamuddin's Shrine or Amir Khusro's Tomb.

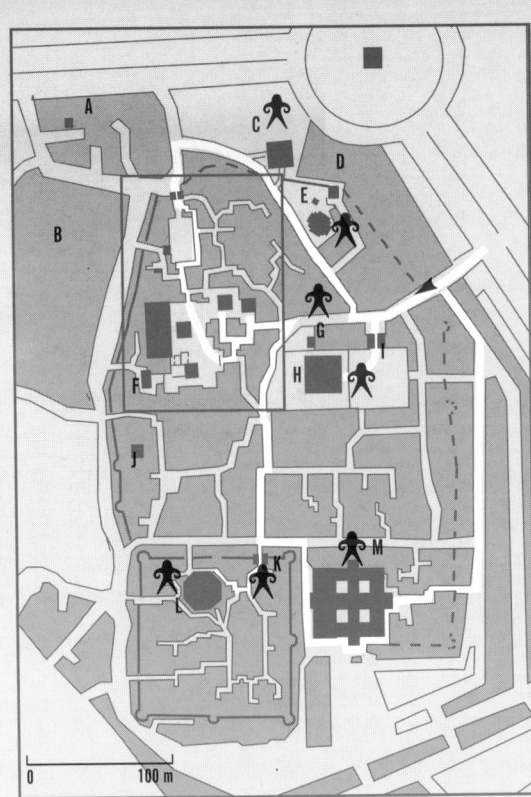

Map 10.4 Nizamuddin village

A. Do Sirihya Gumbad 15th c.
B. This is a burial ground but with houses now constructed among the graves and tombs.
C. Barah Khamba 15th c. (p.170)
D. Tomb 16th or 17th c.
E. Lal Mahal ?13th c. (p.169)
F. Khan-e-Dauran Khan's mosque, early 18th c. This small mosque is surrounded by graves, including the remains of a small tomb at the back, which dates from an earlier period. Khan-e-Dauran Khan was a courtier of Muhammad Shah and was killed by Nadir Shah's army.
G. Ghalib's grave and Ghalib Academy 19th & 20th c. (p.169)
H. Chausath Khamba 1623 (p.169)
I. Gateway, late 16th or early 17th c. (p.169)
J. Dargah Hazrat Inayat Khan 20th c. Inayat Khan (1887-1927) was born into a family of musicians. His career started in music but mysticism was important to him too and in 1904 he became a sufi, a calling which eventually took him to Europe. His Dargah has pleasant modern buildings and regular recitals of excellent sufi music.
K. Kotla Nizamuddin, mid-14th c. (p.173)
L. Khan Jahan Tilangani's Tomb, died 1368 (p.173)
M. Kali Masjid 1370 (p.173)

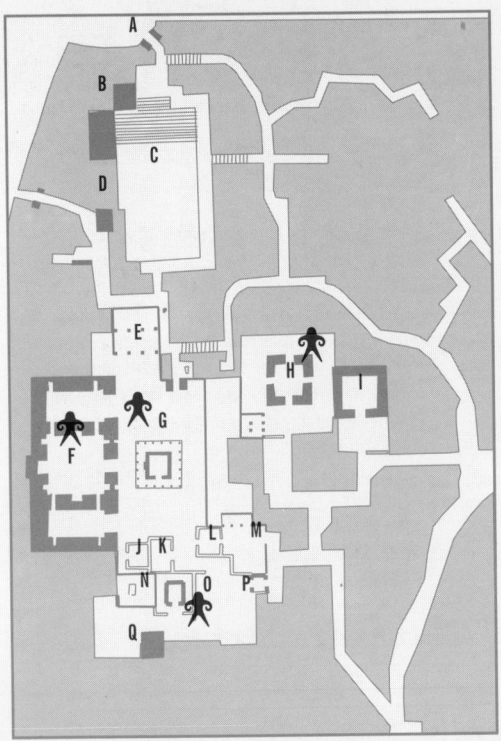

Map10.5 Nizamuddin's Dargah

A. North Gate, originally 15th c. (p.170)
B. Tomb 1563 (p.170)
C. Baoli 1321 (p.170)
D. Tomb of Bai Kodaldai 1541 (p.170)
E. Majlis Khana 16th or 17th c.
F. Jamaat Khana Mosque, early 14th c. (p.174)
G. Nizamuddin's Shrine, mainly 19th c. (p.171)
H. Atgah Khan's Tomb 1566 (p.175)
I. Bari ka Gumbad (unknown roofed building – possibly a gateway)
J. Jahanara's grave enclosure, died 1681 (p.171)
K. Muhammad Shah's grave enclosure, died 1748 (p.172)
L. Mirza Jahangir's grave enclosure, died 1832 (p.172)
M. Gateway, late 18th or early 19th c.
N. Tomb 1678
O. Amir Khusro's Tomb 1605 (p.172)
P. Gateway 1881 (p.172)
Q. Dalan of Mirdha Ikram 1801 & Langar Khana 14th c. (p.172)

A pilgrim's village

Near the pedestrian underpass on Mathura Road a very busy road leads into Nizamuddin. Shortly after the second turning to the left there is a large **Mughal-era gateway**, which was either never completed or has lost the top of the wall. It was probably the entrance to a garden or *serai* but now it leads through to an open space with a large, fairly modern pillared hall on one side. On the other side is the **Chausath Khamba** (1623). The name means 'sixty-four pillars' and, despite first impressions, you will notice that there are indeed sixty-four pillars, the outside row on each side being double. Constructed in white marble as a mausoleum for a family, there are several beautifully carved cenotaphs inside. It was built by Mirza Aziz Kokaltash, the son of Atgah Khan, whose tomb is not far away (p.175), and the father-in-law of Jahangir's hapless eldest son Khusrau. Mirza Aziz had spent some years as governor of Gujarat and may have got inspiration from the fine mid-15th century tomb of Sheikh Ahmad Khattu at Sarkhej, near Ahmedabad; the exterior screens are very similar. The building is especially interesting as it typifies an architectural style that had

Chausath Khamba

Chausath Khamba

developed by the end of Jahangir's reign, marking the transition from the heavy red sandstone architecture of Akbar to the light white marble of Shah Jahan. There are very few mausolea built in this hypostyle form.

Lal Mahal Tower

The building to the right of the gateway is the Ghalib Academy, honouring the great Urdu and Persian poet, and round the corner, next to the outer north wall of the Chausath Khamba is **Ghalib's Tomb** (19th c.), a delicate little edifice in white marble. Although Mirza Asadullah Khan Ghalib (1797-1869) lived in Shahjahanabad for most of his life he was buried here, near the shrine of Nizamuddin, and just north of the Chausath Khamba. His life is described in greater detail on p.203, but there is a small and dusty museum on the third floor of the Academy where, among such curiosities as models of epicurean feasts that Ghalib would have enjoyed, there are a few interesting old photos of Delhi.

The road divides here. Straight ahead it leads to the Dargah, but you should take the road on the right, which takes you past the 13th century **Lal Mahal**. The name means 'red palace' but it is not known for certain what these dreadfully decayed buildings were. There are references in early literature to the Kushaki Lal (an out of town palace) built by Balban before he became Sultan in 1266 and it is not impossible that this was part of it. What is left now is a single-storey building that seems originally to have consisted of a central domed chamber with three-bayed *dalans* projecting forward on each side with a *chatri* above each of them. The open *dalans* have recently been enclosed and the interior is presently full of rubbish but, by putting one's eye to cracks in the collapsing doors, it is possible to glimpse carving on the stone ceiling, more visible in the two-storey tower nearby. Perhaps once connected physically with the domed building, this is certainly connected stylistically. The tower is built in local stone to first floor level and above that in red sandstone.

Lal Mahal. Some improvements have taken place since this photo was taken

Beyond this is the 15th century **Barah Khamba**. This is an unusual tomb, prefiguring the type of Mughal tomb that consists of a central chamber surrounded by interlinking arcaded rooms (e.g. Humayun's Tomb and the Bara Batashewala). The name means twelve

Barah Khamba

columns, referring here to the number of double columns that surround the central chamber. The tomb's history is unknown. It is thought to date from the Lodi period, but it may be slightly earlier.

Continuing on the same road, at the T-junction turn left for the **North Gate** of the Dargah, where you will have to remove your shoes. The gateway takes you straight into the rather magical ambiance of the 14th century *baoli*, magical at any rate in the complete contrast with the bustling commerce outside the gate. This is the place that caused so much trouble to Ghiyasuddin Tughlak (p.49). It was built by Nizamuddin in the early 14th century, presumably to serve the needs of people visiting him, most of whom would have walked the considerable distance from the old city (Lal Kot and Siri at that time) or from new Tughlakabad. On its completion he blessed the well and it is deemed to have acquired miraculous powers, especially for expelling evil spirits and curing skin disease. During colonial times local people jumped from the surrounding roofs into the water for money; and this is sometimes still done, mainly for fun; the jumping is combined with a spectacular display of climbing to get to the jumping-off point. The *baoli* itself is built from large blocks of close-fitting quartzite and is surrounded by several buildings that are identifiable in early 19th century drawings. In the northwest corner a dome covers the inaccessible **Tomb** (1563) of two women. The graves have Persian inscriptions saying that one of the women was 'pitied and pardoned' while the other 'departed plaintively'. Unfortunately that is all we are told. One of the few accessible tombs can be found by taking the narrow lane off the passageway leading south towards the Dargah. This is the small marble **Tomb of Bai Kodaldai** (1541). Once open on all sides, now only two sides are open. The tomb is in a sad state and has been defiled with blobs of red paint. There are traces of a few other old buildings around it.

Tomb of Bai Kodaldai

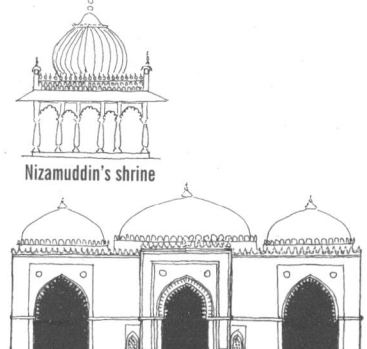

Nizamuddin's shrine

Jamaat Khana mosque and Nizamuddin's shrine

Jamaat Khana mosque

The walkway south from the *baoli* eventually leads you into the **Dargah** itself, usually throbbing with life. The most interesting buildings are the 13th century **mosque** (p.174) and several burial places, including Nizamuddin's own and several members of the Mughal royal family. **Nizamuddin's Shrine** is directly in front of the mosque. The original plain grave has been much embellished over the years. Firoz Shah Tughlak built the first structure (14th c.) but this was replaced in 1562 when the marble screens were erected by a nobleman of Akbar's court. A series of additions were made, starting in 1608 with the wooden canopy with mother-of-pearl inlay, an unusual survival from so long ago. This was erected by Sheikh Farid Bukhari, Governor of Delhi during Akbar's reign. A new red sandstone veranda was built in 1652 but was subsequently replaced in 1808 by the marble pillars we see today. The veranda ceiling was replaced in 1820. Finally the dome was replaced in 1839.

Nizamuddin's shrine detail

Nizamuddin's shrine is surrounded by numerous other buildings and countless graves of people who wished to be buried near the saint. Among these, four are of architectural interest: **Jahanara's grave enclosure** (died 1681) is very close to the south end of the mosque. Jahanara, the eldest and favourite daughter of Emperor Shah Jahan and Mumtaz Mahal. She took on the duties of Mumtaz Mahal after her death and was a major patron of Shahjahanabad, building a vast garden and *serai* inside the walls of the city. When she died, Jahanara's wish was to be buried very simply: 'Let nothing but grass cover my grave; for that is the covering meet for the lowly.' The mossy patches inside the elegantly carved marble cenotaph in the centre of the enclosure should, by rights, be sporting tiny lawns. This type of grave became very common in late Mughal times; Aurangzeb is buried in an even simpler grave near Aurangabad. The graves either side of Jahanara's are those of children of later Mughal emperors.

Jahanara's grave

Immediately beside Jahanara's is **Muhammad Shah's grave enclosure** (died 1748). This is even finer, in more intricately carved white marble. The solid marble doors are particularly eye-catching. The largest of the cenotaphs inside is that of Muhammad Shah himself, who was placed on the throne in 1719. During his reign Delhi was sacked and the Peacock Throne and other treasures carried off by Nadir Shah of Persia. Also

Muhammad Shah's grave

'carried off' was a girl of the Imperial family who was married to Nadir Shah's son. The girl died in childbirth and she and her baby were buried in this enclosure. Other graves are of Muhammad Shah's wife and grandson. Opposite is **Mirza Jahangir's grave enclosure** (died 1832). Again built from white marble, it contains the graves of Mirza Jahangir and his brother. Mirza Jahangir was the eldest and favourite son of Akbar Shah II and was banished to Allahabad after firing a pistol at the British Resident in 1808. He led an eventful but drink-sodden life and always chafed against British rule. He died at thirty-one and his remains were brought back to Delhi. Beyond the grave enclosure are a *dalan* and a late-Mughal gateway, The *dalan* is called the house of Mirza Jahangir but was obviously not, since he did not live in Delhi and would certainly not have lived here.

Up a few steps on the right is **Amir Khusro's Tomb** (1605). This tomb has been variously embellished over the years but, unlike Nizamuddin's, it is rather less easy to see owing to the enclosure wall, which was built during

North Gate of Dargah

Humayun's reign. The tomb itself was reconstructed during Jahangir's reign by one of his officials. Amir Khusro Dehlavi (1253-1325) was a great poet and chronicler and was favoured by several Sultans. He wrote in Persian, the official language of the Muslim court, but he embellished traditional Persian poetic forms with indigenous Indian imagery, including parrots, mangoes and local flowers. The famous line 'If there is paradise on earth, it is here, it is here, it is here', inscribed in the palace of Shah Jahan, was written by Amir Khusro in a great poetic eulogy to the Delhi of his time. He was a close friend and disciple of Nizamuddin and, it is said, died of grief shortly after Nizamuddin's own death.

South of Amir Khusro's Tomb are an early 19th century *dalan* and the Tughlak **Langar Khana**. The **main gate** is in the northeast corner of this courtyard. Formerly the entrance to the outer enclosure of Amir Khusro's tomb, there is little to see of its original form. Once outside the Dargah turn to the left and go out past shops selling devotional artefacts and such like. Up a few steps go left, pushing aside a cloth barrier if necessary, down a couple of steps and turn right. This will lead you into the tiny enclosure of the exquisite 16th century **Tomb of Atgah Khan** (p175). Continue past the shops and into a triangular space where there are generally knots of destitute people waiting for food to be bought for them at one of the

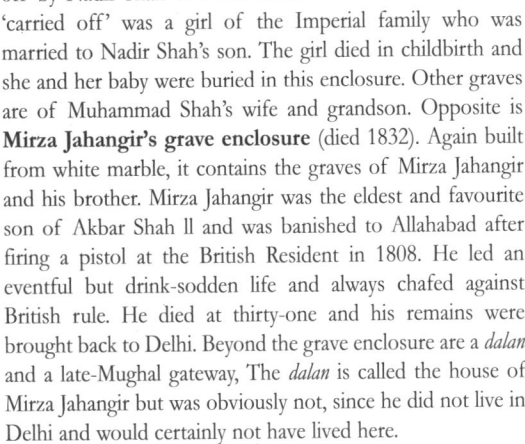

restaurants there. The current rate is Rs 5 per person, so a Rs 100 note will feed twenty.

Turn right here and follow the lane more or less due south until it intersects with another busy lane. Opposite is the main **Gateway** to the **Kotla Nizamuddin** (mid-14th c.). This is quite a substantial walled enclosure and was, perhaps, built as the enclosure to the tomb inside, although the actual relationship is unknown. A clear comparison can be made with the nearly contemporaneous Qadam Sharif enclosure, where the walls are also very impressive but, similarly, do not have any close geometric relationship with the tomb.

The Kotla contains the first octagonal tomb in Delhi, that of **Khan Jahan Tilangani** (died 1368), which is found by taking the second lane on the right after entering the Kotla and then right again. This will bring you to the only wall of the tomb that is fully visible. This is the only important building inside the Kotla and is in fact the first octagonal tomb ever to have been built in India. Unless you have visited other octagonal tombs, for instance in the Lodi Gardens, it will be difficult even to understand its form. There are families (who have been there for many generations) living in the veranda and small yards have been created in front of most of the dwellings. Some of the incised stucco decoration on the external walls is visible in places, as is the collapsing *chajja*. The main dome is surrounded by small domes over the centre of each side, the precursors of the *chatris* which occur in the equivalent position on later octagonal tombs. The tomb was built for Firoz Shah Tughlak's first *wazir* (prime minister), Khan Jahan Tilangani. The name Tilangani comes from his birthplace, Tilang or Telengana, the heartland of what is

Khan Jahan Tilangani's Tomb

Khan Jahan Tilangani's Tomb

now Andhra Pradesh. Khan Jahan was captured by Muhammad Tughlak in 1322 during his campaign in the south, converted to Islam and became one of Muhammad's trusted courtiers. He was appointed *wazir* by Firoz Shah on his accession to the throne and served him for twenty years. Indeed, one contemporary described him as the real ruler of Delhi. When he died his position went to his son, Khan Jahan Junan Shah, famous for having built seven great mosques, one of which is nearby, just outside the walls of the Kotla.

Back in the main east-west lane the first turning right after the gate takes you to the rear of the **Kali Masjid** (1370). This is one of the seven mosques just referred to. The inscription over the main entrance gives a date of 1370. Its name is probably due to the black (*kali*) patina that once encrusted the rendering. In layout it is most similar to the Khirki Masjid (p.70), having four courtyards but with different proportions. Unfortunately the building was in ruins at the beginning of the 20th century and restoration has eliminated many contemporary features. A few survive on the exterior, in particular the typical tapering bastions at the corners of the projecting entrances.

From here it is easy to walk back to your starting point up the modern road outside the village proper. There are several other minor buildings on the west side of the village that can also be explored.

Kali Masjid interior

Jamaat Khana Mosque (13th century)
Map 10.5 (p.168)

Jamaat Khana Mosque dome

The history of the mosque is somewhat obscure and there are various theories attached to it. One tradition has it that Alauddin Khalji built the mosque as a reward because he had offered Nizamuddin a lakh of rupees (then a vast sum of money) and it had been refused. Because the mosque is painted all over, it appears at first glance to be quite different from the contemporary Alai Darwaza, the only extant remains of Alauddin's mosque at the Qutb Minar. However, on closer inspection, it is possible to see that the buildings are very similar, both in proportions and decoration. An alternative story is that the central chamber was built by Alauddin's son Khizr Khan as a tomb for the saint but that Nizamuddin did not wish to be buried under a roof. The tomb was therefore not used and was subsequently converted into a mosque with the addition of side chambers, but the appearance of the façade, where the masonry appears well bonded, does not altogether bear this out. An historical source (Iqtidar Husain Siddiqui quoted in Troll) seems to indicate that Nizamuddin was buried 'in the wilderness according to his will' and that Firoz Shah built the mosque for pilgrims to the shrine. Stylistically however it fits best with a Khalji foundation.

This is an interesting mosque architecturally because of its probable date, over a hundred years after the first part of the Qutb Minar Mosque was constructed (the additions by Iltutmish and Alauddin seem to have followed the general pattern of the early building) but some decades before the rash of Tughlak mosques. In plan it resembles the Begampur Mosque and the Tohfe Wala Gumbad in Siri, in that the central square chamber is only marginally connected with the side chambers. The side chambers are, however, very different,

consisting of a single narrow bay with domes at front and back rather than a pillared hall. The façade is moderately severe, depending on the decoration of the *pishtaq* and arches for any relief. The interior is more ornate and, like the façade, the decoration is heavily dependent on calligraphy. The architectural form is familiar, with squinch arches and a sixteen-sided band above them supported on pendentive corbels. What is unusual is that the dome starts directly above this and there are tiny niches, every other one giving light, around the base of the dome itself.

Jamaat Khana Mosque interior

Atgah Khan's Tomb (1566)

Map 10.5 (p.168)

Atgah Khan's wife, Ji Ji Angah, was one of Akbar's nine nurses, chosen because of Atgah Khan's devotion to Humayun. He was with Humayun at his defeat by Sher Shah and helped him escape. Later he served Akbar loyally and was eventually appointed chancellor, putting out of countenance several rivals at court. Among them was another of Akbar's ex-nurses, Maham Angah and her ambitious son, Adham Khan, who assassinated Atgah Khan in 1562 (p.223). This tomb was erected by Atgah Khan's son, Mirza Aziz Kokaltash, whose own family mausoleum is the stylistically very different Chausath Khamba nearby. The verses on the tomb refer directly to Atgah Khan's assassination.

This tomb is one of the hidden architectural masterpieces of Nizamuddin. Built at about the same time as Humayun's Tomb, it is a charming synthesis of the traditional square tomb form, profusely ornamented with carved marble, inlaid marble, carved red sandstone and red sandstone *jali* screens. Because of its modest proportions there are no windows, other than the screened openings in the main arches, so it is dim inside; nevertheless it is still possible to see the remains of what must have been a handsome interior with an incised and painted plasterwork ceiling and superbly inscribed calligraphy.

There is also a small *dalan* with columns and arches typical of late Mughal work. Next to it are what appear to be the remains of a small wall-mosque with the remains of colourful encaustic tile decoration.

10 - 175

Further Afield

Near Nizamuddin there are a number of tombs, graves and small mosques that were clearly built in its orbit. Apart from the many already discussed above, and others such as the ones in the Delhi Golf Club, there are several to be found in the surrounding open spaces. Of particular architectural interest are:-

GOL GUMBAD (15th century)
Map 10.2 (p.150)

Although this austere and featureless building has a Tughlak appearance from the outside, the interior has some features typical of later tombs, in particular the dome drum with four openings for light.

Gol Gumbad

GATEWAY AND TOMB (15th century)
Map 10.2 (p.150)

Gateway outside Oberoi Hotel

These buildings once formed a large complex: the gateway (described as the Dargah Fatamabi) was the entrance to a walled enclosure containing a square tomb, similar in concept to the Bara Batashewala, although less elaborate. The original external tomb wall can be seen on the north side, while the interior, now also described as a Dargah, has been elaborately renovated with shiny broken tile work.

DELHI GOLF CLUB TOMBS

Only a little further away there are a number of Mughal tombs on the golf course (see p.131). These were among a number of other historic buildings around Nizamuddin and Humayun's Tomb that were listed by the ASI in 1916. A few of these remain, such as the Mosque and Tomb in Kaka Nagar, but so altered as to be of little architectural interest.

18th century tomb

Lal Bangla Gate interior

SHAHJAHANABAD

As we rode over the bridge, the first view of the city was the finest and most solid sight of eastern magnificence that we have seen. Such gateways, and the enormous Palace with its two miles of walls and battlements round it, and old mosques without end rising from among the other buildings. The streets too look busy, and though the King is no longer the rich King he used to be, the city looks as if pains were taken to keep up the buildings worth preserving.

Fanny Eden, 1838

Shah Jahan

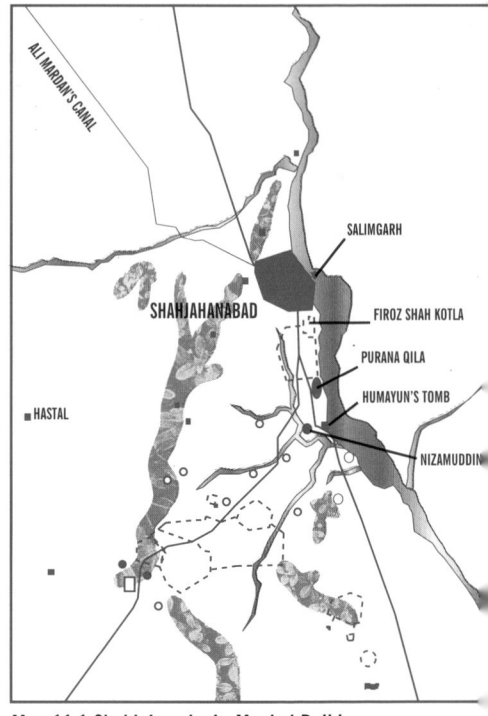

Shah Jahan inherited the throne in 1628, after the kind of fratricidal bloodshed that had been commonplace during the Sultanates but refreshingly uncommon during Mughal times. His behaviour presaged nearly two centuries of increasing violence as the great Mughal empire fell apart. Despite his unloving behaviour towards many of his close relatives, Shah Jahan was capable of complete devotion to his wife, Mumtaz Mahal. After her early death, caused by the birth of their fourteenth child, he erected the Taj Mahal in her memory, arguably the most beautiful building in the world. It is for this and for the exquisitely delicate white marble pavilions in his palaces at Delhi, Agra and Lahore that Shah Jahan is most famous.

Map 11.1 Shahjahanabad - Mughal Delhi

Shah Jahan brought Delhi back onto the centre-stage of Indian affairs after more than a century in the wings, by moving the court back to a new site, north of the old cities of Delhi. He was finding Agra impossible: the fort too cramped, the city too congested and the riverbanks seriously eroded. Apart from the significance of reoccupying a longstanding capital, it was natural for him to found a new city; as an 18th century biographer wrote, 'exalted sultans always had it in mind to cause the world to remember [their reigns] by a permanent monument' (Shah Nawaz Khan in *Ma'asir al-Umara* quoted in Blake).

While Shah Jahan was occupied in his various building projects trouble was brewing among his sons. Knowing what problems had befallen Jahangir from the liberty he had been allowed as a favourite son himself, Shah Jahan kept his eldest and favourite son, Dara Shikoh, beside him at court, where the latter built a great mansion north of the fort. Dara Shikoh was a popular and cultivated man, open, like Akbar, to many different ideas. Away from the court was Shah Jahan's militarily competent third son, Aurangzeb, firmly and puritanically Muslim. He spent many years in the Deccan, attempting to enlarge the Empire, but was thwarted at every turn by Dara Shikoh, who would persuade Shah Jahan to make terms with the besieged just as Aurangzeb was near victory.

When Shah Jahan fell seriously ill in 1658 all three of Aurangzeb's brothers made a bid for power, but Aurangzeb was the eventual victor and pronounced himself Emperor. Dara Shikoh fled but made repeated attempts on the Empire. He was eventually captured by Aurangzeb, who paraded him in an undignified manner through the streets of Delhi, much to the distress of the people. This was enough to persuade Aurangzeb that he would be safer without popular rivals to the throne and several were killed, starting with Dara Shikoh.

Shah Jahan survived another eight years, confined in the Agra Fort by his son Aurangzeb and attended to by his eldest daughter Jahanara. He died in 1666. Meanwhile Aurangzeb was troubled by uprisings, especially in Rajasthan and in the Deccan, where his favourite son allied himself with his enemies. In 1681 Aurangzeb moved into the Deccan, never to return to the north. He was, at first, militarily successful and in 1689 the Mughal Empire was at its largest, after which Aurangzeb struggled unsuccessfully to hold it together. With his power slipping away and haunted by his bloody deeds in the past, Aurangzeb died in 1707 in his late eighties. He left seventeen direct descendants, a recipe for the strife that followed. Aurangzeb's second son managed to secure the throne and ruled for five years. His reign was followed by two short ones before the start of the longer reign of Muhammad Shah Rangila, in 1719.

Aurangzeb's departure for the Deccan had been a blow for Delhi. Only one-sixth of the population remained and the palace and great houses were left empty and unfurnished until the court returned in 1712, when the city regained its former size, if not its glory. Problems of overcrowding were compounded by a series of natural disasters: heavy rain caused huts to collapse killing over two thousand people in 1716, a series of earthquakes did substantial damage in 1719, there was an epidemic of plague in 1730 and then heavy rain caused the canal to flood in 1735. On the other hand court patronage flourished and several fine mosques were constructed.

An event almost as traumatic as Timur's invasion befell Delhi in 1739 when Nadir Shah, a powerful Turk who had just seized the Persian throne, descended on Delhi. Injudicious behaviour by its citizens, for instance quarrelling over the price of grain, led to the city's sacking. The main bazaars were burnt, 20,000 people killed, and vast quantities of money, jewellery and other treasures, including Shah Jahan's Peacock Throne, were carried back to Persia, where the spoils were so great that the population could be relieved of taxes for three years. It is likely that the damage was localised because, while some contemporaries wrote that Delhi was left with the 'appearance of a plain consumed by fire', others lived through the period but fail to record it.

It certainly seems that the situation cannot have been too desperate, because things returned to normal for the next ten years. By 1747, indeed, the city was lauded as extending from the Arab Gate (i.e., the Arab Serai, beside Humayun's Tomb) in the south to the Salt Market in the north, a total of twelve kilometres. However, the next fifty years saw conditions deteriorating lamentably for the citizens of Delhi. The country suffered from repeated assaults from Afghanistan as well as endless fighting among the numerous states that had grown out of the disintegrating Mughal Empire. During the 1750s the inhabitants of the suburbs moved elsewhere or retreated inside the city walls due to the lawlessness outside them. Even inside there was trouble, because there was insufficient revenue from the small territory still attached to Delhi to pay the soldiers. The situation gave rise to a whole new genre of Urdu poetry, *shahr ashob* (ruined city), in which the poets wrote of the decadence and corruption of urban life that had brought the city to such a pass.

The next decade was no better, with the Emperor Shah Alam exiled in Awadh and Maratha marauders stripping the silver inlay from the ceiling of the *diwan-i-khas* in the Red Fort. By 1775 a third of the city was in ruins, mansions were dilapidated, canals clogged with debris and the suburbs abandoned. But still more tribulations were to come. In 1784 the city was taken by the Marathas under Madho Rao Scindia of Gwalior, who 'took the emperor [Shah Alam II] under his protection'. A description of the city at that time says that the 'houses are low and mean, the streets despicably poor and thinly inhabited'. Despite this unpromising appearance a couple of years later yet another group of marauders, Rohillas from the area northeast of Delhi, were digging up the palace for treasure. In their rage at finding none they blinded Shah Alam and then stripped bare what was left of his palace. Scindia retook the city in 1788 and managed to retain it until 1803.

Shahjahanabad

Typical haveli doorway

Shahjahanabad, commonly referred to as Old Delhi or the Walled City, was built by Shah Jahan after he made the decision in 1638 to move his court from Agra, which had superceded Delhi in 1506 under Sikander Lodi. While it was already common for rulers to build new palaces and even new cities, nobody was more likely to follow this custom than Shah Jahan himself, who was particularly interested in architectural projects.

The Red Fort like the one at Agra, was built beside the Yamuna, adjacent to a smaller fort, Salimgarh, which had been built during the Suri interregnum (1540-55). There were also several older buildings on the site of the new city, probably with small settlements around them. In the south were Shah Turkman's grave (c 1240), the 13th century grave of Iltutmish's daughter Raziya, and the 14th century Kalan Masjid. To the west, now behind the Fatehpuri Masjid, there was another pre-Mughal mosque and beyond that, outside the walls, the important complex of the Qadam Sharif (p.93). To the south of the new city were the remains of the older cities, no doubt in a rather less ruined state than when sketched by avid travellers in the 19th century. It is thought that the buildings closest to the new city, for example Firoz Shah Kotla and the extensive suburbs that surrounded it, were used as a quarry.

Unplanned housing

In common with other fortified cities (e.g., Tughlakabad) the fort or citadel lay on one side of the city and was separated from it by a moat and high walls. The palace was completed within ten years, with white marble pavilions lining the top of the riverside wall. At that time the riverbed was closer to the city and a branch flowed between the two forts, right up against the walls of the Red Fort when it was full. Most of the year, however, there was a broad beach below the fort and it was here that the people gathered to see the Emperor and watch elephant fights and similar entertainments. On this side the fort does not seem well protected, the palace pavilions being plainly visible. We have to assume that Shah Jahan did not really expect an attack on Delhi; the great walls on the north, west and south sides were surely only for show.

The city contained the houses of princes and senior courtiers, each of whom maintained households that were smaller versions of the Emperor's own and, to a remarkable extent, self-sufficient. Each establishment was set within a walled compound and contained mansions, gardens, a mosque or temple and all the workshops and tradesmen necessary for the household's requirements. As well as these huge urban estates there were the smaller mansions of lesser nobles and merchants that were scattered quite evenly and widely within the walls. Bernier, a French traveller who lived in Delhi during the 1660s, described these latter as being built of clay and straw although a few were partly of brick and stone. However, he also says that they were 'airy and pleasant, most of them having

Haveli construction detail

courts and gardens, being commodious inside and containing good furniture'. Surrounding these was a sea of straw thatched huts that formed the residences of all those servants and soldiers who did not get accommodation within their patrons' walls.

Outside these great houses bazaars developed along the main thoroughfares, where independent merchants traded in imported goods and other merchandise. The main bazaar streets were lined with single storey arcades in which the merchants laid out their wares, their storerooms being behind, with residential quarters above. Specialist markets developed and some may have remained in the same areas for centuries; for instance, a description of Delhi from around 1850 mentions fireworks being sold on the street on the north of the Jami Masjid, brass and iron merchants at the west end of Chowri Bazaar and dealers in grain and druggists behind the Fatehpuri Masjid. All these markets still exist today and might have existed long before 1850.

In addition to the houses and bazaars there were mosques, temples, *serais* (inns), wells, huge gardens such as that of Jahanara, Shah Jahan's eldest daughter, and an extensive open space around the walls of the Fort, which was used for recreational and military purposes. A canal, originally built by Firoz Shah to irrigate land north of Delhi, was repaired and

Lane with gateway

extended from Karnal to Shahjahanabad by Ali Mardan Khan, the nobleman to whom Shah Jahan entrusted much of the building work of the city. It flowed through the northern suburbs and into the city where it divided into two main channels, one down the main bazaar, Chandni Chowk, and one through Jahanara's garden and then into the palace.

During the reigns of Shah Jahan and Aurangzeb, when Shahjahanabad was supported by the wealth of a vast empire, it was clearly at its richest and most splendid. It has to be emphasised how impressed European visitors were by Delhi; the size of the city and luxury of the palace and noblemen's houses far surpassed anything they had seen at home although, at the same time, they saw little to praise in ordinary people's housing and shops.

It is frustratingly difficult to get a really good idea of what the city looked like (even as late as the 19th century, since most European drawings or photographs are only of Chandni

Courtyard corner

Chowk or the Red Fort), but one source is a detailed map of uncertain origin produced during the 1840s (a facsimile is now available in *Shahjahanabad / Old Delhi,* ed. Ehlers & Krafft). While it obviously tells us a great deal about conditions at that time, it also gives us clues about earlier years. In particular we can get an idea of the size of the mansions, which covered large sites and are shown in great detail. By the 1840s only a few of these establishments still existed, although some others remained in name alone, with perhaps the only building still standing being the entrance gate, beyond which a maze of narrow lanes had replaced the original courtyards and pavilions (usually leaving the property boundaries unchanged and traceable). One such surviving building, the largest at the time the map was made, had been occupied by Sa'adat Khan, the first Nawab of Awadh. This was located south of the canal near the Kabuli Gate. It is clear from the map that it consisted of several large buildings with courtyards and numerous outbuildings (p.195).

Modified haveli courtyard

In the 18th century, as the Empire diminished, Shahjahanabad became a more permanent base for the Emperor, a fact that must have led to the city becoming more built up, with a greater number of *pucca* buildings. The increasing political troubles of the later Mughal rulers meant that there was no longer sufficient wealth to maintain the glittering standards of the past, but it is wrong to assume that this had a completely calamitous effect on Shahjahanabad, where a sophisticated urban life continued even as the built environment deteriorated. Lucknow under the powerful Awadh Nawabs actually superseded Delhi as the capital of Indian Islamic culture, although the number of 18th century mosques and temples in Delhi testifies to the continuing patronage of the arts and religion here as well. A negative effect of the political unrest was that the suburban population moved into the city, adding to the congestion. The journal of a Mr Cruso, who travelled in the mid-1780s, talks of the entrance through the Delhi Gate of the city into a 'long street of miserable appearance, containing one very handsome masjid, with gilded domes' (i.e., Faiz Bazaar and the Sonehri Masjid), but then goes on to describe in fascinating detail the vast mansion of 'Asuph ul Daulah' where he and his party lodged for a few days. There was a series of rooms with wonderfully carved and painted ceilings, a *harem* where all the rooms were lined with mirrors, a 'teh konna' (*taikhana* - underground room), gardens and accommodation for 5,000 troops and 500 horses.

Following the British occupation in 1803 there were just over fifty years of relative peace and prosperity during which the urban culture of the city revived, albeit under the yoke of the British administration. By 1811 it looked prosperous and bustling and restoration work was done on the city walls and the Jami Masjid. In 1821 the canal was cleared and reopened. An 1823 description spoke of 'new sturdy houses of brick and stone set amid a landscape of ruined mansions.' A year later Bishop

Haveli doorway

Heber of Calcutta, travelling through India to get to know his diocese, commented on the fine houses, mosques and streets inside the city walls but contrasted them with the desolation outside and also the 'lamentable state of squalor' of the Emperor's palace inside the Red Fort.

During the reign of the last Emperor, Bahadur Shah ll, there was a great cultural revival, with Delhi regaining the pre-eminent position it had lost to Lucknow. However there was, inevitably, a great change in the social organisation of the city. The economy of the city was no longer dependent on the great households alone. The East India Company army had to be supplied, cash crops played an important new part in the country's economy and a new class emerged of professional people. Real estate registration was reintroduced and taxation was reduced. All this

Collapsing house

increased the confidence of citizens who built energetically but not on the same scale as before. It was during this time that some of the *havelis* that survive today were built, as well as many of the existing Jain and Hindu temples. They share a particularly pretty and delicate style of architecture and decoration. Most residents lived in caste or craft-based *mohullas* (neighbourhoods or, in those days, groups of buildings around a single, gated, lane or alleyway), sometimes built within the ruins of the old mansions. In 1845 no less than 576 such *mohullas* were listed, while the population of the city was given as 137,000, with a bit more than 20,000 outside the walls. The two main religions were equally represented.

Typical lane

The areas to the north and south of the Red Fort were the most Europeanised parts of the city, where houses are shown on our map in the middle of gardens, inside walled compounds, the very reverse of the Indian *havelis* where the gardens are within courtyards, overlooked by rooms and *dalans* on all sides.

Momentous changes took place after the Great Uprising in 1857. The army took over the Fort and large areas of the city were destroyed in order to create a larger open space around it (see over). Jahanara's garden and a part of the city north of it were later taken for the new railway line and station. Jahanara's *serai*, part of her garden complex, which had already turned into a warren of tiny alleyways, was replaced by the Town Hall, with gardens behind and around it. The style of architecture changed, with a distinctive European decorative style creeping into buildings, even those with a thoroughly Indian use such as *havelis* and temples; for instance, Gothic doorways to *havelis* are ubiquitous in some areas.

Rooftops

The relocation of the British Indian capital from Calcutta to Delhi in 1911 brought more changes to Shahjahanabad. The additional population put a strain on the infrastructure of the city, increasing rents dramatically and resulting in Old Delhi becoming and remaining the most congested city in India. Interestingly, even though plots were available in New Delhi and elsewhere outside the walls, many families still continued to build inside the walled city, not only in the relatively spacious Daryaganj, recently released by the army, but also along the narrow lanes of the old city, where handsome art-deco houses can be found in large numbers.

Things changed even more rapidly after Independence in 1947 when a massive number of refugees from Pakistan poured into the city and others, in slightly smaller numbers, poured out. Even after the immigrants had been re-housed in the numerous colonies that developed in south and west Delhi, there was still fast growth inside the walled city, both of residential population and of commerce. Needless to say, a great many *havelis* were redeveloped to cater for this massive explosion. Many were completely gutted and now consist of a dreary passageway with shuttered shops either side, although even here the owners sometimes preserved the original doorway. Others were redeveloped as residential neighbourhoods in an organic way with individuals gradually eating into the open courtyards as they added tiny dwellings. These areas now consist of intricate neighbourhoods of winding lanes with dwellings slotted, as if in a three-dimensional puzzle, around each other.

Elsewhere, wholesale redevelopment has taken place and lanes were laid out with rows of individually built houses or a pattern of small ground floor dwellings interspersed with stairs up to more on the upper level. There is a fourth category in which the original courtyard is still visible but the *haveli* is lived in by many different families. There are still some *havelis* that are in single family occupation. The most common type of courtyard is square with similar enclosed rooms on each side, often with pointed 'gothic' arches. It is not unusual, however, to find more traditional rectangular courtyards with a raised platform at one end. Open *dalans* with round-arched arcading look onto the courtyard on each side but the main *dalan* is on the platform (this is sometimes occupied by one family while others live in the side rooms). A problem for both landlord and tenant is that nobody can afford repairs, so it is not far-fetched to say that the old city is literally crumbling under the strain. Even so there are many areas of the city in which there are pleasant living conditions. The back lanes and courtyards are very quiet and have great environmental benefits: for instance, the fact that the sun cannot penetrate the narrow lanes means that in summer they are several degrees cooler than wider streets. Many areas are therefore worth preserving and, moreover, can be learnt from.

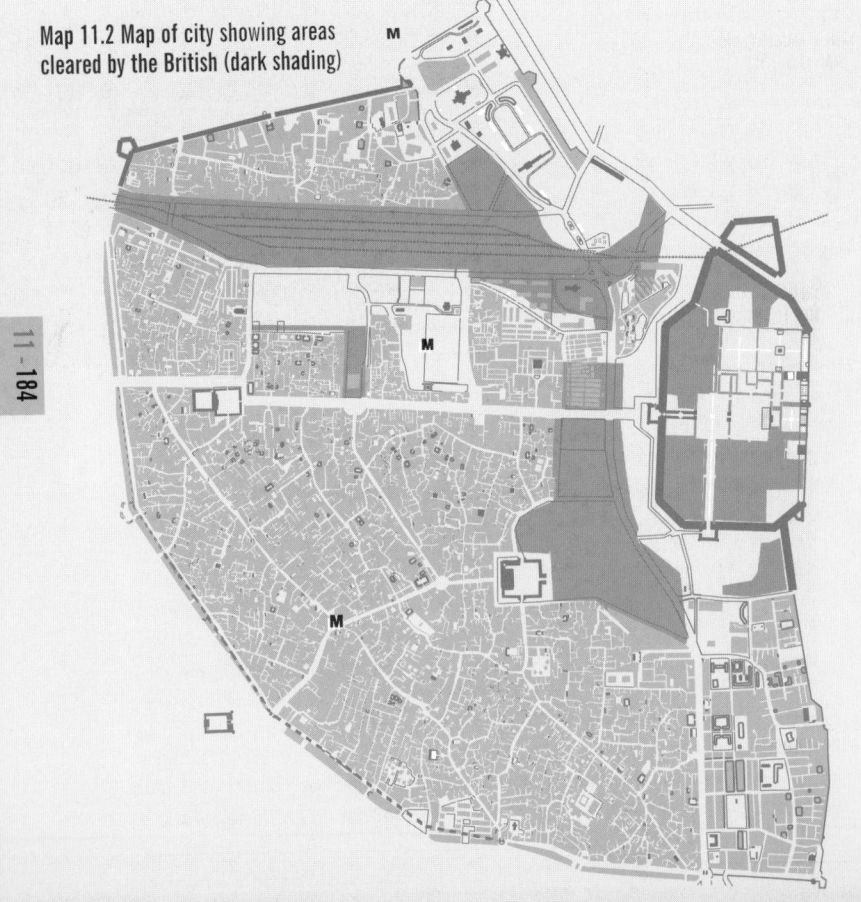

Map 11.2 Map of city showing areas cleared by the British (dark shading)

Exploring Shahjahanabad

S hahjahanabad is a difficult and, at first, an off-putting place to visit. The city is the largest and busiest 'medieval' city in India and therefore confusing, but well worth visiting. There are tiny manufacturing units all over the city, strictly segregated by product (e.g., embroidery, metal bashing, paper goods, costume jewellery, etc.) It is also an unbelievably busy wholesale market (probably the biggest in India for many unlikely items such as fabrics and paper) for a vast range of products that are all carried, through narrow alleyways, into crumbling *havelis* and gimcrack modern storerooms, to be carried out again, once sold, to their ultimate retail outlet. There are also retail shops and a proportionate number of shoppers, besides numerous residents going about their daily lives in the midst of this colourful mayhem.

In this chapter the city has been divided into twelve areas, each with a detailed map showing buildings of particular interest. Traditional doorways and courtyards are shown with a dot or heavier lines respectively. A walk is indicated in each area, taking in as much of interest as possible. Exploration everywhere is rewarding but it is very easy to lose one's way. The best approach is to know where you want to return to and take a bicycle-rickshaw back there at the end of your walk.

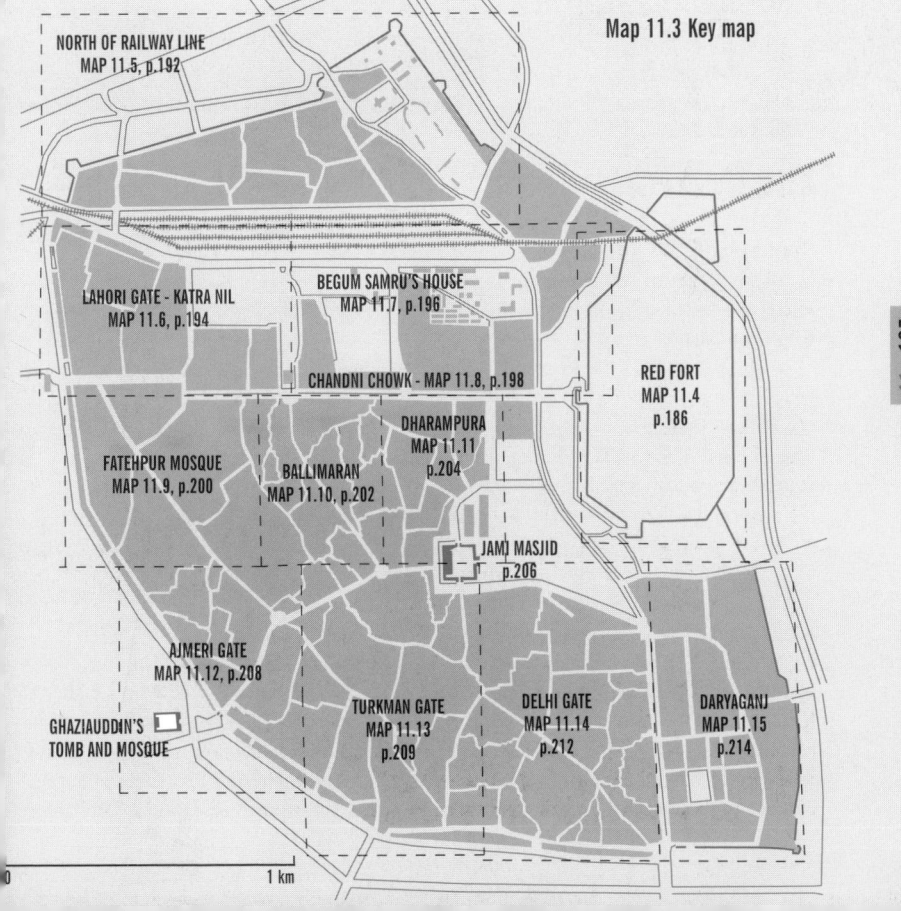

Map 11.3 Key map

NORTH OF RAILWAY LINE
MAP 11.5, p.192

BEGUM SAMRU'S HOUSE
MAP 11.7, p.196

LAHORI GATE - KATRA NIL
MAP 11.6, p.194

CHANDNI CHOWK - MAP 11.8, p.198

RED FORT
MAP 11.4
p.186

DHARAMPURA
MAP 11.11
p.204

FATEHPUR MOSQUE
MAP 11.9, p.200

BALLIMARAN
MAP 11.10, p.202

JAMI MASJID
p.206

AJMERI GATE
MAP 11.12, p.208

GHAZIAUDDIN'S
TOMB AND MOSQUE

TURKMAN GATE
MAP 11.13
p.209

DELHI GATE
MAP 11.14
p.212

DARYAGANJ
MAP 11.15
p.214

11 - 185

1 km

Khass Mahal Burj

Khass Mahal screen

The Red Fort

Since visitors are not allowed to enter many of the buildings binoculars are helpful for seeing details of the interiors. The lower ASI fees apply (Rs 100 for foreigners, Rs 5 for Indians).

The palace at Delhi was the culmination of Shah Jahan's building projects. In his private sleeping quarters (*khass mahal*) there is an inscription recording the date and cost of construction and comparing the palace to heaven. It needs a powerful imagination to equate it with heaven now, with only a few pavilions remaining and their former context of courtyards and gardens gone.

The chief architect was Ustad Ahmad Lahori, who had worked with the Persian architect Ustad Isa Khan Effendi at the Taj Mahal. The work was begun in 1638 at

Khass Mahal detail

a time selected by astrologers as being supremely auspicious. The main entrances were Delhi Gate, so named because it led towards Delhi (the old cities), and the Lahori Gate, aligned with Chandni Chowk, which led towards the road to Lahore. It is the Lahori Gate that was and still is used by the public, while the Delhi Gate gives access to the large army compound that is finally being vacated from the Fort. Both gates were augmented with projecting protective bastions by Aurangzeb during the lifetime of his father, the captive and deposed Shah Jahan,

Naubat Khana interior

Bhadon pavilion

much to the latter's displeasure. Inside, the
eastern half of the Fort was reserved for the
Emperor and his household. The southern
part of this was the *zenana* (women's quarters),
only accessible to women, the Emperor, his
sons and certain servants. The northern part,
where the Emperor carried out his business,
was more public, but still largely restricted.
This area included the largest and finest of the
many gardens in the palace. The western
half of the palace was the truly public area,
containing the workshops, bazaars, stables,
etc. The intersection of these zones was at the
Diwan-i-Am courtyard, that part of the palace
where the general public were admitted to the
Emperor's daily court.

   As the Mughal Empire contracted the
later Emperors found it difficult to keep up
standards in the palace. By the early 19th
century, according to European accounts,
much of the interior of the Fort was derelict.
Part of the public area had become a warren
of streets and alleyways very similar to the city
outside, where hundreds of descendants of
Shah Jahan lived in the utmost destitution.
However, there were still buildings that
impressed visitors when they saw them after
the Great Uprising, even though they had
suffered in the anarchic, revenge-filled
months immediately following the re-taking
of the city. After .1857 the whole area,
excluding the very few buildings deemed
worthy of preservation, was cleared to make
way for barracks and army offices.

Diwan-i-Khas

Moti Masjid

Note the variation in the arches. Above is the Rang Mahal with simple cusped arches.

The garden pavilions (right) have the same type of arches.

Below is the Shah Burj, built slightly later, which has more mannered cusped arches and more elaborate junctions with the pillar capitals.

THE JHAROKHA IN THE DIWAN-I-AM

The jharokha, under which the Emperor sat, exemplifies a departure in architectural style, thought to show significant European influence, by way of pictures imported into India showing royalty or religious figures framed in little pavilions, with semi-circular arches and bulbous ('cypress-like') columns. This 'vegetabilisation' is explicitly referred to in contemporary descriptions of the palace, the buildings being compared with paradise and therefore with a garden. Of course, some of the inspiration, such as the curved bangla roof, came from closer to home, but the idea of this conflation of royalty, divinity and gardens through distorted European imagery is persuasive (See Ebba Koch).

The other element of the platform is the inlaid niche behind the jharokha. This is a fascinating piece of work and has been the subject of some controversy as to its provenance: whether the inlaid work that decorates the back surface is wholly a product of Indian workshops or not. It was almost certainly a mixture, made up from sets of small pietra dura panels imported from Italy, while the setting and the surrounding plant and bird inlay work on white marble was almost certainly done by local craftsmen, who might well have made a few black panels as well, in order to complete the whole scheme. Pietra dura means 'hard stone' in Italian, referring to the thin slivers of polished hard stone cut into shapes and fitted to create realistic pictures. The ones used here are typical of the many sets that were manufactured for incorporation into pieces of European furniture such as cabinets. The most famous is the small arched panel at the top (very difficult to see), depicting the Greek God Orpheus playing to animals. The Mughal court was well aware of European art and Jahangir, especially, was fascinated by the realism of the pictures. The Court would have been similarly fascinated by the detail of these panels.

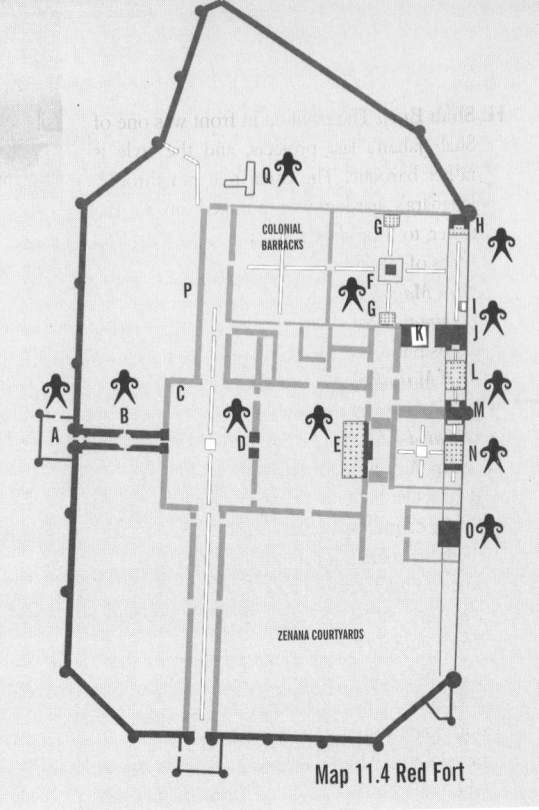

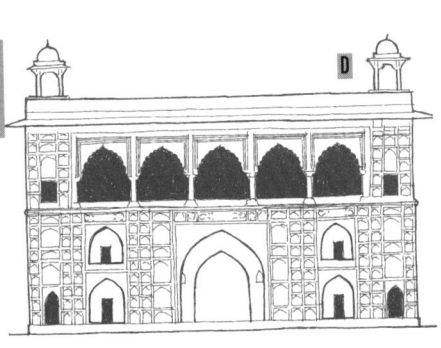

Map 11.4 Red Fort

A. Lahori Gate

B. *Chhatta chowk.* The main public market in the Palace, modelled on a Persian market at Shah Jahan's request.

C. Shaded areas show the position of buildings before the post-1857 demolition.

D. *Naubat khana* (drum house). Here visitors to the court had to dismount.

E. *Diwan-i-am,* where the Emperor held his public audiences.

F. *Hayat bakhsh.* The only surviving garden. The pavilion in the middle of the pool was built by Bahadur Shah ll.

G. *Sawan* and *bhadon* pavilions. *Sawan* and *bhadon* are the two rainy months in the Hindu calendar.

H. **Shah Burj.** The pavilion in front was one of Shah Jahan's last projects, and the style is rather baroque. The canal that ran through Jahanara's garden was pumped up to the tower, to drop down the chute and then along the terrace, through the series of pavilions. It was known as the *nahr-i-bihisht* (river of paradise).

I. *Hira Mahal.* Built by Bahadur Shah ll.

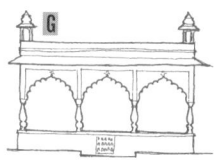

J. *Hammam* (bath house). There is fine inlaid work on the floor and dados but it is difficult to see.

K. *Moti Masjid* (Pearl Mosque). Built by Aurangzeb. It has been closed to public for several years.

L. *Diwan-i-Khass* (hall of special or private audience). The decoration is elaborate but would have been even more spectacular in the past, living up to the inscription on the inside of the central hall which quotes Amir Khusro's famous line 'If there be a paradise on earth, this is it, this is it, this is it' (p.172).

The ceiling, flat and covered in an ornate diamond pattern of carved and painted timber, was once encased in silver, stolen during the anarchy of the late 18th century.

M. *Khass mahal* (special palace). Where the Emperor slept. Like the *hammam,* the *khass mahal* is asymmetrical about the east-west axis because both buildings formed the corner pavilions of the courtyard that would once have enclosed the *diwan-i-khas.* Thus, while the north side related to the semi-public *diwan-i- khas,* absolute privacy was needed on the south side of the *khass mahal,* where the *zenana* began. This was achieved by reducing the visual connection between the two sides to the astonishingly elaborate marble *jali* screen and panel over the *nahr-i-bihisht,* set back inside the north-facing three-bayed alcove (the screen was recently damaged disgracefully during ASI 'restoration work'). Access to the interior of the building was normally from the south, from an elaborately adorned open arcade. At either end of the arcade there are cusped arches with *jali* screens below and translucent marble or alabaster panels above. On the river side an opening is left for viewing activities on the sands below, while the Emperor could show himself from the the *burj-i tila,* the projecting octagonal tower.

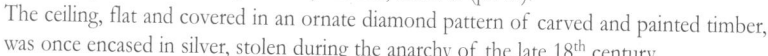

N. *Rang mahal* (coloured palace). Like the other pavilions the *nahr-i-bihisht* flowed right through the building but here it included a highly ornamented pool where a fountain erupted out of the centre of a flattened lotus flower. At either end of the pavilion are semi-enclosed rooms that are finely decorated with inlaid glass and feature well-defined net vaulting in the half domes at each end.

O. **Museum** in a much altered pavilion.

P. **Mutiny museum.** This is one of the colonial buildings erected in the Fort and houses a museum on the Uprising.

Q. *Baoli.*

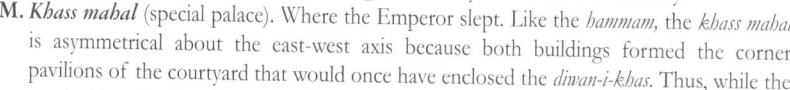

North of Railway Line

The area east of Kashmiri Gate once contained the mansions of Shah Jahan's oldest son, Dara Shikoh and Ali Mardan Khan, Shah Jahan's courtier responsible for much of the work to the new city such as the canal. Their vast mansions covered well over ten hectares between them! These estates passed through several hands before being used by British administrators when they first occupied Delhi in 1803. The area was the centre of administrative power during the early East India Company days and there are a number of early colonial buildings. Later on, the area along the city wall (Nicholson Road) became fashionable, being conveniently situated between the Civil Lines and the railway station, so there are a number of interesting early 20th century buildings here, mainly administrative or educational, some still in the same use today.

Map 11.5 - North of Railway Line

A. **Asha Mansion** 1926.

B. **Dargah Panja Sharif** 18th c. Although nothing remains of the original buildings this is an important Shia site, where a handprint of Ali is kept.

C. **Maulvi Muhammad Baqar's mosque** 1854.

D. **Tomb beside Maulvi Ataullah's mosque** 18th c.

E. **Colonial house** 19th c.

F. **NCC offices** 1890s. This was one of Sultan Singh's houses. He was a prosperous banker, who must have bought the greater part of James Skinner's estate.

G. **House** 1900s Another of Sultan Singh's houses.

H. **Colonel James Skinner's estate** early 19th c. There are two small colonial buildings that might have been in Skinner's garden.

I. **Kashmiri Gate** 1650s. Quite different from the other remaining gates, this once formed a polygonal square inside the gate, very similar in plan to the polygonal *chowks* that stood at the junctions of some of the main roads elsewhere in the city.

J. **Bengali Club** 1925. Many Bengalis moved to Delhi when the capital was transferred from Calcutta in 1911.

K. **Kashmiri Gate Market** 1890s. Built by Lala Sultan Singh.

L. **Lal Masjid** or Fakrul Masjid 1728-29.

M. **Madrasa Amima Islama Arabad** 1880s.

N. **St Stephen's College Building** 1891. Built for the college, which remained, until it moved to the Delhi University campus in the 1940s. Now houses the Election Commission offices.

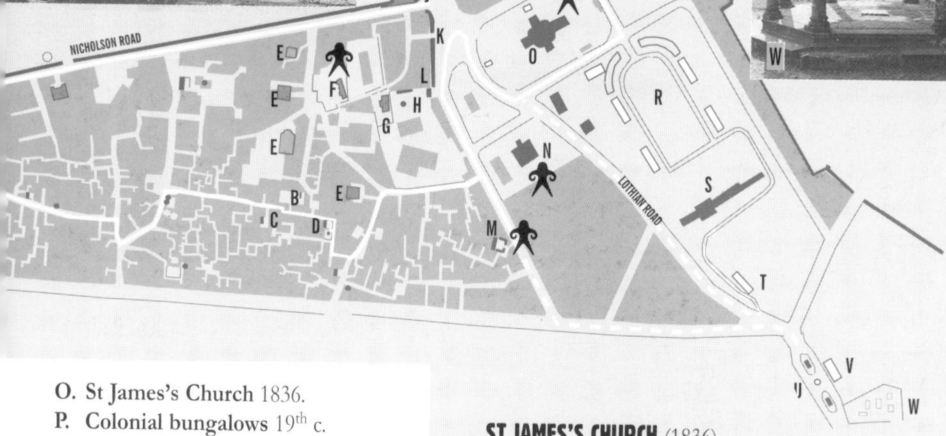

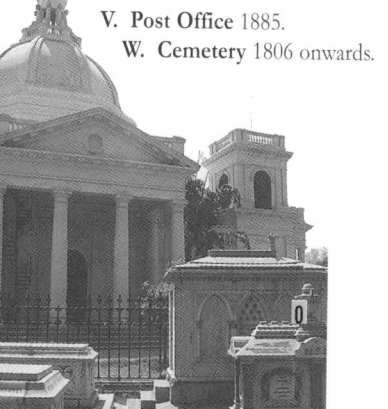

O. **St James's Church** 1836.

P. **Colonial bungalows** 19th c.

Q. **Early colonial residence** early 19th c. This was built for the Deputy Resident in place of the mansion of Ali Mardan Khan over the original *taikhana*.

R. **Guru Gobind Singh Indraprastha University** mid-20th c. Built as the Delhi College of Engineering.

S. **Archaeological Museum** 1650s and 1800s. Tradition has it that this was originally Dara Shikoh's library. It later became the British Residency.

T. **Delhi Institute of Technology** Early 1900s

U. **Magazine** 1820s. All that remains of the British magazine, blown up in 1857.

V. **Post Office** 1885.

W. **Cemetery** 1806 onwards.

ST JAMES'S CHURCH (1836)

This was built by Colonel James Skinner, the result of a private promise that he had made, when he lay wounded on a battlefield in 1800, that if he survived his injuries he would build a church. The building has recently been saved from structural collapse by INTACH.

The design of the church was probably given by army engineers, which is not as odd as it sounds, engineers being, effectively, the only European 'architects' then practising in India, and depending on copybooks for the European classical features, as seen here. The church is well proportioned with an unusual plan. Instead of the more normal cruciform shape with a dome sitting over the crossing of the transepts, here the dome is supported on an octagonal arcade and the circular space under the dome is, effectively, the nave, where the congregation sits. The chancel contains the remains of the inlaid marble cenotaph which once stood over William Fraser's tomb, the remains of which stand in front of the church (see p.251 for more on Fraser). On the north side of the church is the Skinner family's burial ground and, at the rear, the tomb of Thomas Metcalfe, who lived in Delhi for forty years from 1813 until his death in 1853, during which time he served as Agent and Commissioner.

Skinner, born in 1778, was the son of a Scottish military officer and his Rajput wife. At the age of eighteen he joined Mahadji Scindia's army under General de Boigne. At this time there were a number of mercenaries from Europe fighting for the major Indian powers, men such as de Boigne from France and Walter Reinhard from Luxembourg, whose Indian wife (Begum Samru — p.197) became an important figure in Delhi's history. Skinner himself became a successful soldier and a wealthy man. He took arms with the British in 1803 and led an irregular cavalry corps, made up initially of troops that had served under Scindia. This unit became the famous Skinner's Light Horse, which still exists and still has many connections with the surviving Skinner family.

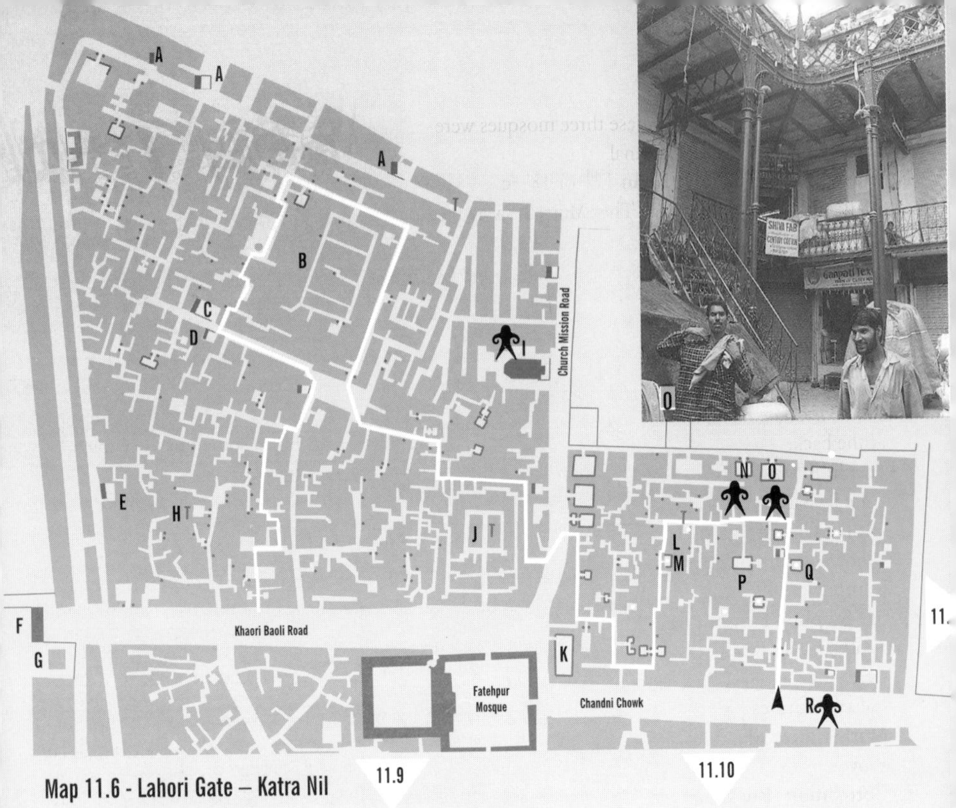

Map 11.6 - Lahori Gate – Katra Nil

11.9

11.10

Lahori Gate and Katra Nil

This area is pleasant to walk around, and contains interesting buildings and markets, such as a huge cloth market in the northeast section near the railway, and the fascinating chemicals and spice market near Khaori Baoli Road. The area around Katra Nil has an astonishing number of *shivalayas*, octagonal domed pavilions that shelter an arrangement of small idols surrounding a lingam (marked as white spots on the map). Although most of them were probably originally family shrines attached to *havelis*, these have mostly gone, leaving the shrines behind. There are fewer mosques in this area than other parts of the old city. Around the northern perimeter of the area there are a number of *dharamsalas* that would have served passengers from the nearby railway station.

The larger area to the west is interesting because it once contained several large *havelis*, whose imprints are clearer than in other parts of the city. The Haveli Nawab Sa'adat Khan was extant until relatively recently and redevelopment took place very much within each distinct courtyard. On the other hand the market on the corner opposite the Fatehpuri Mosque had already been redeveloped when the 1840s map was made, and been changed little since.

A. **Mosques** 18th and 19th c. These three mosques were all built over or beside the canal.

B. **Haveli Nawab Sa'adat Khan** 17th or 18th c.

C. **Mutasib's Mosque** 1723. The Mutasib was the court inquisitor.

D. **Ramzan Shah's Mosque** 1801. The mosque appears to have been founded by the mother of a courtier of Shah Alam (not in fact called Ramzan Shah).

E. **Masjid Dilkushad** 19th c. This is an unusually ornate mosque with windows overlooking the street at the back.

F. **Sarhindi Masjid** 1650. Built just outside the Lahori Gate by Sarhindi Begum, a wife of Shah Jahan.

G. **Walled City Museum** (converted from an early 20th c. house – currently closed).

H. **Temple** late 19th c.

I. **St Stephen's Church** 1867. The Cambridge Brotherhood, who founded St Stephen's College, were originally based here. The brick building is in Italian Romanesque style.

J. **Market area**: Mentioned in introductory paragraph above.

K. **Coronation Building** (probably commemorating the 1911 coronation). Built on the site of 'Namak ki Haveli', which belonged to a servant of the Maratha court who betrayed them by aligning with the British, thus being 'false to his salt (*namak*)'. An original door can be seen to the north.

L. **Ghanteswara Mandir Shivalaya** 1850.

M. **Dhumimal Khanna's Shivalaya** mid 19th c.

N. *Haveli* **courtyard**, now a temple and school.

O. **Dharamsala** (1, Bagh Diwar) late 19th c.

P. **Ladliji ka Bara Mandir** mid 19th c.

Q. **Shivalaya Kunniji Maharaj** 19th c.

R. **Chunna Mal Haveli** Built after 1857 (p.198).

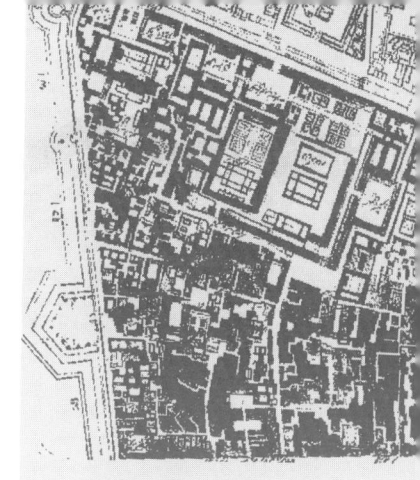

DETAIL OF 1840s MAP

The largest mansion shown on this map is the Haveli Nawab Sa'adat [Shahadat] Khan, built in the 17th or 18th century. Several gates remain, along with the distinctive street pattern resulting from relatively recent redevelopment. Sa'adat Khan was the uncle and father-in-law of Safdarjang and both of them lived in Delhi while serving (or ruling) the Mughal emperors. Safdarjang himself is supposed to have lived in part of Darah Shikoh's mansion, while Sa'adat Khan's name remained attached to this building. A previous courtier could have built it, but it seems likely to have been built by Sa'adat Khan as he was responsible for repairing the neighbouring canal during Muhammad Shah's reign (thereby earning a handsome income). Delhi was visited in 1793 by a British traveller, Franklin, who talked of the splendour of the great houses and mentions specifically the baths (hammam) in Sa'adat Khan's house, 'a set of beautiful rooms, paved, and lined with white marble; they consist of five distinct apartments into which light is admitted by glazed windows at the top of the domes'.

11 - 195

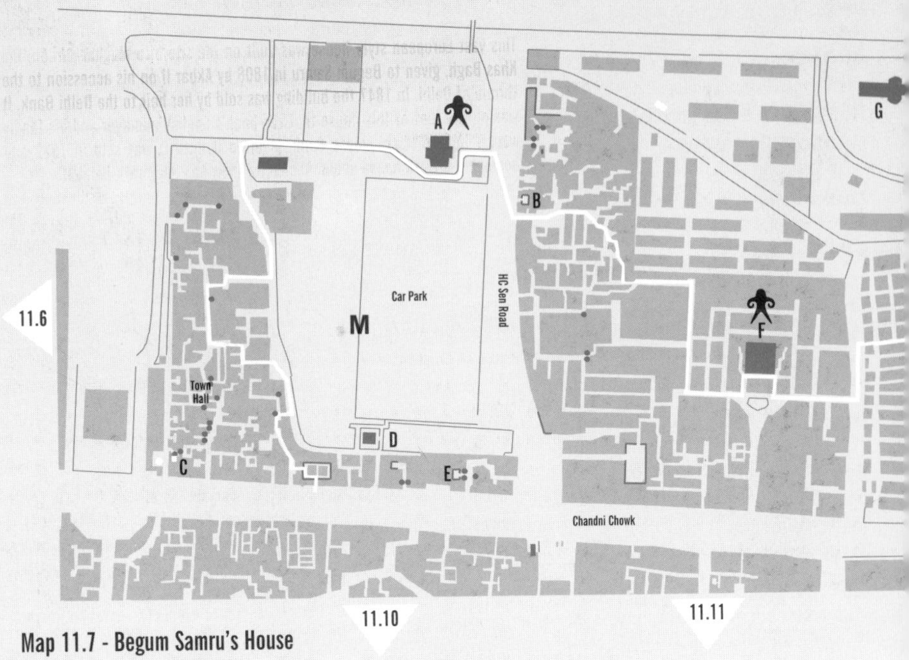

Car Park

HC Sen Road

M

Town Hall

C

D

E

B

A

F

G

Chandni Chowk

Map 11.7 - Begum Samru's House

Begum Samru's House

The huge grounds of Begum Samru's House and a part of Jahanara's garden formerly took up most of the area. This is now mostly a vast area devoted to car parking and (currently) Metro construction, while Begum Samru's garden was developed relatively recently, hence the grid pattern of streets. Begum Samru's garden is now a wholesale market for medical and electrical goods and wares. Apart from a small residential area cleared after the Great Uprising, where the Lajpat Rai Market now is, the only other formerly urbanised areas in this section of the city are now busy markets selling fabrics, metalwork and jewellery. Another old area, opposite Lajpat Rai Market and beneath the walls of the Red Fort, must have been excluded from the post-1857 clearances because of the cluster of temples.

A. **Hardayal Municipal Public Library** 1916. The collection originated in the Lawrence Institute Library, once housed in the Town Hall. This building opened in 1916 as the Hardinge Municipal Public Library and renamed in 1970 after one of the accused in Hardinge's assassination attempt.
B. **Courtyard** early 20th c.
C. **Courtyard temple** late 19th c.

BEGUM SAMRU'S PALACE (1823)

This vast European style house was built on the site of a Mughal garden, the Khas Bagh, given to Begum Samru in 1806 by Akbar II on his accession to the throne of Delhi. In 1847 the building was sold by her heir to the Delhi Bank. It was on the roof of this house that the bank's English manager and his family were killed in 1857. Lloyds Bank acquired it until it was sold in 1922 and became a private house again, becoming known as Bhagirath Palace.

Begum Samru was the widow of Walter Reinhard, a European mercenary officer who commanded a small army maintained by the estate of Sardhana near Meerut. After his death she displaced his son by his first wife and became the 'commander' herself. She seems to have skilfully backed every horse going and was in a good position, when the British took over, to cash in on her earlier conversion to Christianity. She had already become a curiosity as a Christian ruler; now she was able to live in all worlds, accompanying female visitors to the King's zenana in the palace during the day, and at night sitting with the gentlemen smoking her hookah after dinner when the rest of the ladies had withdrawn.

D. **Modern temple.**

E. **Courtyard** early 20th c.

F. **Begum Samru's House** 1823.

G. **St Mary's Church** 1865. This was a Roman Catholic chapel built on land cleared after 1857. Like St Stephen's Church it is in the Italian Romanesque style.

H. **Lajpat Rai Market** 1950s. Built for Punjabi refugees after Partition.

I. **Temple complex** 17th c. These shrines are connected with a sadhu, Madhavadasa, who is said to have impressed Akbar by performing a miracle, turning grinding stones remotely!

J. **Line of aqueduct.** Houses are now built over the aqueduct that carried the canal from Jahanara's garden to the Red Fort, and here passed over a branch canal that flowed down Chandni Chowk and eventually discharged into the river beside the Nigambodh Darwaza.

K. **Mosque** Sadly, recently rebuilt. This is shown on the 1840s map at the place, known as the 'shutr-gulu' or 'camel's neck', where the water collected before being pumped up to the palace.

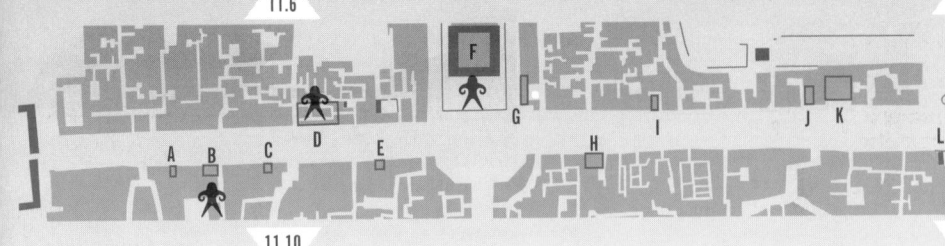

Map 11.8 - Chandni Chowk

Chandni Chowk

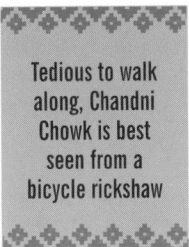
Originally Chandni Chowk was an important market with shops lining the road with residences above, interspersed with chowks. The frontages were interrupted by gateways to mansions and roads. Most of the buildings were redeveloped in the 19th century and much grander buildings erected, some of which survive. It is sometimes difficult to spot them, but there are quite a few ostentatious houses, often with rooftop terraces behind screens, flanked by rooms on either side. There is an astonishing range of styles, from extraordinarily ornate screens that look rather like elaborate cake icing, to sober classical façades.

A. **Mahalakshmi Building** 1910.

B. **Union Bank of India Building** 1930s.

C. **Oriental Bank of Commerce Building** 1930s.

D. **Lala Chunna Mal's Haveli** after 1857. Lala Chunna Mal prospered in the years immediately following the Great Uprising, when the British displeasure with the Muslim community benefited the Hindus. Already a successful merchant and banker, with a small *haveli* on Katra Nil, he was in a good position to take advantage of the low prices prevailing for land in the city. He later became an important figure in local government and a great charitable benefactor to city institutions. His descendants still live in the *haveli*, while the ground floor is a busy cloth market.

E. **Allahabad Bank Building** 1930s.

F. **Town Hall** 1864. This was originally built as the municipal offices and housed the European Club, the Lawrence Institute and its Library. The building replaced what remained of Jahanara's serai. The junction with the newly created Nai Sarak opposite formed a semi-circular urban space in front of the Town Hall, acknowledging the pre-existing octagonal *chowk* in front of Jahanara's serai (the original Chandni Chowk).

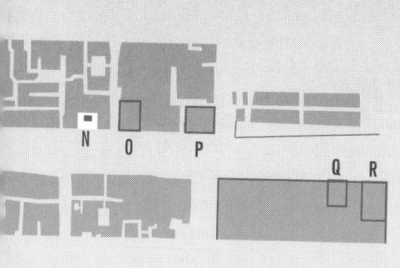

G. Police Station late 19th c.

H. Punjab National Bank Building 1920s.

I. Residence 1920s with a particularly ornate façade.

J. Central Bank of India Building mid 20th c.

K. Mahavir Jain Bhawan Early 20th c. The Delhi Jain community is long-standing and prosperous. The building had an insubstantial, delicate, arcaded façade that was recently replaced by an appalling concrete frame. The roofline remains the same.

L. Sunehri Masjid 1721. Built by Roshan-ud-daulah Zafar Khan, a corrupt official at the Mughal court. It was from the raised courtyard of this mosque that Nadir Shah watched the massacre of citizens in 1739.

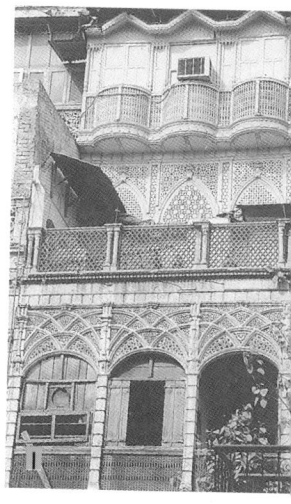

M. Gurudwara Sisganj (mainly modern). Like other Gurudwaras in Delhi, the buildings, of which there are several, are modern. The site is historic, commemorating the spot where the ninth Guru, Tegh Bahadur, was beheaded on Aurangzeb's orders at the Kotwali (Mughal police station), which occupied this site.

N. Central Baptist Church 1858. One of the earliest churches in Delhi.

O. State Bank of India early 20th c.

P. Fort View Hotel early 20th c. This was part of a new group of buildings that were eventually allowed to be built on land that had been cleared after 1857.

Q. Gaurishankar Temple 1760s. This temple is supposed to have been founded by a Maratha courtier of Scindia and survived the post-1857 clearance. There are a series of shrines at first floor level, the main one being highly ornate, with silver walls and ceiling.

R. Lal Mandir (1656 foundation, but the buildings are newer: mainly 1878). Located on the first floor level, the original temple, on the north (right) side of the courtyard, also seems to have survived the post-1857 clearance. It originated as a temple erected for the Jain members of Shah Jahan's army camping in the then much larger open area in front of the Fort. There is an unsavoury bird hospital behind the temple.

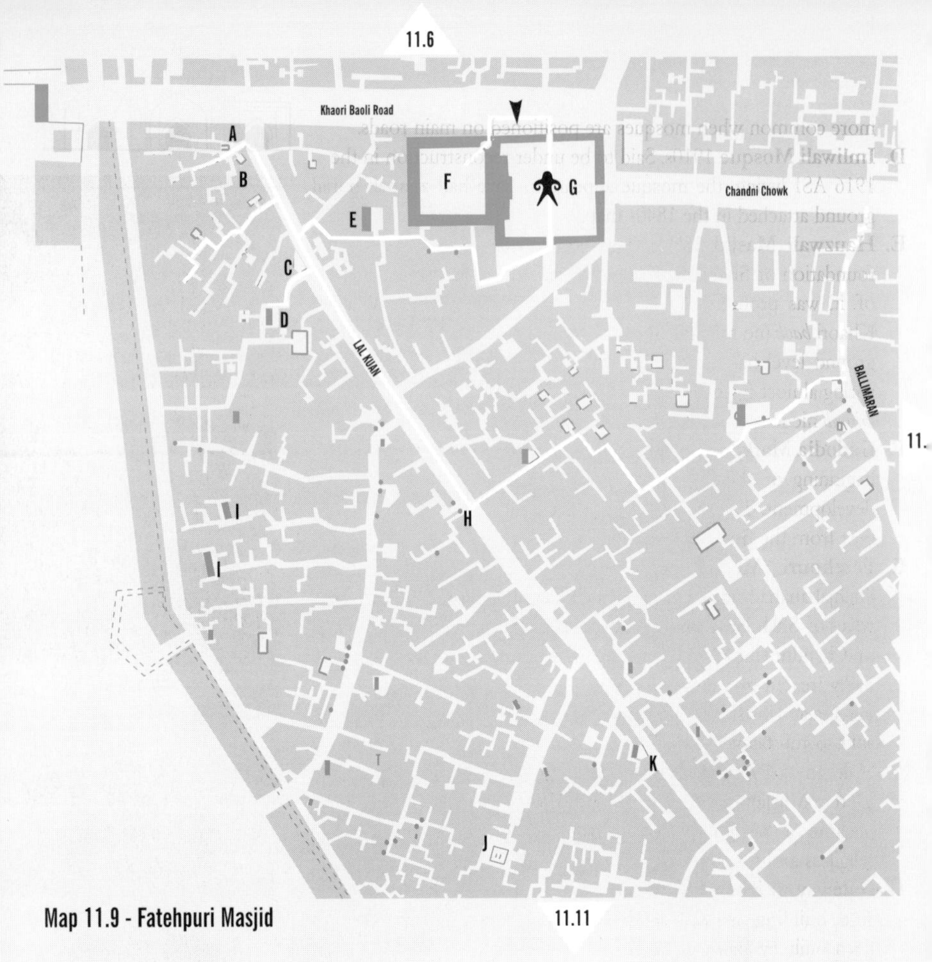

Khaori Baoli Road

A

B

F ⚜ G

E Chandni Chowk

C

D

LAL KUAN

11.

I

I

H

K

J

Map 11.9 - Fatehpuri Masjid 11.11

Fatehpuri Masjid

Most of this area consists of a network of tiny lanes that grew organically among the ruins of old *havelis*. The area to the southeast of the mosque is very different, with regular lanes. This is probably because it had a group of large *haveli* courtyards in the mid 19th century and redevelopment was done in an organised way. There are some very charming markets here: a huge wholesale spice market is located on either side of Khaori Baoli, while paan ingredients are sold at the top end of Lal Kuan.

A. Open pavilion.
B. Temple mid-19th c.
C. Tahawwur Khan's Mosque 1727.
   This would have been built by a courtier and is a typical upper floor mosque with shops below, noticeably

more common when mosques are positioned on main roads.

D. Imliwali Mosque 1910s. Said to be under reconstruction in the 1916 ASI listing, the mosque appears to have had a small burial ground attached in the 1840s map.

E. Hauzwali Masjid 15th c. This is a mosque that pre-dates the foundation of Shahjahanabad. Lal Kuan, the main road southwest of it, was probably an old road and this mosque and adjacent Khaori *baoli* (no longer existing) may have been a resting place. The ground level has altered drastically – inside, the arches seem to spring almost from the floor and only the very top of the original *mihrab* niche is visible. A simple *minbar* has been built recently.

F. Gadodia Market early 20th c. The building was constructed at the beginning of the 20th c. as a mixed commercial and residential development. The quite fine but eclectic architecture can be seen best from the first floor or roof.

G. Fatehpuri Masjid 1650. The third largest mosque in Shahjahanabad was built by Nawab Fatehpuri Begum, one of the wives of Shah Jahan, and occupies a prominent position, at the end of Chandni Chowk. This mosque and courtyard were particularly badly treated by the British after the Great Uprising, when it was sold to the banker, Lala Chunna Mal. In 1877 it was restored to the Muslim community and became a popular venue for religious and political debates.

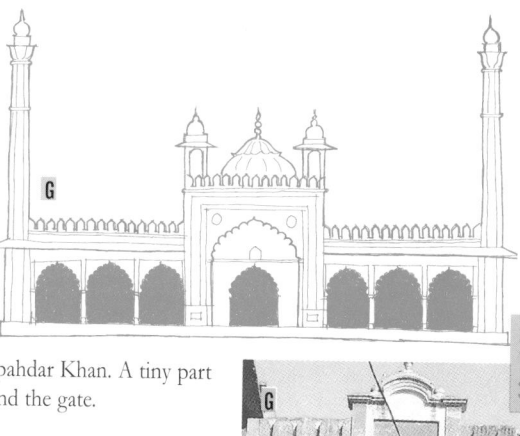

H. Gateway to Zinat Mahal 1846. The building is said to have been built by Bahadur Shah II's favourite wife, Zinat Mahal, although the 1840s map describes the group of buildings behind the gateway as belonging to Sipahdar Khan. A tiny part of the original building is visible beyond the gate.

I. Mosques 19th c.

J. Graves of Nawabs Iradatmand Khan and Musa Yar Khan 1774. Nawab Iradatmand Khan seems to have founded a *madrasa* here during Muhammad Shah's reign. Musa Khan may have been a relative.

K. Mosque 1781.

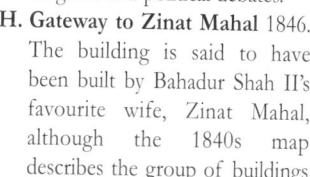

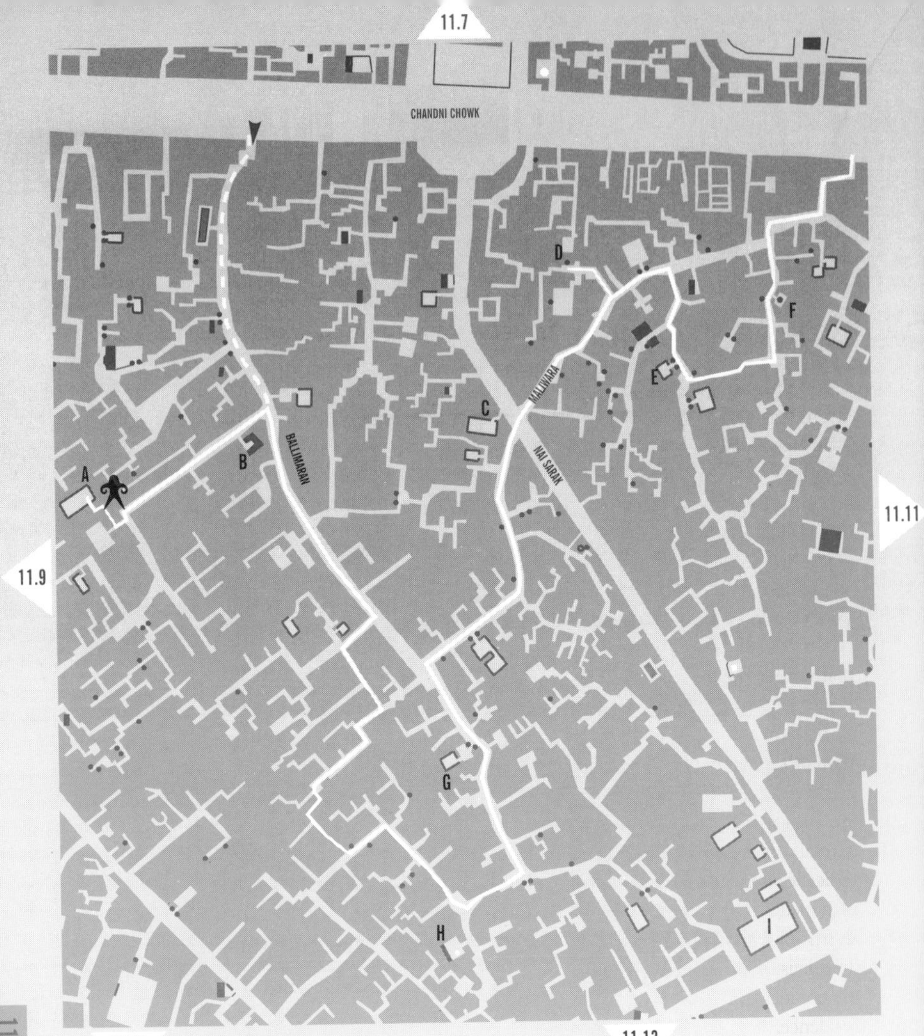

CHANDNI CHOWK

D

F

MALIWARA

C

E

BALLIMARAN

HAI SARAK

B

A

G

H

I

Map 11.10 - Ballimaran

C

Ballimaran and Maliwara

This area has a number of interesting *havelis*. The most interesting courtyards are indicated as a bold square or rectangle on the maps. They are often accessible to the public because they are in multiple occupation or in institutional use, but if doors are clearly shut the privacy of the occupants should obviously be respected. All the existing *havelis* in the walled city date from the 19th or early 20th centuries, when the vast households of the past no longer existed. The pattern, at any rate from the mid-19th century, was a single-courtyard *haveli*, sometimes preceded by a small yard or long entrance passage. The entrance gateways were always highly ornate, generally with a projecting balcony above. Sometimes on either side of the doorway,

D   E   G

especially on busy lanes, there were shop units. The courtyard was surrounded by rooms, some enclosed, but many taking the form of open room or *dalans*. The main *dalan* would have been the men's entertaining room, with the women able to look down from screened side rooms. On the roof there were generally bedrooms in the corners, with terraces between them where people would have slept during the hot weather.

G

A. **Ghalib's wife's family's *haveli***. Reputed to be that of Ilahi Baksh Maruf (Ghalib's father-in-law), it seems to have been owned by one Ammi Naw ad-din Khan in the 1840s.

B. **Ghalib's haveli**. This is said to be where the poet Mirza Asadullah Khan Ghalib lived at the end of his life. While he always lived in this area, he moved several times. This structure seems to have been radically altered: it appears on the 1840s map as part of a medium sized *haveli* and its entrance at that time was from within, in other words not from the street. The division of the property and bare brickwork give us no idea of how it might have appeared as a residence.

C. **Large courtyard** late 19th or early 20th c.

D. **Window in *haveli* wall** (Recently demolished).

E. ***Haveli* doorway**.

F. **Temple**.

11 - 203

G. ***Haveli* courtyard** early 19th c. If there is one threatened building in the walled city that needs attention it is this, probably the finest *haveli* in the city, beautifully proportioned and detailed, and very little altered since it was built. The 2003 monsoon brought down part of its roof and more damage could easily occur again.

H. **Temple complex** 18th c. The temples are connected with the life of Sant Charandas, a holy man who was born in 1703.

I. **Raghu Gunj** 1930s Commercial building.

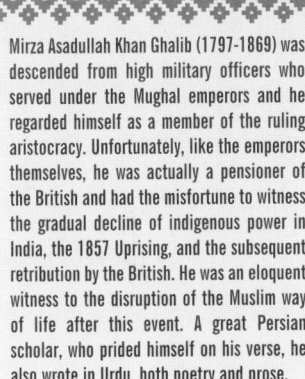

H

I

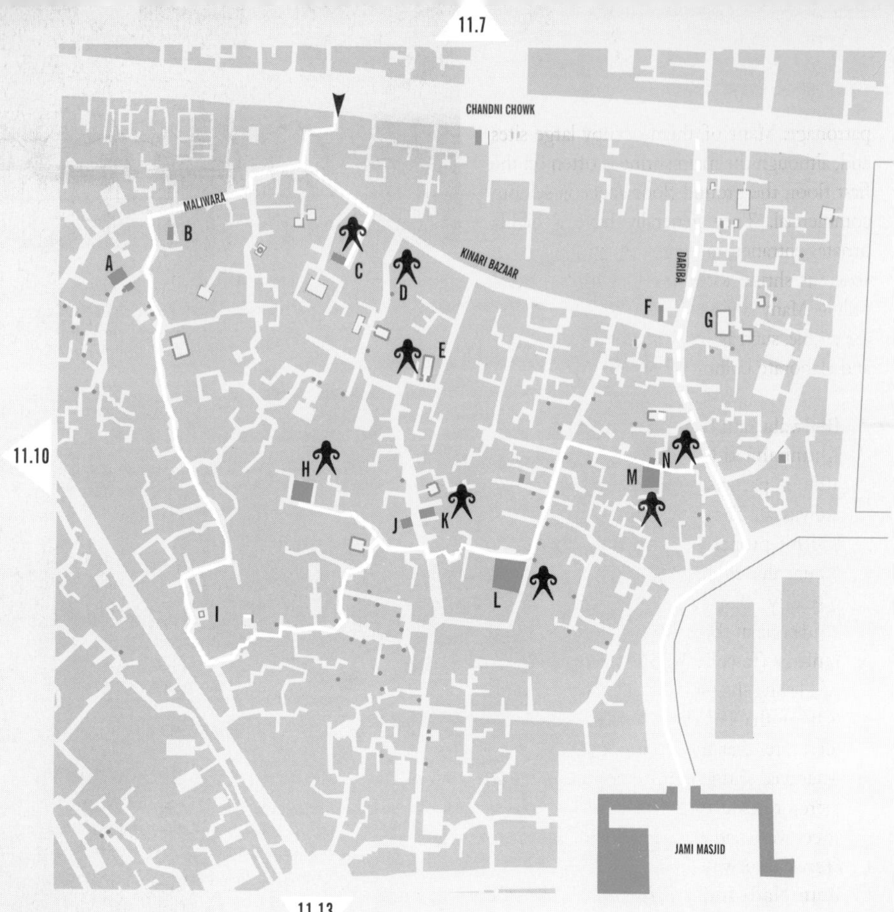

CHANDNI CHOWK

MALIWARA

KINARI BAZAAR

DARIBA

11.10

B

A

C

D

E

F

G

H

N

M

J K

I

L

JAMI MASJID

Map 11.11 - Dharampura

11.13

Dharampura

This is one of the more prosperous parts of the old city. Considering the area is so central it appears to be surprisingly uncommercial, although needless to say there are small industries tucked away in dark little rooms everywhere. The most commercial street is Kinari Bazaar. Kinari means trimmings or edging and it is here that you can buy ribbons and all kinds of haberdashery items, but most particularly the various essentials for weddings.

This area also houses many Jain temples. The Jain temples in Old Delhi are remarkable for their size, wealth and level of

patronage. Many of them occupy large sites and, although the main shrine is often on the first floor, the ground floor space is seldom commercial. They generally have a highly ornate entrance, a large courtyard and a spacious shrine with a sumptuously painted ceiling. Many late-Mughal decorative features are visible, such as *bangla* roofs, ribbed domes and elaborate bulbous columns.

G

A. **Bedwala Jain Mandir, Maliwara** mid-18th c.

B. **Khunbaha ki Masjid** early 18th c. This is a Shia mosque that is named after a particular incident rather than a community or founding individual. The incident was a murder, following which the murderer had his property confiscated and given to the family of the victim; Khunbaha means 'received as fine paid for murder'. Part of the property was converted into this mosque. The tomb with the headstone at the entrance is said to be that of the victim.

C. **Jauhri's (Jeweller's) Temple, Naugharana** ?17th – 19th c. In the 1916 ASI listing the temple is described as having been rebuilt in the second half of the 19th century but repaired only ten years later. It is likely, therefore, that the repairs were to an older, surviving part: surely the octagonal shrine embedded in the back of the building, which might therefore date from the 17th century. The nine houses in this pretty street were and are inhabited by jewellers, hence the name.

D. *Haveli* doorway.

E. **Ram Nath Inder Trust** 1850. At the moment this *haveli* is more or less in its original condition although the decorations are not.

F. **Nawab Sahib ki Masjid** 1722-23. Another Shia mosque.

G. *Haveli* courtyard.

H. **Jain Panchayati Mandir** mid 18th c.

I. **Dargah Mir Sadar Jahan.** This is one of several hundred mainly Sufi shrines that existed in Shahjahanabad. They were centres of popular culture, focussing on spiritual leaders, with regular celebrations and rites.

J. **Sri Padmavati Puraval Digambir Jain Panchayati Masjid, Masjid Khajoor.**

K

L

K. **Sri Digambir Jain Meru Mandir, Masjid Khajoor** mid 18th c. This is probably the most interesting Jain temple in the city with a marvellous façade and an unusual interior. The main shrine is filled with a forest of bulbous pillars surmounted by small *chatris*, each containing a four-sided image.

L. **Shri Digambir Jain Naya Mandir** 1807.

M. **Sri Digambir Jain Bara Mandir, Kucha-i-Sethi** 1834..

N. **Sri Digambir Jain Chhota Mandir, Kucha-i-Sethi** 1840.

Jami Masjid (1650 – 56)

The mosque can be visited at any time outside the main prayer times (i.e., not early, late or at mid-day). Those unsuitably dressed will have to wear a wraparound skirt or top. Shoes can be left outside the gates for a small fee. There is a larger camera fee. Visitors can climb the south minaret but women have to be accompanied by a man.

The Jami Masjid, or Friday Mosque, is the main mosque of Shahjahanabad. Built by Shah Jahan, it stands ten metres above the level of the city, the elevation achieved by building on a natural hillock. Wide flights of steps lead up to the three gates on the north, east and south sides. In the 1840s Emily Metcalfe, Sir Thomas Metcalfe's daughter, was puzzled that five thousand worshippers could all successfully reclaim their identical footwear, left lined up on these steps from top to bottom. Nowadays the population for the Friday prayers is even greater and the congregation spills out over these steps and lines up, prayer mats in front of them, on the white lines marked on the steps. Inside,

more lines demarcate the prayer positions in the vast mosque courtyard.

The mosque is similar in layout to earlier congregational mosques in Delhi, although it is grander in size and conception. There is a main East Gate, used by the Emperor to attend prayers, which has almost the same overpowering magnificence as Akbar's South Gate at Fatepur Sikri, especially when seen from the bottom of the steps. The North and South Gateways are less grand, being smaller in every dimension and not projecting in such an imposing way from the main wall. Between the gates runs a delicate arcade, open on both sides so that the city can be seen from the courtyard. Another feature of the mosque, shared with the one at Fatepur Sikri is that the prayer hall is pulled forward from the arcade, this time even more prominently, so that it almost stands independently inside the courtyard. The façade has a very prominent pishtaq, almost twice the height of the five-bayed façade of the prayer chambers on either side. The minbar (pulpit) is carved from a single block of marble. The Prophet's relics are kept at the eastern end of the north arcade.

MOSQUE AND MADRASA OF GHAZIUDDIN (founded 1692)

Ghaziuddin was a leading member of the Mughal court during the reign of Aurangzeb and his successors. His son became the first Nizam of Hyderabad. Ghaziuddin built a complex that included a large mosque, madrasa and his grave enclosure. The madrasa became Delhi College in the 1820s, mainly funded by a large endowment given by Itimad-ud-daula, the Nawab of Awadh.

The entrance to the complex is through a handsome red sandstone U-shaped building. The present access is via passageways either side of the central opening, now used as a classroom laboratory. Inside, two elegant jharokhas face the courtyard. Two-storey arcades enclose the courtyard, giving access to rooms that are used as hostel accommodation for Zakir Husain College as well as housing the Anglo Arabic School.

Map 11.12 - Ajmeri Gate

Ajmeri Gate and Hauz Qazi

This is a busy commercial area, soon to be made even more so by the opening of the Metro station at Hauz Qazi. There are a number of interesting mosques as well as the fine mosque and *madrasa* of Ghaziuddin just outside the gate. Like the other gates, Ajmeri Gate gets its name from the destination (Ajmer) of the road that started here.

A. **Sirkiwalan's mosque** 18th c. This was attached to Haveli Badl Beg Khan. Behind it is an open area that once formed a courtyard of the *haveli* – a few fluted bulbous columns can be found among the debris. Immediately to the west was an even larger courtyard and remnants can be seen here (access from Lal Kuan).

B. **Masjid Mubarak Begum** 1822. Mubarak Begum, wife of Sir David Ochterlony, first British Resident, died in 1878. Her property reverted to the Government. On her death her estate consisted of a very dilapidated house with an attached mosque (described in the legal papers as 'a nice little showy building') and shops.

C. **Masjid Qabr Wali** 1786.

D. **Unchi Masjid** late 18th or early 19th c.

E. **Masjid Hauz Qazi** originally 1718. Although an older foundation, it appears to have been rebuilt in the late 19th century.

F. **Mosque and Madrasa of Ghaziuddin** founded 1692.

G. **Ajmeri Gate** 1640s.

Turkman Gate

This area contains a fascinating group of contrasting neighbourhoods. In the west is the quiet residential neighbourhood of Kucha Pati Ram. In the north, towards the Jami Masjid, is the surprisingly hilly Imli Pahari (or Bhojla Pahari).

South of this is one of the poorer neighbourhoods of the city, surrounding some pre-Shahjahanabad sites that originated with the burial site of **Shah Turkman** who, like the better-known Sufi saints of Ajmer and Mehrauli (Qutb Sahib), probably came to India during the reign of Iltutmish. He was also known as Biyaban, because he lived in the forest and did not like society. He had many followers including Begum Raziya Sultan, the only female ruler of Delhi. Shah Turkman died in 1240 and was buried here, some distance from the then city of Delhi.

A. **Masjid Nawab Rukn ud Dawla** founded 1807, rebuilt 1913. The façade is particularly ornate, with high relief carvings of foliage, mannered cusped arches and the same sort of parapet ornament as seen, for instance, at the mosque in Qudsia Bagh.

B. **Factory site.** This once housed a heavy industrial unit, closed in 1984. At first glance it is a tangle of rusting metalwork, but scattered around the site are the remains of the huge *haveli* that the factory replaced. There were obviously several substantial buildings here with elegant *dalans* looking onto a series of courtyards.

C. **Mosque and *madrasa* of Husain Bakhsh** 1851. This is a large complex built on the site of an old *haveli*. Husain Bakhsh was a Punjabi merchant.

D. **Courtyard temple**

E. **Entrance to Haksar *haveli*,** believed to be where Nehru's wedding took place. The gateway has been demolished recently.

F. **Begum Raziya Sultan's grave** died 1240. The graves themselves (the second is thought to be her sister's) are completely devoid of interest, although the surrounding wall is built from large blocks of well-dressed local stone.

G. **Imli Pahari lane.** One of the scenes from the film *Monsoon Wedding* was shot on the roof of a building at the top of the hill.

H. **Amrudwali Mosque** 1735.

I. **Kalan Masjid** 1387. This is the most northerly of the seven mosques built by Firoz Shah's prime minister, Khan Jahan Junan Shah, probably to honour the burial place of a famous saint. This mosque is the only one of the series that is both intact and in use. Until recently it was prettily decorated with white, pale blue and green paint, but it has now been crudely despoiled with brightly coloured gloss

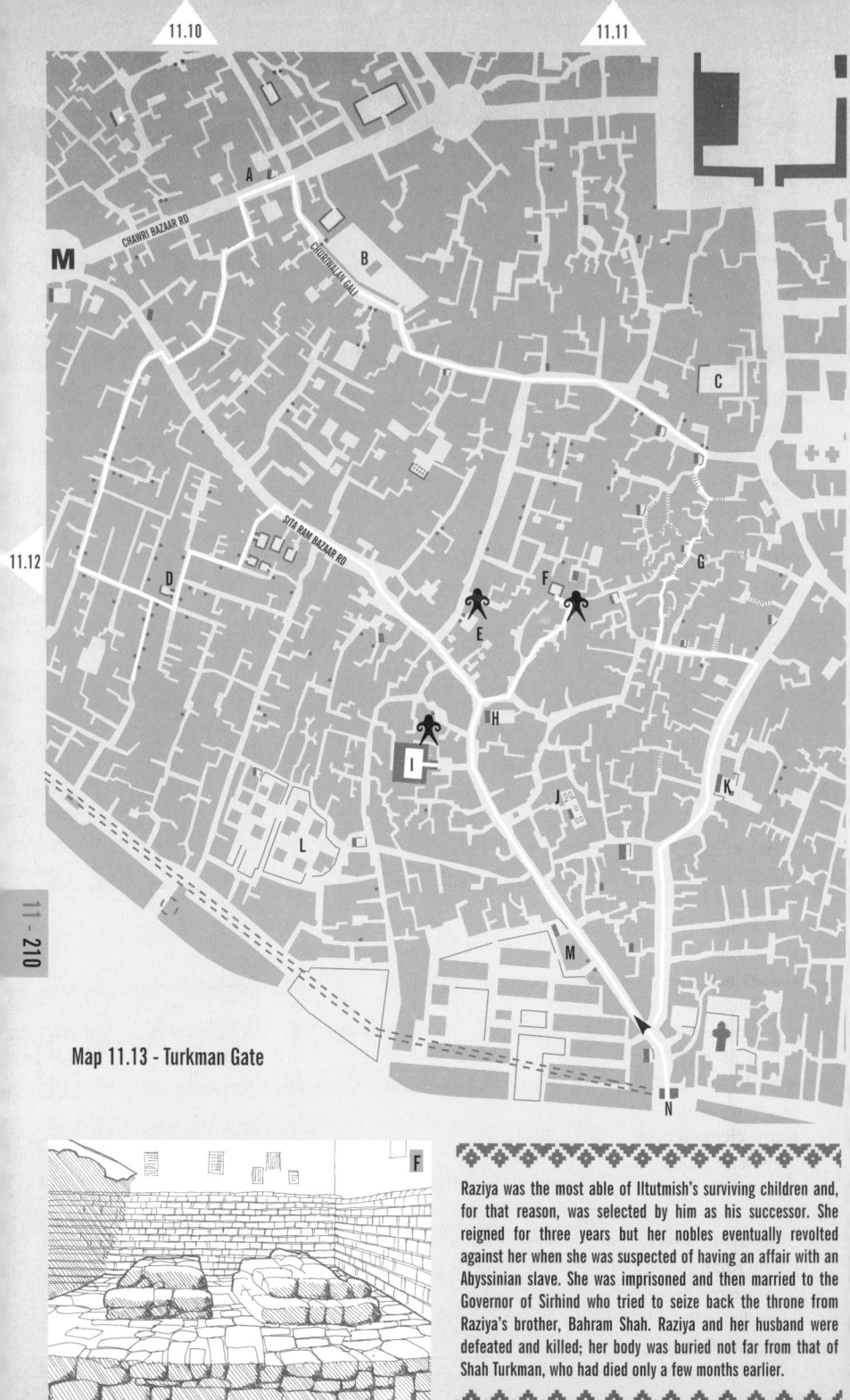

CHAWRI BAZAAR RD

A

CHURIWALAN GALI

B

M

C

11.12

SITA RAM BAZAAR RD

D

F

E

G

H

I

J

K

L

M

N

11 - 210

Map 11.13 - Turkman Gate

F

Raziya was the most able of Iltutmish's surviving children and,
for that reason, was selected by him as his successor. She
reigned for three years but her nobles eventually revolted
against her when she was suspected of having an affair with an
Abyssinian slave. She was imprisoned and then married to the
Governor of Sirhind who tried to seize back the throne from
Raziya's brother, Bahram Shah. Raziya and her husband were
defeated and killed; her body was buried not far from that of
Shah Turkman, who had died only a few months earlier.

paint. From the rooms on the right side a staircase leads up to the roof where you can see the thirty domes that cover the bays below.

J. **Shah Turkman's Dargah** died 1240. The evident change in ground level indicates the ancient origins of this site. Interestingly, the 1840s map shows few buildings in the immediate vicinity, although an enormous number of graves are indicated, so it is possible that the rise in ground level might have had less to do with constant demolition and rebuilding of buildings and more to do with burials being carried out one on top of another. The saint's shrine, with fairly modern embellishments, is found in a separate, lower enclosure, through the arch in the corner.

K. **Mosque and Dargah of Shah Gulam Ali** 1781 onwards. This immaculately maintained enclosure is the site of a popular *khanqah* founded by Shah Gulam Ali where his spiritual leader, Mirza Mazhar Jan-e Jahan was buried in 1781 after a political assassination. Both were leaders of a reformist, puritanical, *sufi* order.

L. **Modern housing replacing slum clearance**, a considerable improvement on the older 'modern' housing to the left of Turkman Gate.

M. **Gateway to Haveli Nawab Mir Fakhr Khan** 17th c. This is one of the few remaining gateways from an original mansion.

N. **Turkman Gate** 1650s.

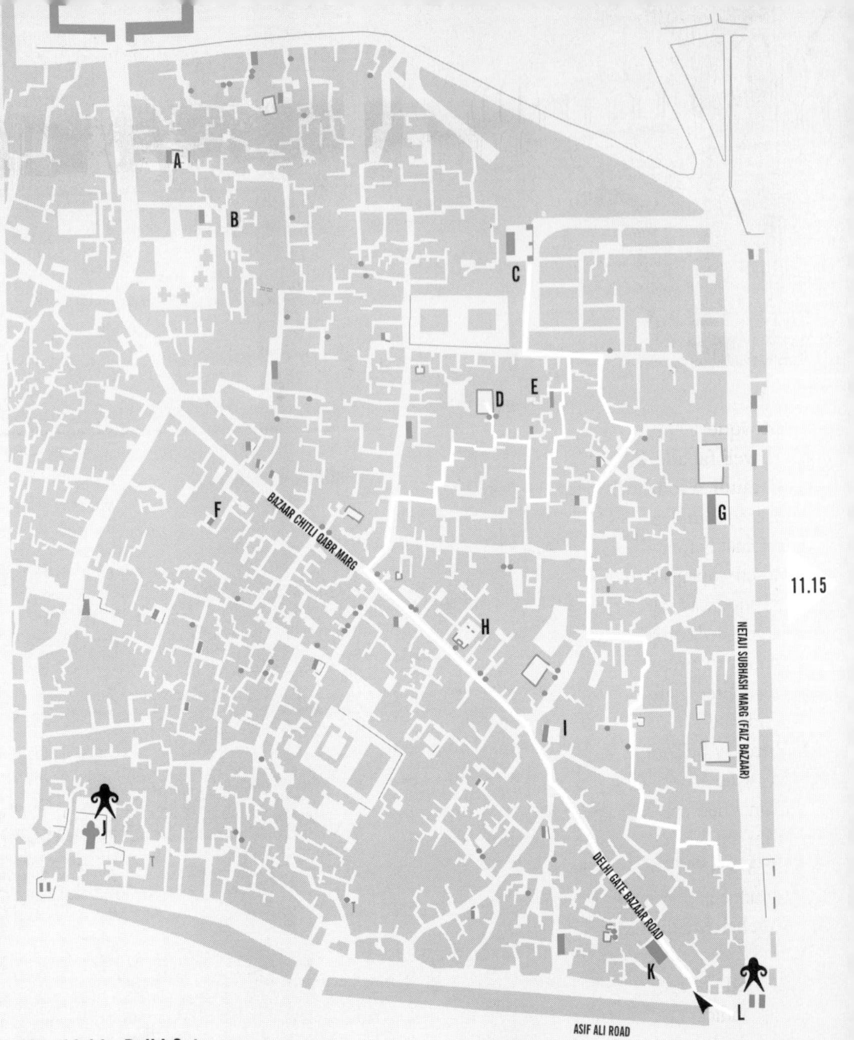

11.14

11.15

A

B

C

D

E

F

G

BAZAAR CHITLI QABR MARG

H

I

J

NETAJI SUBHASH MARG (FAIZ BAZAAR)

DELHI GATE BAZAAR ROAD

K

L

ASIF ALI ROAD

Map 11.14 - Delhi Gate

Delhi Gate

Although this area does not contain many well-known buildings it has some attractive quiet residential neighbourhoods (as well as some desperately poor and squalid ones such as the butcher's area east of Turkman Gate). The original street pattern prevails and, like in other similar areas, old gateways, mosques and temples can be found. A part of the northern part of this area was cleared after 1857. A new street pattern is discernible in the area near the new road to the Jami Masjid, but it soon merges with the old.

L

A. **Mosque** 19th c.

B. **Haveli façade** 19th c.

C. **Pataudi House Masjid** 18th c. This exceptionally pretty complex consists of a mosque as well as the original gate and two pavilions at either corner of the raised courtyard. When the 1840s map was made the mosque was standing in a uniquely open area, part of a large *haveli* complex that seems to have been called Kala Mahal. Its present name must derive from its proximity at a later date to the Nawab of Pataudi's Delhi residence.

D. **Primary School in** *haveli* **courtyard.**

E. **Mosque** 19th c. This mosque has been particularly well maintained and new construction has taken place away from the façade.

F. **Ek Minar Masjid** 19th c. This mosque has an unusual entrance and interior.

G. **Sunehri Masjid**, Faiz Bazaar 1744.

H. **Ruined** *haveli*. The 1840s map indicates that its courtyard had a classical façade at the back (presumably the owner fancied some westernised modernity) and, among the existing ruins, there are remnants of just such a façade in front of some traditional cusped arches.

I. **Masjid Daiwali** 1653.

J. **Holy Trinity Church** 1905.

K. **Shri Digambir Jain Mandir**, Delhi Gate 19th c.

L. **Delhi Gate** 1650s. It is named thus because it faced what was then thought of as Delhi, the pre-Mughal cities to the south.

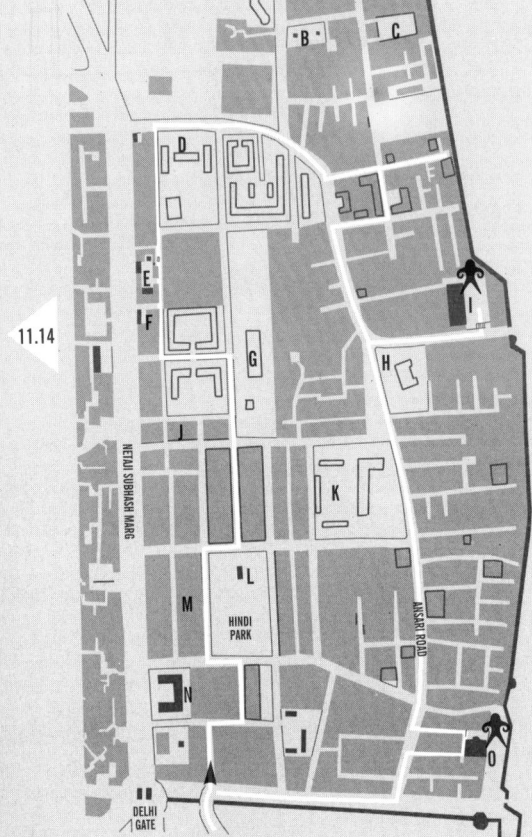

Map 11.15 - Daryaganj

Daryaganj

Daryaganj, along with the Kashmiri Gate area, differs from other parts of the Walled City in that it was developed first as a series of great mansions overlooking the river. Like in the Red Fort the ground was level with the top of the wall, which still forms a substantial barrier, even though it has been largely rebuilt and has been given a mock battlemented facing (a more intact stretch of wall runs along the south side of Daryaganj). The area was taken over by the army during the time of the East India Company and remained largely in army hands till the beginning of the 20th century. This prevented the sort of haphazard development that created the fascinating intricacy of the rest of the city but, instead, gave rise to one of the best agglomerations of early 20th century domestic architecture in Delhi when the land was finally released for private development (the most interesting buildings are indicated with a heavier line). There are a number of colonial style buildings, but the majority are in a simple Art Deco style. Northwest Daryaganj is dominated by institutional (mainly educational) buildings. Daryaganj became the heart of the publishing industry in Delhi.

A. **Sunehri Masjid** 1751. This mosque was built by Qudsia Begum, but it is in a more restrained style than her exuberant garden and mosque north of the city (p.247). It was located just beyond the much larger Akbarabadi Masjid, one of the great mosques built by several of Shah Jahan's wives. It is interesting that the Sunehri Masjid was saved while the Akbarabadi mosque was demolished after 1857.

B. **Colonial House** late 19th c.

C. **Times of India offices** 1930s.

D. **Anglo Sanskrit Victoria Jubilee School** 1919.

E. **Dargah Shah Shabir Baksh** 1821.

F. **Masjid Beriwala** 1635.

G. **Schroff Eye Hospital** 1926.

H. **Radha Krishna Bhawan** early 20th c.

I. **Zinat al-Masjid** 1707. It was built by Zinat al-Nisa, daughter of Aurangzeb.

J. **Commercial Buildings** 1930s. These, and the buildings along Netaji Subhash Chandra Marg, must have made fine terraces when first built.

K. **District Institute of Education and Training** 19th c. This is a good group of colonial buildings: pleasant rooms face onto open courtyards.

L. **Mosque in Hindi Park** 18th c. This was probably attached to a former mansion but, by the 1840s, seems to have been incorporated into the compound of the 'Bail Park Company'.

M. **Hindi Park housing** 1930s.

N. **Police station** 1930s.

O. **Dr Ansari's House** 1900s. This large house would once have had large gardens and a good view of the river. Dr Ansari was a leading member of the Indian National Congress and many political meetings were held here. The house is still a residence and has won an Urban Heritage Commendation.

11 – 215

Hastal

Needless to say, there are a number of mid to late-Mughal buildings, contemporary with the development of Shahjahanabad, that were built outside the city walls. Typically they are tombs or walled gardens. These are generally included in other chapters but a few lie in areas that are not otherwise covered in this book. Shah Jahan's hunting lodge north of Palam is one of these. Of the three remaining buildings two are *dalans*; the most interesting is the *minar* in the centre of the village, Hastal (Janakpuri). This can be seen clearly as one enters the village – walk anti-clockwise around it until you get to a narrow alleyway that leads to the entrance door. The tower was built from red sandstone and has alternate round and square fluting, like the Qutb Minar. Only the first two 'storeys' survive from what must have been a taller tower. Similar isolated *minars* exist elsewhere, sometimes alongside a mosque but often not (e.g., Fatepur Sikri and Banassar Qila near Bayana). This tower cannot be as easily linked to hunting as, for instance, the Hiran Minar at Fatepur Sikri with its projecting 'tusks', but it seems likely that all these structures were used as look-outs.

The future of Shahjahanabad

It is difficult to imagine what will become of this fascinating area. There are some parts that are so decrepit that ultimately they will have to be redeveloped, and various models are available. Rebuilding on the old street pattern is obviously one, and this has taken place piecemeal in most parts of the city, where small blocks of flats are fitted onto awkward sites. A more radical solution was exemplified in the notorious Turkman Gate clearances of 1976, which saw traditional housing bulldozed and replaced by dreadful barracks. There are some better examples of this type of housing not far to the west but, nonetheless, this type of development totally negates the existing urban structure and abandons some of the undoubted benefits of traditional housing. Indeed, there are many areas that presently provide just such accommodation, with streets full of solid, spacious houses only lacking, perhaps, the sanitary amenities standard in modern housing. But how much longer will families want to live in these circumstances, the lack of modern amenities compounded by the distance from vehicular roads? More prosperous families tend to move to new suburbs, leaving behind those less able to maintain properties.

Over most of the area there are dynamic wholesale markets, but how much longer will this method of business continue? If the wholesale markets start to leave the walled city (and it is impossible to imagine that this will not happen if India's economy grows as much as anticipated) what will happen to the thousands of buildings that are left empty? Ideally, the vibrancy of the markets would be maintained with retail business alone but here again, as shoppers are provided with more modern facilities elsewhere, the importance of the old city will fade. It is obvious that the problem is a difficult one and, sadly, a short-term pragmatic solution will not be one in which the architectural heritage of this area is considered. Ideally, the population would decrease, allowing remaining household to occupy more space. Ideally, also, the area would retain some commercial importance, perhaps as a centre of craft production.

MEHRAULI

There lay the ruins of palaces, villas, mosques, sepulchres, caravanserais, and gardens of bygone ages…

Leopold von Orlich, 1843

Mehrauli village

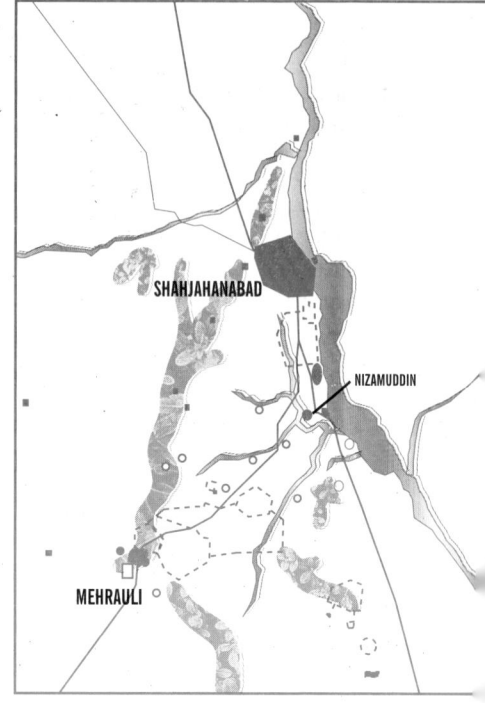

SHAHJAHANABAD

NIZAMUDDIN

MEHRAULI

Although hundreds of thousands of people visit the Qutb Minar every year, very few explore the deeply historical area beyond the monuments. Standing in Iltutmish's Tomb, behind the Qutb Minar mosque, the visitor is all too aware of the buses that swirl, horns blaring, round the back of the Qutb site to Mehrauli village. From the green area to the south of the Qutb Minar, it is possible to see the trees of the Archaeological Park, tantalisingly close. Unfortunately, getting from the Qutb to either of these places is not as simple as it sounds; it is actually some distance and not a particularly agreeable walk to either of them. They require separate visits because there is so much to see in both the village and the adjacent Archaeological Park: in the park are the prettiest *baoli* and the best preserved tomb interior in Delhi, a series of enchanting abandoned mosques, and woodland sprinkled with romantic ruins. In the village, a *sufi* shrine and a late Mughal palace are among the better known sites, while west of the village centre a quiet residential neighbourhood climbs the hill towards Kishangarh (see map opp.). Here, a network of quiet winding lanes thread their way past modest traditional houses, a contrast with the seething bustle of the main bazaar road.

To give an idea of the architectural and historic importance of the area we need only notice that the INTACH listing includes 245 entries for Mehrauli (of which little more than 30 entries have been covered in Chapters 3 and 4), while giving 251 for the whole of the walled city of Shahjahanabad.

The village grew up around the shrine of Qutbuddin Bakhtiyar Kaki (Qutb Sahib), the second in the line of great *sufi* saints, the fourth and fifth of whom were also active and buried in Delhi (at Nizamuddin and Chiragh Delhi). The shrine and therefore the village were outside the city walls, along with other naturally extra-mural places such as the *Idgah* and the great tank (Hauz Shamsi) built by Iltutmish to provide water for the city. The village would have been much smaller in the past but it is likely always to have been strung out along the old main road, as it is now, with the shrine at one end and Iltutmish's tank at the other. Around this core there remains a vast collection of mosques, tombs and secular buildings from the Sultanate and early Mughal period, mostly ruined but some still in good repair. The village grew in importance when the late Mughal kings built a palace beside the shrine, visiting it periodically from the Red Fort. Others copied them and built a number of substantial houses in the village. Sir Thomas Metcalfe, resident in Delhi almost without break from 1813 to 1853, bought a tomb and converted it into a country retreat, adding a substantial garden and various outbuildings. Even after 1857, when the court no longer existed, the village was clearly a prestigious place to live, as is demonstrated by the remaining buildings.

The old main road is still the main bazaar of the village, always fantastically busy, compounded by the number of people who contrive to drive vehicles down it. Standing in the main bazaar, traffic and crowds permitting, it is worth glancing at the eclectic variety of mainly early 20th century façades above the shops. Like in Shahjahanabad, the evidence for great urban pride is striking. On either side of the main road the streets are far more tranquil.

Because of the sheer number of old buildings in Mehrauli and their heterogeneous nature, they are much more endangered by development than ancient buildings in other parts of south Delhi. As in Shahjahanabad, we get a panicky sense that we must see it all quickly before it disappears; an astonishing number of old buildings were demolished even during the last decade of the 20th century and many of the remaining ones are threatened.

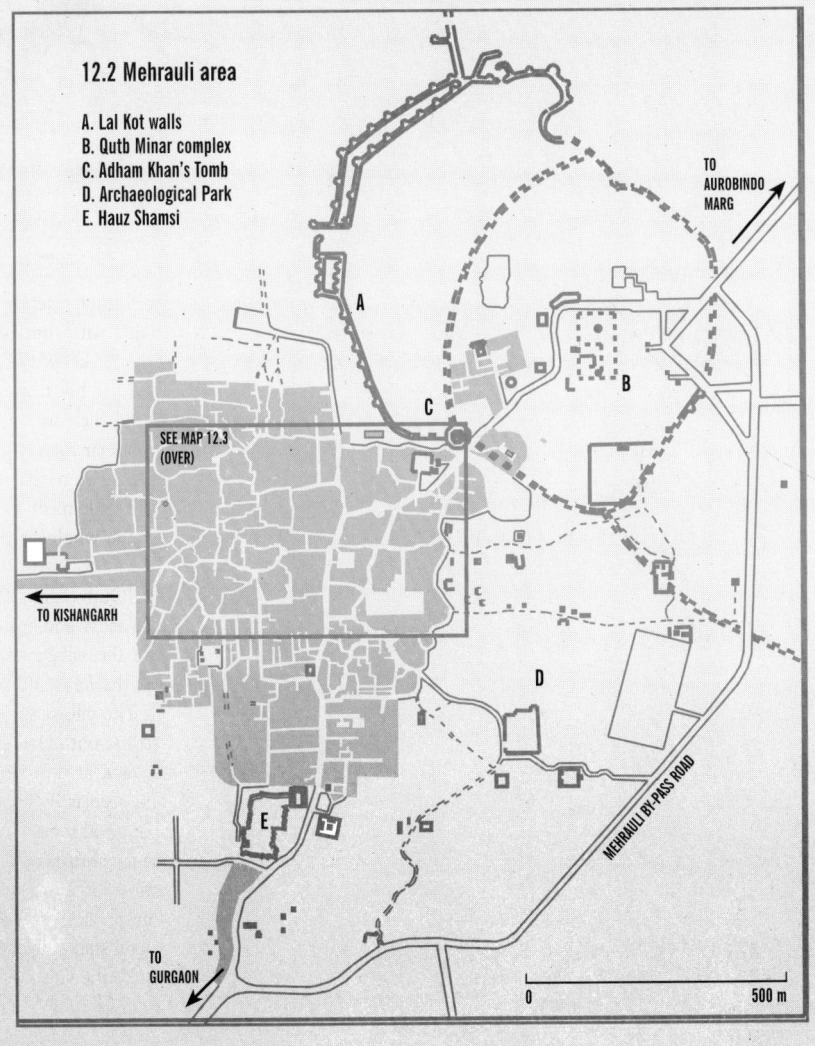

12.2 Mehrauli area

A. Lal Kot walls
B. Qutb Minar complex
C. Adham Khan's Tomb
D. Archaeological Park
E. Hauz Shamsi

TO AUROBINDO MARG

A

B

SEE MAP 12.3 (OVER)

C

TO KISHANGARH

D

E

TO GURGAON

MEHRAULI BY-PASS ROAD

0   500 m

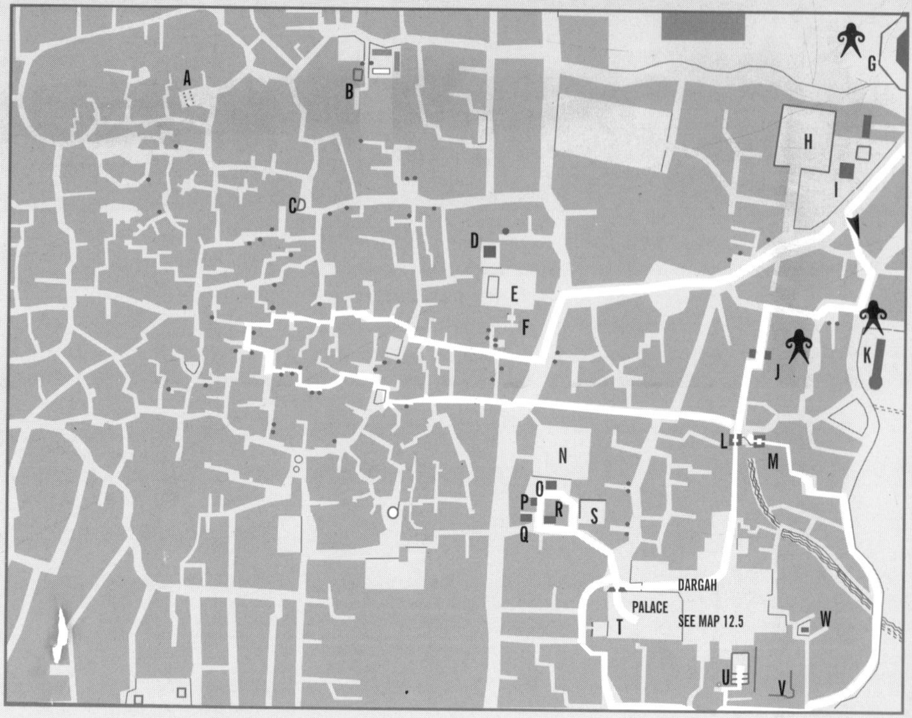

Map 12.3 Mehrauli village centre map

0   100   200 m

The Village centre

A. *Chaupal* – meeting hall, used as primary school

B. Colonial houses

C. Remains of *baoli*

D. Chaumachi Khan's Tomb 16th c. (p.223)

E. Ram Lila ground

F. Temple

G. Adham Khan's Tomb 1562 (p.222)

H. **Walled compound.** This is supposed to have been where Bahadur Shah II's bullock carriages were kept. Nearby is the **Mosque of Quazian,** a late Mughal mosque with one onion dome now used as a residence.

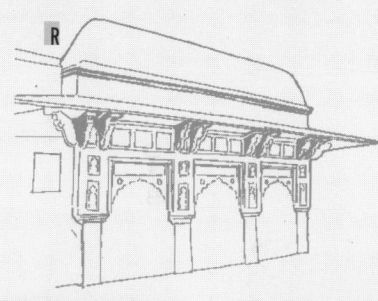

Lodi tomb, converted to Government dispensary
Naubat Khana, mid-16th c. (p.222)
Gandhak ki Baoli 13th c. (p.231)
North gate of Dargah 1541 (p.222)
Gate to Majlis Khana 15th or 16th c. (p.223)
Fruit and vegetable market. This was once
the courtyard of a *haveli*
Tomb 16th c. (p.222)
Gateway 15th c. (p.223)
Tomb 16th c. (p.222)
Tomb of Sheikh Sulaiman 1537 (p.223)
Walled burial ground 16th c. (p.222)
Remains of late Mughal courtyard,
perhaps part of the **palace,**
early 19th c. (p.223)
Late Mughal courtyard, early 19th c. (p.223)
Remains of walled garden. early 19th c.
Mughal tomb

Adham Khan's Tomb elevation (top) and section

Haveli detail

Haveli doorways (top and above)

Walk

Through the village centre

Start at Adham Khan's Tomb near the bus stand.
Warning: parking is not easy in the area.

The most prominent building in Mehrauli is **Adham Khan's Tomb** (1562), built on the ruined walls of Lal Kot. It makes an interesting contrast with earlier octagonal tombs. Although it shares their most basic features, it differs in significant ways, for instance the double drum on the exterior, the circular engaged columns that replace the heavily battered corner buttresses, and the minimally articulated surface decoration. The interior follows a typical pattern but, again, the decorative treatment is more reminiscent of Humayun's tomb, say, than of Isa Khan's. An interesting contrast is with Atgah Khan's tomb in Nizamuddin, which is small but elaborately decorated. Perhaps the grandiosity of the one and the loving detail expressed in the other reflects the characters of the two men, or at least how they were perceived.

From Adham Khan's Tomb walk down the busy main village street and take the second turning on the left and then the first on the right. There is an elegant doorway on your left that would have been the entrance to a grand *haveli*. Ignore the first turning on the left and take the second, to the **Naubat Khana** (mid-16ᵗʰ c.), a generally overlooked pair of buildings standing either side of the road, which were once the outer gateway to Qutb Sahib's *Dargah*. The western building is in a more original condition while the other one has been taken over by a Gurudwara and undergone some extremely crude restoration. The road brings you out onto a busy narrow lane opposite the entrance to the **Dargah**. Remove and carry your shoes and go through the Dargah, where there are numerous buildings of historical interest but few of overwhelming architectural worth. Leave by the west gate and go into the **Palace** through the fine Zafar Mahal gateway (see Map 12.4 (p.224) for both Dargah and Palace).

Leaving the palace, a short detour ahead and to the left takes you to a group of **Mughal tombs**. On the right there are the remains of an old **burial enclosure**. Turn right and at the end of this lane is a 16ᵗʰ century rectangular **tomb**. Turn to the left and on the right as

12 - 222

Adham Khan was Akbar's foster brother, the son of Akbar's politically influential wet-nurse, Maham Angah. When Akbar was in his late teens Maham Angah became fearful that power was slipping out of her and her son's hands, and into those of Atgah Khan, the husband of another ex-wet-nurse. This led, in 1562, to an injudicious assassination that enraged Akbar. He had Adham Khan thrown from the walls of the fort at Agra (twice, it is said, because he was alive after the first fall). It is to be remembered that the present Red Fort had not yet been built; the harem terrace off which he was thrown was said to be no more than 'the height of a man and a half'). The affection of the Emperor for the family meant that they were allowed to erect a suitably grand tomb for the son. Maham Angah was also buried here, having died of grief soon after the event.

you walk back to the road is a 15th century **gateway**, half buried in the ground. Beyond this are two more rectangular **tombs**, the one on the left being the **Tomb of Sheikh Sulaiman** (1537), a venerated saint of the early 16th century.

Village lane

Now return to the Zafar Mahal and follow the road round to its right, to encircle the Dargah. A very narrow entrance on your left leads you to an open space, once a **palace courtyard** with a fragment of an ornate arcade. A more substantial late-Mughal courtyard can be seen by continuing downhill, taking a lane on the left and then the third lane on the left after that. At the end go right up some stairs and then left, under three arches into a once fine **late-Mughal courtyard**, that might have had some connection with the Dargah, being so close to it. Now return to the road and continue round the Dargah (see map), passing its back entrance, before descending steeply to a junction where a path on the left takes you back to the Dargah entrance lane.

Zafar Mahal

Alternatively turn right, to a motorable road, and then left to zigzag through some graves and houses and through the **Gate to the Majlis Khana** (15th or 16th c.). This gate, in an appalling condition, was originally the entrance to an assembly house (Majlis Khana), which became a burial ground for those who died while visiting the shrine. The building was highly ornamented; it is just possible to make out the smoke-blackened fluted ceiling.

Go left along the lane until you reach the frantically busy main bazaar road. From here follow the marked walk past the market area into a hilly residential neighbourhood with numerous traditional, though not grand, houses. Back in the main bazaar road turn left and take the next left to see **Chaumachi Khan's Tomb** (16th c.) over-

Chaumakhi Khan Tomb

Zafar Mahal

looking a small Ram Lila ground. This is an early Mughal tomb that was enclosed within a square enclosure, of which one of the corner turrets remains. The ground plan is a Baghdad octagon and has features found in other contemporary tombs. An unusual feature outside is the yellow sandstone facing on the south side of the tomb, especially the engaged columns at either end and the white plaster 'pointing' to give the façade a more grandiose appearance. This was perhaps the tomb of someone whose self-image surpassed his wealth. The name of the tomb is probably a corruption of the owner's name.

From here you can return straight up the main road to Adham Khan's Tomb.

The Dargah of Khwaja Qutb-ud-din Bakhtiyar Kaki (Qutb Sahib)

Qutb Sahib (died 1235) was born in Persia and came to India during Iltutmish's reign as a disciple of Khwaja Muinuddin Chishti of Ajmer, from whom he inherited the mantle of leader of the Indian *sufis*. It is said that he got the name Kaki because, while meditating, he was fed small cakes known as kák. An alternative story is that he made gifts to debtors and the families of dowry-less girls of a 'ka-ka' of gold or silver. Although his original grave was plain earth covered with a cloth, the complex grew and was embellished over the centuries by numerous additions. The greater interest shown in this shrine by the later emperors might be because political conditions made continued patronage of the Ajmer shrine impossible. Although not as busy as Nizamuddin's Dargah this is still one of the most important in India and has many visitors.

Shrine

Map 12.4 Dargah and Palace, Mehrauli
Palace buildings: A to G
Dargah buildings: 1 to 24

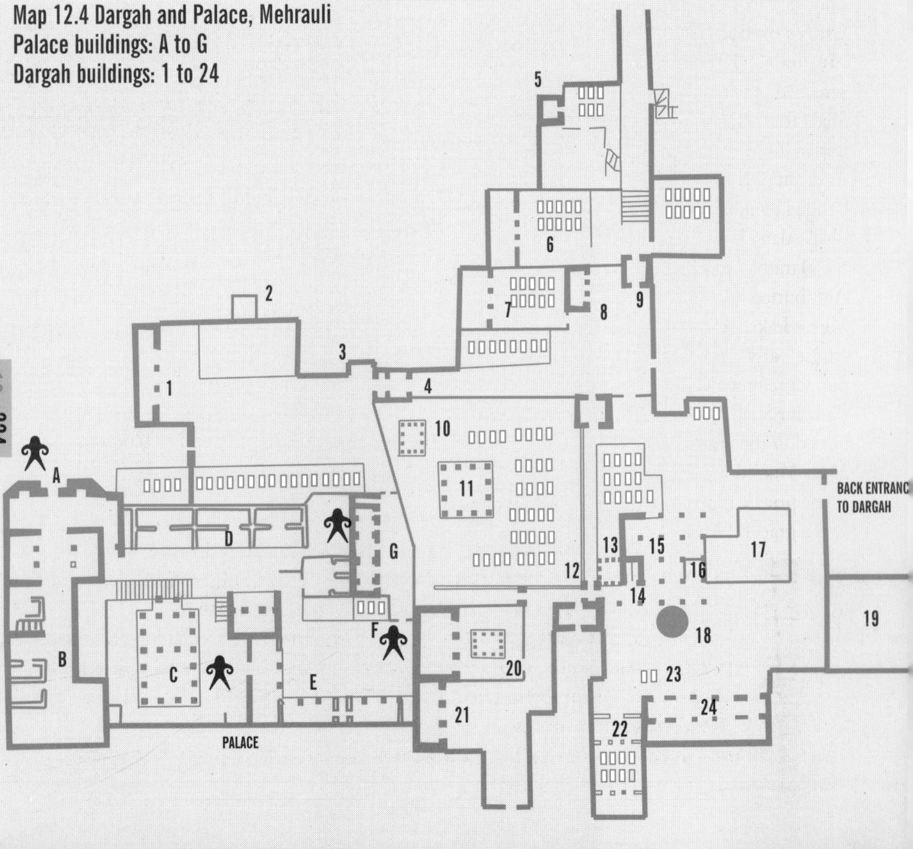

5

6

2

7   8   9

3

1   4

10

11

BACK ENTRANCE
TO DARGAH

A

D

G

13   15   17

12   16

14

F   18   19

B

C   E

20

21   23   24

22

PALACE

PALACE

A. **Zafar Mahal** (early 19th century). This was reconstructed by Bahadur Shah II to allow the entrance of elephants. Inside the palace it is worth climbing to the top floor where there is a pretty multi-chambered *dalan* with a terrace on the palace side and a view out over the entrance on the other.

B. **Remains of a two-storey arcade**, rather like the Chhatta Chowk in the Red Fort, which once led to further palace buildings beyond.

C. **Tomb** (13th century). By tradition it contains the grave of Alauddin, nephew of Iltutmish and another belonging to a disciple of Qutb Sahib.

D. **Two-storey European style buildings** (19th century). It is possible to make out external decorations that included pilasters painted with pretend pointing, a kind of poor man's 'rustication'. These pilasters 'support' a frieze decorated with a tendril pattern. On an inside wall there is a pure classical fireplace.

E. **Dalans** (19th century). This was clearly the more 'Indian' part of the palace.

F. **Graves of Bahadur Shah I and other late Mughals** (19th century). The marble-screened enclosure was built by Jahandar Shah for his father Bahadur Shah I. Also buried here is Shah Alam II, perhaps the most pitiable of the late Mughals, who was blinded by the Rohilla leader, Ghulam Qadir. Shah Alam II was puppet emperor, first of the Marathas and then of the British (p.179). Also buried here are his son Akbar Shah and Mirza Fakruddin, the last emperor's heir, whose early death signalled the end of the puppet regime even before the events of 1857 finally finished it. The last emperor himself, Bahadur Shah II, another strong runner in the Mughal misfortune stakes, was to have been buried in the empty grave in the middle but died in exile in Rangoon.

G. **Moti Masjid** (early 18th century). This was probably built by Bahadur Shah I (died 1712) as the private mosque of the royal family and later incorporated into the palace compound. It is a graceful little building in white marble, typical of the era.

DARGAH

1. **Mosque** (early 19th century)
2. **Tomb** (Mughal)
3. **Grave of Murad Bakht** (wife of Shah Alam ll) – now used as residence
4. **Western gateway to Dargah** (1707). Once the main inner gate to Dargah

5. **Dargah and Mazar of Saika Baba** (16th century). Beside this rather altered tomb is the grave of Khwaja Hasan Khaiyat (15th century). Both men were presumably connected to the shrine in some way.
6. **Grave enclosure of Nawabs of Jhajjar** (19th century). This family were ennobled by Lord Lake in 1803 but came to grief in 1857.
7. **Grave enclosure of Mu'atmad Khan** (late 17th century). Mu'atmad Khan was a eunuch in the court of Aurangzeb. Also in this enclosure are the graves of the family of Ilahi Baksh, a descendant of the last Mughals.

8. **Mosque** (15th century). This small mosque is clearly pre-Mughal in style. The ground level has also risen around it, a sure sign of antiquity.
9. **Gateway to Northern Courtyard** (late 18th century). This was constructed by Maulana Fakhruddin, buried just behind Qutb Sahib's mosque. Maulana Fakhruddin was a popular Chishti saint who died in 1784.
10. **Grave of Khwaja Abdul Aziz Bastami** (late 19th or early 20th century). Built later, over the grave of an early saint about whom little is known.
11. **Shrine of Qutb Sahib** (late 19th and early 20th century). Unlike Nizamuddin's shrine, Qutb Sahib's

preserved its bare simplicity until well into the 19th century. Before that it remained as a mound of earth, with a simple cloth covering. By mid-century the grave was enclosed by wooden railings. The marble balustrade that surrounds the grave dates from 1882, the domed building over it from even later. The rear wall of the enclosure may have been built by Qutb Sahib's successor as a prayer wall. It was decorated with ceramic tiles by Aurangzeb, probably early in his reign, while he was in Delhi and before his orthodoxy prevented him from visiting the tombs of saints.

12. **Gateways and screen** (1710s). The gateways at the corner of the screen and the screen itself were built during the reign of the late Mughal Emperor Farruksiyar, whose family graves are beside the entrances to the Dargah. The screen includes finely carved *jalis*, normally covered with little cotton prayer offerings. For women,

who make the offerings, it is the closest they are allowed to the grave, visible inside.

13. **Grave of Maulana Fakhruddin** (1807). See building 9.

14. **Graves of Sheikh Nizamuddin Abulmoiyad and his mother** (13th century). These two graves used to be open to the sky but have now been incorporated into the enlarged mosque. The Sheikh was a disciple of Qutb Sahib.

15. **Qutb Sahib's Mosque** (mid 16th century onwards). The mosque was rebuilt by Islam Shah Suri (1545-54), added to by Farruksiyar, and much altered since then.

16. **Grave of Bibi Hambal** Bibi Hambal is supposed to have been Qutb Sahib's wet-nurse. The enclosure is obviously Mughal.

17. **Langar** and other new buildings.

18. **Modern minar.**

19. *Baoli* (1846). It appears that the buildings around the *baoli* were built in 1846, but the well probably existed before then. It used to have wide steps leading down in three flights from the west end of southern court. It is unclear from early descriptions how much of this was covered by 'double storeyed arched rooms' but on maps it appeared to take up most of the courtyard area. The steps have now been built over with a series of unused open platforms.

20. **Mazar of Hazrat Qazi Hameeduddin Nagauri** (18th century). Qazi Hameeduddin was a contemporary of Qutb Sahib. Clearly this is another tomb that was constructed over the grave long after the burial.

21. **Mosque** (1785).

22. **Grave enclosure of Nawabs of Loharu** (1802). This is an enchanting little burial ground, with elegant bulbous columns and cusped arches surrounding a collection of white marble graves, belonging to the Loharu family who, like the Jhajjars, were enobled by the British but, unlike them, remained in favour after the eruptions of 1857. This is the family, related to the poet Ghalib, that was involved in the scandal of William Frazer's murder.

23. **Graves of Zabtah Khan and his wife** (18th century). These are elegantly carved gravestones on a small platform. Zabtah Khan was the father of Ghulam Qadir, who blinded the Emperor Shah Alam.

24. **Majlis Khana** (18th century). This large assembly hall, built by Zabtah Khan, has cusped arches and fluted bulbous columns.

The
Archaeological
Park

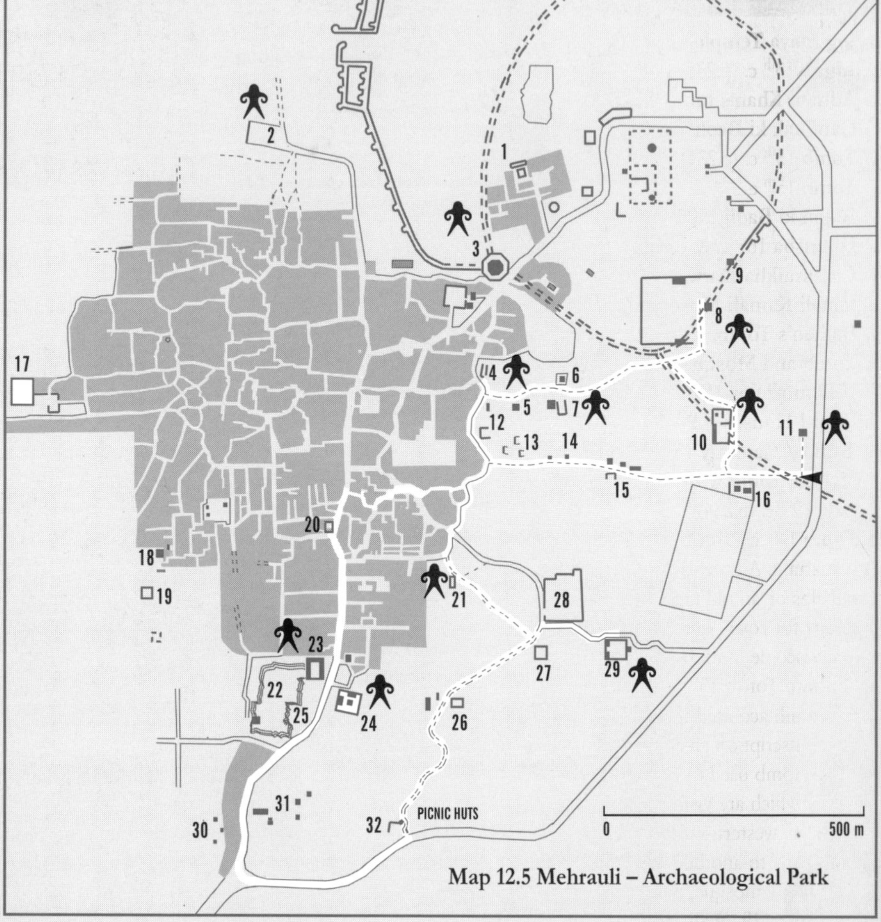

2

1

3

9

8

17

4

6

5

7

12

13

14

10

11

15

16

20

18

19

21

28

27

29

23

22

25

24

26

31

30

32   PICNIC HUTS

0   500 m

Map 12.5 Mehrauli – Archaeological Park

19

18

1. **Jog Maya Temple,** mainly modern with a few 19th c. buildings
2. **Idgah** 13th c. (p.235)
3. **Adham Khan's tomb** 1562 (p.222)
4. **Gandhak ki Baoli,** early 13th c. (p.231)
5. **Tomb** 15th c. (p.231)
6. **Tomb** 15th c.
7. **Rajon ki Baoli** 1506 (p.235)
8. **Dilkusha** 16th c. & early 19th c. (p.236)
9. **Chaumukha Darwaza** ?14th c. (p.236)
10. **Jamali Kamali Mosque and tomb** 1528-9 (p.237)
11. **Balban's Tomb,** late 13th c. (p.231)
12. **Tomb and Mosque** 15th c. (p.232)
13. **Wall mosques** 15th c.
14. **Guard Houses / Pavilions** 19th c. (p.234)
15. **Tomb / Gateway** 15th c.; **Mosque of Maulana Majduddin** Mughal; **Tomb with wall mosque** 16th c.; **Stables** late 18th or early 19th c. (p.234)
16. **Tomb** 16th c.; **Tomb of Khan Shahid** ?16th c. (p.231)
17. **Gaushala.** A little way up the road to Kishangarh there is the remains of an old tank, several **temples** and a Gaushala, a refuge for cows, which live in more spacious conditions than many people in Mehrauli.
18. **Saubate Tomb** 1375. It is not known why this twelve-pillared tomb acquired the name or who was buried here. The inscription gives a date but no name is discernible. The tomb used to be surrounded by low walls, fragments of which are visible to the south and east. The western wall formed a prayer wall and was linked to another enclosure with a simple three-bayed mosque, now used as a shed.
19. **Wall mosque** 18th c. This formed quite a large enclosure with a gate on the east side. It is very ruined and is only just accessible.

20. **Hijron ka Khanqah** 15th c. (p.233)
21. **Takya of Kamli Shah** 19th c. (p.232)
22. **Hauz Shamsi** 13th c. (p.233)
23. **Jahaz Mahal** 15th c. (p.233); on other side of road: **Tomb** 15th c.; **Mosques** 15th c.
24. **Jharna** 1700 (p.233)
25. **Aulia Masjid** 1191 onwards. This backs onto the Shamsi tank. Although it is known originally to have been the earliest mosque in Delhi, founded in 1191 and thus pre-dating the tank itself, it has been completely rebuilt and the present buildings are of no historic or architectural interest.
26. **Wall Mosques** 15th c.
27. **Bagichi ki Masjid**, early 16th c. (p.232)
28. **Dadabari Jain Mandir**, mainly modern (p.232)
29. **Madhi Masjid** 15th c. (p.232)
30. **Tombs and mosques,** mainly 15th c. There are several Lodi buildings in this area but they are more difficult to find because the area is being built-up. One of the buildings is a twelve-pillared tomb where a famous saint, Makhdum Samauddin was buried.
31. **Tombs**, mainly 15th c.; **Sohan Burj** 15th c. (p.233)
32. **Wall mosque** 15th c.

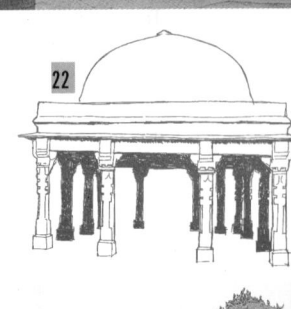

The Archaeological Park

A convenient starting point is the wide straight path leading into the park on the Mehrauli by-pass road. There is parking beside the road at the entrance into the park (indicated by a DDA sign prohibiting various activities).

Ceiling decoration in Khan Shahid's Tomb

Balban's Tomb (late 13th c.) is a short distance away on the right, through the surviving but solitary gateway. He was one of the most powerful of the Slave Sultans and, although there is no firm evidence, it is likely that this was his tomb. It is said to have been the first building in India built with true arches, and consists of three interlinked but ruined chambers. The central one is supposed to be that of Balban while the smaller chamber on the east side might have been the burial site of his son, Khan Shahid. On the west side is another similar chamber with a cenotaph and a small amount of elaborate incised plaster on the east wall. This arrangement of three interlinked burial chambers is unusual; the only other place it is found in Delhi is in the Tin Burj at Muhammadpur (p.111).

Around the tomb excavations have revealed a large number of buildings, indicating a fairly urbanised settlement at some point in the past. Further along the path there is a **walled platform** with two tombs inside it. The first is a fairly conventional Mughal tomb, but the second on the right is unusual. Tradition ascribes this tomb to Khan Shahid, the son of Balban, but the chamber adjoining Balban's own tomb seems a far more likely place for his burial. Besides, its rectangular shape and the ceiling covered in elaborate, shallowly incised, monochrome decoration make it almost certain that it is Mughal.

Tomb near Rajon ki Baoli

At this point turn right to **Jamali Kamali**. This is the large group of buildings on the left as you walk uphill (p.237). Opposite on the hill is one of Metcalfe's follies, of which more below (p.236). Turn left after Jamali Kamali and walk through an open park to a footpath below a steep bank. If you turn right and uphill you will find the former **garden and houses of Sir Thomas Metcalfe** (Dilkusha, p.236).

Returning from Metcalfe's house walk westwards along the path towards Mehrauli village. Near the bus stand (you will know by the noise and rubbish) there is a twelve-pillared tomb on a platform on the right and the **Rajon ki Baoli** enclosure on the left (p.235). A little further on is a **15th century Tomb** with three wide arched openings on each side, making it a hybrid between the standard square Lodi tomb and a twelve-pillared tomb.

Rajon ki Baoli

Continue on the path into Mehrauli and turn right for the **Gandhak ki Baoli** (early 13th c.). This *baoli* is said to have been built by Iltutmish, making it the oldest in Delhi. It has a simple form, with narrow walkways at each level leading to the well at the back. A large part of one wall collapsed in the 2003 monsoon but has been repaired. Turn back and walk down the metalled road, past several ruined mosques and tombs on the left. The most conspicuous are a **15th century Tomb and Mosque.** The tomb is in the form of an eight-sided *chatri* and was built in an enclosure with a wall mosque and gate. Interestingly, a couple of the columns of the tomb appear to be temple columns. Both the tomb and mosque have scraps of coloured decoration still attached. Where the road crosses the drain from Mehrauli it is possible to return to the car via a good path through the forest (p.234, under 'drain crossing' for this part of the walk).

Bagichi ki Masjid

Madhi Masjid interior

For a longer walk continue down this road until you meet another road coming up from the left. Just past this, a path branches off to the left towards the **Takya of Kamli Shah** (19th c.). Bahadur Shah is reputed to have built this house for Kamli Shah, a young lady who became a mendicant. Although the building itself is uninteresting, there is an excellent view from the roof. Continuing down the hill will bring you to a wide path opposite the ruined **Bagichi ki Masjid** (early 16th c.), a burial ground. You should make a detour here to visit the curious Dadabari Jain Mandir and the **Madhi Masjid** (15th c.), further down the road. This has a large courtyard, with the remains of what appear to be grave platforms in the centre. The unusual feature of the mosque is that, although it appears to be very similar to other wall mosques, here the prayer wall consists of two covered halls either side of the three central bays, which are uncovered.

The **Dadabari Jain Mandir** is an interesting group of buildings, dedicated to a Jain saint, Manidhari Shri Jinchandra Suriji, who lived in the 12th century. Although the site is historic the present buildings are mainly modern. The main temple is to the left and is an open hall with white marble columns with ornamental brackets often seen at Jain temples. Straight

Born near Jaisalmer in 1141, Manidhari Shri Jinchandra Suriji is supposed to have renounced the world at the age of six. He had mastered all the Jain texts along with the philosophies of other religions by the age of eight, and was appointed a spiritual leader. By the age of fourteen he was the head of the Jain community. When he was twenty-six the Raja of Delhi, Madan Pal, invited him to spend the monsoon season at Lal Kot. Falling fatally ill, he warned his followers that they should not stop on their way to the river to cremate his body, and that they should have a bowl of milk ready to receive the mani jewel that would fall from his forehead. This injunction was forgotten and the body was put down to rest at this spot. When they came to pick it up again they could not lift it. Neither could four elephants, so he was burned here, the jewel falling out into a bowl of milk held by a Muslim fakir.

Dadabari Jain Mandir

ahead is a hillock that is covered with a collection of small shrines with a little path that wanders among them. They all contain Jain images of varying quality.

Returning to the track past the Bagichi ki Masjid, follow it past several ruined mosques to the main road. Turn right here and walk round to the road into Mehrauli. A short distance up on the right is the **Sohan Burj** (15th c.). It is an illegally occupied (but cared for) five-bayed building that was probably attached to the adjoining wall mosque as a *serai* or a meeting hall. Beyond it is a collection of mainly 15th century **Tombs**. The area is of interest (at the time of writing) if only because this is one of the few necropolises in Delhi that is still inhabited. This is the state in which many of the tombs mentioned in Chapter 8 would have been before the ASI set about clearing them. Among them is a grave-covered platform known as the **Chihaltan Chilhalman**, the 'graveyard of Mohammadan saints'.

Returning to the road and walking on into the village you pass the **Hauz Shamsi** (13th c.) on your left. This great tank, built by Iltutmish, was originally much larger. The **pavilion** (1311), now attached to the west bank, was formerly in the

Hauz Shamsi

Hauz Shamsi pavilion

middle of the tank; it is supposed to cover the footprint of a horse, ridden by the Prophet, who told Iltutmish in a dream where to build the tank. On the other side of the road is the **Jharna** (1700), found, rather improbably, beyond a fuelwood store yard (look out for the notice at the back of the yard). This was a garden built to make use of the overflow from the Shamsi tank. The first building was that which forms the waterfall and the little *dalan* in front of it, plus the tank. The two last emperors made additions to the garden: the side pavilion having been built by Akbar Shah (1806-37) while Bahadur Shah II built the central pavilion, just as he did in the *hayat bakhsh* pool in the Red Fort.

Beyond this the next building of note is the **Jahaz Mahal** (15th c.). This is an interesting building, U-shaped now, though probably once part of a rectangular courtyard. It is possible that it was once a *serai* or even a pleasure palace beside the tank, hence its nautical name (*jehaz* means ship). There is a *mihrab* niche on the west wall, probably a private mosque. The roof is adorned with six *chatris* with, variously, six, eight and twelve pillars. Inside there are a matching variety of squinches in the various chambers.

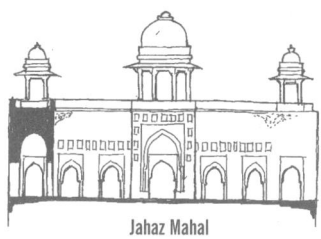

Jahaz Mahal

You are now back in the village. Continue up the road and look out for the narrow entrance to the **Hijron ka Khanqah** (15th c.) on the left. This wall mosque dates from the Lodi period but became the burial ground of the Delhi eunuchs. It is beautifully maintained and a startlingly tranquil place, just off the main road. Continue on the road a short distance and take the second turning on your right, which meets a wider road going downhill. Follow this, past a wide junction, and take a narrower road that continues downhill. This rejoins the metalled road near the **drain crossing** (the end of the walk extension).

Hijron ka Khanqah

Take the path through the forest, passing a number of wall mosques on either side. The next group of buildings are all buried to some depth in the ground and many of them have recently been restored by INTACH, along with many others nearby. The stream (now drain) from Mehrauli must have brought down the silt in which the buildings are now engulfed. The stream has been partially culverted and it is to be hoped that when the work is finished it will be possible to explore this path with pleasure – at present it is very smelly. Beside the path there are some **Guard Houses or Pavilions** (19th c.) at either end of a retaining wall. A ramp in the middle connects the two levels. It is unclear what this is: perhaps part of a garden layout. Near it is a small domed building, even more deeply buried than the rest, probably 15th century. Beyond these is a **Tomb or Gateway** (15th c.). Only the very top of the south door is visible and either side of it are projecting balconies at the present ground level. These are very similar to the balconies of the gateway at the Khwajah Sara Basti Khan complex at Defence Colony (p.120), giving a clue that this might have been a gateway rather than a tomb.

Tomb or Gateway

Next is a **Tomb and wall mosque** (16th c.). Normally a wall mosque attached to a tomb stands on the west side, as if it were enclosing it. There are a few examples of tombs being built right behind mosques (such as the small tomb behind the *idgah*) but these are normally clearly subsidiary to the mosque. This arrangement, where a tomb stands behind a subsdiary wall mosque, is curious. Beside this is a long building with a double-sided arcade, thought to be late Mughal **stables**. Opposite these buildings is a wooded compound containing the Mosque of Maulana Majduddin and three graves from the early 13th century. The earliest has a touching inscription: 'The most dear son, the brightness of the eye, the fruit of the heart Asad, son of Husain…who learnt the Quran by heart at the age of seven years…'. Fittingly there is a small *madrasa* in this compound. The path eventually takes you back to the main path, near Jamali Kamali. Go straight ahead for your car.

Tomb (with wall mosque to east - Mih detail below)

Idgah (13ᵗʰ century)
Map 12.5 (p.228)

This can be found at the end of the road north from Mehrauli village. It was built for the population of Delhi (Lal Kot, etc.) at the great Islamic festivals of Id. It was to this *Idgah* that Timur went to receive the leaders of the city and made the unfulfilled promise that their lives would be spared. It is a long wall with seventeen *mihrab* niches and substantial round turrets at either end, now truncated. Almost certainly there would also have been other projections, for instance over the central *mihrab*. The front of the wall has been restored so extensively that it could date from any period. At the back, accessible through a passage to the right of the central *mihrab* (like at the Hauz Khas *idgah*), there is a small building against the rear wall that might have been a tomb.

Burial ground on high platform near Idgah

Some way beyond the *idgah* is a strange complex of buildings dating from the early years of the Sultanate. A **high platform**, originally

Chillagah of Baba Sheikh Fariduddin Shakar Ganj

with corner bastions, is said to be where Muhammad of Ghor's soldiers were buried after dying in the attack on the Fath Burj gate of Lal Kot nearby. The over-modernised *chatri* in front of it is the tomb of a Muslim saint, one Sheikh Shihabuddin Ashiq, about whom little is known. On the other side of the platform is a vaulted cell, the **Chillagah of Baba Sheikh Fariduddin Shakar Ganj** (the main disciple and successor of Qutb Sahib and Nizamuddin's predecessor), where he is supposed to have meditated. This is the equivalent of the Chilla Nizamuddin just outside the walls of Humayun's tomb.

Surrounding the mound are a number of graves hidden among the undergrowth. Not far away is the Fath Burj and the grave of Baba Haji Rozbih (p.30).

Rajon ki Baoli (1506)
Map 12.5 (p.228)

This is the prettiest *baoli* in Delhi, its beauty enhanced by its forest location. The name, perhaps, comes from the word for masons (*raj*) although it seems unlikely that the name refers to its users. There are four levels, with arcades and internal rooms, the water level generally being below the third of these (when it is not completely dry) but it is obvious that in the past the water has often been a few feet above the

Rajon ki Baoli mosque

second level, leaving a distinct high-water mark. The most elaborate *baolis* are found in Gujarat, where it is clear that they were far more than merely functional buildings. Many hours must have been spent among the ornate surroundings of some of them; here also, we can see that the *baoli* would have been suitable for whiling away the heat of the day. The most functional element of a *baoli* was always the well at the back, from where water could be conveniently drawn up in a bucket, while the steps were used for access directly to the water.

Rajon ki Baoli

Linked to the *baoli* is a mosque and twelve-pillared tomb, which has an inscription saying that it was built in 1506 during Sikander Lodi's reign by Daulat Khan Khwaja Muhammad. It is likely that the whole complex was built by the same man, the *baoli* as a contribution to the welfare of his fellow citizens (a popular form of philanthropy) and the mosque and tomb as welfare for his own soul. The *baoli* is not aligned precisely north-south, meaning that the mosque is at a slight angle to it. The mosque is built in a standard style with a plaster coat over random rubble masonry. The tomb is quite elaborately decorated, with the remains of coloured tiles on the parapets and a patterned dome, rather like the petals of a flower.

Rajon ki Baoli mosque

Dilkusha (16ᵗʰ century & early 19ᵗʰ century)
Map 12.5 (p.228)

This is the tomb converted to a residence in the 19ᵗʰ century by Sir Thomas Metcalfe, who gave it its name (meaning 'heart attracting'). Sir Thomas was one of those early East India Company servants who really loved and admired India (but who also amassed considerable wealth). His principal residence was Metcalfe House, a substantial house north of Shahjahanabad. Other British officials had country houses to the north of the city, but Metcalfe chose this area, famous then as a tourist spot, just as it is now. Moreover the Emperor had a house at Mehrauli and Thomas Metcalfe followed the court.

He bought the 16ᵗʰ century tomb of Quli Khan, brother of Adham Khan, from his descendants, extended it on each side, and surrounded it with a formal garden, augmented, where these did not already exist, by picturesque ruins (follies) on distant rocky outcrops.

Dilkusha

Follies were part of the picturesque landscapes created around gentlemen's country houses in England. Some people were lucky enough to have genuine ruins on their estates, most had to create them. Here in India Sir Thomas Metcalfe had plenty of both. Two of these are beside the Qutb coach park, a square ziggurat and a round spiralling one. The **Chaumukha Darwaza** nearby aligns with the original Lal Kot walls and is described as Tughlak in the INTACH listing on account of its heavily battered walls, but with an arched opening on all four sides it is difficult to imagine why it was built, unless as another of Metcalfe's follies.

There is very little left of Metcalfe's house apart from the original tomb and one ruined room. The tomb chamber was used as a dining room while the surrounding rooms were living rooms, bedrooms and bathrooms. The tomb has recently been restored and very pretty plaster decorations have been exposed. Covered over is evidence that Hindu temple remains were still being used as building material when this tomb was first built, several fragments of Hindu carved pillars being built into the walls.

There were two guesthouses or service wings, built against the north and south walls of his garden. The one on the north side seems also to have been converted from a tomb.

Jamali Kamali Mosque and Tomb
(1528-29)
Map 12.5 (p.228)

This is the high spot, architecturally, of the Archaeological Park, a lovely mosque and an exquisite tomb. Jamali was the pen name of Sheikh Fazlullah, a poet and traveller who died in 1536 and was buried here, in the tomb he had had constructed in 1528-29. The mosque is slightly later than the Moth ki Masjid (p.116) and of course pre-dates the Qila-i-Kohna (p.140) and Isa Khan's mosque (p.160) and is rather more ruined than any of them.

The tomb is in a beautifully swept and tranquil enclosure beside the mosque. It is worth a lot of time and effort to find the *chowkidar* to let you into the tomb, which is sensibly kept locked. Going inside is like stepping into a jewel box. The decorations are almost perfectly preserved and are the epitome of elegance and charm. The almost flat ceiling is ornamented with a glorious pattern in incised plasterwork, painted red and blue. The walls

Jamali Kamali Tomb interior

combine incised plasterwork with inlaid encaustic tiles. Particularly fine are the roundels in the squinches and the decorated panels over the door and windows, all of which are done in different geometric patterns. There are two handsome, matching, marble graves inside; we can assume that the more central one was Jamali's. Nobody knows to whom the other grave belongs; it is thought that the name Kamali is purely alliterative.

Jamali Kamali mihrab

Jamali Kamali mosque

Lado Serai

The village stands in the middle of the Qila Rai Pithora extension to Lal Kot. It got its name from a *serai* on the north side of the Mehrauli Badarpur road. It is likely, therefore, that it dates from the founding of the *serai*, or rather its demise, when houses were built inside the walls. Several tombs were also built nearby, inside the original city walls, indicating that the land inside this walled area was then mainly rural. The village is now a centre for furniture design and manufacture.

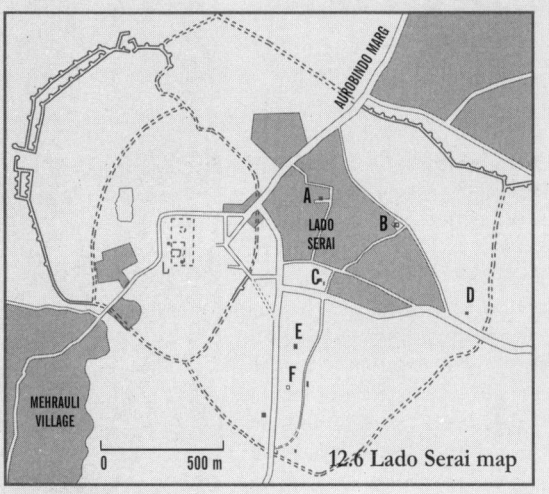

12.6 Lado Serai map

A. **Tomb** (15th century). Originally an elegant Lodi tomb it is now being used for storage.

B. **Mosque** (15th century). This small wall mosque is inaccessible because it was built on a high platform and is now without steps. The west wall has large turrets at either end.

C. **Tomb** (15th century). This small tomb has recently been restored, giving us a hint of what these buildings must once have looked like.

D. **Tomb of Sheikh Haidar** (1357). Sheikh Haidar was a disciple of Nizamuddin.

E. **Azim Khan's Tomb** (14th century). This is one of the buildings that would have formed part of Sir Thomas Metcalfe's romantic landscape. It is a plain affair, with Tughlak characteristics such as the absence of any decoration either side of the projecting entrance bays.

F. Behind the ridge on which the tomb and temple stand are a number of ruins scattered among the trees and farmland.

G. **Jain temple** (modern) with a monolithic sculpture of Mahavira on the top platform. From here is it possible to see one of **Metcalfe's follies**, a tower on a further rock outcrop looking a little like a Kos Minar, the 'milestones' erected along main roads by Jehangir.

NORTH DELHI

THE CIVIL LINES

...towards the northern end the hills dwindle into a mere rocky ridge only, a few yards broad. That 'Ridge', however, since the memorable hot weather of 1857 is a name not likely to be forgotten by Englishmen.

Oswald Wood, 1872

The British

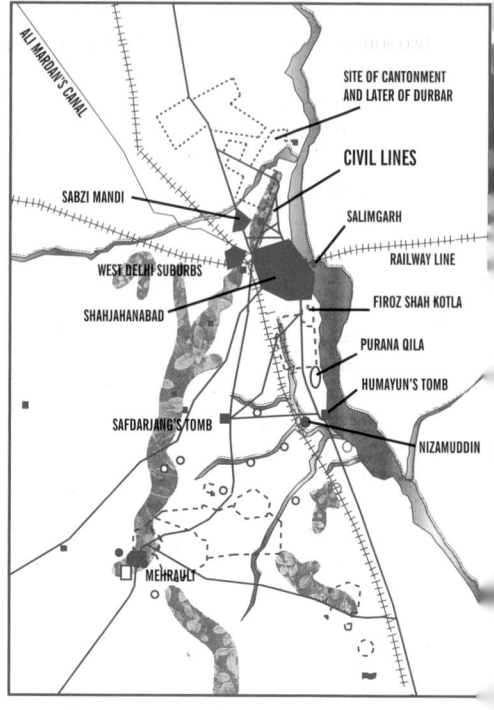

General Lake defeated the Marathas under Scindia at Patparganj in 1803 and took over the territory around Delhi. The city was incorporated in the North-Western Provinces, for a time the frontier of British India, and governed from Agra. Delhi, despite being the more important city, was not made the provincial capital because of the presence there of Shah Alam, who was given protection by the British and allowed to retain the throne and title of Emperor but only on very demeaning terms. He was allowed an income from the small territory that was ruled in his name but he had virtually no authority outside the Red Fort. The real authority was vested in the Resident and the civil administration, the most senior among them being British. The first British residents lived within the city, and were markedly more given to Indian customs than during later times. At first they took over existing buildings but it would not be long before they were building in an entirely European tradition. The British were enthusiastic about Delhi, impressed by the remains of the great mansions and, influenced by the European Romantic movement, enchanted by the ruins outside the city.

The more peaceful conditions that now prevailed helped to improve circumstances within the city, where there was a great deal of restoration and rebuilding. In 1828 the decision was made to move the European troops out of the city to a cantonment beyond the Ridge. The triangle formed by the Ridge, the river and the north walls of the city was the area that became the Civil Lines, where lived some of the European population.

The Great Uprising in May 1857 came as a horrifying surprise to the British and was far from expected among the Indian population. At first the sepoys from Meerut were met with more enthusiasm by the Delhi townspeople than by the Indian soldiers (or the poor old Emperor) but by the end of the first day most of the army companies had joined the mutineers. Many British and Christian families were killed but others managed to escape, often with the help of their servants. The Emperor, Bahadur Shah II, despite his initial reluctance to get involved, was made the figurehead for the 'mutineers'. The sepoys held the city and, at first, the high ground of the Ridge. Help arrived for the British in a little under a month and the Ridge was retaken. The British held on to the Ridge throughout the summer and were subjected to spirited attacks throughout that time. Eventually on 14 September 1857 the British were strong enough to try an assault through the Kashmiri Gate. It was successful and after a few days of fighting through the streets the entire city was back in the hands of the British. The British showed the same ruthlessness as the sepoys had done, killing sick and wounded soldiers found abandoned by their comrades. The Emperor's family, who were found taking refuge at Humayun's Tomb, fared little better. They were led back to the city and two sons and a grandson of Bahadur Shah II were summarily executed on the way, the officer in charge claiming that he feared the crowd if they saw the princes alive. Over the next few months trials were held in the Red Fort and many men were executed. The Emperor himself was exiled to Rangoon.

Delhi United Christian Senior Secondary School

The Uprising had a profound effect on relations between the British and the Indians. From now on the British kept a greater distance both socially and physically from the Indians and this was manifested in the much greater seclusion of the European population from the Indians. A dramatic change in Shahjahanabad was that the British army moved into the Red Fort. They then created a *cordon sanitaire* between them and the city by demolishing a great swathe of houses and shops to clear a wide space (p.184); the only happy result was that the Jami Masjid was fully exposed to view. Other large areas were later demolished for the railway and the Town Hall. Although the railway was earnestly desired by local merchants, conservation-focussed hindsight informs us that the railway smashed through the city in a particularly insensitive way: slicing through Salimgarh Fort, the lines then clipped the edge of the Red Fort before cutting a wide path through the area to the north of Jahanara's garden, isolating a small section of the city beyond the tracks.

For the Indian population life for a few years after the Great Uprising was wretched. At first the entire population was expelled and forced to camp among the ruins south of Shahjahanabad. After a while the Hindus were allowed back, but it was some time before the Muslim population was free to return. For several years after their return the Muslims still had to submit to the humiliation of the desecration of their religious buildings. Several mosques were demolished completely; the Fatehpur Masjid was sold to a Hindu merchant as a warehouse and the Jami Masjid was used as a ballroom. Decayed though the state of the Red Fort had been before the Uprising, it was almost destroyed by the changes made by the British. A few of the finest pavilions were spared but most buildings were destroyed and utilitarian barracks built in their places.

Life eventually returned to normal and prosperity was restored to Delhi. A considerable number of institutional buildings were erected inside Shahjahanabad in solidly European style, a style that found favour with a few Indians as well, although most still built traditionally arranged *havelis*. The European community lived to the north of the city while the Indian suburbs spread out to the west, expanding the old market centres of Subzi Mandi, Kishanpur (Sadar Bazaar) and Paharganj. The population by 1881 was slightly down on the pre-Uprising number at just over 100,000 but outside the walls it had gone up to about 50,000. The number of Hindus was by then slightly greater than Muslims.

Although Calcutta was the capital of British India, Delhi's historical significance persuaded the British to hold three Durbars here. The first was the Imperial Assemblage of 1877,which brought an extra 70,000 people into Delhi, followed by the two coronation durbars of 1902-03 and 1911-12, both attended by even more people and the second by the King and Queen themselves. Each one was held at the same spot, on open ground to the north of the cantonment area. The encampments of all those attending spread for miles. The Viceroy and Governors of the various provinces were camped where Delhi University now stands and a light railway connected them with the Civil Lines in one direction and the Parade Ground and Proclamation Dais in the other.

North Delhi and the Civil Lines

This area of Delhi attracts few tourists. Apart from a few ruins on the Ridge (mentioned in Chapter 7) there are no Sultanate buildings. From the Mughal period more remains because this was the city's recreational area, where several great gardens were built. Some of these gardens, as well as *serais* and other places, still exist, but the buildings on the whole are sadly neglected. Others are remembered in name only. The British, when they came to Delhi in 1803, also concentrated their activities north of Delhi, so for the Colonial period, as for the Mughals, the Kashmiri Gate was a major communications hub, as it has now become again.

The main physical feature bisecting this area is the Ridge, a much more noticeable hill than its manifestation further south. Between the Ridge and the river there is an area of flat land narrowing towards the north. Beyond the Ridge lies a larger area known as the Barari Plain that is low lying, flat, and bisected by the Najafgarh Jheel canal.

The Mughals built gardens on both sides of the Ridge; in 1793 a British traveller, Franklin, described the area as crowded with the remains of spacious gardens and country houses of the nobility. The Shalimar Garden, built by a wife of Shah Jahan, was some distance away to the northwest; Franklin wrote that it contained many buildings, was enclosed by a high brick wall, and from here 'the prospect… towards Delhi, as far as the eye can reach, is covered with the remains of extensive gardens, pavilions, mosques and burial places'. Other gardens included the Roshanara Gardens, built by Shah Jahan's daughter Roshanara, the Tees Hazari garden, just outside the north walls of the city and the Qudsia Bagh (mid-18th c.), probably then in better repair, having been created more recently by Muhammad Shah's wife, Qudsia Begum.

The very earliest European inhabitants lived mainly in the area to the south of the fort, in Daryaganj. Between 1803, when the British took control of Delhi, and 1857 (the Uprising), the British lived in the northeastern section

Street in Ram Nagar, West Delhi

House with octagonal corner turrets

of the walled city or in the suburbs to the north, while the army was stationed in Daryaganj. In 1828 the European troops were moved to the new military cantonment situated on the far side of the Ridge. Stocqueler's Handbook of British India (published 1854) describes the cantonment as 'an alternation of bungalows, huts, and groups of gaudy trees (*sic*)'. Between the Ridge and the river was the Civil Lines, containing the Customs House and some large gentlemen's residences, such as Ludlow Castle (bulldozed in the 1960s) and, further north, Sir Thomas Metcalfe's house, still standing and visible from the Ring Road. Although the great gardens had fallen into disrepair, or been converted into European pleasure gardens, there were still many orchards and vegetable gardens, especially around Sabzi Mandi. Meanwhile, to the west, more suburban settlements developed, such as Kishanganj, founded by Diwan Kishan Lal, and near it the Punjab grain market, which was made over to the city merchants, in order to keep the grain carts out of the city.

Things changed after 1857. The European community moved out of the walled city and lived in the Civil Lines, while the military moved in, occupying the Red Fort and Daryaganj. The Civil Lines was gradually developed with bungalows for rent while their owners continued to live in the walled city. Many of these houses still exist but others, along with their large gardens, have been redeveloped, although not as many as might be expected considering their potential. To the west of the walled city there was further major expansion, where the Sadar Bazaar area became very built-up.

The site of the military cantonment became the venue for the Durbars of 1877, 1903 and 1911, and their vast encampments covered an area many times the size of the city. In 1903 the scheme included a dedicated railway system and the encampments spilled out south beyond Paharganj. The 1911 Durbar was even grander and the official camp housed 300,000 people. It was attended by King George V and Queen Mary, on the first visit to India by a reigning British monarch, and it was here that the King announced the removal of the capital from Calcutta to Delhi, up till then a closely guarded secret.

Qudsia Bagh mosque interior

House on Shamnath Marg

Original Butler School (on the site of the existing Butler Memorial Girl's School, no. 23 map p.248)

This event caused an immediate change to North Delhi, which became the temporary capital for some years while New Delhi was built. For five months of the year, therefore, when the government functioned on the plains rather than in Shimla, the Civil Lines were crowded with civil servants and rents shot up. Many families were even housed in the tented camp designed for the durbar. In the early days of New Delhi the Imperial city more or less surrounded the old city, because so many people still lived in the Civil Lines and there was much traffic from here to New Delhi. For a while the local people were sceptical about the permanence of the new capital and investment was lacklustre. Eventually, however, New Delhi dominated and North Delhi took on a different aspect. Many of the government buildings were taken over by Delhi University. For a long time after its foundation in 1922, the University's personnel consisted only of the Vice Chancellor and the Registrar, whose offices moved between temporary buildings in the Civil Lines, while the colleges stayed on in their existing buildings at Kashmiri Gate. It was felt increasingly that this half-hearted situation was inappropriate for the capital city but money was not forthcoming for building on the allocated New Delhi site, so the former Viceregal lodge site was selected instead. The University offices and library moved here in 1933 but the colleges did not follow till the forties. The Civil Lines bungalows were occupied more and more by those prosperous Indian families who, by that time, had adopted a fairly western lifestyle. Many glimpses of the Civil Lines during the this period can be had from reminiscences of ex-colonials or upper class Indians, for it is to here that most such people refer when they talk of having been brought up in 'Old Delhi'. Here is a description in Anita Desai's *Clear Light of Day:*

> 'On either side of their garden were more gardens, neighbours' houses, as still and faded and shabby as theirs, the gardens as over-grown and neglected and teeming with wild, uncontrolled life. From the roof-top they could see the pink and yellow and grey stucco walls, peeling and spotted, or an occasional *gol mohur* tree scarlet with summer blossom.
>
> 'Outside the sagging garden gate the road led down to the Jumna river. It had shrunk now to a mere rivulet of mud that Tara could barely make out in the huge expanse of sand that stretched out to the furry yellow horizon...'

Mutiny Memorial

NORTH DELHI NOW

Because of the drift of commercial activity southwards following the building of New Delhi, North Delhi has been under slightly less development pressure in recent decades than many parts of South Delhi and there are some breathtakingly huge and empty sites in the area. Parts of the Civil Lines, therefore, retain a tranquillity that is unusual. Of course the most protected area is the Delhi University campus, which itself contains many pleasant colonial buildings, as well as some interesting new ones.

Mughal North Delhi

pool edge decoration

SHALIMAR BAGH (1653)

On Eicher map there is an entrance to the gardens on Maharaja Agrasen Marg. Follow the path more or less straight on and you will eventually come to the original buildings.

The gardens are quite extensive and pleasant to walk in, consisting largely of overgrown orchards. Built by Akbarabadi Begum, one of Shah Jahan's wives, the original layout, consisting of raised paths surrounding square garden plots can be traced in places. However, the most visible remains of the garden consist of the Sheesh Mahal, a canal leading down to a square pool and the two pavilions on the far side of this pool, all very ruined. This is the middle section of the original garden; there were buildings and canals above the Sheesh Mahal and another larger pool below the existing one, discharging into a large tank outside the walls of the garden. The **Sheesh Mahal** is quite a large building, constructed from brick and sandstone. There are ornamental niches on the interior walls and painted decoration can be seen in places, although the existing decoration may be from the colonial period when the garden was used as a country retreat, first by Ochterlony, twice the British Resident, and then Sir Charles Metcalfe. Water flowed through the centre of the building and then cascaded down to the canal below, only parts of which are visible. The pool beyond is better preserved and has holes that must have contained fountains. The edges of the pool are elaborately sculpted with a kind of *kangura* pattern. The two remaining pavilions appear to be parts of a long pavilion that spanned the out-flowing canal, or at least framed it. Again, some decorative features remain. Beyond this, old photographs show that the water dropped again to another square pool with a large central island on which must have stood a pavilion.

In the orchards nearby are the remains of a colonial house: a row of arched openings, two of which have been bricked up.

Sheesh Mahal

Shalimar Bagh

MAQBARA PAIK (16th century)

Correctly marked on Eicher map, near the junction of the Ring Road and Grand Trunk Road.

This is an unusually tall tomb. Its Baghdad octagon plan and mannered dome suggest that it is an early Mughal tomb rather than Lodi, as described in the ASI and INTACH listings.

Maqbara Paik

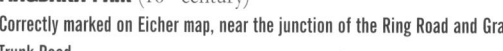

BADLI SERAI (17th or 18th century) 🐙
Visible from GT Rd, where Serai Pipalthala is shown on the Eicher map

The two gates of this *serai* still stand either side of an open space that once contained a village, cleared for conservation purposes at the beginning of the 20th century. The road would once have run through the middle. They are late Mughal buildings and, as an historic site, it was probably given prominence by the British not for its architectural interest, but because it was held by Indian soldiers during the Uprising, and captured in June 1857.

TRIPOLIA (1728) 🐙
On the GT Road, at Ranapartap Bagh

These two fine triple gateways would have formed the entrances to a market place, with the road running through the middle, very like at the Badli Serai, but grander. Mahaldar Khan, an official in Muhammad Shah's court, built the whole complex. Between the gateways there is a late Mughal gate to what was once Mahaldar Khan's garden on the west side and another slightly better-preserved gate further south that was probably the entrance to another garden. The triple gateways themselves have plasterwork decorations both inside and out. The remains of the decorations inside show lavish attention to detail. An interesting feature is the connecting passages between the roadways, which have waist-high sandstone barriers across them, as if they were toll-booths!

Garden gate south of Tripolia

Tripolia

ROSHANARA'S TOMB AND GARDEN (1650) 🐙
Correctly marked on Eicher map, just west of Old Sabzi Mandi

Only two buildings survive: the entrance gate and the central pavilion, which became Roshanara's Tomb. Between them it is just about possible to make out the pool that ran from one to the other. The original *char bagh* arrangement has been obliterated by the conversion of the garden into a European style park in the 19th century, which at the same time incorporated another Mughal garden to the west (now the Roshanara Club). Roshanara was the middle child of Mumtaz Mahal and said not to be as beautiful as Jahanara, Shah Jahan's favourite daughter. During the civil war between Shah Jahan's sons, Roshanara took the side of Aurangzeb, spying on the popular Dara Shikoh.

The pavilion is a finely proportioned building, perhaps more reminiscent of Akbar period buildings than of the more exuberant late Shahjahani style, although the bulbous columns of the arcades certainly follow contemporary design. In the open centre of the pavilion is Roshanara's tomb, a marble grave surrounded by a marble screen, the top part of which was once *jali*-work. The gateway has remians of good tile decorations.

Roshanara's Tomb

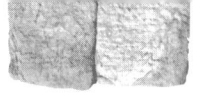

Qudsia Bagh (1748)
Map 13.2 (p.248)

Qudsia Begum was the wife of Muhammad Shah, who lost favour with her husband but regained power when her son, Ahmad Shah, came briefly to the throne. She was the effective ruler, along with her confidant, the chief eunuch Jawid Khan, with whom she also built the Sonehri Masjid south of the Red Fort. The garden was once magnificent, with a three-storey 'wall' along the river that contained internal rooms with balconies and

Qudsia Bagh gateway

views of the river. All that remains now are a gateway and a mosque. Before 1857 the garden was preserved, but it became the site for a battery during the siege, so was badly damaged.

The **gateway** is extremely dilapidated but was clearly once a sumptuous building. Here we have a truly baroque, even rococo, affair, built mainly from brick but with finely carved red sandstone and intricately sculpted plasterwork, much of which has now fallen off. The engaged columns either side have a zig-zag pattern incised on plaster that masked the same beautifully executed pattern in brick, or rather tiles, underneath. The conventional *kangura* battlement pattern has here transmogrified into a row of three-dimensional urns, two of which remain. The interior of the gateway, which contains several chambers, was also elaborately decorated with the complex net vaulting typical of the period.

The **mosque** is in better repair but is no more sober than the gateway. It is actually an attractive building, if you enjoy this style of architecture, which is seen at its apogee in Nawabi

Rear of Qudsia Bagh mosque

buildings in Lucknow. It is once more of brick, with a decorative plasterwork coating. The three domes are as elaborate as they could be, with each band of the fluting clasped at its base by a leaf. The battlements have a more conventional *kangura* pattern but, without the solid support found in Sultanate buildings or the structural integrity of earlier Mughal buildings, they have mostly fallen. The façade is plastered and divided into shallow panels. Each of the entrances is set within an *iwan*, with complex net vaulting in each. Inside there is another display of net vaulting and rococo flourishes. Attached to the back of the mosque are the remains of further vaulted rooms, presumably a garden pavilion.

Qudsia Bagh mosque

Gateway detail

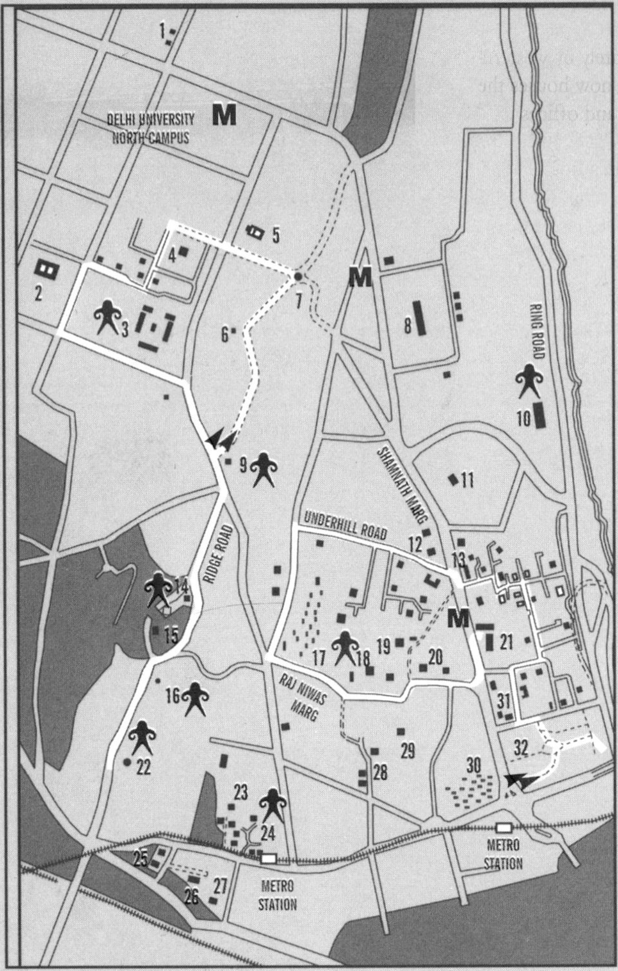

Bungalow behind Sec

13.2 Civil Lines Map

1. **Ammunition stores** 1828
2. **Faculty of Arts** 1947 (p.250)
3. **St Stephen's College and chapel** 1939 (p.251)
4. **Delhi University Office** 1902 (p.250)
5. **Gwyer Hall** 1948. This was designed by Walter George and the detailing of the courtyard blocks are very similar to the Faculty of Arts building.
6. **Guard houses** 1828
7. **Flagstaff tower** 1828 (p.250)
8. **Secretariat** 1912. This huge building was designed by E. Montague Thomas, a British architect, to house Government functions while the North and South Blocks were being completed on Raisina Hill. For a building whose main use was to last such a short time (Viceroy's House and the Secretariat Buildings were expected to be finished much sooner than they were) it is impressively grand, with a central tower flanked by two

three-storey blocks and domed end pavilions inspired entirely by western models. The building now houses the Delhi State assembly and offices.

9. **Chauburj Mosque** 14th & 19th c. (p.90)

10. **Sir Thomas Metcalfe's house** 1835. Only visible from the Ring Road, this was a huge house, built in a European classical style but adapted to the Indian climate with high ceilings, small openings for windows and doors and a deep veranda (the formerly classical façade was drastically altered in 1913). It was taken over by the government after the Great Uprising, having been severely damaged, and has remained in government use till today.

11. **Indraprastha College for Women** 1917. This was originally built as a Guest House, called Alipore House.

12. **Shamnath Marg bungalows**, late 19th c.

13. **Exchange Stores** 1902 (p.252)

14. **Pir Ghaib &** *baoli* 14th c. (p.91)

15. **Hindu Rao's house** 1820s (p.251)

16. **Ashokan Pillar** 3rd c. BC (p.91)

17. **Muslim cemetery** 18th c. (p.253)

18. **Baptist Union of North India Buildings**, mainly 1910s and 20s (p.253)

19. **House at 19, Raj Niwas Marg,** early 19th c. (p.253)

20. **Delhi United Christian Senior Secondary School** 1926

21. **Oberoi Maidens Hotel** 1900 – 07 (p.253)

22. **Mutiny Memorial** 1863 (p.251)

23. **Butler Memorial Girl's School** 1900s

24. **Railway Colony**, late 19th & early 20th c.

25. **Methodist Church** 1931

26. **Queen Mary's School** 1908

27. **St Stephen's Hospital** 1908. St Stephen's Hospital was founded by a group of Missionary women to serve the women and children of Delhi. The first hospital was built beside the Queen's Gardens (Company Bagh) in Chandni Chowk but the hospital was moved here in 1908. It became a general hospital in the 1970s and the new buildings now completely surround the original stone structure.

28. **Cambridge Brotherhood building**, late 19th c.

29. **St Xavier's School** 1900s. The school now occupies buildings that used to be the Cecil Hotel.

30. **Nicholson Cemetery** 1850s onwards

31. **Temporary Secretariat,** early 20th c. Used while the larger (also temporary) building was under construction to the north, this later became railway offices.

32. **Qudsia Bagh** 1748 (p.247)

Exploring the Civil Lines

The map (p.248) shows most of the buildings remaining from the colonial period. Two separate walks could be taken that, between them, include the most interesting of these. The other buildings mentioned in this chapter are situated so far apart that they need to be visited individually, by car, and are described at the end of the chapter.

Flagstaff Tower

THE RIDGE AND THE UNIVERSITY

Starting at the Chauburj Mosque (p.90), walk along the path through the Ridge Forest, much better grown here than further south. The path meets others at the **Flagstaff Tower** (1828). This was originally a signal tower, built on a high point at the edge of the first cantonment. It has to be remembered that the Ridge in those days was covered in nothing more than low scrub (afforestation was carried out from 1910 onwards) so signals from the tower would have been visible from far away. The building is Gothic in style with half-hearted castellated parapets. It was part of the formal design of the cantonment and remained part of the scheme when the area was laid out for the durbars and, later, the temporary capital. Turn left here on a straight road that leads down to the main entrance to the University. The **Delhi University Office** (1902) is on your left. This was originally built as the Circuit House, and was located in the Cantonment area. It later became the Viceregal Lodge, and then the University offices. It is a long low building which has recently been well restored.

University building

University offices

Turning left beyond the University Offices and you will see many of the university buildings. At a T-junction you should turn right, cross the main road at the end and see the **Faculty of Arts** building (1947). This was designed by Walter George and is an excellent

Faculty of Arts

example of his monumental, load-bearing brickwork style. George had come to India to work with Baker on the imperial capital but stayed on after independence, and was President of both the Indian Institute of Architects and of the Institute of Town Planning. His architecture combined well the modernism resulting from new building techniques and traditional Indian building skills evolved from the severe climate and local materials. Retracing your steps on the same road, continue eastwards to **St Stephen's College** (1939) on your right. Walter George designed the whole complex, although the chapel was built slightly later. It is a beautifully maintained haven, amidst the rather less impressive grounds of the rest of the University. The building again displays George's effective use of load-bearing brickwork, horizontal emphasis and shadow.

St Stephen's College

Hindu Rao's house

Turning right on the main road takes you back to Chauburj Mosque. From here you can walk or drive down the Ridge Road, passing Pir Ghaib and the Hindu Rao Hospital. Below the main hospital building is **Hindu Rao's house**. This was probably built by Colebrooke, Resident of Delhi from 1827 to 1829, when he was dismissed for corruption. It is, however, more closely connected with William Fraser, who may have bought it from his friend in 1831. Fraser lived in it till his murder in 1835, the result of being caught up in a complex property dispute between members of the poet Ghalib's family. Hindu Rao, an anglophile aristocrat, and brother-in-law of Daulat Rao Scindia, the Maratha leader, bought the house next. After 1857 the house was used as a convalescent hospital and continues in hospital use up to the present day. The original building has been much altered since 1857, when it was photographed as a ruined relic of the siege: it was once clearly of typical Anglo-Indian construction with the usual high ceilings and deep veranda.

Further down the road is the stump of the Ashokan Pillar, once part of Firoz Shah's hunting lodge (p.91). Below this on the right is the **Mutiny Memorial** (1863). The Memorial is in High Victorian gothic style, perhaps the most gothic building in Delhi. It was built to commemorate the British soldiers, and those Indians who died alongside them, killed in the Great Uprising. There is a modest notice beneath it pointing out that the 'mutineers' were fighting for their country's freedom.

Mutiny Memorial

Near Qudsia Bagh
Map 13.2 (p.248)

Colonial house in area north of Oberoi Maidens Hotel

This is the heart of the Civil Lines, once an area of spacious bungalows in large gardens, some of which have been redeveloped. Start by visiting **Qudsia Bagh** (p.247). From the gardens walk north up the road nearest Shamnath Marg. The buildings on the left were mostly government buildings and have now been adapted for different government purposes. Turn right at the end of the street and then left. There is a pedestrian only barrier half way along. Beyond the barrier there are a number of pleasant buildings from the late 1930s, some built in the same style and much smaller than the older bungalows.

Colonial house in area east of Oberoi Maidens Hotel

Turn left at the crossroads and walk up to Shamnath Marg, passing the side of the **Exchange Stores** (1902) on the right. This handsome row of shops, with apartments above, is said to have been built by Lala Sriram, a big landowner and a member of the Delhi Municipality. The classical details are Palladian in style. Cross the road and take Underhill Road, opposite and slightly to your right. There are a number of large bungalows still left on this road, those on the right having been converted to

Late 1930's house

House on Underhill Road

Exchange Stores

institutional use. At the end of the road turn left on a main road and then left onto Raj Niwas Marg. Soon on the left is the entrance to a large **Muslim cemetery** (18th c.). Near the entrance there are the remains of a walled enclosure or wall mosque with two octagonal pavilions visible at each end. At the north end of the site, past hundreds of graves, there is a late Mughal mosque.

House where John Lawrence may have lived

Further along on the left are the **Baptist Union of North India Buildings** (mainly 1910s and 20s). This vast site contains several pleasant buildings from the early 20th century, now used mainly as schools. At the back of the site is an old **house**, thought to be where John Lawrence (later to be Governor-General) lived when he was Collector of Delhi and Panipat. Opposite it is a small **chapel**, dated 1918, with an attractive external veranda. This road eventually returns you to Shamnath Marg, where you can turn left for the **Oberoi Maidens Hotel** (1900 – 07). This was first constructed as a

Muslim cemetery grave

single storey building and extended seven years later. For a long time it was the smartest hotel in Delhi; it was here that Lutyens and Baker stayed on their early visits to Delhi, while working on New Delhi. It is unrelentingly European in style, like many other post-1857 buildings. The introduction of air conditioning has of course changed the architecture considerably, as the verandas and upper level corridors have been rather crudely enclosed.

Baptist Union building

Chapel at the back of Baptist Union building

Oberoi Maidens Hotel

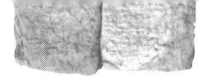

West Delhi

When the walled city spilled out in this direction in the 19th century, the area was already well bestrewn with suburbs, villages, *serais*, two *Idgahs*, and other ancient ruins such as the Qadam Sharif. The area of inner west Delhi that dates from the colonial period is a struggle to visit, because the older part of it, that nearest to Shahjahanabad, is even more congested than the walled city itself because the wider streets allow access to many more wheeled vehicles. Moreover, unlike the walled city or, indeed, many other parts of Delhi, it would be impossible to say with which particular period of history this area is most closely connected, as it has always been a suburb and never the centre. It was, for instance, the only large suburban area mentioned by Bernier, a French traveller at the time of Aurangzeb, who spoke of a 'long chain of buildings on the side of Lahore'. A glance at the (locally inaccurate) Eicher Map will betray its heterogeneity. We can see that there are old village areas and old roads, 19th century organic layouts, planned grid layouts and, superimposed on all of this, an attempt at a modern road scheme.

IDGAH (17th century)
Correctly marked on Eicher map

This huge *Idgah* (its size is its most interesting feature) was supposedly constructed during Aurangzeb's reign. Another smaller *Idgah,* rather closer to Shahjahanabad, is shown on early maps and mentioned in the 1916 ASI listing. An *Idgah* would have been a necessity before Aurangzeb's time and the smaller one might have been built by Shah Jahan, but superseded by Aurangzeb's.

Beyond the *Idgah* is a Muslim burial ground beside the old village of Sidipura that contains a few Mughal-era *chatris*. In the village there is a mosque built in 1743-44.

JHANDEWALAN TEMPLE (mainly modern)
Correctly marked on Eicher Map

This is a Devi temple of considerable antiquity but it has been much modified in recent years, having been remodelled on the lines of the Vaishnodevi shrine in Jammu and Kashmir.

RAM NAGAR (early 20th century)
Correctly marked on Eicher Map

This area is a surprisingly well-preserved relic from late colonial days, a grid layout of large houses built in local style with internal courtyards, but sporting mainly western decorative features. This area, enclosed on three sides and still in residential use, is remarkably tranquil despite its tumultuous surroundings.

Ram Nagar house detail

TIBBIA COLLEGE (1921)
Correctly marked on Eicher Map

This is an attractive complex of buildings with many revivalist features such as *chatris*, *jalis* and *kanguras*. The college was founded in 1880 inside the walled city to teach Ayurvedic and Unani medicine. It was inaugurated on this site by Mahatma Gandhi in 1921.

NEW DELHI

LUTYENS'S DELHI

Whatever one's opinions may be of the aesthetic value of these palaces, one cannot help trying to discover the significance of this monumental display. One ends up by finding it in the necessity to impress upon the Indians, from the millionaire potentate to the starving sweeper, a respect for British power.

Maurice Dekobra, 1931

New Delhi

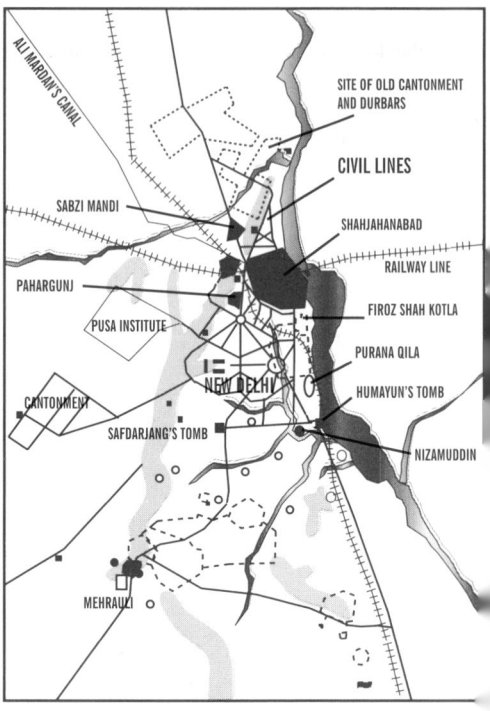

A t the 1911-12 Durbar the announcement was made that henceforth Delhi would be the capital of British India. There were several reasons for the change of capital from Calcutta to Delhi. Firstly, Curzon's 1905 partition of Bengal had caused great offence and led to considerable unrest in Calcutta. After only a few years it was felt expedient to reverse the partition but it was important not to go back to the old system, with the provincial government under the nose of the Viceroy. The solution was to give Bengal the same status as the other Presidencies (Bombay and Madras), and to move the capital to a neutral location, Delhi. It was also thought, perhaps mistakenly, that the climate of Delhi had an

advantage over that of Calcutta. Another undoubted advantage was that the distance between Shimla, the summer capital, and the winter capital would become more convenient.

There was, however, prejudice against Delhi as the capital, even setting aside the cost involved. Lord Curzon, for instance, thought that such a location, 'the dead seat of Muslim kings', surrounded by the ruins of earlier cities, was not a good advertisement. He also thought it smacked too much of the Mughals and the money could be much better spent on the development of industry and railways. From the other side of the political spectrum Gandhi recognised its inappropriateness in a country with inadequate housing and regular famines, complaining that it was 'in conflict with the best interests of the nation'.

The plan for the change of capital was a well kept secret and came as a great surprise to

Rashtrapati Bhawan

everyone. The implications for Delhi were huge; the city was going to have to receive and accommodate the whole central administrative service and all the services attached to it. At first it was assumed that the site would be where the British had already established themselves north of Delhi and a foundation stone was even laid there, but views changed once an architect had been appointed. The main architect and planner was Edwin Lutyens, at that time best known in Britain for his modestly sized English country houses. On his first visit to Delhi various possible sites were considered and his selection was the low hill near the village of Raisina, surrounded by the ruined remains of older cites. As Robert Byron, a visitor to the newly completed capital, remarked later, 'on every hand, tombs and mosques from Mughal times and earlier, weathered to the colour of the earth, bear witness to former empires'. The monuments were considered quite carefully, mapped and surveyed. As well as these ruins there also happened to be several villages, obviously considered less important because they (or at least the domestic buildings) were swept aside where necessary.

It was blithely assumed that Delhi would never be short of space like Bombay or Calcutta with 'its streets confined within ramparts of domestic masonry', and the layout reflects this. The plan also acknowledged the pre-existence of buildings from Delhi's glorious past, accommodating many of the ancient buildings; it would take several more decades before the oldest cities would become part of Delhi.

Typical New Delhi privately built house

One of the pre-existing buildings - Jantar Mantar

Connaught Place - A focal point of the plan

New Delhi

Residents are justifiably proud of New Delhi, the result of the last extravagant burst of colonialism in India. Likewise, visitors new to the city are amazed by the wide tree-lined avenues and, above all,

Rashtrapati Bhawan at night lit for Republic Day

by the magnificence of the buildings on Raisina Hill: the Rashtrapati Bhawan and North and South Blocks. The city was conceived as the capital of an Indian empire that would last for centuries. At the laying of the original foundation stone, the Viceroy said that in comparison to previous cities in Delhi 'assuredly none ever held promise of greater permanence or of a more prosperous and glorious future'. And yet, by the time the capital buildings were finished, it was generally acknowledged that India would soon be free from the yoke of colonialism. In fact, the inauguration in 1931 was in the same week that the delegates returned from London after the first Round Table Conference to discuss some form of independence.

New Delhi's design was deliberately un-urban, a blend of monumental 'Beaux Arts' with Garden Suburb. The criticism that this kind of layout was inappropriate to the hot summer climate can be partly countered by the fact that it was designed only as the winter capital, although this is hardly a valid argument, because only a small minority of the population made the annual migration to Shimla. Now, in the twenty-first century, it can only be said that New Delhi is a city-planner's nightmare, leaving what is now a huge metropolis with an impractically hollow centre. However, despite the obvious problems, in architectural and visual terms parts of New Delhi are sublime and have to be viewed in that light.

DEVELOPING THE PLAN

As mentioned earlier, the shift of the colonial capital from Calcutta to Delhi came as a complete surprise, but afterwards the planning moved forward very swiftly. Lutyens was appointed consultant in 1912 and became a member of the Delhi Town Planning

Teen Murti garden front

Committee (DTPC), with a brief to design a Master Plan. An early rival to Lutyens was another consultant, H. V. Lanchester, an urban designer who was sensitive to the worth of traditional Indian towns and who followed Ebenezer Howard in favouring garden city developments outside them rather than the wholesale redevelopment of older areas. Also heavily involved was the Viceroy himself. Lanchester produced the early plans, but by 1913 he had left Delhi and Lutyens worked up the proposal eventually favoured by the DTPC. When the Viceroy, Lord Hardinge, said that the capital had to be finished in four years Lutyens proposed that Herbert Baker, an old friend with experience of colonial building in Africa, should join him. The timeframe was, of course, wildly underestimated. The outbreak of the First World War held things up considerably and then the scale of the project and mounting costs delayed things when peace returned. The central buildings were not inaugurated until 1931 and empty sites languished until well after the Second World War.

At first the assumption was that the capital would be built north rather than south of Shahjahanabad, making use of the infrastructure already there, such as some residential accommodation. However, the very fact that the north was already built up meant that this would be the more expensive option as far as land acquisition went. It was also a more constricted site. On the other hand, it had better natural features, such as the Ridge and the nearby river. In the end, however, the south was preferred for its cheaper land, more space and greater healthiness, being further from swamps. Ironically, although cost had originally been a factor in preferring the southern site, the shift of site later became an excuse for raising the estimate!

The town planning decision-making was not straightforward. A core idea was to link the new capital with the older cities of Delhi. Several links with Shahjahanabad were proposed, such as a main vista that would link Government House with the Jami Masjid via a circus (Connaught Place), which was to be the site of the railway terminus. There were also to be improvements in the old city, with attempts at decongestion and the provision of more open space. The river was another element of the landscape the DTPC and others had wanted to incorporate into the scheme. While the north / south debate was going on, for instance, there was a proposal that the river be dammed opposite Firoz Shah Kotla. This would provide water for bathing throughout the year and get rid of the seasonal swamps that formed in the riverbed in the dry weather. It was proposed that part of the riverbed could also be reclaimed, releasing more land for the construction of the capital on the northern site. When the plans for the capital shifted south the dam plan was relocated further down the river. This would form a lake at the end of a vista from Government House to the Purana Qila, in which the old fort would be picturesquely reflected, but the idea was not taken up, partly because it was realised that raising the level of the water here would inevitably lead to swamp formation in other places. The other problem was that the railway line would cut the city off from the river. Clearly, abandonment of the river connection was cheaper, but how different Delhi would now be if the river had been effectively incorporated into the scheme.

The existing layout was eventually decided upon, although many of the original ideas, especially as regards Shahjahanabad, had been abandoned, partly because the northern development of the new city was hampered by the existence of Paharganj (with a population of 15,000, numerous shrines and temples, and property in many different private hands), but also because the realigned railway would lie between the old and new cities. Government House was located on Raisina Hill, with the main vista, known then as King's Way, now Rajpath, ending at the north gate of the Purana Qila. The main north-south road (Queen's Way, which became Janpath) started at Connaught Place and terminated at a circle south of Rajpath. Lutyens designed a group of buildings at the junction between Rajpath and Janpath but the idea was rejected because it was felt that they would interrupt the ceremonial way from India Gate to Government House (only the National Archives building exists, a small element of this scheme). Between Connaught Circus, Government House, India Gate, etc., a network of intersecting roads was laid out and repeated as a mirror image south of Rajpath, with modifications to accommodate pre-existing buildings.

As it was for Shah Jahan when he built his new city, so it was for the British: there were already a number of buildings and villages scattered across the area where the new city was planned. Some of the most important monuments, such as the Jami Masjid, Safdarjang's Tomb and the Purana Qila, became the focal points in the layout of streets, and many other buildings were incorporated in one way or another. The private houses of villagers, on the other hand, were swept away. Buildings deemed of historical or architectural interest were identified in the 1916 ASI survey, which concentrated almost exclusively on recording either places of worship or real antiquities. The worth of a picturesque urban environment had long been appreciated, but the means of conserving streetscapes (which means preserving ordinary domestic and commercial buildings as well as the monuments) was still a long way away, even in Europe.

It is curious in hindsight that the British considered this expansive design as suitable for a capital city (the same question applies to other new colonial cities as well). Why, for instance, did they think such vast residential plots were suitable in Delhi, when they knew that no such thing existed either in the centres of major Indian city centres (Bombay, Calcutta, Ahmedabad, for example), or in European capitals? However, we should not transpose modern thinking about city planning onto earlier decades. In those days people's horror of over-crowded urban environments and love of 'good air' far outweighed other considerations. If our modern concerns about access, public transport and mixed-use development had existed in the 1940s it seems unlikely that Nehru, with his austere lifestyle, would have blithely moved into a house with a six acre garden within easy walking distance of the Parliament building. Perhaps it is more surprising that the status quo has been maintained for so long and that, despite the population pressures, so many New Delhi bungalows continue to be used for their original residential purpose (although over the years some have been transferred, legally or otherwise, into institutional use). Admittedly, on the north side of Janpath many areas are being redeveloped, in particular the extensive junior staff housing (which is probably the most sustainable kind of colonial housing in terms of land-use), but even here an astonishing number of the original buildings remain. Unlike Shahjahanabad, therefore, which has kept much of the original street pattern but precious few of the buildings, the Colonial Capital still has much of both. The street pattern is more or less unaltered and a remarkable number of buildings still exist, mainly because they are in Government hands and are thereby, to some extent, protected.

THE BUILDINGS

The detailed plans for the layout having been approved, attention turned to the buildings. At first it was proposed that there would be an architectural competition for the main buildings but this idea was abandoned and, in 1913, Lutyens was appointed to design Government House (it was renamed Viceroy's House in 1929 and at Independence the Rashtrapati Bhawan) and Baker the Secretariat buildings.

After the layout of the city was agreed upon, there arose a problem: there were not enough buildings to fill such a huge area. The government offices would not be big enough to line the roads and single-storey bungalows right on the road were thought to be even more incongruous. One solution would have been large establishments for the rulers of the princely states but Lord Hardinge, the Viceroy, was against this, feeling that they should be off governing their states, not living it up in Delhi. The only remedy was the planting of trees to line the roads, a long-term (but hardly urban) vision that we are the beneficiaries of today.

There was also the question of architectural style. Advice came from all sides: was it to be English, Renaissance or Mughal? The great English Arts and Crafts architect Voysey got closer to the right answer, saying that 'considerations of local conditions, especially climate and traditional character, were the premises for fine buildings'. Hardinge, influenced by the

Indo-Saracenic architect Sir Swinton Jacob, favoured a Revivalist approach. The foremost historian of Indian Architecture, E. B. Havell, campaigned for genuine Indian architecture, proposing that the design and construction should be undertaken, as in the past, by a 'master builder' who, with traditionally trained craftsmen, would be bound to produce something suitable. This idea, although supported by many Indians, was not taken up, because it was felt that modern office requirements were too different from what traditional buildings provided. In the event the building was heavily reliant on the skills of Indian craftsmen, although the architectural concept and details were tightly controlled by the English architects. There were several contractors involved in the construction of New Delhi, the best-known being Sujan Singh and his son Sobha Singh (writer Khushwant Singh's grandfather and father). Haroun-al-Rashid was the main contractor for the Rashtrapati Bhawan.

The architects themselves, Lutyens and Baker, were, surprisingly, no admirers of Indian architecture. Baker complained that Hindu architecture 'merely aped wooden construction in stone, with grotesque meaningless carvings'. He approved rather more of Indo-Islamic architecture, but thought that it consisted of little more than 'masses of brick and concrete covered with decoration'. He did, however, admire *jalis*. Lutyens was equally scathing about Indian buildings. In fact, even if he had been an admirer of Indian architecture he disapproved of fixing on a particular style for mere ornamentation. He would equally, as Robert Byron felicitously put it in his 1931 article, have 'hesitated to rear a poem by Kipling in stone'. Instead, he said the buildings should be 'built as an Englishman dressed for the climate'. The path that each architect took was different, but the combined result is highly effective. They both, in fact, borrowed features from Indian architecture and united them with the classical style that they felt to be appropriate to the imperial capital. In the case of Lutyens his greatest inspiration came from the Sanchi *stupa* and railings, while Baker made good use of the *chatri* and *jali*.

NEW DELHI NOW

Although some areas of the garden city have been changed drastically, especially around Connaught Place, a far greater area has changed remarkably little. North of Rajpath there has been a great deal of redevelopment but, even here, there are still large pockets of original PWD bungalows. Some are in a pitiable state, many of them occupied by organisations that have no interest in maintaining them. In the northwest segment of New Delhi there are still a few original rows of low-income housing. Even these were spaciously laid out and provided generous accommodation, so that in the few places where they have not been demolished they have clearly become desirable residences. South of Rajpath the bungalow area is remarkably intact and even when the original bungalows have been replaced it has often been with similar large houses. In addition, the service areas behind the bungalows too have been left fairly untouched, even though development here would do very little damage to the ambience of the great tree-lined boulevards.

School building on Bangla Sahib Lane

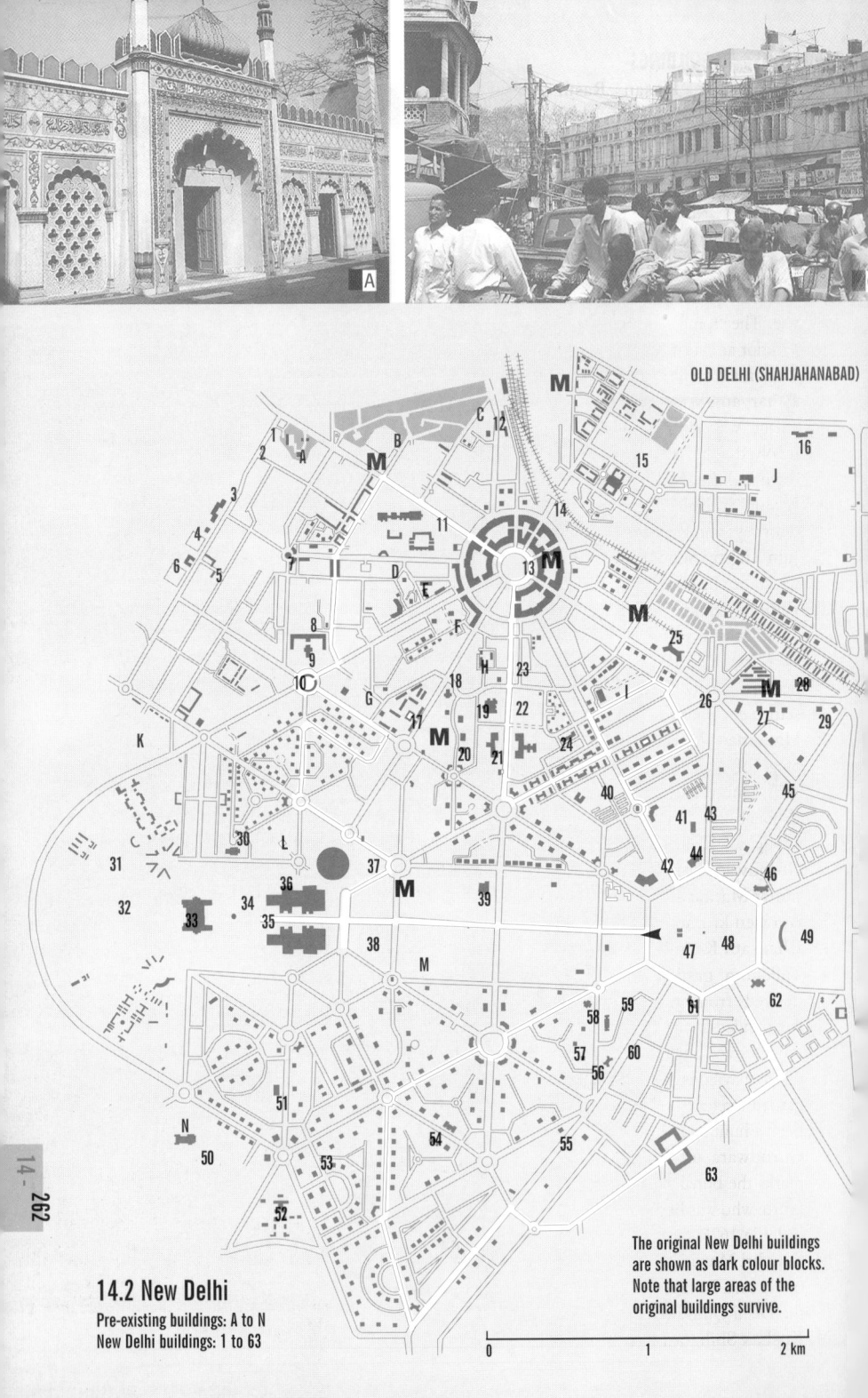

A

C

OLD DELHI (SHAHJAHANABAD)

M

M

M

M

M

M

M

M

M

M

M

1
2
A
3
4
6
5
7
B
C
12
11
D
E
F
8
9
10
G
H
31
18
19
22
23
20
21
24
40
41
43
44
42
25
26
27
29
28
45
46
47
48
49
K
30
L
36
37
33
34
35
38
39
32
31
58
59
61
57
60
62
56
63
51
N
50
53
54
55
52
15
16
J
13
14

The original New Delhi buildings
are shown as dark colour blocks.
Note that large areas of the
original buildings survive.

0   1   2 km

14.2 New Delhi

Pre-existing buildings: A to N
New Delhi buildings: 1 to 63

PRE-EXISTING BUILDINGS

A. **Dargah of Hasan Rasul Numa** 1691. Hasan Rasul Numa was a popular saint during Aurangzeb's reign. The complex contains the gateway and the tomb itself, various outbuildings and a mosque. The mosque is later in date, rather elaborately decorated and in use. The 'tomb' consists of an enclosure wall with an arcaded exterior and a completely plain interior containing several graves.

B. **Indian Christian Cemetery.**

C. **Paharganj**. Redevelopment of Paharganj, more of a town than a village, was avoided because of the amount of private property involved. The 1916 ASI survey mentions a few mosques in the town and the INTACH survey lists about half a dozen buildings. Like in Shahjahanabad there are a number of houses with fine doorways and a few mosques and temples.

D. **Jain Happy School**. Another Jain temple in a walled enclosure, which has been converted into a school.

E. **Chhota Mandir & Bara Mandir,** late Mughal. These temples, together with a few others were listed in Jaisinghpura, the village of Mirza Raja Jai Singh of Amber, great-grandson of Akbar's famous general Man Singh. It was the largest settlement south of Paharganj.

F. **Hanuman Mandir**. This was rebuilt by Man Singh of Amber and has now been rebuilt in the 20th century so the building is not historic, although the site is supposed to be of great antiquity. It is always thronging with devotees.

G. **Gurudwara Bangla Sahib**, modern (p.270).

H. **Jantar Mantar** 1724 (p.280).

I. **Agrasen ki Baoli** 15th c. (p.272).

J. **Chausath Khamba** 1370s (p.98).

K. **Talkatora garden** 18th c. The name probably derived from the cup-like (*katora*) hills that surrounded a tank (*tal*). In front of the tank was a long terrace forming the bund, along which were built ornate pavilions, some of which survive. Below this a long garden stretched down the slope. The buildings may have been a hunting lodge built for Muhammad Shah.

L. **Gurudwara of Teg Bahadur**, modern. The gurudwara marks the burial site of Guru Teg Bahadur, the ninth Sikh Guru, who was beheaded in Shahjahanabad on Aurangzeb's order in 1675.

M. **Sunehri Masjid** 18th c. This is all that remains of the village of Raisina. It was listed as being in Hakim Ji's garden beside the Delhi Qutb Road.

N. **Kushak Shikara** 14th c. (p.97).

NEW DELHI BUILDINGS

1. **St Thomas's Church** 1932 & **School** 1935. These were built to serve the poorer segment of the population. The church was designed by Walter George.
2. **Police Station** 1930s.
3. **N P Boys Senior Secondary School** 1940s
4. **Hindu Mahasabha Bhawan** 1930s. Designed by Sris Chandra Chatterjee (see 6).
5. **Harcourt Butler Senior Secondary School** 1930s.
6. **Birla Mandir** 1938. The grandest building on Mandir Marg was commissioned by the Birlas and designed by Chatterjee, leader of the revivalist Modern Indian Architectural Movement, the aim of which was to recover the cultural talent of former times. He strongly disapproved of the work by Lutyens and others in New Delhi and here created an exuberant temple using purely traditional features.
7. **Gole Market** 1920s.
8. **St Columba's School** late 1930s.
9. **Sacred Heart Cathedral** 1934 (p.270).
10. **Gol Dak Khanna** 1930s (p.270).
11. **Lady Hardinge Medical College** 1920s This became one of the first colleges of Delhi University.
12. **Lady Hardinge Serai** 1931. Built for destitute travellers, one of the two building in Delhi designed by A. G. Shoosmith, th

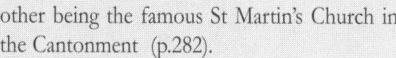

other being the famous St Martin's Church in the Cantonment (p.282).

13. **Connaught Place** 1933 (p.271).
14. **Minto Bridge** 1933.
15. **Government Press** 19th or early 20th c. This is in an anachronistically early colonial style, having been built before the bulk of New Delhi. A government press was set up in the 1840s but there is no evidence of a building in this position in 19th century maps.
16. **Lok Nayak Hospital** 1930.
17. **Police Station** 1930s. This courtyard building is entered through a double-columned colonnade. There are original residential buildings on quite a large site behind the office building.
18. **Free Church** 1927.
19. **Sardar Vallabhbhai Patel Smarak Trust Building** 1920s.
20. **Kerala House** 1927.
21. **Western Court** 1930s (p.271).
22. **Imperial Hotel** 1930s (p.271).
23. **Freemasons' Hall** 1935 (p.271).
24. **P. T. Chummery Quarter Complex** 1930s (p.272).
25. **Modern School** 1930s.
26. **Nepalese Embassy.** Once a private house. The central panels on the side wings have been changed with the addition of Nepalese style window mouldings.
27. **Bhawalpur House** 1939.
28. **Lady Irwin College** 1930s. This is a markedly simple building designed by Walter George. There are alternating arched and square opening and very interesting brick detailing.

29. **Houses**, a fine group of non-PWD buildings.

30. **Cathedral Church of the Redemption** 1935. This Anglican church was designed by Medd. It was to have occupied the main roundabout on Janpath south of Rajpath but it was realised that the location would put it too far away from the bulk of the congregation, who lived on the north side of the city. The architectural concept is interesting, building up in massive blocks to the central domed tower, but the use of rough, non-ashlar sandstone on the walls and the red tiled roofs make it untypical of its surroundings.

31. **The Estate** (p.276).

32. **The Garden** (p.275).

33. **Rashtrapati Bhawan** (p.274).

34. **Jaipur Column** (p.276).

35. **Gates** (p.276).

36. **North and South Blocks** (p.278).

37. **Parliament building** (p.277).

38. **Vijay Chowk (Great Place)** (p.269).

39. **National Archives building** (p.269).

40. **Lady Irwin Senior Secondary School** 1930s.

41. **Travancore House** 1930 (p.272).

42. **Hyderabad House** 1928 (p.268).

43. **Faridkot House** 1938. This is a modernist building with Art Deco features.

44. **Baroda House** 1936 (p.272).

45. **Tehri-Garhwal House** 1940s. This was probably one of the last of the Princes' houses to be built and is in solid colonial style.

46. **Patiala House** 1938 (p.272).

47. **India Gate** 1921 (p.268).

48. **Chatri** (p.268).

49. **National Stadium** 1930s (p.272).
50. **Teen Murti House** 1930s. This was originally built as Flagstaff House, the residence of the Commander-in-Chief, and was Nehru's official residence from 1948-1964. It was designed by Robert Tor Russell, head of the PWD architect's department, and is a large imposing house, suitable for the vast size of the site. Because it became a museum after Nehru's death it is possible to see a large part of the austere interior.
51. **Kashmir House** 1930s.
52. **Gymkhana Club** 1928.
53. **Indira Gandhi Memorial** 1930s. This is a typical PWD bungalow. The official residence of Indira Gandhi, where she was assassinated. It is preserved as a museum and, although the house is much altered, some of the rooms are authentic.
54. **Gandhi Sadan Smriti** 1930s. This was the Birla house, where Gandhi lived while in Delhi and where he was assassinated in 1948. Now a museum.
55. **Kashmir House** 1930s.
56. **Kapurthala House** 1940s.
57. **Patani House** 1940s.
58. **Darbhanga House** 1930s.
59. **Jaisalmer House** 1939. This was built in the modern International Style, which was far more popular on mainland Europe than in England. The style is characterised by both a lack of ornament and an internal concrete frame that allows for unbroken rows of window.
60. **Kota House** 1938. This is a modernist building, but in the more decorated Art Deco-inspired style seen at Faridkot house.
61. **Bikaner House** 1939 (p.273).
62. **Jaipur House** 1936 (p.273).
63. **Sujan Singh Park** 1940s (p.273).

33, 34, 35

38

40

41

42

Exploring New Delhi

New Delhi was designed for the private motor car and it is fairly impossible to see it in any other way than by driving round it. The following describes a drive that introduces you to the main features of this area.

Start at **India Gate**. This is a 138 ft high War Memorial Arch, finished in 1921, and designed by Lutyens, who had designed others in Europe and Britain. Behind it is a *chatri,* built to contain the statue of George V, which stood here until 1968

India Gate at night

(it now stands rather forlornly in the Coronation Park, at the site of his proclamation of the new capital). The *chatri* is situated in the middle of what was known as Princes' Park, around which large sites were allocated to the Indian princes. The most impressive is **Hyderabad House** (1928), visible straight ahead as you drive from India Gate into Rajpath. This is the best preserved of the Princes' houses and was designed by Lutyens. It has been kept in good condition because it is used by the Government, specifically the Ministry of Foreign Affairs, for formal meetings and entertaining. Unfortunately air-conditioning has had a sad effect on

LUTYENS'S BAKERLOO

The original plan was for Government House (Rashtrapati Bhawan) to sit at the top of Raisina Hill, with the Secretariat buildings below it. Baker, however, proposed that the Secretariat buildings also be put on the hill and Lutyens immediately agreed, even though he realised there would be an extra cost involved in clearing and flattening a larger area of the hill. It also, crucially, meant pushing Government House back, away from the edge of the hill. Baker designed the road up between the two wings of the Secretariat with a 1:22.5 incline, to finish before the main entrances of his buildings. Lutyens saw perspectives of the three buildings, which were also displayed at the Royal Academy and in the press. Rather surprisingly, he failed to take adequate notice of the fact that they were drawn from an impossible viewpoint, level with the top of the hill and therefore hovering some distance above Rajpath. He was particular though, and pressed to see sections that would show the road in relation to all three buildings, but it was only after two years, in 1916, that he finally saw them. He was horrified. The sight line from the Great Place (Vijay Chowk) was interrupted by the steep gradient and at this point only the dome of Government House would be visible. He fought to have the road changed for six years but the expense and inconvenience to circulation between the Secretariat buildings was going to be too much and he was defeated. He wittily called the debacle his Bakerloo, and remained on difficult terms with Baker for years. Robert Byron, writing an appraisal of the city for the British Architectural Review in 1931, found the effect of the isolated dome moving, because he thought of the dome as a 'pure monument'. This notion was probably of little consolation to Lutyens.

India Gate closeup

the façade because the verandas and balconies have all been enclosed, drastically altering the original architectural concept and leaving a somewhat shadowless, bland exterior.

Drive down Rajpath. At the crossing with Janpath Lutyens designed a monumental group, out of which only part of the **National Archives** building was constructed. Continue down Rajpath. As you approach the great ensemble of buildings ahead you will see the façade of the Rashtrapati Bhawan disappear, and by the time you reach the Great Place, now known as **Vijay Chowk,** only the dome is visible. This effect results from changes in the design, which Lutyens regarded as a catastrophe (see Lutyens's Bakerloo).

Vijay Chowk is the culmination of the processional way along Rajpath before it starts its final ascent to the Rashtrapati Bhawan. The main features are the six fountains, the commencement of the long pools that line Rajpath on both sides. Each fountain features an obelisk supported by concentrically arranged 'dishes', designed so that the water flowed evenly over each edge into the one below. At each end the area is enclosed by a screen wall, the inspiration for which came largely from the Sanchi railings. Cross it and drive up between the Secretariat Buildings, now known as **North and South Blocks** (p.278), to the **Rashtrapati Bhawan**, built as the Viceroy's house (p.274).

Return to Vijay Chowk and turn left and then right to drive round the **Parliament Building** (p.277). Drive straight on at the roundabout opposite Parliament, but take the fourth turning at the next roundabout to drive though a well-preserved area of **bungalows**. A few of the New Delhi bungalows were designed by particular architects (Baker designed a few bungalows that became known as 'Baker's ovens'), but the rest were left to the Public Works Department (PWD) and they came up with a series of pleasant, spacious buildings all sitting on big plots of land. These, like most other

Pavilion on east side of Vijay Chowk

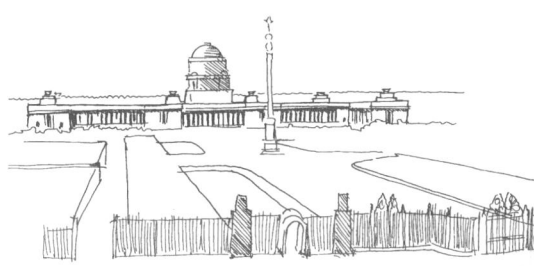
Bird's-eye view of Rashtrapati Bhawan

View of North Block

View of South Block

New Delhi bungalows, are mostly official residences for politicians and Government employees. In this area the houses are more modest in size, being midway between the grand houses south of Rajpath and the humble clerks' housing northwest of here. Whatever the size of house, however, the pattern was always the same, with the main road giving access to the front of the house and a service lane at the back, an arrangement that persisted in the building of many modern colonies.

Bungalow with modern porch

Turn right, slightly backwards, along another residential street, which swings round to the left onto Ashoka Road. Turn left again. On the right is the **Bangla Sahib Gurudwara** (20th century). This was the site of Mirza Raja Jai Singh of Jaipur's *haveli*, where the eighth Guru, Har Kishan, stayed with Mirza Raja during the Sikh succession quarrel in 1664. The building has been rebuilt many times; the present ornate structure is 20th century. At the end of the road is a very busy roundabout with the **Gol Dak Khanna** (1930s) marooned in the centre. This Post Office was designed by Robert Tor Russell, head of the PWD architects department, as part of Lutyens's town planning scheme. North of the circle is the **Sacred Heart Cathedral** (1934). This is the Roman Catholic Cathedral, built in a style that is rather untypically fussy for Delhi. It was designed by Medd, Russell's successor as Architect to the Government of India.

Bungalow on Teen Murti Marg

Take the first turning left after the Cathedral. Where this road meets Shaheed Bhagat Singh Marg there is a small area where a number of original buildings survive. Drive across the main road and go straight ahead. There are several open courtyards of pleasant **clerks' housing** on the left. Built around large greens, these row houses typically have front verandas, several rooms and backyards. Smaller versions had a similar layout but fewer rooms. Similar rows of

Clerks' housing - police lines

Clerks' housing - railway

Clerks' housing

houses were built in various other places, such as on some of the Princes' undeveloped plots. These were clearly meant to be temporary but many of them still stand, providing rather attractively spacious low-cost housing. Wherever this type of housing survives it seems to be well loved and is, of course, much more suitable to the needs of modern Delhi than the grander bungalows that ironically survive in much greater numbers.

Informal housing on undeveloped Prince's plot

Turn right on Panchkuian Marg, which will bring you to **Connaught Place**. Named after George V's uncle, who visited India in 1921, this was yet another project supervised by Russell. Although moderately functional, with its well-shaded arcades and good-sized shops, the architectural design works less well because the scale of the buildings do not really suit the size of the circle. It is most effective at the linking roads, where the buildings are more in scale with the width of the streets. The opening of the Metro station here (planned for mid-2005) will, it is to be hoped, produce more pedestrian-friendly landscaping in the central area, once a large park but now much reduced by parking.

Hawker at Connaught Place inner circle

Leave Connaught Place by Janpath. This is the segment of the city that has been most intensively redeveloped, with massive office blocks on most of the axial roads leading southwards from Connaught Place. However, there are still many original buildings left, even in this area. On Janpath you will pass the **Imperial Hotel** (1930s) on your right. This hotel eclipsed the hotels in the Civil Lines. Although fairly featureless on the outside, the interior has been well preserved and recently renovated. Just before the hotel, also on the right, is the **Freemasons' Hall** (1935). Of a pseudo-religious nature, this is a suitably forbidding building but not very visible from the road. On the other side of the hotel are the **Western & Eastern Courts** (1930s). Western Court still serves its original purpose as a hostel for legislators. The much more dilapidated Eastern Court is now the Central Telegraph Office. They were part of Lutyens's original scheme and were designed by Russell.

Hanuman Lane housing

At the roundabout turn sharp left and drive up Firoz Shah Road, between a rare type of housing. Fairly small houses are built to be a part of a grander-seeming scheme. This is a modest version of the 'palace façades'

Semi-detatched bungalow behind Firoz Shah Road

of 18th century urban England, where narrow houses were built to look as if they were part of a single magnificent edifice. At a main crossroads turn left on Kasturba Gandhi Road and then second right on Hailey Road. On the left of Kasturba Gandhi Road is an area of quite modest houses for the Post and Telegraph staff. In the same area is the **P. T. Chummery Quarter Complex** (1930s), built as shared accommodation for single men. Immediately on the left in Hailey Road is a narrow lane leading to the **Agrasen ki Baoli** (15th century), one of the many historic buildings that existed on the site of the new city. This deep *baoli* was reputedly built by Raja Agrasen, the founder of the Aggarwal community, in pre-Lodi times and is one of the handsomest in Delhi. As well as the circular open well at the back of the *baoli* there is a square covered well between them, accessible from the steps, which would have been used for sitting out the heat of the day. The attached mosque may be of a slightly later date.

'Palace façade' housing on Firoz Shah Road

Two-storey houses - Non-PWD (above and below)

Returning to the main road continue eastwards and take the next turn on the right, then right and immediately left to a junction with Firoz Shah Road. The area northeast of here seems to have been mainly developed privately; there are a great number of non-PWD houses nearby, for instance along Barakhamba Road and Sikandra Road. Cross Firoz Shah Road and take the second right, a quiet street lined with semi-detached bungalows. At the bottom turn left on Kasturba Gandhi Marg. Just beyond the roundabout on the left is **Travancore House** (1930 - picture

p.267). This house, originally built as a princely residence, is now occupied by the State Bank of Mysore. It is a handsome building with a butterfly design. A two-storey colonnade at the front of both wings has, on either side, roundels featuring the State Emblems, prancing elephants.

Drive around India Gate, passing in this order: **Baroda House** (1936), designed by Lutyens. Its present use as Railway offices means that it has not benefited from the same tender loving care as Hyderabad House and the modifications have been of a different nature. In both designs the awkward shape of the plot was dealt with by designing a butterfly shaped building so that the front doors face the approach road on the hexagon, while the wings have a sensible relationship with the adjoining roads; **Patiala House** (1938), now the Delhi Law Courts; **Jaipur House** (1936), now the National Gallery of Modern Art and another of Lutyens's buildings, sharing the same characteristics as Hyderabad and Baroda Houses, with a butterfly layout and central dome; the **National Stadium** (1930s), built against Lutyens's wishes. Between the Patiala and Jaipur plots the long waterway starting at the fountains in Vijay Chowk was to have ended in a garden, the romantic silhouette of the Purana Qila as backdrop. However, it was decided that this was an appropriate site for the National Stadium and this was started in 1931 by the PWD under Russell. The main entrance is dominated by five large arches; above them the four *chatris* are an afterthought suggested by Lady Willingdon. The last building is **Bikaner House** (1939). This is less palatial than the other Maharajas' houses on India Gate and much more like a typical New Delhi bungalow.

Turn left on Akbar Road, the second turning after Bikaner House. Continue on this road, with large bungalows on indecently large plots either side, until you reach the third roundabout, where you should take the second turning past further well-preserved **bungalows**. Even in this area, where all the bungalows were designed for the same kind of 'market', it is possible to find several different PWD bungalow types, while each road's bungalows are the same, they vary. Houses on corner plots were given an appropriately different treatment.

Continue south, crossing Aurangzeb Road, until you meet Prithviraj Road, where you should turn left. This has a great number of modern houses, the only such road in the area south of Rajpath, although they still sit on huge plots. Take the second turning on the right, down South End Road, and turn left at the Lodi Gardens, to follow the original southern boundary of Lutyens's scheme. On the left there are a number of post-Independence PWD housing schemes, and beyond Khan Market is the interesting **Sujan Singh Park** (1940s), an unusual departure for the private sector in New Delhi, but one that was to become ubiquitous, albeit with only two storeys, in numerous PWD schemes: apartment blocks set round communal gardens. An early PWD scheme of this type was the Lodi Colony (1940s). Although actually only two storeys, rooftop servants' quarters give them greater stature. Both these schemes were designed by Walter George. A distinctive feature, common to both projects are the great entrance arches that dominate the façades, although in the case of the Lodi Colony buildings the arches only give access to the service yards.

A perennially empty site on Janpath

Small butterfly house

Small bungalow on Teen Murti Marg

Large bungalow on Krishna Menon Marg

14 - 273

Rashtrapati Bhawan 🚶

Map 14.2 (p.262)

The Rashtrapati Bhawan is not open to the public. The official website gives views of several rooms. Visits for groups can be arranged through the President's office but security considerations mean that it is not straightforward. The garden can be visited in the spring (see opposite).

Lutyens designed the Rashtrapati Bhawan as Government House and he made it suitably monumental. The changes wrought by the Montagu-Chelmsford reforms of 1919 meant that its function was reduced to serving as the office and residence of the Viceroy, as another building was required to house the expanded legislature. It was therefore used for formal functions and large-scale entertaining, as it is today. Lutyens's attention to detail was all-encompassing. To quote Byron again, he designed a building that 'might serve a film-producer as Babylon, yet please the visitor with its soap-dishes'.

The centrepiece of the building is the great dome, built, as was the rest, using red and cream sandstone from the quarry at Dholpur (where much of the red sandstone used by the Mughals came from). Below the drum sits the vast mass of the house, one of the biggest residential buildings in the world. It is essentially a two-storey building, with a cream-coloured *piano nobile*, articulated by long colonnades that link solid, battered-wall pavilions. The ground floor is expressed as a monumental platform in red sandstone, interrupted only by a few arched openings and square windows. At the front a wide staircase leads up to the main entrance, which leads straight into the Durbar Hall.

The interior has a total of 340 rooms. On the principal floor are the main reception rooms situated in the central block while private rooms, offices, etc., are in the wings. Beneath the dome is the Durbar Hall, decorated in different coloured marbles, all from India except

Beating the Retreat at the Rashtrapati Bhawan. Note the disappearance of most of the building in the background (see p. 268).

for the Italian red marble pillars, virtually the only use of marble in the building. Along the garden front are a series of great reception rooms, the most splendid being the ballroom, with a superb ceiling painted in 1932-33 by Indian artists under an Italian master, Tomasso Colonnello, in Persian style. This ceiling was commissioned by Lady Willingdon, the vigorous wife of the seventeenth Viceroy, only the second actually to live in the building (Lutyens was horrified by many of Lady Willingdon's additions to the building).

The ground floor contained an array of offices that recreated the *karkhanahs* of Mughal times, with vast numbers of people employed on household maintenance and affairs. In colonial times there were, for instance, sixty men employed in the printing press alone, producing invitations, menus and general 'court circulars'. Running through the centre of the building from north to south are the carriage drives that deposited guests at the foot of a magnificent double staircase that ascends to the staterooms. The stair hall is actually an external courtyard but the walls end with deep coving, as if the sky above was the ceiling.

THE GARDEN
Map 14.2 (p.262)
The garden is open to the public for a few weeks in February / March when the annual flowers are at their peak (Tuesday – Sunday 9.30 – 2.30). Entrance is free but you are not allowed to carry in anything. An opportunity to visit the gardens while they are dormant should not be missed as this makes it possible to fully appreciate the sculptural qualities of the garden's design.

The garden was designed in its entirety by Lutyens and consists of three main elements. The magnificent layout near the house consists of pools, fountains, severely trimmed trees and formal beds. From here a path leads down under a stone pergola to the circular garden.

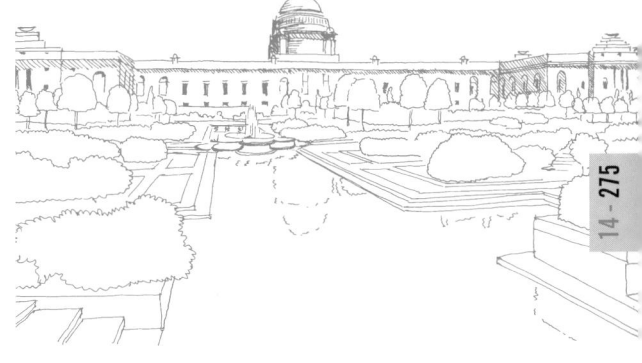

The pergola is structurally ingenious, with the cantilevered beam over the path counter-balanced by a hanging bracket that looks almost like an elephant's trunk. The circular garden is perhaps the most English part of the garden. The least formal element of this garden, its equivalent might be encountered as the most formal area in the garden of a contemporary country house in England.

14 – 275

THE ESTATE

Map 14.2 (p.262)
This is not accessible to the public.

The huge estate of the Rashtrapati Bhawan contains a number of buildings left much as Lutyens designed them. As with the Rashtrapati Bhawan itself, Lutyens was constrained by a budget, but this did not deter him from some suitably monumental designs, their magnificence of course relative to their usage, ranging from the quarters for senior staff through stabling for the Viceroy's horses to servants' quarters.

Jaipur Column with Rashtrapati Bhawan behind

JAIPUR COLUMN

Map 14.2 (p.262)

Halfway between the gates and the Rashtrapati Bhawan is the column presented by the Maharajah of Jaipur, who owned much of the land that was acquired for the building of the city. It is a rather conventional commemorative column with a distinctly peculiar crown: a glass star springing out of a bronze lotus blossom. Although it enhances the view from the entrance of the Durbar Hall eastwards, it is doubtful whether it improves the view in the other direction, blocking a clear view of the dome from the gates, which is most people's closest view of the Rashtrapati Bhawan.

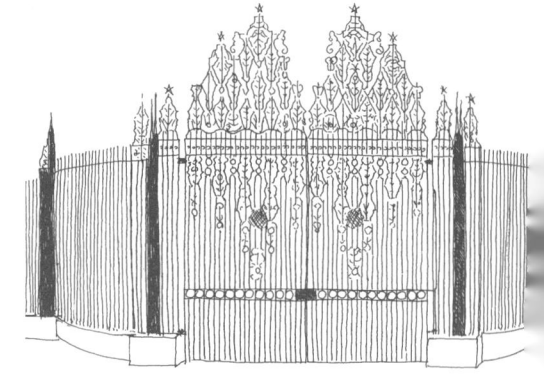

GATES

Map 14.2 (p.262)

The screen that divides the public road from the Rashtrapati Bhawan is a highly effective element in the original design. Solid stone posts and horse-guard boxes interrupt the line of exquisitely made fencing. The whole run is unusually tall, with an intricate pattern at the base. At the centre it swells outwards to frame the main gates. These and the subsidiary gates are prettily designed with an imaginatively asymmetrical design.

Parliament Building 🚶

Map 14.2 (p.262)

The commission for the Parliament Building came a few years after the layout of the city had been agreed, hence its rather subordinate location, below North Block. When the city was first planned it was envisaged that the Council chamber would be in Government House (Rashtrapati Bhawan) but after the 1919 Montagu-Chelmsford reforms, which somewhat expanded Indian participation in government, it was necessary to provide additional accommodation. The commission was given to Baker, whose brief was to provide assembly chambers for the Council of State, the Legislative Assembly and the Chamber of Princes. A fourth chamber would serve as a library. Baker's original idea was for a three-pronged building but Lutyens fancied a Coliseum-like building and it was his proposal that was accepted by the New Capital Committee in 1920. Baker therefore had to fit a complex set of chambers inside a circle.

Given Baker's impossible task, the plan is quite ingenious. Each chamber is semi-circular and is linked via large lobbies to the important central chamber. This was where the 1947 hand-over of power took place, when Nehru made his 'tryst with destiny' speech. It is still the venue on occasions when both houses of parliament are addressed together. Surrounding the chambers is a doughnut shape with offices and service rooms, all with access from the veranda that rings the building. The defect of the veranda is that the colonnade and roof do not offer sufficient protection from the sun for all-year use and, although the openings in the inner wall are always aligned with openings in the colonnade, their irregular sizes and heights are too apparent from outside.

The result, constrained by a tight budget, has never been considered a great success and it was not improved upon by the belated addition of an extra floor, which seriously undermines the relative simplicity of the original drum. The drawing-in of the purse strings can be seen in the finishes: the interior is moderately plain and the exterior walls are finished in painted plaster rather than stone. A too-small dome surmounts the central chamber; this particular feature came in for particularly savage attack from Robert Byron, who felt it was far too weak an element in the overall design. Perhaps the only redeeming feature of the extra floor is that it virtually obscures the dome, although it is unfortunate that from a distance the lantern can still be seen peeping over the parapet.

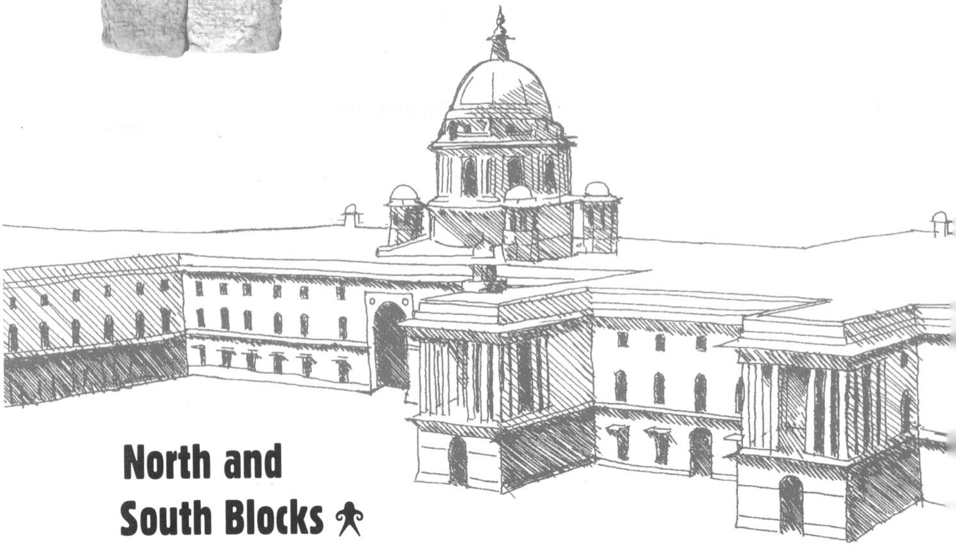

North and South Blocks ☆

Map 14.2 (p.262)

These are not open to the public.

Baker was a less original architect than Lutyens, but he was a sound choice to entrust with the design of the Secretariat buildings, at the time the second most important buildings after Government House. Like their neighbour, the buildings are built from cream and red Dholpur sandstone, the red forming the base and the cream the principal floors. Whereas Lutyens created entirely new architectural forms, Baker stuck to more conventional elements but created buildings that together make up a composite whole that cannot fail to raise the spirits of those who pass by. He described the principle of his design, which was to 'weave into the fabric of the more elemental and universal forms of architecture the thread of such Indian traditional shapes and features as may be compatible with the nature and use of the buildings'. The traditional features of which he approved were *jalis,* as well as great expanses of bare wall, interrupted by deeply shadowed and often ornately decorated openings.

North Block east tower

North Block pavilion

North Block detail

The buildings are so arranged that they form two 'squares', the first where the building is set back for the main entrances and the second in front of the Rashtrapati Bhawan gates. The elevations are punctuated by short projecting wings terminating in a colonnaded balcony, a treatment that is strikingly similar to Baker's 1910 Union Building in Pretoria. Like the Rashtrapati Bhawan, the façade is strongly articulated by light and shadow while the main decorative features are found on the roof. The centre of each building is marked by a dome with a rather Renaissance flavour, except for the fine *jalis* in the large windows. A great disappointment to Baker was the requirement, as an economy, to reduce the size of the towers on the eastern façades of each block.

In the large square created by the open courtyards in front of the main entrances stand four columns each crowned by a 'stately galleon', symbolising the oceanic connections of the dominions that gave them: Canada, Australia, New Zealand and South Africa. By the time these were unveiled in 1930, it was assumed that India would soon become a Dominion as well. The arches of the entrance doors themselves are carved with an inscription, in English on the North Block and in Urdu on the South, the former expressing an astonishingly patronising opinion: 'Liberty will not descend to a people. A people must raise themselves to liberty. It is a blessing that must be earned before it can be enjoyed.'

The interior of the building was designed around a series of courtyards. Some space for expansion was incorporated into the interior of the building but of course, by now, this additional space is a drop in the ocean, an ocean that has spilt over either side of Rajpath and into a large area to the north of it, which now houses a majority of the government departments.

South Block south entrance

South Block detail

14 - 279

Jantar Mantar (1724) 🚶

Map 14.2 (p.262)

The Jantar Mantar was built by Sawai Jai Singh, great-grandson of Mirza Raja Jai Singh of Amber, who owned land in this area and had a house and village called Jaisinghpura nearby. Sawai Jai Singh inherited the territory of Amber at the age of thirteen in 1699. His main interest was in astronomy but his other achievement was to build the city of Jaipur. The building of the observatories resulted from his dissatisfaction with the existing astronomical tables, which he resolved to improve upon. In 1724, having 'to accomplish the exalted command he had received [from Muhammad Shah], he bound the girdle of resolution about the loins of his soul, and built here several of the instruments of an observatory.'

Ram Yantra

The most prominent instrument here, the **Samrat Yantra** ('supreme instrument'), is the easiest to understand. It is, in effect, a sundial and the time of day can be read off the

Jai Prakash

curved quadrants below the gnomon, the large triangular centrepiece. The additional refinement is that the sun's height in the sky can be found by observing what part of the gnomon casts the shadow on the quadrant. The steps up the gnomon would have been used for making this observation.

The small instrument beside the Samrat Yatra is the **Misra Yantra**, the 'mixed instrument'. This is not mentioned in Jai Singh's papers, so was probably built by his son, Madhu Singh. This could be used for making various different observations. The quadrants below the gnomon are inclined at different angles and correspond to the meridians at observatories in other parts of the world. The other elements were used for making particular observations, such as the altitudes of celestial bodies at the meridian.

Behind the Samrat Yantra are the two most attractive instruments, the **Jai Prakash**. These are basically identical hemispheres but dissected so that each is the reverse of the other, thus enabling observers to accurately record the position of the shadow of cross-wires that would have been fixed across the centre of the hemispheres. This was another measurement of the position of the sun, although the approximate positions of stars could be measured by placing the eye at a point on the hemisphere where it most closely aligned with the cross-wires.

At the back are another two complementary structures, the **Ram Yantra**. These were used for reading horizontal and vertical angles. The height of the walls and the central pillar is equal to the distance from the inside of the wall to the edge of the pillar. Sighting bars would have spanned the openings in the wall (these can be seen in existence at the equivalent instrument at Jaipur).

The buildings were seriously damaged by neglect and vandalism during the late 18th century and most of the original marble pieces, with their graduations, were lost. The maharajas of Jaipur financed restoration in 1852 and 1910; much more work has been done since then, including replacing much of the marble so that the graduations will be permanent.

Misra Yantra

Delhi Cantonment

Baird Place housing

Delhi Cantonment, like New Delhi, has altered comparatively little since it was built and, like New Delhi, it exemplifies the ludicrously low densities in the colonial areas, contrasting with astonishingly high densities else where. It still contains a large number of Army establishments, spread out over hundreds of acres of land. There is a much lower percentage of colonial buildings than in New Delhi, because a good number of modern housing blocks have been constructed, but nevertheless the spacious ambience remains. Although large parts of it have restricted access it is well worth a visit. To visit **Baird Place** is to step into a time warp: about a dozen red-tiled and red painted bungalows, the official residences of senior army officers, stand amid mature trees around an oval 'green'. They are intriguingly different from the New Delhi bungalows and are probably better adapted to the normally hot climate, with their tiled, as opposed to flat, roofs. In layout, however, they are similar, with high-ceilinged central rooms lit by clerestory lighting, corner bedrooms and deep verandas. They could have been built in any part of India, at any time during the colonial period.

ST MARTIN'S CHURCH (1931) 🏮
Correctly marked on Eicher Map

Worth visiting is the garrison church designed by Shoosmith, an English architect, who came to India to interpret Lutyens's drawings for the local contractors. This is only one of two buildings he designed here, the other being the Lady Hardinge Serai (no. 12 on map p.262). It is a monumental, solid brick affair with remarkably few openings or ornamental flourishes. The brickwork is of a very high standard, with very narrow joints adding powerfully to the monolithic appearance. The few openings are severely Romanesque, with the main west door alone being celebrated by receding brick arches. Inside, handsome plain arches articulate the bays. The whole of the interior is plastered and painted. It is in use during the week as a multiple classroom for the attached school, so access is possible while the children are playing outside.

St Martin's Church

There are two main bazaar areas, which have some original buildings remaining, albeit much altered.

THE PUSA INSTITUTE
This is another area that seems to be trapped in a time warp. It was first established in 1905 at Pusa in Bihar as an agricultural research centre. It moved to the outskirts of Delhi after the terrible earthquake of 1934 but is now well inside the city, continuing with the same work. As in the Cantonment, there are some attractive colonial institute buildings lining the residential streets at generously spaced intervals.

MODERN DELHI

After Independence, the city became a major centre of commerce, industry and education.... Civic amenities have not kept pace. Unabated in-migration has compounded the problem. Land use regulations have been flouted. The green cover has dwindled.

Government of India's
White Paper on Pollution in Delhi, 1997

Independence and beyond

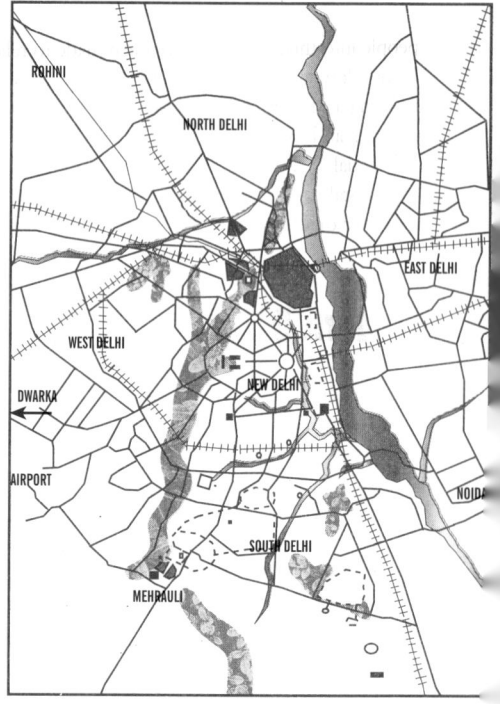

I ronically, by the time Lutyens's New Delhi was completed in 1931, it was known to most people in India and Britain that India was on her way to some sort of independence. What sort of independence this was to be was debated up to the very last minute, when suddenly Partition was declared inevitable and the handover date brought forward. The haste with which the British withdrew no doubt added to the appalling turmoil of Partition. The result for Delhi was a complete upheaval of its population. Many Muslims moved to Pakistan and an even greater number of Hindus and Sikhs moved into Delhi. At first some of the ancient monuments were used for housing the refugees. For instance, the Purana Qila was used to shelter Muslims until they could get away. Incomers squatted in numerous other buildings for a much longer time. A large number of people ended up in very cramped accommodation in Shahjahanabad. Over the next few decades the city expanded to many times its size at Independence.

Local governance changed gradually. The colonial Delhi Improvement Trust became the Delhi Development Authority (DDA) in 1955 with a remit to acquire land and develop it. They are also responsible for producing the Master Plan for Delhi; the first, provisional, one was published in 1956 and the final version followed in 1962, was modified in 1990 (MPD – 2001) and is now being modified again to anticipate conditions in 2021. The New Delhi Municipal Committee, created to administer the Imperial capital, continued to exist until 1994 when it became the New Delhi Municipal Corporation (NDMC). The rest of the city continued to be administered separately, from 1957 onwards by the Municipal Corporation of Delhi (MCD), which was an amalgamation of various local bodies. These two bodies deal with matters such as public streets, drains, markets, public health and numerous other matters.

In 1985 the city became the National Capital Territory (NCT) with its own Government, covering an area of 1,486 sq kms. This body deals with most matters normally dealt with by State governments such as local taxation, Public Works, transport, social welfare, health and education. Full statehood is unlikely to be far away, enabling the current multiplicity of authorities to be simplified. The NCT is part of a wider National Capital Region, an area of 30,241 sq kms covering parts of neighbouring states, created with a view to initiating regional planning, including the optimistic idea of turning district headquarter towns into magnet cities around Delhi that would reduce immigration to Delhi itself.

Despite all this, Delhi has, of course, suffered the same fate as other large and successful cities in the developing world. Rural and urban populations have expanded exponentially and the greater opportunities available in urban centres have sucked yet more people into them. Efforts have been made to relieve the pressures on the existing population by developing alternative, satellite centres outside Delhi such as NOIDA and Gurgaon; by building a Mass Rapid Transport System; by attempting to improve the electricity and water supplies and by trying to organise land use by regularising illegal colonies, developing new residential areas and clearing slums. Unfortunately none of these measures can keep up with the natural expansion of the city and access to land and services is, inevitably, grossly skewed in favour of the affluent.

Modern Delhi

Independent India experienced rapid industrialisation and rapid urbanisation. Delhi grew faster than the other Indian metropolitan cities, due in part to the fact that the effects of the transfer of government from Calcutta to Delhi did not fully materialise until after Independence. The growth of the city in the 1920s and 1930s was surprisingly slow, developers showing a cautious reluctance to invest in the new city. However, all

Slum behind DDA housing

this changed after Independence, the population growing by over 100 per cent in the months following Partition. Although there was a massive Muslim exodus they were more than replaced by almost half a million refugees from Pakistan as well as people from various states in India, in particular over a quarter of a million from Uttar Pradesh. The result was that the population rose from 695,686 in 1941 to 1,437,134 in 1951. It then continued to grow, at a rate of well over 50 per cent every ten years. It is now probably about 13 million. This has been a massive challenge to both town planners and architects.

PLANNING PROBLEMS

Planning guidelines were first set by the Delhi Government and then by the Delhi Master Plan, in force from 1962, and now being revised. The 1962 Master Plan was produced by foreign experts and followed principles that were well established in the West. However, conditions in western cities could not be more different from Delhi, the most obvious being that western cities no longer have to plan for rapidly expanding populations, so it is far easier for them to work towards some sort of an ideal city layout. However, despite the extra difficulty of overwhelming growth, the Delhi Master Plan nonetheless aimed at an 'Ideal' and some of the ideas became reality: industrial zones, Ring and arterial roads, District Centres such as Nehru Place, large housing schemes for public sector workers and other huge schemes involving private developers, such as Rohini in the northwest, said to be the largest housing colony in the world. Land was also allocated for educational institutions and open spaces.

Problems arose from the beginning because there was always a greater population than the public and private housing stock could cater for. There were also a great many people who could not afford the kind of housing that was made available through public or private developments, either because the rent was too high or because they could not afford the high commuting costs of living in cheap accommodation miles away from their work. All through the decades, therefore, squatter settlements have sprung up on unoccupied land everywhere in the city. The inhabitants (who, even now, probably amount to as many as one third of the entire population) are always in the unfortunate position of violating planning laws and are at risk of losing their homes at any time. The brave ones invest

Slum

in their houses, using *pucca* materials to improve the quality of their lives, hopeful that, in the end, their colony will be regularised rather than bull-dozed, an eventuality that has a lot more to do with local and national politics than with actual compliance with the Master Plan. It says a lot for the size of the population explosion and for the inadequacy of current planning that it is not only the poor who live in unauthorised colonies. All over Delhi commercial encroachments have recently been demolished and there are some large and smart residential colonies, such as Sainik Farms, that were built illegally.

Quite outside normal planning restrictions are the approximately 150 villages that have been swallowed up by development. Unlike in Colonial times, when villagers such as those at Raisina or Khairpur (Lodi Gardens) were compensated but shifted right away, nowadays the villagers are compensated for the loss of their fields (if they have not already sold out to land-sharks) but are allowed to stay in their villages. The village *abadi* (residential) land necessarily falls outside normal planning guidelines, meaning that house owners can develop their plots at very high densities, another compensation of sorts. However, this has led to some of the worst over-development and congestion in precisely those areas where conservationists would like to have seen some preservation of the quality of the townscape (for instance, at Mehrauli, Kotla Mubarakpur and Shahpur Jat). A result of the difference between planned and non-planned areas is the vast difference in population densities. Overall figures from the 2001 census give densities ranging from 4,165 people per sq km in Southwest Delhi and 4,908 in New Delhi to 25,760 in central Delhi, 22,637 in East Delhi and an amazing 29,411 in the northeast (trans-Yamuna). Locally of course the population densities are far higher: In the 1990s the population inside the walled city was as much as 2,500 per hectare (equivalent to 250,000 per sq km)! Such wild discrepancies make service provision particularly difficult.

The other zone of intensive development is in the belt around Delhi, where there are satellite towns, such as Gurgaon, Noida, Dwarka and Rohini, which were designed originally to take the pressure off Delhi itself, but in fact are not far enough away to act as freestanding urban centres. Instead, they have largely become dormitory suburbs, adding to the pressure on the roads, although some, Gurgaon in particular, are also important industrial and commercial centres attracting commuters *from* Delhi.

MODERN ARCHITECTURE

Over two thousand years ago the Roman architect Vitruvius wrote that the fundamental requirements for buildings are Commodity, Firmness and Delight. Commodity means its ability to serve the purpose for which it was built. Firmness means whether it will stand up and survive the assaults of time and the elements. Delight is self-explanatory, but most people nowadays would say that good architecture should give delight to both users and passers-by. Delight does not necessarily result from deliberate architectural invention; non-architect-built (vernacular) buildings provide very pleasant environments. This is often because they fulfil so well the requirements

Pragati Maidan

Indira Gandhi Arena

for commodity and firmness, looking exactly right in that place and climate. Monuments and old buildings from the past generally give us delight but they are probably unrepresentative of their age in that they were the important, permanent, architect-designed, buildings. Obviously they were built for commodity and firmness and most were also built with a view to delight, although some would have been built with the additional aim of inspiring awe and respect in the beholder. Many modern buildings make the same sort of statement about importance, although most modern patrons will not want to intimidate people.

Vitruvius's three requirements are still acknowledged by architects today, although the emphasis put on each has varied and the element of delight is sadly missing from an enormous amount of modern architecture produced in the decades immediately after Independence. By contrast, the privately built housing put up in recent decades demonstrates how important people perceive delight to be; a surprising number of clients will pay that bit extra just to have an extra flourish on the roof-line or a fancy façade, a distressing fact to modernist architects who were taught, among other things, about the importance of 'truth to materials'. Recently architects have acknowledged that symbolic elements do have a place in architecture and are prepared to use them and other devices to create delight in buildings, alongside the delivery of commodity and firmness.

Utilitarian modern offices - Connaught Place

Exuberance of private housing

Modern Architecture in Delhi

Independent India saw a considerable break in architectural style, caused both by a rejection of colonial styles of architecture and the need for rapid construction. Colonial architecture was fairly conservative and the PWD bungalows in New Delhi were designed using pure classical motifs. Some private architectural firms still designed classical buildings, although a few had embraced Art Deco ideas. In Shahjahanabad and the expanding suburbs private builders chose from an eclectic variety of styles: at the turn of the century builders had used classical or gothic models or stuck to more indigenous styles, but from the 1930s onwards Art Deco was much in vogue and there are a considerable number of buildings with striking Art Deco façades, with special emphasis on stair-towers and entrances. European Modernist architecture had little influence here, probably because it was less enthusiastically embraced in Britain than in mainland Europe. A few of the Princes' houses are in this style, such as Faridkot and Kota houses, near India Gate (see map 14.2), both from 1938.

In the immediate post-Independence era it was inevitable that most Indian architects looked to **Modernism** for inspiration, and various strands of modernist thinking developed. The vast majority of early modern buildings in India fell into the category of **Utilitarian Modernism**, defined by Jon Lang as the mingling of two strands of pre-war modern architecture. The first was the Art Deco style 'simplified to meet modernist demands' and the second was International Modernism 'adapted to the climatic nature and construction processes of India'. These buildings are ubiquitous, in the form of schools, hospitals, local government offices and housing schemes. Of course, many

Empiricist - Lotus Temple

Modernist - Auditor General's Office

Modernist - World Health Organization building

Utilitarian Modernist buildings are not designed by architects at all – the style became the basic vernacular for builders throughout India and is seen everywhere, generally poorly constructed and ill-maintained.

For those striving for a little more delight, there was strong support for **Revivalism**, which meant imitating (reviving) styles from the past. This grew out of a political belief in the perfections of a golden past (the Gothic Revival in industrial 19th century Britain had exactly the same origins). The idea behind revivalism is that human behaviour and life-styles can be moulded by architecture; if you put people back into the imagined physical surroundings of this golden age they will behave in the (imagined) desirable way of their golden age ancestors. In reality revivalist ideas did not get much further than the superficial adornment of buildings with elements such as *chatris* and *chajjas*, although in some cases the ideas could go further, as in many of the new temples built in Delhi.

Revivalist thinking also had an influence on the group of architects thought of as **empiricists**, whose philosophy was that buildings should derive from their context (the site) and use, rather than ideology or any pre-determined style. The work of Joseph Stein in the Lodi Estate is the best known example of this genre but more recently architects, such as

Revivalist - Supreme Court building

Empiricist - India International Centre

cist - Akshya Pratishthan, Vasant Kunj

Empiricist - Parliament Library

Revathi and Vasant Kamath, have mixed modern and traditional materials and techniques very successfully.

The same attitude as the revivalists, but from a different ideological viewpoint, was behind the modernist **Le Corbusier**'s '*La Ville Radieuse*' in which daily life would be efficient and well-ordered, moulded by the buildings (grandiose tower blocks set in sterile park-like open space). It was this school of thought that ultimately had a greater, and on the whole baleful, impact on architecture and town planning in India. Unfortunately, throughout the world, *Ville Radieuse* planning has been a disaster in most cities where it has been tried. It was even less suited to Indian conditions than to European, because tower blocks require sophisticated servicing and public open spaces require maintenance and modern civic behaviour. Interestingly, the style of architecture that was most inspired by Le Corbusier, which became known as Brutalist in Europe, was more successful in India. In Europe its rationale was of 'honesty', a truth to materials that involved concrete work being left with the marks from the shuttering visible and pipework exposed to view. It is generally disliked there. In India the philosophy was more logical because the need for economy was more urgent and the style actually suited the relatively low skill levels of modern construction workers here. A less ideological Modernism created '**engineered buildings**', in which the technical aspect of enclosing space predominate.

In recent years architects have been eclectic in their inspiration. Many designers are still heavily influenced by international developments in architecture, while others have taken their inspiration more from regional conditions and styles. The fact that there is no precedent for many new building types means that architects inevitably draw their inspiration from a wide variety of sources. The effect of the existing street pattern and building codes in the newer parts of Delhi, where most modern 'architecture' has been built, has tended to mean that buildings have been seen as objects in space rather than as components of a streetscape, but there have also been some successful attempts to enhance the urban character of the city.

Corbusian - ISBT, Kashmiri Gate

Engineered - SCOPE building

Object in space - LIC building

Housing

In any city most of the best-known and prominent buildings are administrative, educational and commercial, but these are a minority. The majority of buildings in cities are residential and it is largely by the quality and disposition of residential accommodation that a city functions well or not.

Immediately after Independence and Partition there was gross overcrowding in places like Shahjahanabad, but the Delhi government rose to the challenge with some extensive housing developments. Much of the development was carried out by the CPWD (Central Public Works Department) and later the DDA (Delhi Development Authority). The desire for speed in production and minimised expenditure led to a utilitarian style of architecture generally involving schemes of considerable uniformity. Despite the uniformity, the estates are pleasantly and spaciously laid out, far more extravagant of land than the equivalent privately developed plotted colonies, at every socio-economic level. They are also entirely out of keeping with traditional Indian design, although the layouts were very much in keeping with the garden city tradition introduced by the British. Typical early CPWD estates vary as to layout, depending on the economic group that inhabits them, but they are virtually always two-storey. Some have detached

Asian Village housing

PWD housing

PWD housing

PWD housing - President's Estate

houses, set in relatively large gardens for the most senior officials, but most were built as apartments either side of central staircase towers. While the layouts of these colonies seem to be modelled on English garden suburbs, the architecture itself derives more from the European modern movement: horizontal windows and sunshades being the only relief in the rendered and painted wall surfaces. Unfortunately the climate makes the garden component of the layouts somewhat difficult to maintain, leading to the impression today of a great deal of surplus land (in which there is more than enough space for cricket and car parking). Later it was realised that these schemes were too low density and more utilitarian designs were built, with four-storey slabs set in rows interspersed with much less outdoor space. More recently an awareness of urban values has crept back into the design of large-scale developments, with an attempt to create neighbourhoods based around pedestrian courtyards, a good non-PWD example being the Tara Apartments in Alaknanda, South Delhi.

There is a dramatic contrast when one looks at those areas of the city that were released to private groups for development, or the large estates often laid out by the CPWD in which families were sold serviced plots to build on. Under market constraints different socio-economic groups were able to achieve different things, but the type of layout tends to be the

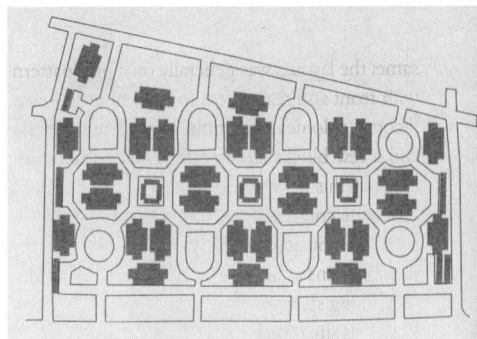

Rabindra Nagar plan - public

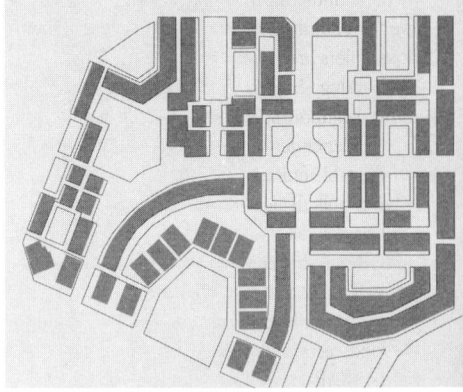

Nizamuddin East plan - private

Tara Apartments

Modernist PWD housing

same: the layouts was generally on a grid pattern with front and rear access to each plot (in lower income colonies sometimes only front access) and a few blocks left free for small local parks. Most of this privately built housing suffers from moderate congestion, with individually built but attached housing on narrow plots with small front gardens at best. The narrow roads and lack of parking space on the house plots are leading to a crisis situation in many areas, now that more and more of the middle class have become car owners. In the more elite colonies, largely found in South Delhi, roads are wider and house plots are larger, allowing for easier car parking, bigger private gardens and more neighbourhood parks. In the early post-Independence period there was considerable uniformity of style in private houses, still detectable in early colonies such as Sundar Nagar (1950s-60s). The thing that is common to the more recent colonies is the extreme eclecticism of the architecture, constrained only by the citywide restrictions on the Floor Area Ratio (FAR), height restrictions, and certain setback requirements.

Small plots in Rohini

Modern housing, West Delhi

Looking to the future

There are numerous problems associated with Delhi that do not appear to have ready solutions. Some of the causes are easy to identify: it is widely understood, for instance, that low-density development creates traffic congestion. In the case of Delhi the situation is exacerbated by the lowest densities occurring in the ring that encircles the commercial heart of the city, while higher densities occur further out. The metro system, being built at impressive speed, will improve the situation, although the proposed network is not extensive enough. Although there is some use of the railways for commuting, choice of transport is limited, effectively, to public buses (and dedicated services to schools and major institutions), auto- and bicycle rickshaws, private cars, scooters and bicycles. The socio-economic layout of the city is given away simply by observing the make-up of the traffic entering the city centre on different routes: wait at traffic lights at one of the crossings in South Delhi and you will be surrounded by cars, wait at one of the crossing on the Ring Road near the Red Fort, for instance, and there will be a sea of bicycles and bicycle rickshaws travelling in from the northern parts of East Delhi.

Another easily identified problem is the astonishing amount of unused or ill-used land in the city centre, including a surprising amount of decayed industrial land that lies empty. Among many startlingly inept land use decisions must be counted the new Indraprastha Park between the Ring Road and the main north-south railway line near the Yamuna, which is inaccessible by foot from any residential neighbourhood apart from Sarai Kale Khan – surely a prerequisite for an urban park! Another example in exactly the same area is the Government plant nursery north of Humayun's Tomb, an amount of open space that could only perhaps be justified by allowing access to the general public at all times.

A third problem of course is that of transport, already referred to. It is hoped that the Metro system will ease congestion in the north and west but, for the rest of the city, roads will be the only means of circulation for the foreseeable future. The Government is fighting fires with a series of flyovers at the busiest junctions but, as has been proved over and over again elsewhere, more and better roads will only lead to longer journeys and more traffic.

What, therefore, are the solutions? Part of the solution has to come from addressing the problems outlined above. The city, like every other city, will have to wrestle with the problem of getting the affluent out of their cars and onto public transport. Nobody pretends that it is possible to do this with a stick (financial penalties) without providing the carrot of really good trains and buses. For instance, the Metro will ease traffic congestion a bit but it is going to be many decades before a widespread network has been built. Clearly the existing railway system is underutilised, especially the ring railway that passes through some areas of high commercial activity and others that are woefully under-utilised (e.g. Chanakyapuri and the Millennium Park).

Housing is probably the biggest headache of all and clearly has to be considered integrally with employment locations, water supply,

DELHI METRO

Three lines, totalling 56 kms, are already running successfully, having been finshed largely ahead of schedule and below budget. The cost is partly offset by property development at Metro stations, which have been designed as impressive new contributions to the urban landscape. Phase Two involves extensions of the existing lines, with an extension and a branch to the north and west, three lines in all going east of the river, and an extension going south towards Gurgaon. Judging by the success of the existing lines it seems likely that more lines will follow in the future, the projected Phase Three.

drainage and maintenance. The general lack of maintenance is one of the most distressing features of modern Indian life. It is essential, not only for the many heritage buildings that have been discussed in this book, but for private houses, commercial buildings and numerous and varied government buildings.

If these and all the other major problems can be tackled, Delhi might become a more liveable city. It might even attract more than the tiny fraction of global tourists that now visit, a prospect that might seem to be double-edged now, with infrastructure in such short supply, but surely an important consideration for the future, when tourism revenues are likely to become an ever greater part of the global economy. Whatever the myriad solutions are, they are clearly going to need an enormous amount of political will. Not only is massive investment needed but, crucially, it will also be necessary to redistribute resources dramatically.

Select Bibliography

CHAPTER 2

Alfieri, Bianca Maria. *Islamic Architecture of the Indian Subcontinent*. Calman & King, London, 2000. Distributed by Mapin, Ahmedabad.

Asher, Catherine B. *Architecture of Mughal India*. Cambridge University Press, New Delhi, 1995.

Frishman, Martin and Hasan-uddin Khan. *The Mosque*. Thames and Hudson, London, 1994.

Juneja, Monica. *Architecture in Medieval India*. Permanent Black, New Delhi, 2001.

Koch, Ebba. *Mughal Architecture*. Prestel-Verlag, Munich, 1991.

Michell, George. *Architecture of the Islamic World*. Thames and Hudson, London, 1978.

CHAPTER 3

Singh, Upinder. *Ancient Delhi*. OUP, New Delhi, 1999.

CHAPTER 4

Kumar, Sunil. *The Present in Delhi's Pasts*. Three Essays, New Delhi, 2002.

Naqvi S. A. A. 'Sultan Ghari, Delhi' in *Ancient India No 3, 1947*. ASI, New Delhi, 1984:4-10.

Smith, Vincent A. *The Iron Pillar of Delhi and the Emperor Chandra*. Journal of the Royal Asiatic Society, London, 1897.

CHAPTER 5

Shokoohy, Mehrdad and Natalie Shokoohy. 'Tughlukabad, The Earliest Surviving Town of the Delhi Sultanate' in *Bulletin of the School of Oriental and African Studies*. vol LV11, no.3, 1994.

Shokoohy, Mehrdad and Natalie Shokoohy. 'The Dark Gate, the Dungeons: The Royal Escape Route and More: Survey of Tughlukabad, Second Interim Report' in *Bulletin of the School of Oriental and African Studies*. vol LX11, no.3, 1999.

Waddington, H. 'Adilabad: A Part of the "Fourth" Delhi' in *Ancient India No 1 1946*. ASI, New Delhi, 1983:60-76.

CHAPTER 6

Gibb, H. A. R. *The Travels of Ibn Battuta 1325-1354*. Munshiram Manoharlal, New Delhi, 1993.

CHAPTER 7

Banerjee, Jamini Mohan. *History of Firuz Shah Tughluk*. Munshiram Manoharlal, New Delhi, 1967.

CHAPTER 8

Lal, Kishori Saran. *Twilight of the Sultanate*. Munshiram Manoharlal, New Delhi, 1980.

CHAPTER 10

Misra, Neeru and Tanay Misra. *The Garden Tomb of Humayun*. Aryan Books, Delhi, 2003.

Troll, Christian W. ed. *Muslim Shrines in India*. OUP, Delhi, 1992.

CHAPTER 11

Ahmad, Nazir. *The Bride's Mirror*. Permanent Black, New Delhi, 2001.

Andrews, C. F. *Zaka Ullah of Delhi*. W Heffer, Cambridge, 1929.

Asher, Catherine B. 'Mapping Hindu-Muslim Identities through the Architecture of Shahjahanabad and Jaipur' in *Beyond Turk and Hindu*. ed. Gilmartin, David and Bruce B. Lawrence, India Research Press, New Delhi, 2003, pp 121-148.

Bernier, Francois. *Travels in the Mogul Empire 1656-1668*. Translated by Archibald Constable. Asian Education Services, New Delhi 1996.

Blake, Stephen P. *Shahjahanabad; The Sovereign City in Mughal India 1639-1739*. Foundation Books, New Delhi, 1993.

Ehlers, Eckart and Thomas Krafft. *Shahjahanabad / Old Delhi: Tradition and Colonial Change*. Manohar, New Delhi, 2003.

Franklin, William. 'An Account of the Present State of Delhi' in *Asiatic Researches* 4 (1795).

Ghalib, Mirza Asadullah Khan. *Dastunbuy*. tr. Khwaja Ahmad Faruqi. Asia Publishing House, London,1970.

Kaye, M.M. ed. *The Golden Calm*. Viking Press, New York, 1980.

Koch, Ebba. *Mughal Art and Imperial Ideology*. OUP, New Delhi, 2001.

Lall, John. *Begam Samru*. Roli Books, New Delhi 1997.

Metcalf, Thomas R. *An Imperial Vision. Indian Architecture and Britain's Raj*. Oxford Indian Paperbacks, New Delhi, 2002.

Mukherji, Anisha Shekhar. *The Red Fort of Shahjahanabad*. OUP, New Delhi, 2003.

Russell, Ralph. *The Oxford India Ghalib: Life, Letters and Ghazals*. OUP, New Delhi, 2003.

Spear, P. *Twilight of the Mughals, Studies in Late Mughal Delhi*. Munshiram Manoharlal, New Delhi, 1991.

CHAPTER 12

INTACH and Conservation Society Delhi. *Mehrauli Heritage Maps*. INTACH, New Delhi, 1993.

Lewis, Charles and Karoki Lewis. *Mehrauli*. Harper Collins, New Delhi, 2002.

CHAPTER 13

Gupta, Narayani. *Delhi, Between Two Empires, 1803 – 1931*. OUP, New Delhi, 1981.

CHAPTER 14

Byron, Robert. *New Delhi*. Asian Educational Services, New Delhi, 1997.

Metcalf, Thomas R. *An Imperial Vision. Indian Architecture and Britain's Raj*. Oxford Indian Paperbacks, New Delhi, 2002.

Nath, Aman. *Dome over India: Rashtrapati Bhavan*. India Book House, New Delhi, 2002 .

Volwahsen, Andreas. *Imperial Delhi*. Prestel Verlag, Munich, 2002.

CHAPTER 15

Dupont, Veronique, Emma Tarlo and Denis Vidal. *Delhi, Urban Space and Human Destinies.* Manohar, New Delhi, 2000.

Jain, A. K. *The Cities of Delhi.* Management Publishing Co, New Delhi, 1994.

Lang, Jon, Madhavi Desai and Miki Desai. *Architecture & Independence.* Oxford Indian Paperbacks, New Delhi, 2000.

Lang, Jon. *A Concise History of Modern Architecture in India.* Permanent Black, 2002.

GENERAL READING

Ara, Matsuo et al. *Delhi: Architectural Remains of the Delhi Sultanate Period.* 3 vols University of Tokyo, Tokyo, 1970.

Ara, Matsuo. *Dargahs of Medieval India.* University of Tokyo, Tokyo, 1977.

Bullock, Humphrey. *The Fifteen Cities of Delhi.* The Roxy Press, New Delhi, 1949.

Carr Stephen. *The Archaeology and Monumental Remains of Delhi.* Aryan, New Delhi, 2002.

Chandra, Satish.*History of Architecture and Ancient Building Materials in India.* Tech Books International, New Delhi, 2003.

Dalrymple, William. *City of Djinns.* Flamingo, London, 1994.

Dayal, Maheshwar. *Rediscovering Delhi.* S Chand & Co, New Delhi, 1975.

Dube D. N. and Promodini Varma. *Delhi and its Monuments.* Spantech Publications, New Delhi, 1987.

Eicher *Delhi City Map.* Eicher Goodearth, New Delhi, 2001.

Frykenberg, R. E. ed. *Delhi Through the Ages: Essays in Urban History, Culture and Society.* OUP, Delhi, 1986.

Jackson, Peter. *The Delhi Sultanate, A Political and Military History.* Cambridge University Press, Cambridge, 1999.

Kaul H. K. *Historic Delhi - An Anthology.* Oxford University Press, Delhi, 1985.

Lewis, Charles & Karoki Lewis. *Delhi's Historic Villages.* Ravi Dayal, Delhi, 1997.

Masselos, Jim and Narayani Gupta. *Beato's Delhi 1857, 1997.* Ravi Dayal, New Delhi, 2000.

Nanda, Ratish. *Delhi, the Built Heritage: A Listing, New Delhi.* New Delhi, INTACH, 2000.

Nath, R. *History of Sultanate Architecture.* Abhinav Publications, New Delhi, 1978.

Punjab Government. *A Gazetteer of Delhi 1883-4.* Vipin Jain, Gurgaon, 1988.

Sharma, Y. D. *Delhi and its Neighbourhood.* Archaeological Survey of India, New Delhi, 1990.

Sharp, Henry. *Delhi, Its Story and Buildings.* Humphrey Milford, OUP, Bombay, 1928.

Sinha, R. *Lal Kot to Lodi Gardens.* Rupa, Calcutta, 1996.

Smith, R. V. *Lesser-known Monuments of Delhi.* Journalists' Literary Circle, New Delhi, 1999.

Zafar Hasan. *Monuments of Delhi*, 3 vols. Aryan Books International, New Delhi, 1997.

1840s map of Shahjahanabad...............181,195
1849 map, a topographical and archaeological map (1 inch to 1/4 mile)......................103,166
1916 survey / listing, ASI report (see general Bibliography under Zafar Hasan)
..........................45,91,103,127,164,176,260
Abdur Rahim, Khan-i-Khanans....................166
Abu Bakr, Sultan 1388-89 81
Adham Khan 175,223
Adhchini...58,78
Adilabad...49,50,54
Afghanistan, Afghans...................37,38,163,179
Aga Khan Foundation...................................165
Agra 101,102,126,134,147,178,223,240
Ahmad Shah Abdali, Afghan chief who attacked Delhi in 18th century 130
Ahmad Shah, Emperor 1748-74...........130,247
Aibak (see Qutbuddin Aibak)
Ajmer 34
Akbar Shah, Emperor 1806-37 233
Akbar, Emperor 1556-1605
..................................18,146,147,155,175,200
Akbarabadi Begum, wife of Shah Jahan......245
Alai Darwaza (see under Gateways)
Alam Shah Sayyid, Sultan 1445-51 100
Alauddin Khalji, Sultan 1296-1316
....35,41,42,45,107,174
Alauddin's minar 36
Ali Mardan Khan (d.1657)
Courtier of Shah Jahan 181,192-93
Ali, the Prophet's son-in-law ....:...........127
Aliganj..114,127
Amir Khusro Dehlavi (1253-1325), poet
....172,191
Ammunition Stores, Civil Lines...................248
Anang Pal Tomar, Rajput kings in 8th and 11th centuries 27-29
Anang Tal, Lal Kot 30,37
Anangpur...27-29
Ansari's House 215
Ara, Matsuo 77
Arab Serai, Humayun's Tomb......................152
Arabesque: A type of decoration in the form of foliage found on Islamic buildings....12,14
Arabian architecture......................................40
Aravalli Hills 26
Arch netting...16,149
Arch, Arcuate construction: Construction that involves the 'true arch'....................11,40
Arch, cusped 17
Archaeological Park, Mehrauli 218
Archaeological Survey of India (see ASI)
Archaeology, archaeological (see Excavations)

Arcuate (see Arch)
Art Deco...214,288
Ashlar: Square, close cut masonry
Ashoka, Emperor 268-231 BC 26
Ashokan pillar 5,80,82,91,98,249,251
Ashokan pillar building, Firoz Shah Kotla....85
Ashokan Rock Edict.................................26,28
ASI 5,32,69,159,165,191
Asian Games village.......................................44
Asiatic Society, Calcutta.................................91
Astrology 186
Astronomy 91,136,280
Atgah Khan (d.1562), Courtier of Akbar
....175,223
Aurangzeb, Emperor 1658-1707
.....................101,171,178,181,186, 226,254
Awadh 96,127,130,179,182,200
Baba Haji Rozbih, 12th c. Muslim saint 30
Babur, First Mughal Emperor 1526-30
....14,77,134,165
Badli Serai, North Delhi 246
bagh: Garden
Baghdad Octagon 149,161
Bahadur Shah (Zafar) II, Last Emperor 1837-58 182,225,233,240
Bahadur Shah I, Emperor 1706-12
....164,225
Bahlol Lodi, Sultan 1451-89 77,100,101,121
Bahlol Lodi's Tomb.................................76,77
Bairam Khan, Prime Minister to the young Akbar 147,166
Baird Place, Cantonment.............................282
Baker, Sir Herbert (1862 - 1946), architect
.........................4,259,260,261,268,277-79
Bakhtiyar Kaki (see Qutb Sahib)
Balban, Sultan 1266-87 34,35,148,169
Ballimaran, Shahjahanabad 202
bangla: A typical roof shape from Bengal much used in Mughal palace architecture, and later in domestic and religious buildings 17,189
baoli: Step-well 8,9,24
Agrasen ki, New Delhi 263,272
Dargah of Qutb Sahib, Mehrauli.........227
Firoz Shah Kotla.................................85
Gandak ki, Mehrauli 221,229,231
Kotla Mubarakpur 118,119
Mihr Banu's Market, Humayun's Tomb
....152,154
Nizamuddin's Dargah 168,170
Pir Ghaib, North Delhi 91
Purana Qila 138
Rajon ki, Mehrauli.....................229,235-36
Red Fort...191

baradari: generally a twelve-pillared open pavilion often used as a tomb, but used as name for other pillared buildings 104
Baradari, Sadhana Enclave........................60,63
Baradari, Shahpur Jat 45
Bari ka Gumbad, Nizamuddin 168
Barracks, Red Fort 187,241
basti: Slum village
Battered walls and buttress: The wall slopes in significantly towards the top 45,51,88,104
Beam...11
Begumpur...61
Bengal...146
Bernier, Francois, French resident of Delhi 1659-64 180,254
Bharat Scout and Guide Compound...........157
Bharatiyam Gram 157
Bibi ka Rauza, Aliganj 128,129
Bibi Khanum Mosque, Samarkand 84
Bibi Zulaikha Sahiba, Nizamuddin Aulia's mother..78
Bijay Mandal.............................57,59,60,64-69
Bridges
    Athpula, Lodi Gardens 122,123
    Barapula, Nizamuddin 150,156
    Khizrabad 102
    Minto, New Delhi 265
    Wazirabad, beside Shah Alam's Mosque and Tomb..............................90
British 18,38,182,184
British Resident / Residency.................193,240
Buddhist religion 20,28
Buddhist temple architecture 9
Bund: An artificial embankment to contain water in a river or tank. 9,10,29,54
Bungalows 18,243,244,260,269,272-73,282
Burial 22-23,148
Burial ground, DDA Green Area, Humayun's Tomb...157
Burj Mandal, Tughlakabad..........................50,51
Byron, Robert. British writer who visited Delhi in 1930s 103,257,261,268,274,277
Calcutta 241,256
Calligraphy 12,40
Canal 96,181-82,192,195,197
Cantilever 10,11
Cantonment, North Delhi 240,243,250
Cantonment, New Delhi 2,282
Capital city, removal of 5
Capital, Delhi as 101,178,183,243,256
Carr Stephens, 19th century historian and writer..96
Cathedral Church of the Redemption 266

Cathedral of the Sacred Heart, New Delhi 264,270
Cemetery..23,193
Cenotaph: Memorial structure of someone buried elsewhere. Denotes the gravestones that were erected inside tombs, over the chamber in which the body was placed 23
Central Baptist Church 199
chaitya: Round arched halls as in early Buddhist cave temples 21
chajja: Stone projection below parapet, protecting openings below 104
Chamfer: An external right angle with the corner taken off
Chandni Chowk, Shahjahanabad 181,198-99
Chandragupta, Gupta king, reigned 375-415 32
char bagh: Garden laid out symmetrically in four quarters
Chatri, India Gate 266,268
chatri: Literal meaning parasol or umbrella - Pillared pavilion often found on the roofs of tombs and palaces 14,104,161
Chauburj, Ridge..90,249
Chauhan 27
Chaumukha Darwaza, Mehrauli 229,236
chaupal: Assembly room 73
Chausath Khamba, New Delhi 263
chawkidar: Caretaker
Chhatta Chowk, Red Fort 190
chilla: Meditation or place of meditation
Chilla Nizamuddin 150,157
Chillagah of Baba Sheikh Fariduddin Shakar Ganj, Mehrauli.............................235
Chiragh Delhi Dargah 75-77
Chiragh Delhi village 72-77
Chiragh Delhi, Naziruddin Mahmud (d.1356) 63
Chiragh Delhi's shrine 77
Chor Minar..107,108
Christian buildings 23
chuna: Lime plaster, highly burnished, with additives to make it white
Chunna Mal Haveli, Chandni Chowk 195,198,201
Churches 18,23
    St James's Church, Kashmiri Gate 193
    St Mary's Church, Shahjahanabad........197
    St Stephen's Church, Shahjahanabad 194,195
    Chapel, Behind Baptist Union of North India Buildings 253
Citadel: Innermost fort in walled city 48

Civil Lines 2,192,240-43,250,252
Classical (European)..18
Clerestorey: windows between two roofs
Colonial architecture 19
Colonnade: Pillared gallery, often surrounding
 mosque courtyard
Colony, Residential development...................19
Connaught Place 259,261,265,271
Conservation.....................................4,98,286
Corbel: Projecting stone, carrying beam
 or wall above 12,88,105
Crypt: burial chamber
Cunningham, Alexander, 19th century
 Archaeologist.....................................32,143
Cupola, Qutb Minar 36,38
Cusped: Decorative scooped edging to arches
Dado: The area of wall up to about waist
 height
dalan, Arcaded room with one open side,
 generally overlooking a courtyard 9
Dam (see bund)
Daniell, Thomas and William, British artists
 in India in 1780s and 90s 84,153
Dara Shikoh, eldest son of
 Shah Jahan 164,178,192-3
Dargah: Shrine of a Muslim saint. Its literal
 original meaning was 'royal court'
  Bibi Zulaikha Sahiba, Adhchini 78
  Chiragh Delhi 75
  Hasan Rasul Numa, New Delhi...........263
  Qutb Sahib, Mehrauli 45,222
  Shah Turkman, Shahjahanabad 211
  Shahi Mardan, Aliganj 127
  Panja Sharif, Shahjahanabad.................192
  Inayat Khan, Nizamuddin....................168
  Nizamuddin Aulia 171
Daryaganj.....................183,214,242,243
DDA...132
Defence Colony 120
Delhi College..208
Delhi Development Authority (DDA) 284,291
Delhi Gate, Red Fort 186,190
Delhi Gate, Shahjahanabad...........................212
Delhi Municipal Corporation (DMC).........284
Delhi University...............................241,244,250
Delhi University Office 248,250
Delhi University, Faculty of Arts 248,250
Delhi University, Gwyer Hall 248
Dharampura, Shahjahanabad 204
dharamsala: A charitable rest-house
 for pilgrims or travellers 194,195
Dholpur sandstone 274,278
Dilkusha, Metcalfe's house, Mehrauli ..229,236

Dinpanah 135,136,146,147
diwan-i-am, Red Fort......................187,189,190
diwan-i-khas, Red Fort 187,191
djinns 85
Dome 10-12,14,22-23
Dome, double 16-17,149
Dome, onion 17
Double triangle design...................................12
Drum, dome 16,88,104
Durbars 241,243,256
East of Kailash 28
European architecture, art 17,183,189,240
European historians 130
Excavations 5,26,28,64,136,139
  Purana Qila 28
  Tughlakabad 52
  Jahanpanah 66,68
Exchange Stores, Civil Lines 252
Faridabad 62
Fateh Khan (d.1376),
 Firoz Shah's oldest son.....................83,91,93
fateha: Offering
Fatepur Sikri 147,206,216
Fatima, the Prophet's daughter 129
Finch, William, 17th c. British traveller 91
Firoz Shah (Tughlak), Sultan 1351 - 88
4,80,82,87,93,98,101,171,173,174,181
Firoz Shah Kotla 84-85,180
Firozabad 81,82
Flagstaff Tower 248,250
Follies 236,238
Fortifications (see Walls)
Franklin, William. Wrote an account
 of Delhi in 1793. 195,242
Fraser, William.....................................193,251
gali: Lane or alleyway
Gandhi Sadan Smriti 267
garbha-griha...20
Gardens 5,37,181,242
  Aliganj 127
  Dilkusha, Mehrauli................................236
  Humayun's Tomb 155,165
  Jahanara's 196,241
  Lalit Kala Academy Studios, Garhi......132
  late Mughal, Qutb Minar........................43
  late Mughal, Lodi Gardens 121,123
  Rashtrapati Bhawan 266,275
  Qudsia Bagh 242,247,249
  Roshanara, North Delhi 242,246
  Shalimar Bagh, North Delhi 242,245
  Talkatora, New Delhi 263
  Tees Hazari 242
Garden City 19

Garhi...132
garuda, vehicle of Vishnu.................................32
Gateway
    Naqqar Khana, Aliganj 127,128
    Nizamuddin's Dargah..............168,170,172
    Oberoi (near) 150,176
    Purana Qila 137,138
    Qadam Sharif...93,94
    Qudsia Bagh 247
    Qutb Minar Serai 43
    Serai Shahji..60,62
    Turkman, Shahjahanabad...............209,211
    Zinat Mahal, Shahjahanabad 201
    Delhi, Shahjahanabad 212
Gaushala, Mehrauli...229
George, Walter, Architect 250,251,265,273
Ghalib, Mirza Asadullah (d.1869)
    Poet...203,251
Ghalib's grave, Nizamuddin 168,169
ghazal: A short poem or ode, generally sung
Ghiyasuddin Tughlak, Sultan 1320-24 48
Glacis: Masonry reinforcement at the
  base of a fort wall 51
Glasshouse, Lodi Gardens.....................122,123
Golf Course tombs 114,131
gopura..20
Government House, New Delhi (see
  Rashtrapati Bhawan)
Government Press, New Delhi 265
Grand Trunk Road...135
Grave (see Burial)
Grave enclosure of Mu'atmad Khan 226
Grave: 'grave' is used in the context of
  gravestones in the open (see cenotaph).
Great Place (now Vijay Chowk) 266,269
Great Uprising 6,183,187,198,201,240,251
Greater Kailash...19
Green Park...109
Gujarat 24,236
Gujjars 49
guldasta: Small decorative tower at the
  corners of parapet walls 105,161
Gulmohar Park...107
Gupta Dynasty, ruled from 375 for
  approx 200 years 27,32
Guru Nanak 21,102
gurudwara...21
    Teg Bahadur, New Delhi.......................263
    Sisganj, Chandni Chowk 199
    Bangla Sahib, New Delhi...............263,270
    Damdama Sahib, Humayun's Tomb 157
    Sadhana Enclave...60
Gwalior...134

Gymkhana Club 267
Haji Begum, wife of Humayun 153
Hamida, Humayun's wife and mother of
  Akbar 146,164
hammam: Bath house
  Afsarwala's mosque,
    Humayun's Tomb....................................153
    Purana Qila 139
    Red fort 191
Hardayal Municipal Public Library,
  Shahjahanabad 196
Hardinge, Lord, Viceroy 258,260
Harappan culture, Indus Valley culture..........26
Hastal 216
Hauz Khas 58,80-82,86-89,108-10
Hauz Khas Deer Park 110
Hauz Khas Park 86
Hauz Qazi, Shahjahanabad 208
Hauz Rani, Malviya Nagar 59
haveli: Large joint-family house, often with
  several internal courtyards
   24,73,183,184,194,200,202,209,241
Hayat Baksh garden, Red Fort 188,190
hazar sutun 35,64,68
Hindi Park housing 215
Hindu Rao Hospital...91
Hindu Rao's house 249,251
Hindu religion 20
Hindu temples (see Temples)
Hira Mahal, Red Fort.......................................191
Holy Trinity Church, Shahjahanabad 213
Houses, ruined, behind Lal Darwaza 143
Housing 291
Housing, Clerks'...270
Housing, New Delhi................................271,272
Housing, public sector 19
Humayun, Emperor
  1530-40 & 1555-56 135,136,139,146,175
Humayunpur 110
Hunting Lodge (see shikargah)
Hypostyle: A type of hall with rows of
  evenly spaced columns supporting
  a flat ceiling..40,64,65
Ibn Battuta (1304-68),
  traveller 23,52,56-58,59,64
Ibrahim Lodi, Sultan 1517-26 101,134
idgah: Large open air mosque for celebrating
  the Muslim festival of Id 22
    Mehrauli 218,229
    Padmini Enclave 107
    Shahjahanabad 254
Iltutmish, Sultan 1211-36...............................34,38
Imambara, Aliganj..127,128

Imli Pahari, Shahjahanabad..........................209
Imperial Hotel, New Delhi 265,271
Independence...183,284
India Gate, New Delhi...........................266,268
India International Centre...........................123
Indira Gandhi Memorial 267
Indo-Aryan language 26
Indo-Islamic architecture 3,9,13,14,53
Indrapat, Indraprastha..........................26,28,136
Inscription 31,32,38,53,85,103
INTACH (Indian National Trust for Art and
    Cultural Heritage) 3,5,6,218,234,263
Iron Pillar, Qutb Minar 32,36
ISKCON temple..28
Islamic buildings, styles (see also
    Mosques, Tombs) 10-17,22-23
Islamic culture..182
Islamic religion..56,80
iwan: A vaulted hall opening off
    a courtyard.......................13,139,140,149,161
Jahan Numa (see Pir Ghaib)
Jahanara (d.1681), daughter of
    Shah Jahan 168,171,178,181,183
Jahanara's garden...................................196,241
Jahanara's serai 198
Jahangir, Emperor 1605-28...................147,189
Jahanpanah...57-78,121
Jahaz Mahal, Mehrauli 230,233
Jain religion 20
Jain temple (see Temples)
Jaipur Column, Rashtrapati Bhawan 266,267
Jalalaldin Khalji, Sultan 1290-96.....................35
jali: Screen made from geometrically
    carved stone or wood.....................88,104,105
Jama Masjid (see Jami Masjid)
Jami Masjid: Friday Mosque. Muslims say their
    prayers together on Friday 22
        Sultan Ghari's tomb (ruined) 46
        Jami Masjid, Tughlakabad (ruined)....49,50
        Shahjahanabad 182,259
Janpath, New Delhi 259
Jantar Mantar, New Delhi 263,280
Jaunpur 77,101,102
Jawaharlal Nehru Stadium tombs..........114,121
Jharna, Mehrauli 230,233
jharokha: Ornamented projecting window,
    with jali screens if part of the zenana........153
jharokha, Red Fort..189
Jogmaya 101
Jor Bagh 127
Kabul 15,96,134
Kaka Nagar 176
Kalkaji 28,132

Kalu Serai 60,61,98
Kanauj 27,81
kangura : Battlement-like motifs on parapet
    walls, with matching solid and void. ..105,245
Karbala 127,128
karkhanah: Workshops
Kashmiri Gate, Shahjahanabad
   192,240,242,244
katra: A small neighbourhood or market which
    would formerly have been enclosed
Kaykubad, Sultan 1287-90 35
Khairpur...121
Khalji era, Dynasty 35
Khan Jahan Junan Shah, Firoz Shah's second
    wazir (Prime Minister)........................80,83,98
Khan Jahan Tilangani (d.1368), Firoz Shah's
    first wazir (Prime Minister) 80,173
Khan, Sir Syed Ahmad (1817-98), scholar 5
khanqah: A residential centre for Islamic
    religious and spiritual learning
Khaori Baoli / Bazaar, Shahjahanabad 200,201
Kharbuze ka Gumbad 62
Kharera...109
khas Mahal, Red Fort 186,191
Khirki...63
Khizr Khan, Sultan 1414-21........................100
Khizrabad 102
Khuni Darwaza, opp. Firoz Shah Kotla........85
Khusrau Shah, Sultan 1321 35,48
khutba: The sermon preached at the Friday
    prayers. Preaching in the name of a new ruler
    meant tacit approval of that ruler. 81
Khwaja Baqi Billah's grave 96
Kilokri..35,48,102,148
Kinari Bazaar, Shahjahanabad 204
kirti mukha, stylised face 31
Kishanganj..243
Koch, Ebba 139,189
Koran, Koranic...11,23,127
Kos Minar 138
Kotla Mubarakpur 117
Kotla Nizamuddin 168
kotla: Small fort
kucha: Lane
kufic, Arabic script 41
Lado Serai 238
Lady Hardinge Serai, New Delhi...............264
Lady Irwin College 265
Lady Sri Ram College 115
Lahore..34
Lahori Gate, Red Fort 186
Lahori Gate, Shahjahanabad........................194
Lajpat Rai Market, Shahjahanabad........196,197

Lake 54,87,121
Lal Gumbad 62,63
Lal Kot 10,27,29-31,34,59,82,148,222,232
Lal Kuan, Shahjahanabad 200,201
Lal Mahal, Nizamuddin..............35,148,168,169
Langar Khana, Nizamuddin 168,172
Lodi Colony......................................273
Lodi Gardens 14,121-6
Lodi tombs and mosques 104,105
Lotus finial..104
Lotus flower, lotus bud........................12,13,42
Lucknow 3,182,247
Lutyens, Sir Edwin (1869 - 1944), architect
   4,256,258,259,260,261,268,273,275-78
madrasa: Islamic religious school 23
    Alauddin, Qutb Minar 11,42
    Amima Islama Arabad, Kashmiri
    Gate, Shahjahanabad 192
    Hauz Khas 86,87,89
Magazine 193
Mahabharata 26,28,136
Mahal, Mahipalpur 97
Mahal, Serai Shahji 62
mahal: Palace, but word often used for
    non-palatial but old buildings
Maham Angah, Akbar's
    wet-nurse 143,166,175,223
Mahavir Jain Bhawan, Chandni Chowk 199
Mahfilkhana, Chiragh Delhi.................75,76,77
Mahipalpur 96,97
Mahmud Khalji, 15th century Sultan
    of Mandu....................................100,102
Mahmud Shah Tughlak, Sultan 1393-1412....81
Mahmud Shah, Sultan 1245-65 34,35
Majlis Khana, Dargah of Qutb Sahib,
    Mehrauli...227
Majlis Khana, Nizamuddin 168
Majlis Khana, Qadam Sharif...........................95
Maliwara, Shahjahanabad 202
Mallu Khan (d.1405), powerful courtier
    during late Tughlak times 81,107
Malviya Nagar 59
mandapa 20,31
Mandu..............................15,59,102,161
Maqbara Paik, North Delhi 245
Masjid (see Mosque)
Master Plan 284,285
Mauryan empire.....................................26,27
Mausoleum (see Tomb)
Mayfair Gardens 107
Mecca 22,23,73
Mehrauli 45,218-37
merlons: That part of a battlement /

crenellation that projects up, forming the
shelter from attack. A decorative version is
formed by a *kangura* pattern. 105
Metcalfe House, Civil Lines 249
Metcalfe, Sir Charles, Resident 1810-18 &
    1825-28 245
Metcalfe, Sir Thomas,
    Resident 1835-53 193,218,231,236,242
Metro 208,271,293,294
Mihr Banu's Market,
    Humayun's Tomb 152,154
mihrab: Prayer niche, always found
    on the west wall of mosques..........22,104,105
minar: tower
Minaret 22,38
minbar: Pulpit in Mosque, always found
    to the right of the *mihrab* 22
Mirza Jahangir (d.1832), son of
    Akbar Shah 11................................168,172
Modern architecture....................................287
Modern Delhi.............................2,285-94
mohulla: A self-contained group of dwellings
    (and workshops) which would be inhabited
    by a caste or craft-based community 183
Mongol 81,134
Mosque: The Islamic place of worship
    (see also Wall Mosques) 9,22,46,105
    Adhchini..78
    Afsarwala, Humayun's Tomb 152,153
    Amrudwali, Shahjahanabad 209
    Aulia, Mehrauli 230
    Bara Gumbad, Lodi Gardens.................125
    Begumpur 60,69,140
    Chauburj, Ridge.........................90,249
    Chausath Khamba, New Delhi 98
    Chiragh Delhi 76
    Daiwali, Shahjahanabad.........................213
    Darwesh Shah, Hauz Khas 107,108
    Dilkushad, Shahjahanabad 195
    Ek Minar, Shahjahanabad 213
    Fatehpuri Masjid,
    Shahjahanabad 200,201,241
    Firoz Shah Kotla 84
    Ghaziuddin, Shahjahanabad 208
    Golf Course, late Mughal 132
    Haji Langa, RKPuram 108,112
    Hauz Qazi, Shahjahanabad.....................208
    Hauzwali, Shahjahanabad 201
    Hussain Bakhsh, Shahjahanabad 209
    Imliwali, Shahjahanabad 201
    Isa Khan, Humayun's Tomb ..151,152,160
    Jamaat Khana, Nizamuddin 168,174
    Jamali Kamali, Mehrauli.................229,237

303

Mosque *cont.*
Jami Masjid, Shahjahanabad....206,207,241
Kalan Masjid, Shahjahanabad................209
Kali Masjid, Nizamuddin...............168,173
Kalu Serai 60,61
Khairul Manazil, opp Purana Qila..143-44
Khan-i-Dauran, Nizamuddin 168
Khirki 60,70
Khunbaha ki, Shahjahanabad................205
Khwajah Sara Basti Khan,
Defence Colony 120
Kotla Mubarakpur 118,119
Lal Masjid, Aliganj 128,129
Lal Masjid, Kashmiri Gate 192
Lodi Gardens, late Mughal......121,122,123
Makhdum Sahib, Mayfair Gardens107,108
Malik Munirka, Munirka 108,113
Moth ki Masjid, South Extension 114,116
Moti Masjid, Mehrauli 225
Moti Masjid, Red Fort 187,191
Mubarak Begum, Shahjahanabad..........208
Muhammad Baqar, Shahjahanabad 192
Muhammad Wali, Siri 107,108
Muradabad Pahari Fort, Vasant Vihar 108
Mutasib, Shahjahanabad 195
Nawab Sahib ki, Shahjahanabad 205
Nili, Hauz Khas.............................107,108
Pataudi House, Shahjahanabad 213
Qabr Wali, Shahjahanabad 208
Qasai Wala Gumbad, Muradabad
Pahari fort 113
Qila-i-Kohna, Purana Qila 135,138,140-41
Qudsia Bagh 247
Qutb Minar 30,31,40
Rukn ud Dawla, Shahjahanabad 209
Sarhindi, Shahjahanabad 195
Serai Shahji, late Mughal.......................60,62
Shah Alam, Wazirabad.............................90
Shah Gulam Ali, Shahjahanabad 211
Sirkiwalan's, Shahjahanabad 208
Sohan Burj, Mehrauli 230,233
Sunehri, Chandni Chowk 199
Sunehri, Faiz Bazaar, Shahjahanabad ..213
Sunehri, near Red Fort 215
Sunehri, New Delhi 263
Tahawwur Khan, Shahjahanabad..........200
Tohfe Wala Gumbad, Shahpur Jat 44,45
Unchi, Shahjahanabad 208
Vasant Vihar 113
Yussuf Qattal, Khirki 60
Zinat al-Masjid,Shahjahanabad..............215
Mubarak Shah Khalji, Sultan 1316-21............49

Mubarak Shah Sayyid,
Sultan 1421-33 77,100,102,118
Mubarakabad...102
muezzin: The mosque official who makes
the call to prayer 22
Mughal architecture 139
Mughal tombs 149
Muhammad of Ghor (d. 1206) 10,34,37,235
Muhammad Shah Rangila,
Emperor 1719-48 73,168,172,179,246
Muhammad Shah Sayyid,
Sultan 1433-45.....................................100,124
Muhammad Tughlak, Sultan 1388-93......80,81
Muhammad Tughlak,
Sultan 1324-51.........53,54,56-58,64,69,82,101
Muhammadpur 110
Muinuddin Chishti (b. approx 1000 AD), first
leader of the Indian Chishti sufis..35,148,224
Munda Gumbad, Hauz Khas 86,87
Munirka 112
muqarnas: Architectural decoration, unique to
Islam, made up of tiny, repeated cells on the
underside of domes etc 12,16,163,164
Muradabad Pahari Fort 108,113
Museums, Red Fort 191
Mutiny (see Great Uprising)
Mutiny Memorial...................................249,251
Nadir Shah of Persia (d.1747) 179
nahr-i-bihisht, Red Fort 191
Nai ka Kot 54
Najafgarh 129
nallah: Open sewer or stream
nashki, Arabic script...............................12,40,41
Nasiruddin Mahmud, Iltutmish's son 46
National Archives, New Delhi 259,266,269
National Capital Territory (NCT) 284
National Emblem 85
National Stadium, New Delhi...............267,272
Naubat Khana, Mehrauli 221,222
Naubat Khana, Red Fort 187,190
NCC offices...192
Net-vaulting...16
New Delhi 2,19,183,243,256-81
New Delhi Municipal Corporation (NDMC)..284
New Delhi Railway Station 93
New Friends Colony.................................19,102
Nizamuddin Aulia (d. 1325)..49,147,148,157,170
Nizamuddin village 148,167
North and South Blocks
..................................258,266,268-69,278-79
Nusrat Khan, Sultan 1394 & 1398 81
Oberoi Hotel, New Delhi............................151

Oberoi Maidens Hotel, Civil Lines 249,253

Ochterlony, Sir David, Resident
 1803-06 & 1818-21 208,245

Ogee: A particular shape of arch where the tip
 of the arch forms a sharp point

Old Delhi (see Shahjahanabad)

Padmini Enclave 107

pahar, Chiragh Delhi...76

Paharganj 241,243,259,263

Palaces...37

Adilabad 54

Firoz Shah Kotla 83,84

Jahanpanah..59

Mehrauli 218,222,225

Tughlakabad 50,52

Palam...100,216

Panchsheel Park 59

Panchsheel Public School 62

Panipat...34,134,146

Parliament Building 266,269,277

Partition 21,136,284,285

Peacock Throne 179

Pendentive: Hanging carving

Persia, Persian architecture
14,15,16,85,139,146,158,161,163,165

Piano nobile: Italian term to denote a
 raised main floor 274

Pietre dura: 'hard stone', Italian inlaid
 stone work..189

Pilaster 18

Pir Ghaib 91,249,251

pir: A Sufi teacher or spiritual guide

pishtaq: The square façade that surrounds
 an iwan or doorway 13,105

Plasterwork 13,14,69

Population 27,59,80-83,101,183,241,285,286

Prayer hall 40

Princes' Houses, New Delhi

Bhawalpur 265

Baroda...266,272

Bikaner 267,273

Faridkot 266

Hyderabad 266,268

Jaipur...267,272

Kerala...265

Patiala 266,272

Tehri-Garwhal...266

Travancore 266,272

Princes' Park (India Gate)..............................268

Prithviraj Chauhan (d.1192), last Rajput king
 of Ajmer..30,34

Prophet Muhammad 93

Punjab 37,100,102

Purana Qila.......................26,28,137-42,259,284

purdah: The practice of secluding women from
 the sight of non-family men

Pusa Institute...282

PWD (CPWD) 269,273,291

Qadam Sharif 83,92-95

Qadam Sharif, Aliganj 127,128

qawwali: A sufi song with strong rhythm that
 tends to increase in speed

Qila Rai Pithora 27,29,37,238

Qudsia Begum, wife of Muhammad Shah
 Rangila........................127,215,242,247

Quoin: Stones forming an external angle on a
 building

Qutb Minar.....................................12,36,38,40-42,46

Qutb Minar Mosque 10,12,40-41

Qutb Sahib, Bakhtiar Kaki
 (d. 1235)................38,45,148,218,224,226,

Qutbuddin Aibak, First
 Sultan 1206-11 34,37,38

Qutbuddin Mubarak Shah Khalji,
 Sultan 1316-1321 35

Quwwat-al-Islam (see Qutb Minar
 Mosque) 40

Railway 183,192

Raisina Hill, New Delhi 259,268

Rajpath, New Delhi 259,269

Rajput...10,26-32

Ram Nagar, Sadar Bazaar 92,254

Ramayana 26

Ramp 54,67,68

Rang Mahal, Red Fort 188,191

Rashtrapati Bhawan
258-59,260,261,266,268-69,274-76

Raziya, Female Sultan 1236-40
34,46,180,209,210

Red Fort 15,17,180,186,241,243

Revivalist architecture 261

Ridge...91,96,240,250

RKPuram 111-12

Rohillas, Afghan tribe 179

Roshanara Club..246

Round Tower, Lodi Gardens 122,123

Sa'adat Khan (d.1754), first
 Nawab of Awadh..................130,181,194,195

Sadar Bazaar..241,243

Sadhana Enclave 63

Safdarjang (d.1754), Nawab of Awadh and
 Prime Minister to Delhi Emperors 130,195

Safdarjang Enclave 110

Saint: In the Indian context, a holy man 23

Saket 83

Salim Shah, Sultan 1545-55 135,136,147

Salimgarh.................................135,180,241
Samarkand 81,134
Samru, Begum 193,196-97
Serai Shahji.......................................58
Sarkhej..15,169
Satpula, Khirki 58,71
Sawai Jai Singh of Amber 280
Sawan and Bhadon Pavilions,
    Red Fort 187,190
Sayyid Dynasty.............................100,102
Schroff Eye Hospital, Shahjahanabad 215
Scindia, Raja of Gwalior..........179,193,240,251
Secret passage, Tughlakabad 50,51
Secretariat, Civil Lines 248
Secretariat, New Delhi (see North and South
    Blocks)
Secular buildings 24
Sepulchre: tomb
Serai Shahji mahal 60,61
Serai, Qutb Minar 43
Shah Alam II, Emperor
    1759-1806 179,225,240
Shah Alam, 14th century Saint 90
Shah Burj, Red Fort 188,191
Shah Jahan, Emperor 1628-58
   4,15,147,178,180-81,186,254
Shah Turkman (d. 1240) Sufi Saint 209,211
Shah Turkman's grave 83,180
Shahjahanabad 2,4,20,62,143,171,180,
   219,241,259,260,284,288
Shahpur Jat 44,45
Shamsi tank, Mehrauli 34
Sheikh Farid Murtaza's grave 62
Sheikh Hasan Tahir (d.1503), Saint 64,68
Sheikh Kabiruddin Aulia (d.1397) 62,63
Sheikh Serai 58,60,63
Sher Mandal 139,147
Sher Shah Suri, Sultan 1540-45
   83,135,139,146
shikara 20
Shikargah: Hunting lodge 80,83,91
    Bhuli Bhatiyari ka Mahal, Ridge,
    New Delhi....................................96
    Kushak, Teen Murti 97,263,251
    Mahipalpur...................................97
    Malcha, Ridge, New Delhi 96
    Pir Ghaib, North Delhi 91,249,251
shivalaya 194,195
Shrine: In this context the burial place of a
    saint
Sikander Lodi, Sultan 1489-1517
   101,102,116,126
Sikh religion 20,21

Sirhind 77
Siri Fort 35,44,45
Siri Fort Sports Complex 107
Sixteen-sided (dome) drum 104,105,140
Skinner, James 192,193
Slave Dynasty (1192-1290) 34
Soami Nagar..................................58,78
Spandrel: The area between the curve of an
    arch and the square framing it
Squatter settlements 286
Squinch: Transition from a square corner to an
    octagonal corner 12,88,104,105,140,149
St Columba's School, New Delhi................264
St Stephen's College, old building at
    Kashmiri Gate 192
St Stephen's College, North Delhi 248,251
St Stephen's Hospital, Civil Lines 249
Stein, Joseph, Architect 289
Stringcourse: A horizontal band of masonry
    or plaster that runs across a façade
Stucco (see plasterwork)
stupa: Solid mound, generally hemispherical,
    that contains Buddhist relic 21
Subzi Mandi 241,243
sufi, sufism 148
Sujan Singh Park 267,273
Sujan Singh, Contactor who built
    much of New Delhi 261
Sultan Ghari's Tomb 46
Sultanate architecture 10-14
Sun Temple, Suraj Kund 29
Sundar Bagh Government Nursery.............158
Sunehri Masjid, Chandni Chowk 199
Suraj Kund 28-29
Suraj Pala Tomar, 11th century Rajput king ..29
taikhana: Underground room for daytime use
    during the hot weather 193
Taj Mahal 15,100,163,178,186
Tank, reservoir
    Anang Tal, Lal Kot 30,31
    Hauz Khas..................................87
    Munirka 113
    Shamsi, Mehrauli 34,218-19,230,233
    Suraj Kund.................................29
    Tughlakabad 50,51
Teen Murti House, New Delhi................97,267
Temples, Hindu 9,10,20-21,31,40,101,183
    Birla Mandir, New Delhi....................264
    Gaurishankar, Chandni Chowk 199
    Hanuman, New Delhi 263
    Jhandewalan, Karol Bagh 254
    Jogmaya, Mehrauli 229
    Sant Charandas, Shahjahanabad...........203

Temples, Hindu *cont.*
   Temple Complex, Red Fort, ...
   Shahjahanabad 197
Temple columns 31,40,41
Temples, Jain 9,10,31,183,204
   Bedwala, Maliwara 205
   Chhota and Bara Mandirs,
   New Delhi 263
   Dadabari, Mehrauli 230,232
   Jeweller's, Naughrana 205
   Lal Mandir, Chandni Chowk 199
   Mehrauli Gurgaon Road 238
   Panchayati 205
   Shri Digambir, Delhi Gate 213
   Sri Digambir Jain Bara...........................205
   Sri Digambir Jain Chotta......................205
   Sri Digambir Jain Meru 205
   Sri Digambir Jain Naya 205
   Sri Padmavati Puraval Digambir 205
Temples, new Hindu 289
Tibbia College, Karol Bagh 254
Tiles, tilework 13,15,156
Timur, Tamburlaine (1336-1405)
..................................81,83,84,100,134,235
Timurid: Style that originated from Timur's
  homeland (Samarkand, Bukhara, etc.) 149
Tin Burj, Muhammadpur 111
Tin Burj, South Extension 117
Tirthankara 20,21
Tomar...27,29,32
Tomb: Enclosure of a burial place.
  'Mausoleum' is more accurate, but the Delhi
  mausolea are known universally as 'tombs'
 22-23,88,104-05
Tomb (of)
   18th century, Golf course....................132
   Adham Khan, Mehrauli 30,220,222,229
   Afsarwala, Humayun's Tomb 152,153
   Alauddin, Qutb Minar 42
   Amir Khusro, Nizamuddin 168,172
   Arif Ali Shah, Aliganj 128,129
   Atgah Khan, Nizamuddin 168,175
   Azim Khan, Lado Serai 238
   Bagh-I-Alam ka Gumbad,
   Hauz Khas 108,110
   Bahlol Lodi, Chirag Delhi 73,76,77
   Bai Kodaldai, Nizamuddin 168,170
   Balban, Mehrauli 111,229,231
   Bara Batashewala, Humayun's
   Tomb..150,158
   Bara Gumbad, Lodi Gardens ..122,124-25
   Bara Lao ka Gumbad, Vasant Vihar 113
   Barah Khamba, Golf course 114,131

Barah Khamba, Hauz Khas 108,109
Barah Khamba, Nizamuddin 168,170
Barber's, Humayun's Tomb...........152,155
Bare Khan ka Gumbad, South
Extension 117,118
Bhure Khan ka Gumbad, South
Extension 118,119
Bijri Khan, RKPuram.....................108,111
Biran ka Gumbad, Green Park......108,109
Bu Halima, Humayun's Tomb 151,152
Chauburj, Ridge 90
Chaumachi Khan, Mehrauli 220,223
Chausath Khamba, Nizamuddin ..168,169
Chhota Bateshewala, Humayun's
Tomb...150,158
Chhota Khan ka Gumbad, South
Extension 117,118
Chhoti Gumbad, Hauz Khas 108,109
Chiragh Delhi, Dargah tombs 76
Dadi ka Gumbad, Hauz Khas 108,109
Darya Khan Lohani, South
Extension 117,118
DDA Green area 150,157
Dilkusha, Mehrauli 231
Do Sirihya Gumbad, Nizamuddin........168
Fateh Khan, Qadam Sharif 94-95
Firoz Shah, Hauz Khas 88,97
Ghiyasuddin, Tughlakabad 53,161
Gol Gumbad, Nizamuddin 150,176
Golf course tombs 131,176
Haji Khanum, Chiragh Delhi 72,74
Haji Langa, RKPuram 108,112
Humayun.........16,147,148,152,153,161-65
Humayunpur tombs...............................108
Iltutmish, Qutb Minar 36,39
Imam Zamin, Qutb Minar...............36,43
Industrial Training Institute,
Humayun's Tomb 152,154
Isa Khan, Humayun's Tomb ..151,152,160
Jamali Kamali, Mehrauli...............229,237
JN Stadium....................................114,121
Kale Khan ka Gumbad, South
Extension 117,118
Kali Gumti, Hauz Khas Deer Park108,110
Katwaria Serai 108,113
Khan Jahan Tilangani....................168,173
Khan-I-Khanan, Nizamuddin East150,166
Khwajah Sara Basti Khan,
Defence Colony 120
Lal Bangla, Golf course 114
Langar Khan, Zamrudpur 115
Mah Khanum, Jor Bagh................127,128
Makhdum Sahib, Mayfair Gardens 107

307

Tomb (of) *cont.*
    Malik Chand ka Gumbad,
    Humayunpur 110
    Maulvi Ataullah's mosque, beside 192
    Mehrauli tombs 221,222,225,230,234
    Mir Taqi, Golf course 114,132
    Mubarak Shah, Kotla Mubarakpur118,119
    Mughal tomb, Golf Course 131
    Muhammad Shah, Lodi Gardens ..122,124
    Munda Gumbad, RKPuram 108,111
    Muradabad Pahari Fort 113
    Najaf Khan, Aliganj 128,129
    National Stadium 143
    Nila, nr Humayun's Tomb.............150,156
    Nizamuddin Aulia 168
    Nizamuddin tombs 168,170
    Oberoi, opposite 150,176
    Poti ka Gumbad, Hauz Khas 108,109
    Quli Khan, Mehrauli (see Dilkusha)
    Qutb Road, Sadar Bazaar 96
    RKPuram tombs 108,112
    Sabz Burj, Humayun's tomb 150,159
    Sadhana Enclave 60,63
    Safdarjang..114,130
    Sakri Gumti, Hauz Khas 108,109
    Sayyid Abid, Golf course 131
    Shah Alam, Wazirabad..........................90
    Sheikh Sulaiman, Mehrauli 221,223
    Sheesh Gumbad, Lodi Gardens 122,125
    Sheikh Alauddin, Sheikh Serai 63
    Sheikh Ali Gumti, Defence
    Colony....................................114,120
    Sheikh Haidar, Lado Serai....................238
    Sheikh Salahuddin Darwesh, Sheikh
    Serai..60
    Sheikh Serai tombs 60,63
    Sikander Lodi, Lodi Gardens 122,126
    Soami Nagar 78
    Sohan Burj, Mehrauli............................230
    Sultan Ghari, Vasant Kunj 46
    Sundar Nagar Nursery tombs........150,158
    Tin Burj, Muhammadpur...............108,111
    Tuhfewala Gumbad, Hauz Khas 86
    Vasant Vihar 108
    Wazirpur ka Gumbad 112
    Wazirpur, RKPuram............................108
    Yussuf Quattal, Khirki.....................60,63
    Zamrudpur tombs 114-16
Town Hall, Shahjahanabad.............183,196,198
Trabeate: The 'post and beam' system
    of construction. 10,11,105,141
Transport 294
Treasure 52,64,66

Tripolia, North Delhi.....................................246
Tughlak architecture 13,88
Tughlak dynasty 48,56-57,80-81
Tughlak Shah, briefly Sultan in 1388 81
Tughlakabad 13,48-53,82
Turkish, Turks. Turkic speaking tribes......15,34
Turkman Gate clearances 216
Twelve-pillared pavilion 12,104
Urban village 5,9,73,103,112,115,167,286
Urs: Death commemoration
U-shaped building, Qutb Road 96
Vasant Kunj 46
Vasant Vihar...19,113
Victory Tower 38
vihara 21
Village (see Urban village)
Wall Mosque 22
    Hauz Khas Deer Park 110
    Hijron ka Khanqah, Mehrauli........230,234
    Humayun's Tomb 155
    Jor Bagh 127,128
    Lal Gumbad, Sheikh Serai.....................63
    Madhi Masjid, Mehrauli 230,232
    Mehrauli wall mosques 230
    Mihr Banu's Market, Humayun's
    Tomb 154
    Nila Gumbad, Humayun's Tomb..152,156
    Serai Shahji 62
    Sikander Lodi's Tomb, Lodi Gardens ..126
    Wazirpur...112
walled city (see Shahjahanabad)
Walls
    Adilabad 54
    Chiragh Delhi 74
    Firoz Shah Kotla 84-85,180
    Jahanpanah...59
    Kotla Mubarakpur 117
    Kotla Nizamuddin 168,173
    Lal Kot 29
    Purana Qila 137-39
    Qadam Sharif 93,94
    Qila Rai Pithora 30
    Tughlak..13
    Tughlakabad 49
wazir: Prime or chief minister
Western Court, New Delhi 265,271
World Heritage Site.................................3,37
Yamuna River 26,35,102,180,240,259
Zafar Mahal, Mehrauli 225
Zamrudpur..114-16
zenana: The part of a building set aside for
    women in *purdah*......................24,69,187,197
Zoo 138